MW01536067

Walt Disney World®
Orlando & Beyond

HIDDEN®

Walt Disney World®
Orlando & Beyond

Including Epcot, Disney-MGM Studios,
Disney's Animal Kingdom, Universal Studios, Universal
Islands of Adventure, and SeaWorld Adventure Park

Lisa Oppenheimer & Catherine O'Neal

THIRD EDITION

Ulysses Press®
BERKELEY, CALIFORNIA

Published by:
ULYSSES PRESS
P.O. Box 3440
Berkeley, CA 94703
www.ulyssespress.com

ISSN 1527-733X
ISBN 1-56975-380-6

Printed in Canada by Transcontinental Printing

10 9 8 7 6 5 4

MANAGING EDITOR: Claire Chun
PROJECT DIRECTOR: Laura Brancella
COPY EDITORS: Steven Schwartz, Lily Chou
EDITORIAL ASSOCIATES: Kate Allen
TYPESETTER: Steven Schwartz
CARTOGRAPHY: Pease Press
COVER DESIGN: Leslie Henriques, Sarah Levin
INDEXER: Sayre Van Young
COVER PHOTOGRAPHY: Arttoday.com
ILLUSTRATOR: Glenn Kim

Distributed in the United States by Publishers Group West
and in Canada by Raincoast Books

To my family, the best road testers ever.

—L.O.

Write to us!

If in your travels you discover a spot that captures the spirit of Disney World, or if you live in the region and have a favorite place to share, or if you just feel like expressing your views, write to us and we'll pass your note along to the author.

We can't guarantee that the author will add your personal find to the next edition, but if the writer does use the suggestion, we'll acknowledge you in the credits and send you a free copy of the new edition.

ULYSSES PRESS
3286 Adeline Street, Suite 1
Berkeley, CA 94703
E-mail: readermail@ulyssespress.com

What's Hidden?

At different points throughout this book, you'll find special listings marked with a hidden symbol:

◀ HIDDEN

This means that you have come upon a place off the beaten tourist track, a spot that will carry you a step closer to the local people and natural environment of Disney World.

The goal of this guide is to lead you beyond the realm of everyday tourist facilities. While we include traditional sightseeing listings and popular attractions, we also offer alternative sights and adventure activities. Instead of filling this guide with reviews of standard hotels and chain restaurants, we concentrate on one-of-a-kind places and locally owned establishments.

Our authors seek out locales that are popular with residents but usually overlooked by visitors. Some are more hidden than others (and are marked accordingly), but all the listings in this book are intended to help you discover the true nature of Disney World and put you on the path of adventure.

Contents

Maps

OUTDOOR ADVENTURE SYMBOLS

The following symbols accompany national, state and regional park listings, as well as beach descriptions throughout the text.

Camping		Waterskiing	
Hiking		Windsurfing	
Biking		Canoeing or Kayaking	
Horseback Riding		Boating	
Swimming		Boat Ramps	
Snorkeling or Scuba Diving		Fishing	
Surfing			

Games to Play While Waiting in Line

The lines at Orlando's theme parks can try anyone's patience. Fortunately, if you know how to create your own entertainment, the wait can be painless (well, almost).

Kids and adults alike can while away the time, use their creativity and even get a few laughs by playing the games described below. Some of these games relate to specific theme parks, others are appropriate for particular age groups. I have also added trivia questions for extra fun.

If you really want to speed up those waiting lines, create some games of your own!

GAMES FOR ALL AGES

RHYME TIME

Everybody loves to make up rhymes. It's even more fun when you do it together. Begin with a line of poetry. The next player adds a rhyming line, the next player contributes another and so on. The player who rhymes the fourth line gets to start a new rhyme. Example:

I read about Disney World in a book,
And decided I'd go take a look.
I left the dog, but my family I took.
All because of that silly book.

"SENSITIVE" POETRY

Compose a poem that you can see, smell, taste, feel and hear. Give it a try, using the following example as a guideline:

I love the smell of old socks.
I love the taste of ham hocks.
I hate feeling blue,
But I love hearing something new.
As you can see I'm a very good poet, too.

A IS FOR...

Look around you and choose objects that begin with particular letters. Start with "A" and proceed alphabetically. For example: animal, bus, carousel, dirt, exit, etc. Each player must come up with a nearby object that begins with the next letter in the alphabet.

HAVE YOU EVER, EVER, EVER?

Begin this game by reciting the first three lines of the following ditty and inserting an animal or object in the last word of the third line. The next player then provides a rhyming word for the last word in the fourth line:

Have you ever, ever, ever?
Have you ever, ever, ever?
Have you ever seen a MOUSE
Eat a HOUSE?
OH! NO! We never saw a MOUSE eat a HOUSE!

The last line of the verse is said in unison. The second word doesn't need to be a "real" one; in fact, the sillier it is, the more fun you'll have with the children! Some other examples are:

Have you ever seen MICKEY
Be real PICKY?
Have you ever seen a MANGO
Do the TANGO?

STUPID QUESTIONS

Making a fool of yourself is easy. Just ask the stupidest question you can think of. Then have everyone decide whose question is the dumbest. The stupid one is the winner!

PINK FLAMINGOS

Everyone poses a question that has to be answered with the phrase "Pink flamingos." Such as "What did you wear to bed last night?" Pink flamingos. "What did you barbecue for dinner?" Pink flamingos. If you giggle when you ask the question, you're out. The last remaining person is the winner.

SILENCE IS GOLDEN

Here's a game guaranteed to leave your group speechless. (Parents will love this!) Everyone pledges not to talk for a certain time period, say ten minutes. Only sign language can be used. It's a fun way to be imaginative with body language and visual communication. The last person to speak wins.

NUMBER STORIES

Storytelling is even more fun when you use numbers. Begin by using the number "one." The next person adds the word "two," etc. Example: Once upon a time . . . Two frogs went on a date . . . They swam across three lakes . . . Then they saw four speedboats headed for them . . . But they escaped with five seconds to spare. . . .

PICK A NUMBER

One player picks a number between 1 and 100, but doesn't reveal it to the other players. Each person takes turns trying to guess the number. When someone guesses incorrectly, the player will say "higher" or "lower" depending on whether the guess is above or below the secret number. The person who guesses right gets to pick the next secret number.

BODY MOVES

A leader starts the game with a body move, such as winking an eye. The next player performs that move and adds another, like nodding his or her head. For example, they might wink and nod their head. The game continues with each player performing the previous body moves—in the correct order—and adding a new one. Someone who forgets a move, is out of the game.

RHYME, RHYME, RHYME
One player begins the game by saying a simple word, such as "mouse." The next player must say another word that rhymes, like "house." Each person takes turns rhyming the original word. When no one can think of a new word that rhymes, the group goes on to a new word.

SEE AND TELL
A leader asks each person about what they see while waiting in line. Some sample questions: What is the smallest thing you see? What is the prettiest thing you see? What is the brightest thing you see? Other things to look for: tallest, shortest, fattest, skinniest, strangest, funniest, saddest, etc.

STORYTELLING
Children are born storytellers. Encourage kids in your group to create tales based on park characters, rides or situations. If you saw Cinderella yesterday, let your child tell you what Cinderella is doing today while you're visiting SeaWorld—or what a visit to SeaWorld would be like with Cinderella.

COMMON FEATURES
How many people can you find wearing Mickey Mouse ears? How many people have braces? Count them. If you're in line at a ride, count the number of people with black hair, children with cameras, people with hats on. . . . You get it? Add to the fun by guessing the number of people you'll find in each category in five minutes.

HANG LOOSE
Here's an easy way to loosen up while standing in line. Have every player rub their head and pat their leg at the same time. Then have them touch their nose and their back at the same time. Next, have them lift their right leg and grab it with their left hand. Improvise other variations on this theme. Another familiar version is "Simple Simon Says."

QUESTIONS, QUESTIONS
What better way to pass the time than by discussing the highlights of your trip? One player asks the others a variety of questions such as: What is the best beach you've seen? Where is the prettiest place you've been? What is the best ride in all the parks?

COLOR ME PURPLE
One player picks a color and other members of the group try to identify it by asking questions. Each player is allowed to ask up

to three questions before making their choice. Example: Do you see lots of people wearing this color? Are there fruits this color? Is it the color of a grape?

CHALLENGES

Create challenges for your children. Here are four examples: Take ten hops with the left foot then another ten with the right. Count backward from 20. Take as many steps as possible to get from one place to another. Hold your breath for the duration of the song "Zip-A-Dee-Doo-Dah."

20 QUESTIONS

The first player chooses an object. The other players then have (surprise) 20 questions to figure out what the object is. Each question has to be answerable by "yes" or "no." And remember, guesses count toward the 20 questions! A good strategy is to ask general questions in the beginning, such as: Is it alive? Is it very big? Is it soft? As a variation on this classic game, limit the object to things within the theme park. Another alternative is to allow each person five questions. After five tries, the next player takes a turn. The game continues until one of the players comes up with the correct answer.

I SPY

This old favorite is a great guessing game. A player says "I spy something purple," referring to an object clearly visible to the other players. Then the other players ask questions to try to determine what the object is. I Spy can also be played by initially describing the shape, dimensions, smell or sound of an object.

GAMES FOR KIDS 6 TO 90

ODD MAN OUT

The object of this counting game is to avoid saying a particular number. To begin, pick a two-digit, odd number like 25. Go around the circle. The first player can count "1" or "1, 2"; then the next player picks up the count, adding one or two numbers to the progression. For example, the first participant says "1." The next says "2, 3." The third person can say either "4" or "4, 5." Continue until someone (the loser) ends up saying "25."

SWITCH HITS

Pick a simple word. The first player must either change a letter in the original word to make another word or create an anagram. For example, start with "BAT." The next player says "BAR" or "TAB." No repeating words!

Extra challenge: After completing a round, try reciting the sequence of words from last to first.

ALPHABET SOUP

When hunger pangs begin to strike, try moving down the food chain alphabetically. Each player repeats the choices of the previous person. Begin at "A" and continue until you get all the way down to "Z." Here's how: First player: "I'm fond of asparagus." Second player: "I'm dying for asparagus and beets." Third player: "I want asparagus, beets and chicken soup."

HINKY PINKY

This word game begins with a player selecting a secret rhyming phrase like "fat cat." The player then defines the phrase—with a clue like "obese feline" or "tubby tabby"—and tells how many syllables are in the rhyming words by saying "Hink Pink" for one syllable, "Hinky Pinky" for two syllables or "Hinkety Pinkety" for three syllables. The other participants try guessing the rhyming couplet.

How about these? What Santa would say during Christmas: "Remember December." An insane flower: "Crazy daisy."

PATTERN WORK

Players of this game use clues to discover a pattern. For example, you choose "double letters" as the pattern. Some clues you could give are: "Look at the crook" or "Poodles love noodles." Another example, a little easier for younger children, could be the letter "C": "He likes cats and canaries, cars and cartoons."

LINKING UP

Here's a way to bring everyone together. The first player mentions a film, book, celebrity or city. Successive players offer a concept linked to the previous one. Example: First player: Teenage Mutant Ninja Turtles. Second player: Pizza. Third player: Cheesy. Fourth player: Smelly. First player: Socks.

BUZZ

Here's a chance to review your multiplication tables. Pick a number between one and nine. That's the buzz-number. Start counting in sequence around the circle of players. When the multiple of the buzz-number comes up in sequence, the number must be replaced by the word "buzz." Players are out if they forget to say "buzz" or if they say it at the wrong time. Example: Pick multiples of 5. When 10, 15, 20, 25, etc. come up they should be replaced by "buzz."

THE POWER OF NEGATIVE THINKING

One person thinks of a funny activity like trying to catch a greased pig. Only negative hints can be used to describe the activity: "It really smells." "You slip and slide around a lot." "There's a lot of squealing." The player who comes up with the right answer suggests the next mystery activity.

ALPHABET MEMORY

Another fun game involves picking words alphabetically. For example, the first player chooses an "A" word, the second player selects a "B" word and the third player picks a "C" word. Each player must name all the words chosen previously. The game continues through the alphabet, with players being eliminated when they forget the sequence of words.

INTERNATIONAL GEOGRAPHIC

See how well you know your way around. The first player names a country. The second player must come up with a city that begins with the last letter of the previously named country. For example, Greenland might be followed by Denver and Portugal could be followed by London. Continue in sequence through your group.

SPELL CHECKER

Here's an easy game that's a great way to build vocabulary. Pick a word like "Lazy." Then have the players run through the alphabet. When you hit a letter that is in the designated word, say "check." For example: Instead of saying "A" the player will say "check." If you forget to say "Check" for the appropriate word you are out of the game.

COCONUTTING AROUND

Coconut is a noun, not a verb. But you can have a lot of fun with this word when you substitute it for a secret verb. Here's how: The contestant goes out of hearing range or covers his or her ears. Other members of the group pick a verb such as "swim." The contestant returns, and can ask up to 12 questions aimed at discovering the verb but must always use "coconut" in the question. For example: "Can you coconut at the beach?" or "Do kids like to coconut in the bath?" After the first contestant finishes, give everyone else a chance to guess other mystery verbs.

NAME THOSE RIDES

The first player starts by naming a theme park ride, such as Space Mountain, It's A Small World, etc. The next player must name a different ride, and the game continues with each person naming a new ride. Players have ten seconds to answer. A stumped player is excused from the game. The last person left wins!

You could also try naming Disney characters (Mickey Mouse, etc.), Florida cities (Orlando, Tampa) or movies (*E.T.*, *Shrek*, *Spider-Man*).

FANTASYLAND SEE AND TELL QUESTIONS

So you're waiting in line in the Magic Kingdom's Fantasyland. Ask your kids the following questions as you wait with anticipation for the line to move forward:

At Cinderella's Golden Carrousel

❖ How many horses have swords?

❖ How many horses have reins made of braided flowers?

❖ Look at the murals above the Golden Carrousel and see who can answer these questions first:

❖ What color is the staircase where Cinderella leaves her slipper?

❖ What time is on the clock tower?

❖ Who is sitting with Cinderella in the forest?

❖ When Cinderella puts on the glass slipper, what color is her other shoe?

At Peter Pan's Flight

❖ In the scenes outside the ride, what color are the clouds?

❖ In the same scene, how many tepees are on the island?

❖ How many totem poles?

At It's A Small World

❖ How many of the following things can you find in the colorful panels outside this ride? Windmill. Flower. Castle tower. Archways. Nutcracker's face. Tree.

At Dumbo the Flying Elephant

❖ Each Dumbo is wearing a different color hat. How many colors can you spot?

❖ Can you find the little animal that befriends Dumbo?

❖ What do you see that made Dumbo think he could fly?

At Snow White's Scary Adventures

❖ In Snow White's forest scenes, what plant is sprinkled around the base of the big tree?

❖ What shape are the trees near the castle steps?

❖ Who is obviously missing from the forest?

TRIVIA CONTEST

1. Who follows the White Rabbit down the hole?
2. What makes Alice shrink and grow?
3. The butterflies Alice meets are shaped like what food?
4. Who was Dumbo's mother?
5. What's the merry tune you hear on the Dumbo ride?
6. Who was Captain Hook's bumbling sidekick?
7. Who are the children Peter Pan takes to Never-Never Land?
8. What did the crocodile swallow in *Peter Pan*?
9. Who sang "When You Wish Upon a Star" in Disney's *Pinocchio*?
10. Princess Aurora is better known by what name?
11. What was the name of the boy who loved Woody and Buzz Lightyear in *Toy Story*?
12. What was the password for the D-Day invasion?
13. Who was the first voice of Mickey Mouse?
14. What kind of television characters were Britney Spears, Christina Aguilera and Justin Timberlake?
15. Name Snow White's seven dwarfs.
16. Where do Christopher Robin, Winnie the Pooh and friends live?
17. Who is Peter Parker's alter-ego?
18. Who takes care of Curious George?
19. What is the Incredible Hulk's day job?
20. Where does the DNA come from in the movie *Jurassic Park*?
21. How many natural enemies do killer whales have?
22. How many feathers do penguins have per square inch?

Answers:

1. Alice. 2. Eating or drinking. 3. Bread. They are called Bread and Butterflies. 4. Mrs. Jumbo. 5. "You Can Fly, You Can Fly, You Can Fly." 6. Mr. Smee. 7. Wendy, Michael and John. 8. A clock. 9. Jiminy Cricket. 10. Sleeping Beauty. 11. Andy. 12. Mickey Mouse. 13. Walt Disney. 14. Mouseketeers. 15. Sneezy, Sleepy, Dopey, Doc, Grumpy, Happy and Bashful. 16. Deep in the Hundred Acre Wood. 17. Spider-Man. 18. The Man in the Yellow Hat. 19. A doctor. 20. Mosquitoes fossilized in amber. 21. None. 22. Seventy.

ONE

Disney Dreaming

It is the ultimate escape, a real-life passage to Never-Never Land. Walt Disney World, purveyor of storybook illusions and cotton-candy moods, is the most popular travel destination in the world. Every year, millions pass through the Disney door to indulge in its illusions, to drink its dreams.

Naturally, it began as a fantasy. Just a few decades ago, Disney World existed only in the mind of a California dreamer. Walt Disney had built his California Disneyland, but he wanted more. So much more, in fact, he journeyed to the opposite end of the country to get it.

But long before Disney ever set eyes on Florida, the palm-studded peninsula had been indulging dreamers. In 1513, Ponce de Leon came looking for a magical "fountain of youth" and great caches of gold thought to be waiting for ambitious treasure-seekers. He found neither youth nor gold, but instead uncovered a place of balmy breezes and palmy shores and year-round blossoms. He called it "Florida," Spanish for "feast of flowers."

Ponce de Leon left, after exploring the eastern coast, to return again in 1521, this time with the hope of setting up a little colony on the southwestern side of the peninsula. American Indians soon squelched this plan, but by then Florida's reputation as a place worth struggling for had begun to take hold.

By the early 1700s, English colonists began causing trouble for the Spanish. They laid waste the missions across northern Florida, destroyed the little "first colony" and killed many American Indians. As Spain's hold grew weaker, England's desire for the territory strengthened. Finally, in 1763, following the devastating Seven Years' War, Spain traded Florida for Cuba, abandoning the glorious dreams of eternal youth and gleaming treasure.

The English had great plans for Florida but were able to fulfill few of their dreams as their attention soon turned from palm trees and sunny shores to the dark battlefields of the American Revolution. Even the Spanish, who took the colony back from the preoccupied Redcoats, found it impossible to maintain and sold it to the United States in 1821.

By 1845, Florida had become a state, and the golden age of steamboats had begun fueling both tourism and agricultural enterprise. Rumors that a fountain of youth lay at DeLeon Springs near DeLand, and word of incredibly warm and colorful waters at Silver Springs, kept river traffic at a full head of steam. Glamorous steamers, toting produce and freight below, carried the wealthy and powerful on sightseeing tours of Florida's interior.

By the late 1880s, two millionaires with dreams as grand as Ponce de Leon's made accessible the sea-surrounded paradise and set in motion a land development that has steamrolled through the 20th century. It all began when Henry B. Plant and Henry Flagler built railroads down each coast, establishing lavish resorts that summoned the rest of the nation to paradise. In subsequent decades, the nation did indeed come, thousands of people fueled by fantasy. Some sought better jobs or the perennial chance to "start a new life." Others simply wanted to soak up rays and bask in the warm seas.

Meanwhile, the Orlando area was hosting its own brand of dreamer: the Florida cowboy. These earthy, hard-working settlers made a living off the ocali, or scrubland, that proved perfect for raising cattle. When they drove the cows they'd crack their whips, earning themselves the nickname *crackers*. The crackers also planted vast groves of oranges and grapefruit, giving birth to Florida's citrus empire.

But not all citrus farmers fared well. In the late 1800s, a Canadian named Elias Disney lost his 80-acre orange grove to a devastating freeze. Elias had moved from Kansas to Central Florida, hoping to share in this land of promise. Initially he ran a Daytona Beach hotel—one of the first in the area—then bought the grove in nearby Paisley. The hotel failed to draw enough tourists, and the farm went bust. In 1889, Elias moved to Chicago and became a construction worker. He died in the 1930s, never to return to Florida.

How ironic that 30 years later, Elias' son Walt Disney would open his own hotels not far from Daytona Beach. And while his father's hotel had failed, Walt's resorts would become a legacy.

When Walt Disney came to Orlando in the early 1960s, the area was still a babe to tourism and development, "virgin territory," as the crackers called it. In the city's small downtown, low-slung buildings gathered along several blocks. From here suburbs unfolded for a few miles but soon gave in to wide open space where sky met scrubland. Though nearly 90,000 people called it home, Orlando only had two "big" attractions, Gatorland and the Tupperware Museum (which is now closed).

Before Walt Disney ever laid the cornerstone of his fantasy world, the area was already a purist's dreamland: deep pine forests, clear, bottomless lakes and miles of silent frontier. This was

Disney World and Beyond

ATLANTIC OCEAN

Fort Pierce

Cape Canaveral

Canaveral National Seashore

Titusville

Daytona Beach

Melbourne

Florida's Turnpike

Lake Kissimmee

Orlando

Kissimmee

DeLand

Walt Disney World Resort

Lake Apopka

Winter Haven

Lake Wales

Ocala

Withlacoochee River

River

Tampa

Tampa Bay

Clearwater

St. Petersburg

Gulf of Mexico

Suwannee River

20 miles

20 kilometers

important to Disney. What he needed most was untouched land, and lots of it. Lack of land had shut him out of California, where his 100-acre Disneyland was hemmed in by outside development.

In 1964, Disney bought 27,500 acres about 20 miles southwest of Orlando. Then he set about building his kingdom. Disney died in 1966, but his Magic Kingdom became a reality five years later, opening on October 1, 1971. Within a year it drew 10.7 million visitors—more people than lived in the entire state of Florida at the time.

The dawning of Disney World sent Orlando for a spin and launched a cultural and physical metamorphosis across Central Florida. All at once, the cowtown became a boomtown. The opening of the Magic Kingdom also decided how millions of Americans would vacation the rest of this century.

> Until 1845, Orange County was called Mosquito County for the insects that protected their territory so fiercely.

But the Magic Kingdom was just the beginning, a mere pinpoint on Disney's Florida drawing board. His real dream was a city where people both worked and lived: an air-conditioned, computer-controlled community with apartments, stores, golf courses, churches and a hospital. It would be crowned with a glass dome, Disney said, to shut out the heat and humidity. Its name would be Epcot, Experimental Prototype Community of Tomorrow.

Epcot did open in 1982, but not as Walt had planned. Instead, the billion-dollar "community" took root as a theme park housing a permanent world's fair and an array of scientific attractions. In the process, it fueled the fire of growth already blazing across Central Florida. In the ten years since the Magic Kingdom had opened, the Greater Orlando population had almost doubled in size. SeaWorld had opened an oceanarium that competed for Disney World's millions. And dozens of chain motels, fast-food joints and slap-'em-up tourist attractions had latched on to Disney World's perimeter, ready to feast on the Disney pie. Across Florida, Orlando was being called a Mickey Mouse Town, while greater America was pumping millions of dollars into this vacation promised land.

The wildfire development continues today. Just as it lured Elias and Walt Disney, Central Florida remains a magnet to countless visionaries with dreams, schemes and plenty of room to grow. Today's Walt Disney World boasts two water-theme parks, a mammoth campground, 28 resort hotels, more than 150 restaurants, and shopping and nightclub complexes. The Magic Kingdom parking lot alone could hold all of California's Disneyland, the seed of Walt Disney World.

The supply simply can't meet the demand. *Each week*, the Orlando area hosts more than 800,000 visitors—a half of its total population. More than 30 million people fly in and out of Orlando's airport every year. The metropolitan area is adding more than 60,000 residents annually.

Lately, the most exciting player on the Orlando dream scene is Hollywood. Both Disney World and Universal Orlando have opened film and television production centers that double as theme parks. "Hollywood East" is what people are calling Orlando these days.

But Hollywood is only part of the frenzy gripping this fountain of fun. Disney World continues to expand, and is currently adding new attractions, half a dozen major resorts and a new town called Celebration that includes homes, condominiums, schools, churches and a million-square-foot shopping mall.

Outside Disney World, other worlds are evolving. Splendid China, a $100 million outdoor theme park, takes visitors through more than 60 miniature replicas of famous China attractions, including the half-mile-long Great Wall. It is not, however, splendid for most children, as it offers no rides or hands-on activities.

And as the fantasy makers continue to build their worlds, Greater Orlando continues to define its identity. Some say the area grew too fast too soon and tried to please too many. Plagued by traffic, littered with billboards and tinged with tacky tourism, it walks a tenuous line between welcoming growth and resenting it. But that's only half of Orlando's story. The other half is of a place holding fast to its homespun ideals, intrinsic beauty and peace of mind. It is a place with one foot in fantasy, and one planted firmly in reality.

That Disney is a world unto itself is undisputed: At any waking moment, its 43 square miles contain more people, traffic, hotels and restaurants than most cities. But more

Where to Go

than this, Disney World is also a state of mind. In a single generation, Disney World placed its stamp on the American psyche, sharing the dreams of one man with an entire nation. For here, in 1971, Walt Disney offered the world its biggest playground. And the world accepted.

But by no means does the Orlando dream vacation end at Walt Disney World. For the traveler in search of the true Central Florida experience, there is much, much more. There are two other big theme parks, Universal Orlando and SeaWorld. The mammoth Universal Orlando offers a surrealistic patchwork of theme-park fantasy and Hollywood-style illusions, while the smaller SeaWorld combines relaxed touring with a view to the sea. Along the fringes of these meccas are miles of kitschy Americana, where you can lose yourself in places such as Alligatorland and Shell World.

Then there's Orlando, which may well be the region's best-kept secret. The city boasts a sleek modern downtown, turn-of-the-20th-century architecture, fine museums and renovated shops, tony restaurants and avant-garde nightlife. Just outside the burgeoning downtown lies more scenic reality. Citrus groves that stretch to the horizon, see-through lakes cupped in cypress trees, endless pastures where only the cattle roam—they too comprise the "world" beyond Disney World.

This guidebook, *Hidden Walt Disney World, Orlando & Beyond*, takes you through Walt Disney's fantasy world, then shows you the beauty outside it. The focus throughout is on quality and value, the exemplary and the unique, while always keeping families in mind. Why families? Because every day, more and more travelers are choosing the family experience as parents and kids look to share what is offered here: the ultimate vacation.

Throughout this book you'll discover the best of the Central Florida "family friendly" establishments and attractions. You will also find plenty of tips on saving time and money, as well as handling special family needs such as babysitters, breast-feeding and stroller rentals. And the book's short feature articles and one-liner teasers give you insider information, providing local trivia and history and little known hints at a glance.

Each of Disney's major theme parks is featured in a separate chapter. There's the *Magic Kingdom*, the genesis of Disney World and the supreme fantasy factory. The place that children love best, the kingdom features fanciful rides and scenes and happy vibes. More high tech and cultural, *Epcot* combines a permanent world's fair with futuristic attractions that fuel the imagination. At *Disney–MGM Studios*, Hollywood works its movie magic through starstruck stage shows and mind-blowing rides. And go back to nature at *Disney's Animal Kingdom*, where leisurely strolls take you through uncannily recreated habitats, bring you face-to-face with exotic animals and lead you to a couple of pure thrill rides to boot.

Disney's six minor parks are highlighted in the *Rest of the World* chapter. Often considered the jewels in Disney's crown, "the rest" includes Fort Wilderness, a vast wooded campground and family retreat. There's also Typhoon Lagoon, an oasis of raft rides and water slides and tropical lushness; Blizzard Beach, a "snowy" version of Typhoon Lagoon and Disney's largest water park; Wide World of Sports, a complex that houses every athletic event imaginable; and Downtown Disney, a glitzy collection of nightclubs, restaurants and shops.

But the unfolding chapters of this tourist extravaganza don't stop here. There's Universal Orlando, which encompasses two theme parks: Universal Studios and Islands of Adventure. The biggest film and television studio outside Hollywood, *Universal Studios* is fashioned with thrilling movie scenes and rides and fabulous special effects. Next door, *Universal Islands of Adventure* features whiz-bang rides and other attractions based on the likes of Dr. Seuss, Jurassic Park and Marvel Super Hero comics.

Nearby *SeaWorld Adventure Park* delves deep into the mysteries of the ocean. The world's most popular oceanarium, it puts humans in touch with 9000 creatures big and small.

When you're waiting to try all those theme-park rides, you'll undoubtedly want to use *Games to Play While Waiting in Line*. This special fun section, which you'll find near the front of the book, features an assortment of games, poems and theme park trivia to help pass the time in line.

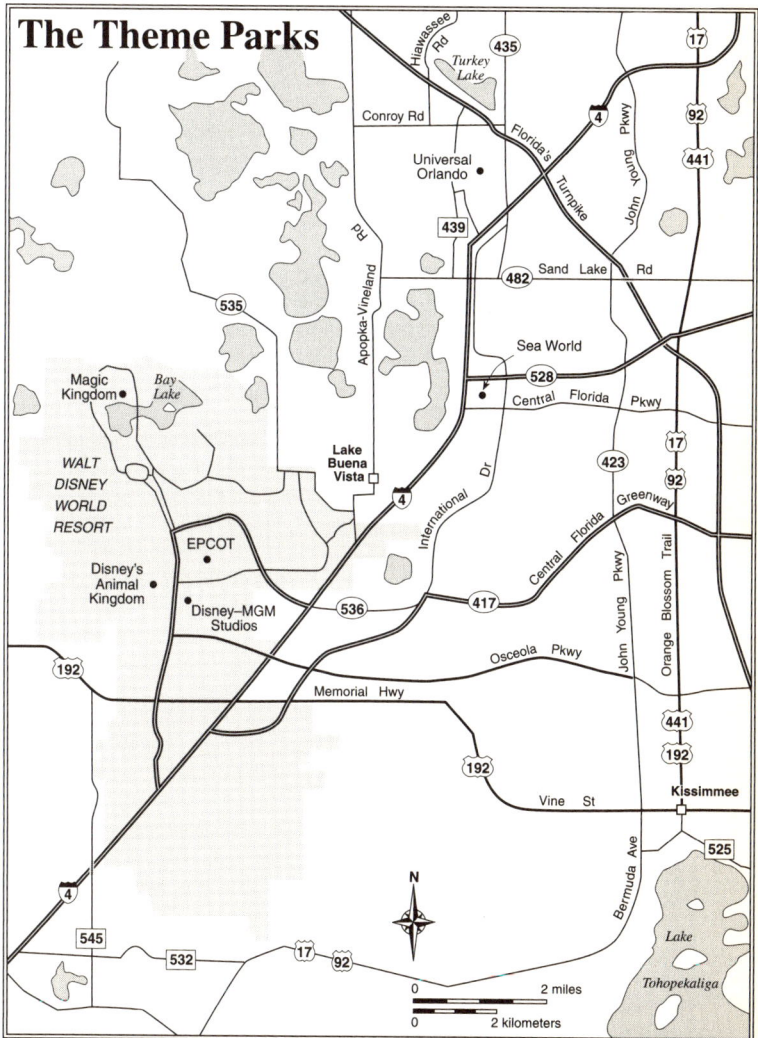

The Theme Parks

Hiawassee Rd

435

Turkey Lake

17

Conroy Rd

Florida's Turnpike

4

John Young Pkwy

92

Universal Orlando

439

441

482   Sand Lake   Rd

535

Apopka-Vineland Rd

Sea World

528

17

Magic Kingdom   *Bay Lake*

Central Florida Pkwy

423

92

WALT DISNEY WORLD RESORT

Lake Buena Vista

4

International Dr

Central Florida Greenway

Orange Blossom Trail

EPCOT

Disney's Animal Kingdom

Disney–MGM Studios

536

417

John Young Pkwy

192

Osceola   Pkwy

441

Memorial Hwy

192

192

Vine   St

Kissimmee

Bermuda Ave

525

4

N

545

532

17

92

Lake Tohopekaliga

0 ――――――― 2 miles

0 ――――――― 2 kilometers

The *Staying, Eating and Playing* chapter offers recommendations on hotels, campgrounds, restaurants, shopping and nightlife in and around the theme parks.

Away from the parks, the *Orlando* chapter portrays picture-perfect neighborhoods, tropical gardens and parks, and shimmering lakes that reflect a mix of historic and modern architecture. The chapter *Side Trips from Orlando* spans two coasts, taking in the Space Coast's lovely beaches and the historic bay scenes of Tampa. It also combs Central Florida's outback, the cowtowns and fishing camps, orange groves and thick woods just outside Orlando.

Together with Orlando and all the theme parks, they form a region poised on the cusp of reality. A place where, on the same day, you can dine in a castle with Cinderella and canoe down a pristine river. Where you can fly through Bedrock with Fred and Barney, then stroll a real city of brick streets and grand old homes. Where you can cruise through a concrete lagoon with brightly painted fish, and catch a real one in a backwoods pond.

Central Florida, the ultimate paradox, is the keeper of both manmade empires and natural treasure. The treasure was there long before the empire. With a little luck and a lot of work, it just may stay a permanent part of the landscape.

SAMPLE ITINERARIES The phenomenal scope of Walt Disney World and surrounding sights makes a short visit stressful, if not maniacal. I recommend staying for at least three days, especially if you're coming from outside Florida. To me the ideal Disney vacation is seven days, with two to three days spent outside the big theme parks. Even the most energetic visitors get tired of pounding pavement ten hours a day, and Central Florida has much to offer in the way of side trips.

However long you stay, rarely do two visitors agree on how to see the Disney World area. Still, there are good ways and bad ways to spend your days, and following a few touring guidelines can help make your vacation less of a hassle. First and foremost: *Arrive Early!*, at least a half-hour before the official opening time. Second, eat a big breakfast *before* you get to the parks. For the rest of the day, eat during "off" hours, which is before or after the dining rush hour. Third, have a good idea of the order you'd like to see the various attractions. This guide's five-star rating system can help you decide what goes at the top (and bottom) of your list. You should also remember that kids (as well as adults!) like to ride their favorite attractions over and over. Allow extra time for riding again.

Last, don't try to cram too much in. Decide what you'd really like to see—then cut that in half. One mother, writing for *Parents* magazine, says she made a "tough decision that enhanced our quality of life in Disney World: We wouldn't try to see everything on this trip."

To help you along, below are itineraries for a family spending four days at Disney World and other theme parks, along with suggestions for fifth, sixth and seventh days if you have time for them.

For the first two days, I've offered two choices: The Magic Kingdom for families with young children three to five years old, and the Magic Kingdom for families without young children. I've also provided two choices for the fourth day: Disney–MGM Studios or Universal Orlando.

These itineraries are guidelines, not marching orders. You may decide, for instance, to visit Epcot instead of the Magic Kingdom on your second day. Because Epcot is an adult-oriented park, I don't recommend it for families with young children. However, if you're determined to take them, consider going to Epcot on the first day. If they see the Magic Kingdom first, Epcot will most certainly be a disappointment to them.

> Take your child to the restroom *before* getting in a long line, especially at Dumbo!

All itineraries assume you're staying at a hotel either inside Disney World or just a few miles outside. If you're staying more than five miles away, you can take the mid-day breaks at a Disney restaurant. And however you plan your days, remember this is a vacation, not a chore.

DAY ONE: MAGIC KINGDOM
(with toddlers)

Early Morning   Be on Main Street early—it opens a half-hour before the rest of the Magic Kingdom—to pick up maps, strollers and other touring essentials. As soon as the rest of the Magic Kingdom opens, head to Cinderella Castle and make 6 p.m. dinner reservations for *Cinderella's Royal Table*. Then proceed to the heart of Fantasyland and ride, in this order:

Dumbo The Flying Elephant
Cinderella's Golden Carrousel
Snow White's Scary Adventure (may frighten small youngsters)
The Many Adventures of Winnie the Pooh
Peter Pan's Flight (may frighten small youngsters)
It's A Small World

Lunchtime   Head back to the hotel for lunch and a nap.

Afternoon   Stroll to Mickey's Toontown Fair and see *Mickey's Country House*. A walk through the Toontown Hall of Fame allows you to visit and pose with your favorite Disney characters.

Late Afternoon to Early Evening   After the show, board the *Walt Disney World Railroad* at Mickey's Toontown Fair. Ride it to Main Street, then disembark and take a jitney or horse-drawn carriage to *Cinderella Castle* for your 6 p.m. dinner.

If you have time after dinner (and aren't too exhausted), take the kids for a twinkling night ride on *Cinderella's Golden Carrousel*, or a visit with the Little Mermaid at *Ariel's Grotto*.

DAY TWO: MAGIC KINGDOM
(with toddlers)

Early Morning   Be on Main Street early once again. When the Magic Kingdom opens, go to Adventureland and ride the *Jungle Cruise*, then see the *Enchanted Tiki Room*. Walk across to Tomorrowland and ride the *Tomorrowland Transit Authority*, and *Tomorrowland Indy Speedway*.

Head to Fantasyland and ride the *Mad Tea Party* (no spinning the teacups). Then repeat other Fantasyland rides the kids like.

Lunchtime   Around lunchtime, go to Frontierland and take a raft over to *Tom Sawyer Island*. Relax while the kids burn off some energy. Have a sandwich at Aunt Polly's Dockside Landing, which is rarely crowded. Ride the raft back to the mainland and see the *Country Bear Jamboree*.

Afternoon   After the jamboree, walk out on Main Street and grab a seat for the *SpectroMagic Parade*.

Evening   Here are some suggestions for the evening: (1) see the *Spirit of Aloha Dinner* (for adults) at the Polynesian Resort in Disney World; (2) have dinner at the *Trails End Buffet* in Disney's Fort Wilderness, then catch the fort's 8 p.m. campfire party.

DAY ONE: MAGIC KINGDOM
(without toddlers)

Early Morning   Be on Main Street early—it opens a half-hour before the rest of the Magic Kingdom—to pick up maps and other touring essentials. As soon as the Magic Kingdom opens, make a mad dash to ride *Space Mountain*. Next head to Frontierland and ride *Splash Mountain*. Then walk to Adventureland for *Pirates of the Caribbean* and the *Jungle Cruise*.

SAFETY FIRST

The advent of several theme park–related accidents in the summer of 2001 has raised eyebrows about ride safety. Just how safe is your average ride? The good news: according to industry trade groups, roughly a half-billion visitors pass through ride-related turnstiles each year, most of whom leave completely unscathed (their wallets notwithstanding). Still, injuries do occur, and many people are rallying for stricter guidelines for the industry. To get information, as well as tips for keeping your family safe during your next trip, log on to www.saferparks.org.

Lunchtime   Return to Frontierland and see *Goofy's Country Dancin' Jamboree*. After the revue, exit the Magic Kingdom, have lunch and spend the afternoon relaxing.

Early Evening   Around 5 p.m., have dinner outside the Magic Kingdom, then return.

Evening   Walk over to Fantasyland and go on *Mad Tea Party*, *It's A Small World* and any other Fantasyland rides you'd like. Walk next door to Liberty Square and see *The Haunted Mansion* and *The Hall of Presidents*. Next go to Frontierland and ride *Big Thunder Mountain Railroad* or do a *Splash Mountain* encore— a great finale to any evening!

If it's summertime or during the holiday season, stay for the *Wishes Fireworks*.

DAY TWO: MAGIC KINGDOM
(without toddlers)

Early Morning   Be on Main Street early. When the Magic Kingdom opens, go to Tomorrowland and ride *Space Mountain* again. Then ride, in this order:

> *Tomorrowland Transit Authority*
> *Walt Disney's Carousel of Progress*
> *The Timekeeper*

Mid-morning   Walk across to Adventureland, stopping to repeat *Pirates of the Caribbean* or any other rides you'd like. Then stroll next door to Frontierland and see the *Country Bear Jamboree*. Afterwards, hop aboard the nearby *Liberty Belle Riverboat* at Liberty Square for a relaxing cruise, or ride *Splash Mountain* another time.

Lunchtime   Grab a bite to eat at the nearby Turkey Leg Wagon.

Afternoon   After your lunch, visit *Mickey's Country House* in Mickey's Toontown Fair, or re-ride the family's favorite Fantasyland attractions. At 3 p.m., head over to Main Street for the *SpectroMagic Parade*. After the parade, exit the Magic Kingdom.

Evening   Some options are: (1) visit *Pleasure Island*; (2) visit *Typhoon Lagoon* or *Blizzard Beach*, if they're open late; (3) have dinner at one of Epcot's *World Showcase restaurants* (assuming you've made a previous reservation), then catch the *IllumiNations: Reflections of Earth*.

DAY THREE: EPCOT

World Showcase opens late in the morning, usually around 11 a.m., so you'll spend the first half of your day in Future World.

Early Morning   Arrive early—*Spaceship Earth* and the surrounding area opens a half-hour before the rest of Epcot. At Guest Relations, you should make a 5:30 p.m. dinner reservation for one of the World Showcase restaurants. Then ride *Spaceship Earth*.

As soon as the rest of Future World opens, walk directly to the *Journey Into Imagination* pavilion and see *Honey, I Shrunk the Audience*. Then get on the *Journey Into Your Imagination* ride. Afterward, explore the rest of the pavilion, including the *Universe of Energy*.

> Spend a day in a theme park and you've walked three to four miles. If you're not in good walking shape, better get moving!

Mid-morning   Walk next door to *The Land*, take the *Living with the Land* boat ride, then see *The Circle of Life* and *Food Rocks*. Next, walk across Future World and explore the *Wonders of Life* pavilion.

Lunchtime   Have a healthy lunch at the Pure and Simple restaurant in the *Wonders of Life* pavilion. Or, if hunger strikes earlier in the morning, grab something tasty and quick from *The Land* food court, called Sunshine Season Food Fair.

Afternoon   After lunch, stroll through the *Innoventions* pavilions, then take an afternoon break outside the park.

Evening   Return to Epcot at 5 p.m., allowing yourself plenty of time to get to World Showcase. Have dinner at 5:30 p.m., then check out the various country pavilions. As the park is closing, find a spot around World Showcase Lagoon to watch the spectacular *IllumiNations: Reflections of Earth*.

DAY FOUR: DISNEY–MGM *OR* UNIVERSAL STUDIOS

DISNEY–MGM

Early Morning   Arrive on Hollywood Boulevard and Sunset Boulevard early—they open a half-hour before the rest of Disney–MGM Studios. Walk to the end of Sunset Boulevard and, when the rest of the park opens, make a beeline for *The Twilight Zone Tower of Terror*. (Note: Children who are shorter than 40 inches are not allowed to ride, and some eligible to ride will find the ride frightening.)

Head across the park and ride *Star Tours*. Afterward, walk around the corner and make a 1:30 p.m. lunch reservation at Mama Melrose's Ristorante Italiano.

If you have small children, skip these and instead go directly to *Voyage of the Little Mermaid*, then catch the mid-morning *Beauty and the Beast* show.

Mid-morning   Go on *The Great Movie Ride*. Then see the *Sounds Dangerous* show.

Lunchtime   Have lunch at Mama Melrose's Ristorante Italiano.

Afternoon   After lunch, there are two options:

(1) If you have young kids, see *Jim Henson's Muppet Vision 3D*, then visit *"Honey, I Shrunk the Kids" Movie Set Adventure*.

(2) Without small children, take the *Disney–MGM Studios Backlot Tour*. This takes two to two-and-a-half hours (including

time in line). If you're not completely exhausted, go for *Who Wants To Be a Millionaire? Play It!*

UNIVERSAL STUDIOS

Early Morning   Arrive 30 minutes before the park opens. At the Front Lot, pick up maps, strollers and other touring essentials. Warm up those legs and, when the park opens, dash to World Expo and ride *Men in Black: Alien Attack* and *Back to the Future.* (Note: Children shorter than 40 inches are not allowed to ride.) Walk around the corner and ride *E.T. Adventure.*

Morning   Keeping up the brisk pace, head to *Animal Planet Live!* Relax. If you have small kids, stroll down the street to *Nickelodeon Studios.* If not, don't miss the *Universal Horror Make-Up Show.*

Lunchtime   Have a late lunch at Mel's Drive-In in Hollywood.

Afternoon   After lunch, peruse Hollywood's street sets and check out *Terminator 2-3D.* Walk around the lagoon to San Francisco/ Amity and ride *Earthquake—The Big One.*

Evening   By now, if you're not totally zapped of energy, catch an evening performance of *Beetlejuice's Graveyard Revue.*

DAY FIVE: DISNEY'S ANIMAL KINGDOM OR UNIVERSAL ISLANDS OF ADVENTURE

DISNEY'S ANIMAL KINGDOM

Early Morning   Arrive extra early (this park has the earliest clos- ing time) and head straight for the *Kilimanjaro Safaris.* Take a walk through the *Pangani Forest Exploration Trail.*

Mid-morning   Grab a quick snack at the Kusafiri Coffee Shop & Bakery (this way you'll avoid the noon rush for lunch). Then walk to Camp Minnie-Mickey and relax at a late morning/early afternoon show of either *Festival of the Lion King* or *Pocahontas and Her Forest Friends.* Follow that up with a walk to DinoLand U.S.A. and ride on *DINOSAUR* (note: children have to be at least 40 inches tall to ride).

Lunchtime   Settle down for lunch on Discovery Island at the Flame Tree Barbecue.

Afternoon   Take in *It's Tough to be a Bug!*, followed by a ride on the *Kali River Rapids* (the height requirement is 42 inches) and a stroll through the *Maharajah Jungle Trek* in Asia. If you still have time, end your day at the last showing of *Tarzan Rocks!* (in DinoLand U.S.A.).

UNIVERSAL ISLANDS OF ADVENTURE

Early Morning   Arrive early and head straight for Marvel Super Hero Island and *The Amazing Adventures of Spider-Man* (if you are a coaster fan, stop first at *The Incredible Hulk Coaster*). Travel through Toon Lagoon to Jurassic Park. If you've got kids, stop at *Camp Jurassic* and the *Jurassic Park Discovery Center.*

Mid-morning Grab a snack at Wimpy's (this way you'll avoid huge lunch crowds) and continue to *Poseidon's Fury.* Then try out *Dueling Dragons* (before lunch!).

Lunchtime Relax over tasty barbecue fare at The Enchanted Oak Tavern, or enjoy a more upscale meal at Mythos Restaurant.

Afternoon Amble around *Seuss Landing* (you'll spend much more time here if you've got kids). End the day by doubling back to Toon Lagoon and riding at least one of those get-you-drenched attractions: *Dudley Do-Right's Ripsaw Falls, Popeye & Bluto's Bilge-Rat Barges* (both in Toon Lagoon) or the *Jurassic Park River Adventure* (in Jurassic Park).

Evening If you're not totally done in, go back and hit some of those roller coasters you may have missed earlier or get a nighttime view of the entire park from the peak of *Dr. Doom's Fearfall.* Otherwise, take in a late showing of *The Eighth Voyage of Sindbad.*

OPTIONS FOR DAYS SIX AND SEVEN

❖ *Disney–MGM* or *Universal Studios.* If you're a real movie buff, see the park you skipped on Day Four.

❖ *SeaWorld.* Kids love the animals, and adults enjoy the break from crowded high-tech attractions.

❖ *Orlando Area.* Explore downtown Orlando or lovely Winter Park.

❖ *Space Coast.* Only 50 minutes away are pretty, white-sand beaches and the Kennedy Space Center.

❖ *Busch Gardens Tampa Bay.* Spend a day at Busch Gardens. If you can, spend the night (it's 90 minutes one-way from Orlando). The next day you can explore Tampa's historic districts or visit Clearwater Beach.

You can also spend these days exploring the minor Disney theme parks, including *Typhoon Lagoon* and *Blizzard Beach.* And definitely use one of the mornings to take the kids to a Disney character breakfast—they'll love you for it.

▼▼▼▼▼▼▼▼▼
When to Go

SEASONS

Timing is the key to a successful Disney World visit. If you go during the busy season, you'll spend too much of your vacation standing in lines and sitting in traffic. Plus, you'll pay top dollar for everything. One family who went to the Magic Kingdom on Easter Sunday (a peak day) calculated they spent 6 hours in line and only 35 minutes riding. By contrast, if you go when it's slow your experience will be the opposite—a *real* family vacation.

Unfortunately for families, summer—when the children are out of school—is high season. Holidays are also a bad time to visit. Disney World has its worst crowd crunch from Christmas

Day through New Year's Day. Thanksgiving weekend takes a close second, followed by the weeks surrounding Easter. During these frenzied days, Disney World and Universal Orlando often reach capacity—more than 80,000 people *per park*—and close their gates by mid-morning. Pity those who make it inside.

You can get an up-to-the-minute Orlando weather report by calling 407-646-3131.

The very best time to visit Disney World is after the Thanksgiving weekend up to the week before Christmas. Other slow times: September and October, and the second week of January through May (excluding holidays).

If you must visit during the busy season, plan to be at the theme parks on Friday or Sunday. Incredibly, because many people travel to and from Disney World on weekends, these are the slowest days. Naturally the reverse is also true: Mondays, Tuesdays and Wednesdays are the craziest. The only exceptions are Typhoon Lagoon and Blizzard Beach, which are popular with locals on weekends.

CLIMATE

Summertime means more than crowds: It also brings sizzling hot days with afternoon showers that arrive like clockwork. The rain takes the edge off the heat, delivering breezy nights with silent lightning that leaps across the black sky. Fall and spring bring chamber-of-commerce weather, those crisp, blue, cloudless days that make your energy level soar. Winter can be warm or freezing—in a matter of hours—though most days are refreshingly cool. Central Floridians, you may as well know, rarely wear coats. To help plan your trip, the following chart lists average highs and lows, as well as rainfall, by month.

AVERAGE TEMPERATURES

	Avg. High Temp. (°F)	Avg. Low Temp. (°F)	Avg. Rainfall (in inches)
January	71	49	2.3
February	73	50	3.0
March	78	55	3.2
April	83	59	1.8
May	88	66	3.6
June	91	72	7.3
July	92	73	7.3
August	92	73	6.8
September	90	72	6.0
October	85	66	2.4
November	79	58	2.3
December	73	51	2.2

CALENDAR OF EVENTS

JANUARY   **Orlando**   The **Citrus Bowl Parade** kicks off the **Florida Citrus Bowl** game on New Year's Day.

FEBRUARY   **Daytona Beach**   The **Daytona 500** marks the culmination of Speed Week with a 200-lap stock car race at Daytona International Speedway.
Tampa   Fabled buccaneer José Gaspar leads a "takeover" of Tampa during the month of February, complete with dancing, feasting, costumes and a lavish parade during the **Gasparilla Invasion and Parade**.

MARCH   **Orlando**   The **Florida Film Festival** features more than 100 films from around the globe.
Kissimmee   Top-name performers appear on stage at the **Kissimmee Bluegrass Festival**.
Daytona Beach   Motorcyclists from across the country descend on the city for races and festivals during **Bike Week**.
Winter Park   Artisans across North America convene for the **Winter Park Sidewalk Art Festival**, one of the South's most prominent art events.
Around Central Florida   Baseball professionals arrive for **Major Leagues Spring Training**. Watch the Houston Astros in Kissimmee, the Kansas City Royals in Davenport, the Florida Marlins in Cocoa, the Cleveland Indians in Winter Haven and the Cincinnati Reds in Plant City.

APRIL   **Walt Disney World**   Mickey Mouse and the Easter Bunny go all out for the **Easter Parade** down Main Street in the Magic Kingdom (sometimes held in March). **The International Flower & Garden Festival** brings more than 30 million blooms to Epcot.
Orlando   It's Shakespeare by the water at the **Shakespeare Festival**, which runs through mid-April. Performances are at the Walt Disney Amphitheater on Lake Eola.
SeaWorld   The **Easter Sunrise Service** features nationally known speakers and singers (sometimes held in March).

MAY   **Daytona Beach**   Join more than 26,000 people at the **Zellwood Sweet Corn Festival**, which features carnival rides, games, and arts and crafts.

JUNE   **Walt Disney World**   The **Gay and Lesbian Day** welcomes thousands to the Magic Kingdom for festivities and special events.

JULY   **Walt Disney World**   **Independence Day** ends with a big bang (of fireworks, that is) at all Disney theme parks and Pleasure Island.

Kissimmee   For ropin', ridin' and square dancin' on horseback, head over to Kissimmee's **Silver Spurs Rodeo**, the oldest rodeo in Florida.

Bartow   The **Bartow Youth Villa Classic** benefits youth projects with an open golf tournament, a dance, a fashion show and more.   **AUGUST**

Kissimmee   The **Anglers Challenge** at the Chain of Lakes **SEPTEMBER** awaits locals and visitors alike vying for "the big one that didn't get away."
Space Coast   Check out Titusville's **Space Fest** for talks by astronauts, science exhibits, a car show and carnival rides at the Miracle City Mall.

Walt Disney World   PGA pros tee off at the **Oldsmobile/Walt**   **OCTOBER**
Disney World Golf Classic, held at the Walt Disney World Resort.
Universal Studios   Check out **Halloween Horror Nights** at the Studio Back Lot. For two weeks it is transformed into a maze of haunted houses, spooky shows and hundreds of roaming monsters and mutants.
Winter Park   The **Winter Park Autumn Art Festival** features local and national exhibitors.

Walt Disney World   One of the state's best art shows, the **Fes-**   **NOVEMBER**
tival of Masters at Downtown Disney Marketplace showcases stellar artwork from across the country.
Kissimmee   Arts, crafts, food and games highlight the **Osceola Art Festival** along Lake Tohopekaliga.
Daytona Beach   The **Turkey Ride Run** is a city-wide event highlighted by an antique car parade.

Walt Disney World   Disney's favorite mouse throws **Mickey's**   **DECEMBER**
Very Merry Christmas Party on Main Street U.S.A. **New Year's Eve** celebrations feature big parties with fantastic fireworks and bands in every theme park and in many Disney resorts.
Orlando   Santa Claus arrives early to lead the gala **Christmas Parade** through downtown.
Around Central Florida   Several cities usher in the season with **Christmas Parades,** tree trimmings and other yuletide festivities.

Nothing makes a trip more enjoyable than a little prep work. Parents can learn the layout of the theme parks   **Before You Go**
and what each has to offer, thus avoiding confusion and hurried decision-making after they arrive. Preteens and teens who plan to sightsee on their own should definitely know how to get around. And young children can prepare (and get wildly excited)

by reading Disney stories and watching the classic animated films. This helps acquaint them with characters and rides they'll see after they arrive. Some families rent Disney videos before their trip and hold movie nights. A few entertaining classics to rent: *Cinderella*, *Peter Pan*, *Alice in Wonderland*, *Dumbo* and *The Wind in the Willows*.

Children should also be told about height restrictions. Certain rides require minimum heights, including the Magic Kingdom's Big Thunder Mountain Railroad (40 inches), Space Mountain (44 inches), ExtraTERRORestrial Alien Encounter (44 inches), Splash Mountain (40 inches), Tomorrowland Indy Speedway (52 inches), Disney–MGM's The Twilight Zone Tower of Terror (40 inches), SeaWorld's Wild Arctic (42 inches) and Universal Studios' Back to the Future (40 inches). The theme parks strictly adhere to these rules. If your kids are too short to ride, it's best they know before you leave.

PACKING

There are two important rules to remember when packing for a "Disney World and Beyond" vacation: Pack light and pack casual. Unless you plan to spend your trip dining in ultra-deluxe restaurants, all you'll need in the way of clothing are some shorts, lightweight shirts or tops, cool slacks, a bathing suit and coverup, and something relatively casual for any special event that might call for dressing up.

The rest of your luggage space can be devoted to a few essentials. These include a good hat, high-quality sunglasses and some insect repellent. You should also take along plenty of strong sunscreen. Even the cloudiest winter days bring out that classic tourist look: scorched skin. A light jacket and rain poncho are also musts. The best ponchos are the hooded kind that come folded in a package the size of your hand. Pharmacies sell them for a few dollars while Disney and other theme parks sell them for several times that amount.

Good, soft, comfortable, lightweight shoes are critical for foot survival. A theme park visitor walks an average of four miles a day (often on blazing hot concrete, no less), so you're going to need sole support. Athletic shoes are ideal for sightseeing; save the sandals and flip flops for poolside.

If you're driving and have extra room, bring plenty of baby formula and disposable diapers. You can buy them inside the various theme parks, but you'll pay dearly. For those afternoon munchies, pack some snacks in ziplocked bags. Crackers, the kids' favorite cereal and popcorn are a few that will hold up well. Juiceboxes are also great substitutes for carbonated soft drinks sold in the theme parks.

Go to the
Head of the Line

Disney rides are legendary not only for their appeal, but also for their long lines. At last, however, Mickey is offering relief. **Fast Pass**, available on select rides (see below), is free and allows riders to check in and get an assigned time for thrills (within a half-hour period). When the appointed time arrives, grab your pass and head directly to the head of the line. You'll find it at the following rides:

Magic Kingdom
Buzz Lightyear's Space Ranger Spin
The Haunted Mansion
Jungle Cruise
The Many Adventures of Winnie the Pooh
Peter Pan's Flight
Space Mountain
Splash Mountain

Epcot
"Honey, I Shrunk the Audience"
Test Track

Disney–MGM
Indiana Jones Epic Stunt Spectacular
Jim Henson's Muppet Vision 3D
Rock 'n' Roller Coaster
Star Tours
The Twilight Zone Tower of Terror
Voyage of the Little Mermaid
Who Wants To Be a Millionaire? Play It!

Disney's Animal Kingdom
DINOSAUR
It's Tough To Be a Bug!
Kali River Rapids
Kilimanjaro Safaris

VISITOR INFO

WALT DISNEY WORLD

General Information: 407-824-4321; www.disney.go.com

Lodging Reservations: P.O. Box 409668, Atlanta, GA 30384-9668; 407-934-7639

Restaurant Reservations: 407-939-3463

Lost & Found Same Day: Magic Kingdom: 407-824-4521; Epcot: 407-560-7500; Disney–MGM Studios: 407-560-3720

Lost & Found Day After: Central lost and found number for all four parks: 407-824-4245

UNIVERSAL ORLANDO

General Information: 1000 Universal Studios Plaza, Orlando, FL 32819; 407-363-8000; www.usf.com

SEAWORLD

General Information: 7007 Sea World Drive, Orlando, FL 32821; 407-351-3600; www.seaworld.com

PARK HOURS

Theme-park operating hours seem to change more often than the Florida tides, but this is to your advantage. Walt Disney World, Universal Orlando and SeaWorld all base their opening and closing times on crowds. If heavy crowds are expected, the parks open early and close late and vice versa. However, there are a few rules of thumb:

When you're sightseeing, carry money and other small items in a fanny pack instead of a purse.

❖ During the summer and holidays, the theme parks stay open late, usually closing at 10 p.m., 11 p.m. or midnight.

❖ In the winter, the parks close around 6 or 7 p.m.

❖ On certain days of the week, Walt Disney World opens portions of the Magic Kingdom, Epcot and Disney–MGM Studios early to anyone staying at a Disney resort. Families who are not opposed to starting out at the crack of dawn can walk right onto some of their favorite rides that would typically be mobbed the rest of the day.

❖ On any given day at Disney World, advertised opening times are not always the real opening times. If the Disney folks expect crowds, they may open the parks 30 to 60 minutes before the scheduled time. There's no way to anticipate this, but you can take advantage of it by being at the park early. I recommend arriving at least an hour early at the Magic Kingdom and Epcot, and 30 minutes early at Disney–MGM Studios and Disney's Animal Kingdom.

TICKETS

WALT DISNEY WORLD   Disney World offers five ticket options: (1) one-day ticket good for one of the four big theme parks (the Magic Kingdom *or* Epcot *or* Disney–MGM Studios *or* Disney's Animal Kingdom); (2) four- or five-day Park-Hopper Pass, which allows access to any combination of the four big parks in any one day; (3) five-, six- or seven-day Park Hopper PLUS Pass, which includes access to Blizzard Beach, Typhoon Lagoon, Wide World of Sports and Downtown Disney, along with unlimited admission to any of the four big parks; (4) Annual Pass good for unlimited admission to Magic Kingdom, Epcot, Disney–MGM Studios and Disney's Animal Kingdom; and (5) Premium Annual Pass, which offers unlimited admission to the big four parks *plus* Typhoon Lagoon, Blizzard Beach, Wide World of Sports and Downtown Disney.

The Park Hopper and Park Hopper PLUS passes let you come and go in the theme parks, entering more than one park on the same day. In addition, these passes are good indefinitely and *do not* have to be used on consecutive days. For instance, you may buy a four-day Park Hopper Pass and go to the Magic Kingdom on August 5, 2004, then use the second day of the pass to go to Epcot on November 10, 2004—or whenever.

Now for the bad news: prices. Considering Walt Disney World continuously raises its admission rates, it's likely the following prices will increase as soon as this guidebook goes to print. However, to give you an idea of what you will spend (and it's a pretty penny), here are the prices, not including tax, as of press time:

	Adults	Children 3–9
		(Under 3 years, free)
One-day/One-park Ticket	$52.00	$42.00
Four-day Park Hopper	$208.00	$167.00
Five-day Park Hopper	$239.00	$192.00
Five-day Park Hopper PLUS	$269.00	$216.00
Six-day Park Hopper PLUS	$299.00	$240.00
Seven-day Park Hopper PLUS	$329.00	$264.00
Theme Park Annual Pass	$369.00	$314.00
Premium Annual Pass	$489.00	$416.00

UNIVERSAL ORLANDO   Together, Universal Studios and Universal Islands of Adventure—along with CityWalk—comprise the park complex known as Universal Orlando.

	Adults	Children 3–9
		(Under 3 years, free)
One-day/One-park Ticket	$51.95	$42.95
Two-day/Two-park Ticket	$96.95	$85.95
Three-day/Two-park Ticket	$111.95	$96.95
Two-Park Annual Pass	$169.95	$169.95

SEAWORLD   Admission options include a one-day ticket, a two-day pass that includes Busch Gardens Tampa Bay and annual passes that include Busch Gardens and Adventure Island.

	Adults	Children 3–9
		(Under 3 years, free)
One-day Ticket	$51.95	$42.95
Two-day/Two-park Pass	$85.95	$72.95
Annual Pass	$84.95	$74.95
Two-Park Annual Pass	$129.95	$119.95
Three-Park Annual Pass	$164.95	$154.95

No matter which theme park you're visiting, the single most important ticket tip is to *buy ahead of time!* If you arrive with ticket in hand, you can avoid standing in long lines.

Most area hotels sell tickets to all the theme parks and will even help plan your itinerary. You can order tickets by mail or by e-mail before you leave home or by telephone: *Disney World* (407-934-7639; www.disneyworld.com); *Universal Studios* (800-711-0080; www.usf.com); *SeaWorld* (407-351-3600; www.seaworld.com).

DISCOUNTS   Everyone who goes to Disney World can get bargains. If you know where to look and whom to ask, you'll find discounts galore for restaurants, hotels, nightclubs, shops and even the theme parks. Disney World itself offers only minimal discounts for:

❖ Members of the Disney Club. Family membership costs $39.95 a year and includes parents and all children living at the same address. A variety of savings on lodging, dining, shopping and vacation packages are featured on a rotating monthly basis. Discounts change frequently; contact the club headquarters at 800-654-6347 or www.disneyclub.com.

❖ Florida residents. During certain months—usually January, May and September—residents receive up to 30 percent off Disney theme park admission. A Florida driver's license is required for proof of residency.

Universal Orlando and SeaWorld have discounts for Florida residents and senior citizens. Check with each park for specifics.

SeaWorld, Universal Orlando, Islands of Adventure and Wet 'n Wild have teamed up to offer the Orlando FlexPass, good for 14 consecutive days at all three parks plus 7 consecutive days at City Walk. Prices, not including taxes, are $175.95 for adults, $142.95 for children ages 3–9. An upgraded version includes admission to Busch Gardens. Cost for that is $209.95 for adults, $175.95 for children.

The best discounts are outside the theme parks. The **Florida Traveler Discount Guide** offers numerous bargains at family-style lodging across Central Florida. To order a copy, send $3 to Traveler Discount Guide, 4205 Northwest 6th Street, Gainesville, FL 32609; 352-371-3948; or contact www.roomsaver.com.

The **Kissimmee–St. Cloud Convention and Visitors Bureau** has stacks of free booklets offering discounts at restaurants, shops, nightclubs and attractions outside the big theme parks. Closed weekends. ~ 1925 East Irlo Bronson Memorial Highway; P.O. Box 422007, Kissimmee, FL 34742; 407-847-5000, 800-333-5477; www.floridakiss.com.

You'll also find motel and hotel bargains advertised in the Sunday travel sections of major newspapers. Many are good deals, but some are not. Beware of inexpensive accommodations that say "close to Disney" but are really out in the boondocks. If the place is more than ten miles away, forget it. You'll waste half your day getting to and from the theme parks. You're better off paying a few extra dollars for convenience and peace of mind.

VACATION PACKAGES

There is a dizzying number of packages available for the Disney World traveler. Whether or not to buy one depends on your individual needs. If you're flying to Orlando and staying at a Disney resort, a package can probably save you money. Check for packages that combine airfare, accommodations, car rental and theme-park tickets; they often save up to 20 percent. Packages also clue you in on what your vacation is going to cost since you pay for much of it up front. And they can eliminate a lot of "what are we going to do?" decisions.

On the down side, many packages come with extras you'll never use. Golf green fees, boat rentals, even meals represent lost dollars if you don't use them. Disney's Deluxe Magic packages, for instance, include everything from a deluxe room and three meals a day to unlimited tennis, boating and golf at an ultra-deluxe price.

MICKEY MOUSE MONEY

Leave it to Disney to come up with Mickey Mouse money. As if your own greenbacks aren't good enough, Disney World offers visitors "Disney dollars." Here's how they work: When visitors enter the theme parks, they can exchange their own U.S. currency for Disney bills, dollar for dollar. Disney dollars are good at restaurants and stores throughout Disney World. Of course, there's no logical reason to buy Disney dollars. They're not more convenient than real money, and they don't provide any discounts. They can, however, tempt you to spend more. Says one mother: "Disney dollars seemed like play money. I could spend them with wild abandon—something I'd never think of doing with my own money."

For some families, these are useless, plus they take away the flexibility of being able to enjoy non-Disney restaurants and sights.

Above all, shop around. Travel agents can help compare package prices and options. Considering the intense competition among area hotels and attractions, you can't help but find a bargain.

LOCKERS & KENNELS

A locker can be a lifesaver. Great for stowing extra items such as jackets, packages and diaper bags, they're available for a small fee at all the big theme parks.

Disney World kennels offer convenient, inexpensive lodging for pets. Besides Fido and Fluffy, the kennels also accept many unusual boarders such as snakes, birds, hamsters, rabbits and goldfish. If your pet falls into the "unusual" category, bring its cage. Kennels are located at the Ticket and Transportation Center, Magic Kingdom, Epcot, Disney–MGM Studios, Animal Kingdom and at Fort Wilderness.

Universal Orlando and SeaWorld provide inexpensive lodging for dogs and cats.

CREDIT CARDS

Don't leave home without your plastic; at Disney World, you're gonna need it. The major cards—Visa, MasterCard and American Express—are accepted throughout Disney World and surrounding attractions. However, theme-park vendors and fast-food restaurants *do not* take credit cards. Bank One, located inside the Magic Kingdom, gives credit-card cash advances.

CAMERAS

What would a trip to the Disney World area be without photographs? Whether you take your camera or camcorder (or both), you will have plenty of opportunities to get those classic Disney shots. If you forget your equipment, you can buy disposable cameras or rent 35mm cameras or camcorders at the Kodak Camera Centers inside the Disney theme parks. Universal Orlando also rents cameras.

Bring your own film and video tapes; you can buy them inside the theme parks—but at premium prices. Two-hour film developing is available at all the Disney parks; one-hour developing is provided by Universal Orlando.

Flash photography is not allowed in most theme-park theaters and on many indoor rides, but other than these few restrictions, there's hardly a bad place to take pictures inside the area's theme parks. Here are some extra-choice spots for great shots of the kids:

❖ With Cinderella, in front of Cinderella Castle (Magic Kingdom)

❖ On Dumbo, before takeoff (Magic Kingdom)

❖ Next to the dancing fountains at Journey Into Imagination (Epcot)

❖ With "actors" and "actresses," in front of The Great Movie Ride (Disney–MGM Studios)

❖ Under an umbrella and streetlight from *Singin' in the Rain* (the umbrella rains when touched), at the back of New York Street across from the Backlot Tour (Disney–MGM Studios)

❖ With Jaws, in the Amity town square; or in front of Brown Derby Hat Shop in Hollywood (Universal Orlando)

❖ Feeding the dolphins, at the Dolphin Cove at Key West (SeaWorld)

STAR SYSTEM

One of the primary goals of this book is to help you sort through the overwhelming number of theme-park attractions, and I've judged them by originality, imagination, design and *overall* family appeal. Obviously, family members aren't always going to agree on the "best" rides, so I've geared my ratings toward the people in charge: the parents. For instance, some rides extremely popular with young children received lower ratings because they don't appeal to adults or even older children.

One Star signifies "one to be missed," a dullsville attraction that's a waste of time. *Two Stars* means it's below average, but with some redeeming entertainment value. *Three Stars* indicates an average attraction, one that shows at least a little imagination but may not appeal to the majority of visitors. *Four Stars* signifies above average, offering ingenuity, fantasy and top-notch design. *Five Stars* is "not to be missed," a very popular, state-of-the-art attraction that makes you want to ride over and over and over.

LODGING

With more hotel rooms (over 75,000) than any other city in the country, Greater Orlando offers a smorgasbord of lodging. From mom-and-pop motels and family-style apartments to lavish resorts that resemble mini-cities, you can choose many ways to sleep

AFTERNOON DELIGHTS

On those sweltering summer afternoons, the last place you want to be is rubbing sweaty elbows in a crowded theme park. Instead, leave the parks and head for:

• Your air-conditioned hotel room (the kids can nap while you catch an in-room movie).

• A Disney resort swimming pool, where you can lay prone in the shade and slurp an icy drink (the Polynesian Resort pools are convenient).

• A Disney hotel restaurant. They're cool and uncrowded in the afternoon.

• Pleasure Island's 24-screen movie complex.

in the Orlando area. No matter where you stay, you should book well in advance. During high season, I recommend reserving Disney resorts a year ahead of time. Disney World is, after all, the world's most popular travel destination.

In *Hidden Walt Disney World, Orlando & Beyond*, I have chosen the best family-oriented accommodations the area has to offer. Included are all the Disney World resorts, as well as nearby lodging with specialties such as children's check-in and kids-only restaurants. Rates referred to are high-season rates, so if you are looking for low-season bargains, it's good to inquire.

Budget hotels are generally less than $80 per night for two adults and two children; the rooms are clean and comfortable but lack luxury. The *moderate* hotels run $80 to $120 and provide larger rooms, plusher furniture and more attractive surroundings. At a *deluxe* hotel you can expect to spend between $120 and $200 for two adults with children. You'll check into a spacious, well-appointed room with all modern facilities; downstairs, the lobby will be a fashionable affair, and you'll usually see a restaurant, lounge and a cluster of shops. If you want to spend your time in the finest hotels, try an *ultra-deluxe* facility, which will include all the amenities and cost over $200.

CAMPING

For families, camping is a great way to stay in the Orlando area. First and foremost, it saves money. Not only is camping much less expensive than staying in a hotel, but it also saves on food bills. By cooking some of your own meals, you avoid falling into the trap of eating overpriced theme-park food three times a day. Camping also provides a physical and mental break from the rigors of theme-park touring. Best of all, most campgrounds are family-oriented, providing myriads of outdoor activities for all ages.

Campers will need basic cooking equipment and, except in winter, can make out fine with only a lightweight sleeping bag and a tent with good screens and a ground cloth. A canteen, first-aid kit, flashlight, mosquito repellent and other routine camping gear should be brought along.

Walt Disney World has its own campground, Fort Wilderness, and there are several private campgrounds just minutes from Disney's door. For campground listings, see Chapter Ten.

DINING

It seems as if Central Florida has more restaurants than people. To help you decide on this army of eateries, I've included my favorite restaurants with family appeal.

Dinner entrées at *budget* restaurants usually cost $10 or less. The ambience is informal, service usually speedy and the crowd often a local one. *Moderate*-priced restaurants range between $10 and $20 at dinner; surroundings are casual but pleasant, the menu offers more variety and the pace is usually slower. *Deluxe* establishments tab their entrées from $20 to $30; cuisines may be simple or sophisticated, depending on the location, but the decor is plusher and the service more personable. *Ultra-deluxe* dining rooms, where entrées begin at $30, are often the gourmet places; here cooking has become a fine art and the service should be impeccable.

On a diet? All the major theme parks offer light, low-calorie fare. Check with guest relations at each park.

Some restaurants change hands often and are occasionally closed in low seasons. In every instance, I've endeavored to include places with established reputations for good eating. Breakfast and lunch menus vary less in price from restaurant to restaurant than evening meals. All restaurants serve lunch and dinner unless otherwise noted.

Strollers and Car Seats   A stroller can be a lifesaver inside a theme park. If you don't bring your own, you can rent one at any Disney World park, Universal Orlando or SeaWorld. I recommend using a stroller for children three and under. Those four to five years old will definitely need one in Epcot and Universal Orlando, but probably not at Disney–MGM Studios (it's much smaller) or Disney's Animal Kingdom, where they will want to stop and smell the roses. At the Magic Kingdom, it's nice to start the day without one, then pick one up later if little legs start to give out. Keep your stroller receipt; stolen strollers are replaced free of charge with a receipt.

TRAVELING WITH CHILDREN

If you're flying to Orlando and renting a car, **Kids in Safety Seats** (407-857-0353, 877-990-5477; www.kidsinsafetyseats.com) will provide car rental seats and strollers. For a small fee, they will deliver in the Disney World area. They can also provide cribs and highchairs. Remember, Florida law requires car seats for young children.

Babysitters   Guests of Walt Disney World resorts can use the **Kids Nite Out** babysitting center, available for infants through 12-year-olds. Reservations should generally be made at least 24 hours in advance by calling 407-828-0920. Disney resorts and most area hotels also offer in-room babysitting, though it's considerably more expensive. Several private services provide bonded babysitters who will accompany you to the theme parks and watch the kids while you're sightseeing. Call ABC **Mothers, Teachers, Nannies and Grannies, Inc.** (407-857-7447) or **Super Sitters** (407-382-2558). Both companies can also provide in-room babysitting.

Baby Services   Available at the Magic Kingdom, Epcot, Disney–MGM, Disney's Animal Kingdom and Universal Orlando, Baby Services offers quiet, dimly lit rooms with changing tables and comfortable rockers for nursing. High chairs, bibs, pacifiers, formula, cereal and jars of food are also on hand for a fee. Disposable diapers are available here and at many Disney stores. The stores usually keep them under the counter, so you'll have to ask.

Nursing Nooks   Disney World's relaxed family atmosphere and abundance of cool, dark attractions make it a good place to discreetly nurse an infant. In the Magic Kingdom, try the quiet theaters at The Hall of Presidents, Mickey's PhilharMagic and Walt Disney's Carousel of Progress.

At Epcot, there are theaters at Future World's Universe of Energy, Wonders of Life (Cranium Command) and The Land (Circle of Life). In World Showcase, France, Canada, China and The American Adventure all have dark cinemas. Over in Disney–MGM Studios, you'll find comfortable seats with some privacy at Muppet Vision 3D and Voyage of the Little Mermaid. At Disney's Animal Kingdom there are several benches tucked away along the Discovery Island Trails. The dimly lit Enchanted Oak Tavern in Universal Islands of Adventure makes for a quiet stop.

For those uncomfortable about these locations, there are comfortable rocking chairs at the Baby Services area of each park.

DISABLED TRAVELERS   For the most part, Walt Disney World and surrounding theme parks are easily accessible to travelers with disabilities. Attractions feature wide, gently sloped ramps, and restrooms and restaurants are designed with the disabled in mind. Wheelchairs and motorized three-wheel vehicles are available for rent at the entrance to every theme park. For hearing-impaired guests, Disney World offers written descriptions of most attractions as well as a Telecommunications Device for the Deaf inside each park. For a small deposit, sight-impaired guests can borrow portable tape recorders and cassette tapes with narrative on each attraction. Braille Guides are also available. Check at the Guest Relations desk. For a brochure listing other services, call Walt Disney World Resort Special Reservations, 407-939-7807 or 407-939-7670 (TDD).

For information on facilities in the area, contact the **Center for Independent Living**. ~ 720 North Denning Drive, Winter Park; 407-623-1070. For advice on general travel, contact **Travelin' Talk**, a network of people and organizations. ~ P.O. Box 1796, Wheat Ridge, CO 80034; 303-232-2979; www.travelintalk.net. Also providing helpful information for disabled travelers are the **Society for Accessible Travel & Hospitality** at 347 5th Avenue, Suite 610, New York, NY 10016, 212-447-7284, fax 212-725-8253, www.sath.org; and the **MossRehab Resource Net**, Corman Building, 1200 West Tabor Road, Philadelphia, PA 19141, 215-456-9600, www.mossresourcenet.org.

Be sure to check in advance when making room reservations. Many hotels and motels feature facilities for those in wheelchairs.

SENIOR TRAVELERS   As millions have discovered, Central Florida is an ideal place for older vacationers, many of whom turn into part-time or full-time residents. The climate is mild, the terrain level, and many destina-

Getting around
Walt Disney World

Walt Disney World is so built up and spread out that it may seem intimidating at first. Not to worry. The Disney folks are quite practiced at getting visitors where they want to go. Theme-park exits are well-marked on all the major roadways. And once you're inside Disney World, all you have to do is follow the signs.

Disney's own transportation network parallels the public transportation systems of many big cities. Yet despite its size and state-of-the-art design, it doesn't always move you quickly or easily. Generally, monorails are the fastest way to travel, and buses are the slowest. But the monorail links only a few places, stopping at the Magic Kingdom, Epcot, the Grand Floridian Beach Resort, Polynesian Resort, Contemporary Resort and the Ticket and Transportation Center, while buses can take you anywhere.

The Ticket and Transportation Center is Disney World's equivalent of Grand Central Station.

If you're staying at a Disney resort, you'll receive maps and detailed instructions on how to get around. For the general public, transportation maps are available at the Ticket and Transportation Center and at the theme-park ticket counters. No matter where you're going, a Disney attendant can tell you the quickest route.

Technically, you must have a special transportation ID to ride the Disney monorails, buses and boats. The ID card is issued to guests of Disney resorts and to those with four- or five-day theme-park passes.

tions offer significant discounts. Off-season rates make the area exceedingly attractive for travelers on limited incomes. During slow season, visitors 55 and older enjoy discounts at Walt Disney World, Universal Orlando, SeaWorld and other local attractions. Florida residents over 65 can benefit from reduced camping rates at most state parks, and the Golden Age Passport, which must be applied for in person, allows free admission to national parks and monuments for anyone 62 and older.

The **American Association of Retired Persons** (AARP) offers membership to anyone 50 or over. AARP's benefits include travel discounts with a number of firms. ~ 601 E Street NW, Washington, DC 20049; 800-424-3410; www.aarp.org.

Elderhostel offers reasonably priced, all-inclusive educational programs in a variety of Central Florida locations throughout the year. ~ 11 Avenue de Lafayette, Boston, MA 02111; 877-426-8056, fax 617-426-0701; www.elderhostel.org.

Be extra careful about health matters. In addition to the medications you ordinarily use, it's a good idea to bring along the prescriptions for obtaining more. Consider carrying a medical record with you—including your medical history and current medical status as well as your doctor's name, phone number and address. Make sure that your insurance covers you while away from home.

FOREIGN TRAVELERS

Passports and Visas   Most foreign visitors need a passport and tourist visa to enter the United States. Contact your nearest United States embassy or consulate well in advance to obtain a visa and to check on any other entry requirements.

Customs Requirements   Foreign travelers are allowed to carry in the following: 200 cigarettes (1 carton), 50 cigars or 2 kilograms (4.4 pounds) of smoking tobacco; one liter of alcohol for personal use only (you must be 21 years of age to bring in alcohol); and US$100 worth of duty-free gifts that can include an additional quantity of 100 cigars. You may bring in any amount of currency, but must fill out a form if you bring in over US$10,000. Carry any prescription drugs in clearly marked

CAR TROUBLE?

If your car breaks down at Disney World, Universal Orlando or SeaWorld, a security officer will come to the rescue. Security vehicles patrol the parking lots, making rounds every five to ten minutes. Simply hail one of the vehicles, which resemble police cruisers. The officers will either start your engine or call someone who can.

containers. (You may have to produce a written prescription or doctor's statement for the customs' officer.) Meat or meat products, seeds, plants, fruits and narcotics are not allowed to be brought into the United States. Contact the **United States Customs Service** for more information. ~ 1300 Pennsylvania Avenue NW, Washington, DC 20229; 202-927-6724; www.customs. treas.gov.

Driving   If you plan to rent a car, an international driver's license should be obtained *before* arriving in Florida. Some car rental agencies require both a foreign license and an international driver's license. Many also require a lessee to be at least 25 years of age; nearly all require a major credit card. Seat belts are mandatory for both driver and all passengers. Children under the age of 5 or 40 pounds should be in the back seat in approved child-safety restraints.

Currency   United States money is based on the dollar. Bills come in six denominations: $1, $5, $10, $20, $50 and $100. Every dollar is divided into 100 cents. Coins are the penny (1 cent), nickel (5 cents), dime (10 cents) and quarter (25 cents). Half-dollar and dollar coins are rarely used. You may not use foreign currency to purchase goods and services in the United States. You may, however, exchange your currency at the Bank One located inside Disney World's Magic Kingdom. Inside Universal Orlando, change your money at Wachovia Bank; at SeaWorld, the Special Services desk provides a foreign currency exchange. Disney World resorts and many area hotels will also exchange your money.

Language Assistance   Disney's Magic Kingdom, Epcot and Disney–MGM Studios provide translated recordings for many attractions. Check with Guest Services inside each park. Universal Orlando's Guest Relations has foreign language maps.

Electricity and Electronics   Electric outlets use currents of 110 volts, 60 cycles. To operate appliances made for other electrical systems, you need a transformer or other adapter. Travelers who use laptop computers for telecommunication should be aware that modem configurations for U.S. telephone systems may be different from their European counterparts. Similarly, the U.S. format for videotapes is different from that in Europe; National Park Service visitors centers and other stores that sell souvenir videos often have them available in European format on request.

Weights and Measures   The United States uses the English system of weights and measures. American units and their metric equivalents are: 1 inch = 2.5 centimeters; 1 foot (12 inches) = 0.3 meter; 1 yard (3 feet) = 0.9 meter; 1 mile (5280 feet) = 1.6 kilometers; 1 ounce = 28 grams; 1 pound (16 ounces) = 0.45 kilogram; 1 quart (liquid) = 0.9 liter.

▼ ▼ ▼ ▼ ▼ ▼ ▼ ▼ ▼ ▼

Transportation

CAR

Several major highways lead to the Orlando area. From the northeast United States, take **Route 95** south to Daytona Beach, then pick up **Route 4** west. Route 4 makes a beeline for Orlando.

From the midwestern United States, pick up **Route 75** south to **Florida's Turnpike**. Head south on the turnpike to Route 4.

Route 4, which runs from Daytona Beach to Tampa, is the major artery through Orlando. Walt Disney World, Universal Orlando and SeaWorld all have exits along Route 4.

AIR

Orlando International Airport is the air gateway to the Walt Disney World area. A state-of-the-art facility, it lies 27 miles northeast of Disney World and 15 miles southeast of downtown Orlando.

◆ ◆

It is served by more than 50 domestic and foreign airlines including Air Jamaica, American Airlines, America West, British Airways, Continental Airlines, Delta Air Lines, Icelandair, Martinair, Northwest Airlines, Southwest Airlines, United Airlines, US Airways and Virgin Atlantic.

To liven up traveling time, take along audiotapes of classic Disney stories.

Once you arrive, the Walt Disney World information desk (main building) can help you get organized. Inexpensive shuttle service to the Disney World area is provided by **Mears Motorshuttle** (407-423-5566, 800-759-5219).

TRAIN

In Central Florida, **Amtrak** (800-872-7245; www.amtrak.com) makes stops in the Orlando area at 1400 Sligh Boulevard; Kissimmee at 111 Dakin Street; DeLand at 2491 Old New York Avenue; and Palatka at 220 North 11th Street. If you're traveling to the Orlando area from the vicinity of New York City, consider Amtrak's **Auto Train**. You can board your car at Lorton, Virginia, four hours from New York, and depart from Sanford at 600 Persimmon Avenue, about 25 miles northeast of Orlando.

BUS

Traveling by bus is not the quickest way to arrive, but it's usually the least expensive. **Greyhound Bus Lines** (800-231-2222; www.greyhound.com) has a station in Orlando at 555 North John Young Parkway; 407-292-3424. There's also one near Walt Disney World in Kissimmee at 103 East Dakin Avenue; 407-847-3911. The Kissimmee station offers van service to the major theme parks and resort hotels in the area.

CAR RENTALS

Companies at the Orlando airport include **Avis Rent A Car** (800-331-1212), **Budget Rent A Car** (800-527-0700), **Dollar Rent A Car** (800-800-4000), **Hertz Rent A Car** (800-654-3131) and **National Car Rental** (800-227-7368). Companies that provide free airport pickup service include **Alamo Rent A Car** (800-327-9633),

Enterprise Rent A Car (800-325-8007) and **Thrifty Car Rental** (800-367-2277).

For car rentals in Walt Disney World, call **National Car Rental** (800-227-7368). Other rental agencies nearby include **Alamo Rent A Car** (800-327-9633), **Avis Rent A Car** (800-331-1212), **Budget Rent A Car** (800-527-0700), **Enterprise Rent A Car** (800-325-8007) and **Hertz Rent A Car** (800-654-3131). Remember: The closer you are to Disney World, the more expensive the gas. Fill up before you get there.

TWO

The Magic Kingdom

To many people, the Magic Kingdom *is* Disney World. For here is where Walt Disney first worked his fantasy formula on Florida, recasting a swath of swampland into fairy-tale architecture, whimsical artistry, flourishing gardens and state-of-the-art attractions. Here the brilliant cartoonist pushed make-believe to its extreme limit, devising a fictional kingdom woven with cartoon characters, simulated towns and jungles, lighthearted music, squeaky clean streets, shimmering lakes and thrilling rides all spun into one colorful, jubilant experience.

The Magic Kingdom takes up only 107 of Disney World's 29,900 acres—little more than a drop in a pond—yet it is the heart of that world. A virtual clone of Anaheim, California's Disneyland, the kingdom is fashioned with 32 attractions, 34 eateries, 44 food carts, 47 shops and 22 merchandise carts spread across seven imaginative—and vastly different—"lands." The most popular is Fantasyland, a dreamy web of storybook architecture, boat rides, carousels and merry music. Adventureland, with its thatched buildings, squawking parrots and jungle journey, offers a tame trek through the wilds of Africa and South America.

Frontierland presents a stony profile of rust-colored knolls and cowboy-and-Indian scenes, while adjacent Liberty Square emulates early America with colonial storefronts and patriotic attractions. Like a page out of the Sunday comics come to life, Mickey's Toontown Fair features roaming cartoon characters, kid-size houses and stores painted in a riot of colors. In contrast, Tomorrowland was originally designed as a series of stark whitewashed buildings. This land portrayed the future as Disney saw it in the 1960s. That vision hasn't endured, however; in 1995, Tomorrowland received a facelift that transformed the monumental white blocks of concrete into a colorfully festooned land of convex Tinker Toy–style shapes. Today, Tomorrowland is best known as home to the park's most popular ride, Space Mountain.

Then there's Main Street U.S.A., the key to the Magic Kingdom and the first sight that greets visitors. Here brick streets, old-fashioned lampposts and intricate building facades create a splendid facsimile of an idealized American town. There's also the colorful depot for the Walt Disney World Railroad, a steam train that chugs around the perimeter of the Magic Kingdom. Just beyond Main Street is a lush park known as Central Plaza that is ringed with indigo water and dotted with grand oak trees and lacquered park benches. The magnificent Cinderella Castle looms ahead, and all day long visitors gather to stare and marvel at its many spires and to dream fairy-tale dreams.

Each area's remarkable attention to detail—from the decorated trash cans to employee costumes and clever restaurant menus—never ceases to amaze even frequent visitors. There is true joy in immersing yourself in the mood of one land and then being transformed by the aura of a thoroughly different realm. Even on the worst days, when the park is crushed with people and the sun threatens to suffocate, it is impossible not to be caught up in the spirit of the Magic Kingdom.

Nighttime brings more illusions to the kingdom, as beads of light trace intricate rooflines and the castle spires glow high in the inky sky. This is the most festive time, when triumphant music pulsates from parades, costumed singers pour through the streets and fireworks blast against the eastern stars.

Since the Magic Kingdom's opening in 1971, Disney World has spawned its other theme parks, including the 260-acre Epcot (more than twice the size of the Magic Kingdom). But despite the competition, the Magic Kingdom remains the ultimate escape valve, the spot farthest from reality. It is a place for children, and a place where adults can think like children. It is a place that tugs on the hearts of dreamers and even those skeptics who chide its corny humor, conservative overtones and idealistic approach.

Anyone who has experienced the fascination of Cinderella Castle, the adrenaline rush of Space Mountain or the happy vibes of *It's A Small World* knows the Magic Kingdom has no parallel. In fact, more people visit the Magic Kingdom than any other theme park *in the world*.

Nuts & Bolts

ARRIVAL

Getting to the Magic Kingdom can be quite a chore, complex and time-consuming. Because of this—and because early arrivers can avoid long lines—it is imperative to get there *one to two hours* before the advertised opening time. Trams and monorails are usually operating two hours prior to opening, and Main Street typically opens 30 minutes to an hour before the rest of the park.

From the Grand Floridian Beach, Contemporary and Polynesian resorts: Take the hotel monorail directly to the Magic Kingdom.

From Epcot: Take the Epcot monorail to the Ticket and Transportation Center, then transfer to the Magic Kingdom monorail or ride the ferry.

From Disney–MGM Studios and Disney's Animal Kingdom: Take a Disney bus directly to the Magic Kingdom.

From the Wilderness Lodge: Take a Disney boat directly to the Magic Kingdom.

From the Yacht Club, Beach Club, Port Orleans, Dixie Landings or All-Star Sports, Music and Movie resorts: Take a Disney bus directly to the Magic Kingdom.

From the Swan or Dolphin hotels or the Caribbean Beach Resort: Take a Disney bus directly to the Magic Kingdom.

From Fort Wilderness, Pleasure Island, Typhoon Lagoon, Blizzard Beach or Downtown Disney: Take a Disney bus directly to the Magic Kingdom.

From area hotels not in Disney World: Most hotels provide shuttles to and from the Magic Kingdom. However, they often run only on the hour or every two or three hours. In this case, it's better to drive.

By Car: On Route 4, look for signs that say "Walt Disney World" exits. Take the Magic Kingdom exit and follow it about two miles to the toll plaza. Here you'll pay a $7 parking fee and be directed to a mammoth parking lot that seems to fall off the horizon. At this point, you're still at least 20 minutes from the Magic Kingdom.

It's imperative to *make a note of your parking row* (sections are named after Disney characters such as Pluto, Goofy and Chip and Dale) or you might not be able to find your car at the end of the day. From here you take a tram to the Ticket and Transportation Center, a sort of Grand Central Station where you purchase admission tickets and board a monorail or ferryboat for the half-mile journey to the Magic Kingdom. The monorails are faster (two minutes compared to the ferry's five minutes), but lines are usually longer because visitors avoid the extra walk to the ferry launch. If the monorails appear crowded, opt for the ferry: it will be quicker and more relaxing.

GAME PLAN Remember once again that it's a good idea to get to the Magic Kingdom an hour or two before the announced opening time. Then it will be easy to plan your morning. For instance, if the Disney people say the park opens at 9 a.m., you can park your car at 7:30 a.m. and be on Main Street between 8 and 8:30 a.m. Here you can rent a stroller or locker, get maps and information, secure reservations for live shows, eat breakfast and stroll Main Street's shops and sights—before all of the crowds arrive.

Most important, you may even get into the rest of the park early. During the summer, holidays and other busy times, the Magic Kingdom sometimes opens as early as an hour before the advertised time for Disney World resort guests. This helps prevent traffic gridlock and record-breaking ticket lines on days when the place fills up—and visitors are turned away—well before noon. There's no way to surmise when this will happen, but one thing is certain: Arriving early can save you *up to several hours* of waiting in line

MAGIC KINGDOM

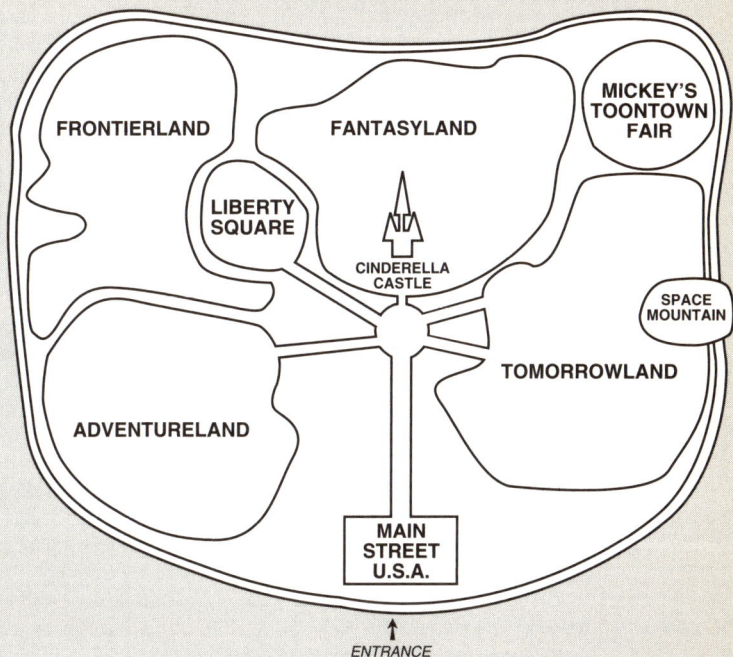

```
                          MICKEY'S
                          TOONTOWN
                            FAIR
FRONTIERLAND      FANTASYLAND

         LIBERTY
         SQUARE
                                        SPACE
                 CINDERELLA           MOUNTAIN
                   CASTLE
                                TOMORROWLAND

ADVENTURELAND

                    MAIN
                   STREET
                   U.S.A.

                  ↑
                ENTRANCE
```

MAIN STREET U.S.A.
Main Street Cinema
Share a Dream Come True
SpectroMagic Parade
Walt Disney World Railroad

ADVENTURELAND
Enchanted Tiki Room–Under New
   Management
Jungle Cruise
The Magic Carpets of Aladdin
Pirates of the Caribbean
Swiss Family Treehouse

LIBERTY SQUARE
The Hall of Presidents
The Haunted Mansion
Liberty Belle Riverboat
Mike Fink Keel Boats

FRONTIERLAND
Big Thunder Mountain Railroad
Country Bear Jamboree
Frontierland Shootin' Arcade
Goofy's Country Dancin' Jamboree
Splash Mountain
Tom Sawyer Island

FANTASYLAND
Ariel's Grotto
Cinderella Castle
Cinderella's Golden Carrousel
Dumbo The Flying Elephant
It's A Small World
Mad Tea Party
The Many Adventures of
   Winnie the Pooh
Mickey's PhilharMagic
Peter Pan's Flight
Snow White's Scary Adventures

MICKEY'S TOONTOWN FAIR
The Barnstormer
Donald Duck's Boat, Miss Daisy
Mickey's Country House
Minnie's Country House
Toontown Hall of Fame

TOMORROWLAND
Astro Orbiter
Buzz Lightyear's Space Ranger Spin
The ExtraTERRORestrial Alien
   Encounter
Space Mountain
The Timekeeper
Tomorrowland Indy Speedway
Tomorrowland Transit Authority
Walt Disney's Carousel of Progress

for attractions. Best of all, it removes the aggravation from an experience that should be pure entertainment and fantasy.

This flexible opening axiom doesn't apply to quitting time, however. Attractions and rides usually close pronto, although Main Street stays open a half-hour to an hour later and buses and monorails operate about two hours after closing. This, of course, is a prime time to see Main Street. While the rest of the park is funneling out, you can experience the sights and shops at leisure. And buying souvenirs just before closing means you won't have to rent a storage locker or lug the bags around all day.

Some other helpful hints:

❖ Check the schedule boards that list current waiting times for the most popular rides, shows and attractions. You'll find a board at the end of Main Street, near the Cinderella Castle Forecourt, and in Tomorrowland next to Astro Orbiter. Disney employees stationed at both boards will also provide sightseeing advice.

❖ Try to see all of one theme area, or "land," before moving on to the next. The Magic Kingdom is so complex it's disastrous to sightsee checkerboard style.

❖ Take your time. Trying to see all of the Magic Kingdom in one day is like trying to watch ten movies in one night. It's impossible!

❖ Eat an early or late lunch—before 11:30 a.m. or after 2 p.m. Ditto for dinner, which should be before 4:30 p.m. or after 8 p.m. You'll avoid the meal crowd crush and have more time to do what you really came here for.

GUEST SERVICES

Stroller and Wheelchair Rentals   Strollers and wheelchairs are available at the Stroller Shop, on the east side of the main entrance.

Baby Services   Located next to the Crystal Palace restaurant on Main Street U.S.A. Services include changing tables and comfortable rockers for nursing. Diapers, formula and other baby needs are also available here, as well as in some stores throughout the Magic Kingdom.

Lockers   Available under the Main Street Railroad Station at the foot of Main Street, and at the Ticket and Transportation Center. Be forewarned: All lockers cost $5 per day plus $2 refundable deposit for unlimited use. Items too large for lockers can be checked at Station Break desk.

Pets   Pets are not allowed in The Magic Kingdom. However, you can board them for the day or overnight at the kennel near the parking toll plaza. If you leave your dog overnight, you are required to walk your pet nightly.

Lost Children   Report lost children to Guest Relations (in the Ticket and Transportation Center) or Baby Services on Main Street.

Package Pickup   Serious shoppers should consider this free service, which lets you forward all your Magic Kingdom purchases to Guest Relations. You can pick up your packages on your way out and avoid lugging them around all day. One note: Package pickup sometimes has human traffic jams between 5 p.m. and 6 p.m., and during the half-hour before park closing.

Lost & Found Report lost or found articles to Guest Relations.

Banking Traveler's check services, cash advances and automatic teller machines are available under Main Street's train station, near the Diamond Horseshoe Saloon in Frontierland and at the Tomorrowland Light and Power Company near Space Mountain. Open from 8:30 a.m. to 4 p.m. every day.

GETTING AROUND

To get a feel for the place, think of the Magic Kingdom as a giant wheel whose spokes lead to seven lands. At the base of the wheel is Main Street U.S.A., which serves as the park's entrance and the place to get oriented. The Walt Disney World Railroad travels the rim of the wheel, while overhead Skyway buckets trickle across the northeast sky.

At the wheel's hub sits Central Plaza, a verdant park in front of Cinderella Castle. The plaza is a good meeting place if your party decides to split up during the day—or if someone gets lost. There are also plenty of broad grassy areas where parents can rest while children release some energy. Families sometimes have picnics here, spreading out blankets under shade trees and sorting out which rides to go on next.

From the hub, bridges and walkways lead to each land. Traveling clockwise, you'll encounter Adventureland, then Frontierland, Liberty Square, Fantasyland, Mickey's Toontown Fair and Tomorrowland. On a map the transitions between lands look fairly easy, though in reality there's plenty to foul you up. The entire kingdom is riddled with sinuous waterways and curving lanes that don't always take you from here to there. Anyone who's just ridden Space Mountain and attempts a dash to Big

STREET SHOWS

You're strolling along Main Street, enjoying the handsome architecture, when suddenly a barbershop quartet breaks into harmony. Dressed in bright-colored pinstriped suits, the men belt out a comical song and lift their hats to a cheering crowd. You round the corner into jungly Adventureland, and there's a Caribbean band tapping away on steel drums. Nearby at Casey's Corner on Main Street, a piano player performs ragtime tunes. Live street shows, lending whimsy and festivity to the Magic Kingdom, are staged daily at various locations across the park. Times change frequently, so check the brochure offered at the entrance for show schedules.

Thunder Mountain Railroad with kids in tow will find he's undertaken a trying trek.

Translation: Use a map to plot your course, taking it slow until you get your bearings. If you get lost, a Disney employee can always help.

Main Street U.S.A.

What finer introduction to an enchanted kingdom than a postcard-perfect street? This replica of a beautiful American town affords a visually exciting collage of wrought-iron balconies, ornate balustrades, gingerbread designs, old-fashioned lampposts, painted benches, shade-giving trees, merry music, espresso and pastry carts, and hanging pots brimming with flowers. Bright-red fire engines clang, jitneys whiz around and horses haul trolleys packed with visitors.

Much of Main Street is lined with clever shops and businesses whose task seems to entertain as well as sell. On the unusual side, there is Uptown Jewelers, which displays gorgeous ceramic eggs. One great spot is the Harmony Barber Shop, where people (particularly children) press their faces against the front window to watch mustached barbers give old-time shaves and haircuts (see Chapter Ten for information on shopping in Disney World).

Interspersed among the shops are nifty sights and eateries that funnel heady aromas out their propped-open doors. There's a pastry shop, an ice cream parlor with red-and-white awnings, and a confectionery where candy makers swirl huge vats of peanut brittle. Each place has its own ambience, some busy and bright, others formal and Victorian, and still others rustic and woody.

There is so much to keep the eye (and mind) busy here that it takes a lot longer than 40 minutes—the average time a visitor spends on Main Street—to absorb everything. Best of all, this area is rarely clogged with people and can be visited anytime. Plan to come between midmorning and midafternoon, when more popular attractions are crowded and the sun is most intense. Main Street is also a good place for one parent to take the kids while the other goes solo on Space Mountain or any other ride closed to small children.

JITNEYS, CARRIAGES AND OTHER WACKY WHEELS

To see Main Street on four (or more) wheels, board one of the zany vehicles that tool around this brick-lined thoroughfare. There are bright red jitneys and fire engines, carts pulled by muscled horses, double-decker buses and horseless carriages. Most make one-way trips from the foot of Main Street to Cinderella Castle. The Main Street trolleys are drawn by husky Belgian and Percheron horses, breeds that were once used to pull plows in Europe.

To explore Main Street, begin by stopping at **Guest Relations** for maps, entertainment and dining schedules, lost and found, and general information.

Vintage Disney flicks, including some great silent cartoons, run continuously at the **Main Street Cinema**. Though it's standing only, the octagonal room with six screens is cool, dark and a welcome respite from lines and summer heat. Kids are often fascinated by these unfamiliar black-and-white cartoons, but it's the adults who can while away a half-hour or more watching such classics as *Steamboat Willie*. The first cartoon with sound, *Steamboat* has a particularly nostalgic story line: a clever mouse named Mickey falls in love with a rosy-cheeked beauty named Minnie. You'll also see a film called *Mickey's Big Break*, a whimsical piece in which Mickey Mouse auditions for the role in *Steamboat Willie*.

Main Street is also home to a larger attraction:

Walt Disney World Railroad ★★★ With their striped awnings, brightly painted bench seats and thunderous choo choo, these old-fashioned steam trains offers loads of fun. You can hop on one of four turn-of-the-20th-century trains that circle the Magic Kingdom, stopping at Frontierland and Mickey's Toontown Fair and traversing what a narrator terms "original Florida frontier"—fern hammocks and scrub palmetto—as well as some hokey Disney character cutouts. Kids love the open-air experience and the chance to ride on what they often call "a real live train." For adults, it's a great way to rest tired bones while getting a splendid introduction to each land. In fact, the train is the only ride that offers close-up views of the Magic Kingdom.

TIPS: Lines frequently form at the Main Street and Frontierland depots but rarely at Mickey's Toontown Fair. Trains run every four to ten minutes.

Share a Dream Come True ★★★★ Most little kids (and many adults for that matter) come to Disney World looking for their favorite princes and princesses, and you'll find many of them at the Share a Dream Come True Parade. Most of the A-list is here (Cinderella, Aladdin, etc.), all performing scenes from some of Disney's most popular animated films.

The parade wends down Main Street every day beginning at 3 p.m. If you're lucky (and early), you might even get a chance to join in the action, waltzing with Cinderella's court, running around with the living objects from the Beast's enchanted castle, or doing a silly hop step with Aladdin's dancing camels. Performance coaches assign "guest stars" about 20 minutes before showtime, but you'll have to be on the parade route even earlier (about 45 minutes) to get a good viewing spot. Don't fret if you're not picked; the audience gets fun things to do, too.

TIPS: Two good viewing spots are in front of Casey's Korner and the Plaza Ice Cream Parlor. Both are home to more than one performance stop.

SpectroMagic Parade ★★★★ The lights had been dimmed and the bulbs had been sold off. But just when you thought you'd seen the last of this Disneyland classic parade, it has been refurbished and reinstalled in Disney World. Folks who missed its long run in California will be pleased to get acquainted with the glowing spectacle featuring 500 bulbs lighting 26 Disney-themed floats. Love it or hate it, the infectious tune gets everyone's toes tapping; you'll probably be humming it long after you leave the park.

The Walt Disney World Railroad's *Lilly Belle* train is named for Walt's wife.

TIPS: The parade played for eons in Anaheim before moving here. If you saw it during your childhood, don't miss this chance for a bit of nostalgia.

Adventureland

The crude wooden bridge from Central Plaza to Adventureland is like a tunnel of metamorphosis: on one side are brick lanes, cropped lawns and the bright orderliness of the plaza; on the other are dim, watery passages, tangles of vines and croaks of toads. Here in Adventureland, Disney's interpretation of exotica thrives with totem poles and carved spears, waterfalls that gush down algae-covered rock and bright blooms that poke across footpaths. The jungly scheme is peppered with the flavors of Africa, Polynesia and the Caribbean: parrots squawk, drums pound and mechanical elephants trumpet. Even the air is heavy with the musty scent of the tropics.

The "faraway place" theme is emphasized by the architecture: a fusion of thatched huts, tin-roofed buildings washed in sherbet hues, and carved wood and adobe facades crowned with clay tile.

One of the best buildings is the Caribbean Plaza, a breezy network of shops where goods are stacked under stucco arches. Pirate hats, bangle jewelry, treasure chests and other "loot" are sold by women in batik prints and harem garb, giving the place a festive, freewheeling feel.

Perhaps of all the lands, Adventureland most appeals to all ages. Families, singles, couples, seniors—they all savor Adventureland. No rides here can be classified as "just for kids," and none prohibits young children. From the mammoth treehouse and adventure-packed jungle cruise to the boat that braves pirate attacks, all the rides feature something for every person.

WHAT TO SEE & DO

The Magic Carpets of Aladdin ★★★ After one feature film, a television series and a couple of direct-to-video sequels, it's about time the fezzed one got his own attraction. A thrill ride it isn't. But going around in circles à la Dumbo, Aladdin's ride has future classic written all over it.

Riders board four-passenger carpets for a twirl around a genie bottle, controlling upward and downward motion as they go. Those folks experienced in endless line-waiting for the aforementioned elephant ride in Fantasyland probably envision hours in line for this attraction, but while it's sure to draw crowds, the ride has 16 vehicles, meaning it can potentially accommodate more visitors than Dumbo. That said, it's still a short ride—little bang for your buck, and probably not one you'd choose to ride if you're visiting the Magic Kingdom sans toddlers. But if you've got little kids, this is one they aren't going to want to pass up. Just grin and bear it. And while you're in the neighborhood, check out the **Agrabah Marketplace**, an open-air "Middle Eastern" bazaar.

TIPS: Watch out for the camels; they spit.

Swiss Family Treehouse ★★★ Some visitors pooh-pooh this attraction as dull and even hard work but most love the challenge of scaling such a magnificent tree. Spanning 90 feet in diameter and boasting some 600 branches, this multilevel banyan treehouse is fashioned after the island home in the classic tale *Swiss Family Robinson*. A marvel of design and ingenuity, the tree boasts some 800,000 perfectly applied vinyl leaves (costing a dollar a leaf in the early 1970s) and a trunk that's stupendous. Though the tree itself is manmade, the Spanish moss on its branches is real. Narrow wooden steps twist around the trunk and through limbs, providing views of rooms furnished so warmly it seems as if the shipwrecked family indeed lives there. Patchwork quilts are tossed across poster beds, and wood pipes deliver fresh water to each room. Notice the spacious kitchen, located at the tree's base, with its stone floors, brick oven and array of pots and pans.

TIPS: The tree requires a somewhat arduous climb that may be too strenuous for small children and seniors.

Jungle Cruise ★★★★ One of Disney's most famous and best-loved rides is this fun-filled, crazy cruise through a skillfully simulated jungle. Visitors sit elbow-to-elbow on bench seats in canopied riverboats with names such as *Nile Nellie* and *Amazon Annie*. A captain, outfitted in safari hat and belted jacket, guides the group on what he warns is a "perilous" subtropical trek. It's one of the few rides narrated by "real" people—a refreshing feature—and these narrators are amusing, with their corny jokes and zany antics. During the ten-minute, action-packed voyage, explorers elude elephants, hippos, zebras, wildebeests, giraffes and pythons. They also dodge waterfalls, escape from pygmies and sneak through a Cambodian temple beaded with humidity. In one shore scene, savages have plundered a camp, leaving a jeep on its back with its wheels still turning and radio blasting.

None of the stuff is real, of course, though some scenes are authentic enough to frighten some preschool children. Most kids are easily calmed, though, and by the end of the ride don't want to get off—despite admonition by the guide to "leave all your jewelry and other valuables but make sure you take your children."

TIPS: This ride ranks with Space Mountain when it comes to perpetual lines. Most aggravating, though, is that lines are deceiving. Every time you round a corner, you realize (miserably) that there are still more lines. Plan to visit first thing in the morning, or try during the 3 p.m. Main Street parade.

Pirates of the Caribbean ★★★★★ Arguably one of Disney's greatest feats, this attraction combines the best of the best rides: realistic scenery, spirited music, nonstop action and a short but stomach-loosening drop. Unlike the bright outdoor scenery of the Jungle Cruise, this boat trip takes you through the dark and clammy hollows of pirates' dens. In early scenes, crooked-toothed, peg-legged men are chained to stone floors and buzzards pick at skeletons strewn on a deserted beach. For most of the ride, the swashbucklers are plundering, frolicking and raising hell on an island. During a chaotic fortress raid, they carelessly fire pistols, chase women and set the town ablaze. Chickens cluck, dogs bark and drunken pigs twitch their legs in strangely realistic ways. Several sights border on the raucous—including the auctioning of women—though Disney manages to make it all seem good fun. The attention to detail is masterful, down to the wiry hair on one pirate's leg.

> To keep the Jungle Cruise jungly when real world temperatures drop below 36°F, 100 cleverly concealed gas heaters and electric fans send warm air to the plants and trees.

TIPS: Small children may be frightened by some of the scenes. Though a very popular ride, lines move quickly and there is rarely more than a 30-minute wait. *Not to be missed.*

Enchanted Tiki Room—Under New Management ★★ Veteran Disney World visitors may recall snoozing their way through this Magic Kingdom stalwart featuring singing "birds" and thundering tikis. It's still unlikely to bowl you over, but the energy level of this animatronic aviary has been upped exponentially thanks to a change in "management." New "owners"—Iago from Aladdin and Zazu from the Lion King—are no birds of a feather. The jangling parrot and the persnickety hornbill bird make for an ornithological odd couple. The two quip and spar their way through dance (as much dance as animatronic birds can do, at any rate) and song including the love-it-or-hate-it Tiki Bird tune.

TIPS: The new incarnation is better than the old, but it will still appeal mostly to kids. If you find yourself short on time, skip it.

Cross into Frontierland, and the caws of Adventureland
parrots transform into the whines of a locomotive (a.k.a.
Big Thunder Mountain Railroad, one of the fastest and
most exciting rides at Disney). Reminiscent of an 1800s mining
town, Frontierland poses a rugged skein of cactus, rust-colored
rock, adobe buildings, trading posts and a town hall coated in
brick. There's Pecos Bill Café, bordered by wood sidewalks; Aunt
Polly's Dockside Landing; Churro Wagon; Westward Ho; and a
Turkey Leg Wagon that serves oversized victuals. Employees are
wrapped in leather duds and occasionally talk with a twang, and
kids dart around with new coonskin caps on their heads.

Frontierland

Big Thunder Mountain, with its ruddy, jagged, vertical profile, is the reason many folks wander into Frontierland, though
they usually stay a while once they discover the multitude of activities. Indeed, the place is a utopia for families: There's a big
woodsy island where kids can run free for hours, a carnival arcade that's mobbed by teenagers, and two family-style revues
that combine good entertainment with relaxation. Plan to spend
some time here; even with minimal lines, it take several hours to
see the best this "land" has to offer.

Big Thunder Mountain Railroad ★★★★★ Wild and rambunctious, this roller coaster easily competes with the big boys. The
plummets aren't steep but they are sudden, and there are enough
curves and speed to get the adrenaline flowing. Set in the Gold
Rush days, the coaster is a runaway mine train that whirls across
two acres of Disney's most creative scenery.

**WHAT TO
SEE & DO**

Keep your eyes open, or you'll miss the mining town caught in
a flash flood, the Audio-Animatronics animals (including chickens,
opossums and donkeys), the falling rocks and the goofy guy in
long johns laid out in an old-fashioned bathtub. There are also
dozens of nifty mining antiques sprinkled across the nubby terrain, and bats that loom overhead. Then there is the mountain:
rising some 197 feet, it took two years and 650 tons of steel to
build. About 16,000 gallons of paint and 4675 tons of cement
were slapped on, along with plenty of good old dirt and rocks.

Once you've ridden during the day, return for a night trip.
With the mountain and rocks aglow, surroundings are supreme.
Arrive about 30 minutes before the park closes, and lines should
be short (or even nonexistent).

TIPS: Children must be 40 inches or taller to ride; not recommended for seniors or the weak at heart. Not to be missed.

Tom Sawyer Island ★★★ One of the few nature-oriented Disney
attractions, this cleverly designed island is a must for families.
Like a reverse doughnut, it rests in the center of the Rivers of
America. Steamboats, rafts and keelboats ply the water, tossing
blue-green ripples against the island shore. Visitors crowd onto

timber rafts (it's standing only) for fun, motorized transportation
to the island.

Cool and woodsy, Tom Sawyer Island offers a retreat from lines
and plenty of places where children can romp: winding footpaths,
hills, bubbling streams, a barrel bridge and old-fashioned swing
bridge, a windmill and grist mill, and a "magnetic mystery mine"
whose moist walls seem dusted with gold. The best spot, though,
is Fort Sam Clemens, a log fortress where you can fire air guns
(with great sound effects) at startled passengers on the Liberty
Square Riverboat. The guns blast incessantly all day and can be
heard across Frontierland.

While kids spend some energy, parents can stroll leisurely or
rest on one of the many benches sprinkled across Tom Sawyer
Island. Families particularly enjoy seasonal Aunt Polly's Dockside Landing, which serves just-squeezed lemonade and peanut
butter and jelly sandwiches. You can linger on the wood loggia
and watch the riverboats go by or mingle with other families.

The island's shady, relaxed environs and lack of crowds make
it an ideal spot to spend steamy afternoons when most other attractions feel the crush of people. A good strategy is to arrive just
before noon and enjoy a picnic lunch.

TIPS: Not recommended for seniors; adults without children
may want to see the island on their second day at the Magic Kingdom. There's rarely a line, so visit when other attractions are
packed. Island closes at dusk.

Splash Mountain ★★★★★ It's not the scariest Disney ride, but it
may be the best, a whole 12 minutes of watery dips and dives
and twists through the hilarious land of three "Brers"—Rabbit,
Bear and Fox. From your perch inside a hollow log, you cruise
upstream and down, past old milling gear and machines, past
Brer Rabbit trying to steal honey from a swarming beehive, and
then past Brer Fox nearly getting gobbled by an alligator. There
are many more zany characters, over a hundred in fact, all right
out of Disney's *Song of the South* and all singing what has become Disney's National Anthem—"Zip-A-Dee-Doo-Dah." Thrill
seekers will get instant gratification with a steep, unexpected plunge
at the beginning of the ride, but the real clincher is a five-story,
47-degree free-fall into the Briar Patch—enough to give you goose
bumps and get you soaking wet! Children as old as ten (and some
adults) may find the drop too scary, but most preteens and teens
think it's "killer." One young Splash Mountain addict summed
it up this way: "When you get on the ride you just get happy."
Zip-A-Dee-Doo-Dah!

TIPS: At the beginning of the big drop, keep your eyes open
for a great view of Cinderella Castle. If you'd rather not get wet,

stay away from the front seat! Age and height restrictions apply. *Not to be missed.*

Country Bear Jamboree **★★★★** A long-standing Disney favorite, this show is an amusing rendition of the world from a bear's point of view. A crew of wacky Audio-Animatronics bears (with remarkably lifelike features and mannerisms) crack jokes, sing songs and tell tall tales to a usu- ally packed Grizzly Hall. The venerable Big Al has become so popular that his mug shows up on Disney hats, T-shirts and postcards.

> The Frontierland Shootin' Arcade's guns are authentic Hawkins 54-caliber buffalo rifles.

Tips: An attraction for all ages, the jamboree draws big crowds for its relatively small auditorium. Plan to visit before 11 a.m. or during the 3 p.m. Main Street parade.

Frontierland Shootin' Arcade **★** Kids are the main fans of this arcade, which is typical of carnival shooting galleries. For a quar- ter you can fire at "wilderness" targets such as cardboard tomb- stones and vultures. The place is nothing special and should be visited on your second day at the Magic Kingdom.

Tips: The arcade costs a quarter for five shots. This attraction won't appeal to many adults and seniors. There's rarely a line here, so visit anytime.

Goofy's Country Dancin' Jamboree **★★** The theater's still called the Diamond Horseshoe Saloon, but the stage show inside is def- initely not of the bawdy saloon variety. Replacing the previous stage show is this live character revue, a strictly-for-kids musical with Goofy, Woody (from Toy Story) and other characters. Twenty-minute shows, performed several times daily, invite kids to get up and boogie with the big guys to familiar tunes like "The Electric Slide," and "Cotton Eyed Joe."

Tips: Definitely one for little kids—if you're a grownups-only party, skip it.

Liberty Square

At first it is difficult to know where Frontierland ends and Liberty Square begins. Both places share the same ambience of American nostalgia, and both are accented with riverboat landings and shady waterfront sidewalks.

But the heart of Liberty Square is quintessentially colonial: saltbox homes tinted in vanilla, storefronts of cranberry-colored brick, gabled roofs, weather vanes, and no lack of American flags. As with most other "lands," Disney's replicas here are ingenious. Tidy shops stock antiques, jams and jellies, and crocheted blankets, and a homey tavern beckons with rough-hewn wood floors and a big stone hearth. With so much coziness everywhere, the humid Florida air almost feels a little brisk.

The flora, too, is nothing short of stunning. Brilliant azaleas and Japanese yews form colorful palettes around trees, along the river and in window flower boxes. Center stage is a vast live oak, appropriately named the "Liberty Tree," that's more than 130 years old. From its branches dangle 13 lanterns recalling the original 13 states.

Liberty Square's homey aura and all-American overtones appeal to families, who often kill an hour strolling the riverfront and shops. Parents will find secluded relaxation behind the Silversmith Shop, where a handful of benches, umbrella-topped tables and big shade trees pose a sort of secret resting place.

WHAT TO SEE & DO

The Hall of Presidents ★★★ When this attraction opened in 1971, it was hailed as a hallmark of Disney achievement. The fantasy makers had duplicated human likeness in robots so well that it was almost eerie. Still today, visitors are awed by the realistic expressions, features, motions and voices of America's 42 presidents. The wrinkles, the eyebrows, the freckles, down to the brace on Franklin Delano Roosevelt's leg, are remarkable. Notice that while Abe Lincoln is calling roll, a few fellow presidents become restless and start fidgeting.

Set in a comfortable theater that seats more than 700, the production highlights U.S. achievement with the expected patriotic overtones. A pre-show film, which is average at best, portrays a textbook story of American history.

Tips: A favorite of seniors; small children may find it difficult to pay attention.

Liberty Belle Riverboat ★★★ It's impossible to miss this triple-decker paddlewheeler as it chugs along the manmade "Rivers of America" through Liberty Square and Frontierland. Steam pours from its stacks, and passengers crowd against white gingerbread railings for nice views of the mainland and Tom Sawyer Island. There's no captain (the boat travels via underwater rail), and the 17-minute ride is super slow and relaxing. It's a great break for parents, who can sit down while their children roam around. Kids love exploring the boat, and getting shot at (with air guns) by other kids camped out at the fort on Tom Sawyer Island. There are usually plenty of seats, but to ensure you get one, be one of the first aboard the boat.

Tips: Covers the same territory as the Mike Fink Keel Boats, and is by far a better ride. If you don't fancy a boat trip, you can explore Tom Sawyer Island on foot. The riverboat draws moderate crowds, with an average wait of 15 to 20 minutes.

Mike Fink Keel Boats ★ These two low-slung craft are named for a Mississippi riverboat captain and renowned marksman who lived from 1770 to 1823. The keel boats explore the same scenery as the Liberty Square Riverboat, so there's no need to ride both—particularly since the keel boats are much less exciting. Passengers are crowded into a small space, and the narrator uses an annoyingly loud microphone to deliver a dull spiel and lackluster jokes. On the positive side, there's rarely a long wait for this attraction.

TIPS: Save this attraction for your second day at the Magic Kingdom—or don't ride at all. This seasonal ride operates during the summer and holidays and at other busy times.

The Haunted Mansion ★★★★★ "Here lies old Fred. A great big rock fell on his head." So reads one of the wacky graveyard epitaphs outside The Haunted Mansion, a vast, ominous house at the crest of a hill. It's a fitting introduction to one of Disney's best-ever attractions, an ingenious design with so many special effects and illusions that you find yourself saying, "I know this isn't real, but. . . ."

To keep the Haunted Mansion good and dusty, crews shoot five-pound bags of dust from a gadget that looks like a fertilizer spreader.

A gloomy butler greets visitors at the front doors and ushers them into an eight-sided gallery with cobwebbed chandeliers and a ceiling that rises—or is the floor sinking? After much doomsaying, he leads everyone to their coffins (called "doom buggies") for a spirited ride through rooms with phantoms, ghoulies and various heebie-jeebies. There's a piano player who's nothing more than a shadow, a spooked cemetery and its petrified watchman, a teapot pouring tea and a screeching raven that won't go away. Voices howl, figures skate across ceilings and ghosts become more vivid as the darkness gets thicker.

All of the special effects are great, but the show stoppers are the holograms. Using advanced technology and imagination, Disney pushed 3D projection to its limits. Life-size human images, dressed in everyday attire, float around and mimic the mannerisms of their living counterparts. In one dance hall scene, holograms whirl around the floor in sync to the music. Perhaps the most fascinating (and talked-about) hologram is the woman's head in the crystal ball: her lifelike image chatters nonstop.

The kicker, though, is at the ride's end, when you gaze into a mirror and see a spook (read hologram) nestled beside you.

Despite the attraction's expert effects, it's not really scary for most people. Small children, however, will likely be frightened by what to them is most certainly "real."

TIPS: Though a popular ride, the mansion is tucked away in a corner of Liberty Square and so has sporadic lines. In fact, lines here are usually dictated by when crowds leave the nearby Hall of Presidents and Liberty Square Riverboat. Every 20 to 30 minutes, both attractions release several hundred people who then wander over to the Haunted Mansion. Translation: Wait till those attractions are *almost* ready to release visitors, and make a beeline for the Haunted Mansion. *Not to be missed.*

▼ ▼ ▼ ▼ ▼ ▼ ▼ ▼ ▼

Fantasyland

Truly a colorful, whimsical place, Fantasyland is a combination of circus-style canopies, gleaming turrets and gingerbread houses, with the whole land crisscrossed by streams filled with shiny pennies. Dominated by the grandiose Cinderella Castle, Fantasyland is fashioned as a palace courtyard. Indeed, strolling these fanciful lanes is like roaming the chapters of a fairy tale.

Fantasyland has more attractions than any other land (11, more than twice that of most lands). Obviously, children are the biggest fans of these rides, which feature the happy lyrics and themes from many of Disney's best-loved films and characters. There are flying Dumbos, whirling Mad Hatter teacups, Cinderella's white carousel horses and Snow White's forest. Most adults enjoy the rides, and those who don't still delight in the imaginative setting and remarkable attention to detail (in true Disney style, even the garbage cans here are splashed with glowing color).

Not surprisingly, Fantasyland is usually the most popular and crowded area of Disney World. Perhaps that's because this make-believe land epitomizes what Disney does best: bring out the kid in everyone.

WHAT TO SEE & DO

Cinderella Castle ★★★★★ Technically, this tremendous structure is part of Fantasyland, though realistically it's *the* frame of reference for all of Disney World. Towering 180 feet above Main Street and encircled by a rock-rimmed moat, the castle is a masterful facsimile of the medieval palace in the classic French fairy tale. Its royal blue turrets and gold spires glisten in the sun, and its myriad towers, parapets and balconies provide visual inspiration. Cinderella's Golden Carrousel is a 1917 gem built by Italian woodcarvers working for the Philadelphia Toboggan Company.

◆◆◆

FAMILY MAGIC: A SCAVENGER HUNT

After dozens of forays through the Magic Kingdom, you may think you've seen it all. But take this wildly fun guided romp, and you'll see the park in a whole new light. A scavenger hunt/guided tour, the adventure starts with a treasure map and leads you skipping, hopping and who-knows-what-elsing through the streets of Fantasyland and beyond. Guides play their parts to the hilt, recruiting guests to perform some pretty silly stunts. Sure, other folks will look at you askance, but your family (and this is definitely one to do with the kids) will be having way too much fun to care. The price is $25 per person (the cost does not include admission into the park, which is required). Call 407-939-8687 for information about this and other tours.

The castle is beautiful even from miles away. Indeed, each year dozens of couples marry at Disney resorts, using the castle silhouette as a romantic backdrop. And some hotels even advertise rooms "with a castle view."

TIPS: Musical shows are offered throughout the day in front of the castle. Check the schedule in the castle forecourt, and plan *not* to peruse the castle during those times. Another time to avoid the castle: during the 3 p.m. Main Street parade when crowds gather all along the route. *Not to be missed.*

Cinderella's Golden Carrousel ★★★ As carousels go, this one's a showpiece. From the hand-painted scenes across the canopy to the fiberglass steeds that go up and down, everything is beautifully detailed and animated.

The 18 scenes, taken from Disney's 1950 movie *Cinderella*, depict the cinder girl in vivid, cinematic colors. Below, horses are embellished with gleaming swords, chains and even yellow roses. Notice that although most horses are white, no two are identical. Also, instead of traditional merry-go-round music, this carousel organ renders such Disney song classics as "Chim-Chim-Cheree" and "When You Wish Upon a Star." Together with the melodies, the glittering lights, mirrors and almost constant motion make this a singular experience for all ages.

TIPS: As with most carousels, lines don't move fast. Arrive before noon or after dusk, when a profusion of lights makes this one of the prettiest rides at Disney.

Peter Pan's Flight ★★★ Small children love this air cruise in colorful pirate ships. The setting is Never-Never Land, from Sir James Matthew Barrie's 1904 fairy tale about a half-elfin boy who "couldn't grow up." Passengers glide around brightly lit indoor scenes for rendezvous with Tinkerbell, Captain Hook, Mr. Smee and other favorite *Peter Pan* characters.

Because of its popularity with families, the short (two-and-a-half-minute) ride typically has long lines. My advice: If the wait is more than 20 minutes, skip it. No matter how good it is, a two-and-a-half-minute ride is not worth a long wait.

TIPS: Not popular with seniors and adults without children.

It's A Small World ★★★★ This leisurely cruise in sherbet-colored boats takes you through glittery scenes of hundreds of singing and dancing dolls. There are red toy soldiers, hip-swaying hula girls, leprechauns, kings and queens and nursery rhyme stars such as Little Bo Peep and Jack and Jill. The theme of world unity shines through in the detailed costumes and settings from countries around the globe. A favorite (if not *the* favorite) Disney ride of small children, it is a feel-good experience with lighthearted lyrics you can't get out of your head.

TIPS: Though a very popular ride, it has fast-moving lines and rarely more than a 15-minute wait.

Dumbo The Flying Elephant ★★★ Disney's version of a carnival midway ride is based on the endearing elephant with oversized ears. Super tame but fun, it features 16 Dumbos that glide in a circle when riders press a button inside. Young children beg to go on this attraction again and again—which explains the notoriously long lines for this two-minute ride. Even with 16 Dumbos, lines still creep along.

TIPS: Parents with small children should make this the first ride of the day. If there is a long wait, one parent can stand in line while the other relaxes in the shade of the adjacent Fantasyland Pavilion.

Snow White's Scary Adventures ★★★ Disney has brightened up this spookhouse-style ride with wooden cars that careen by evil witches and toothy crocodiles and lurch through the merry house of Audio-Animatronics dwarfs. The idea, of course, is that you accompany Snow White on her perilous journey through the forest. Though it's not scary to older kids, small children are often frightened. As the sign outside says: "Beware the Wicked Witch. Some scenes may frighten young minds."

TIPS: Not popular with seniors and adults without children. Traditional long lines have eased up here, so ride anytime.

The Many Adventures of Winnie the Pooh ★★★ The fact that kid-less grownups are waiting alongside families for this new attraction is a testament to the endurance of A. A. Milne's "silly old" bear. From the *Winnie the Pooh and the Blustery Day* story, the ride transports guests via moving honey pot through scenes from the animated film. My favorite part: Pooh's "out of body" dream sequence (you'll know it when you see it). The "Hephalumps and Woozles" are pretty cute as well.

TIPS: Like the Peter Pan and Snow White rides, this one attracts long lines of all ages. But you can forego at least some of the waiting by lining up during the parade or fireworks when Fantasyland temporarily clears out.

Mad Tea Party ★★ The madness here is that you spin in one direction for two minutes at can't-see-a-thing velocity.

When it's over, you still can't see a thing—and feel like you've gone mad. Nonetheless, the midway-style ride can be a blast. Indeed, some teenagers head straight here after Space Mountain, waiting in line for consecutive rides in the giant pastel teacups. The attraction's fanciful theme is taken from an *Alice in Wonderland* scene where the Mad Hatter throws a tea party for his unbirthday.

TIPS: If you don't like getting the spins, skip this ride.

The
Castle

Despite its granite-like appearance, Cinderella Castle is made of fiberglass and steel beams and sports a 500-gallon coat of paint. Lining the archway of the Castle are spectacular mosaics that qualify as one of Disney's premier creations. Five panels—each spanning 15 feet high and 10 feet wide—tell the moving tale of a little cinder girl, her hateful stepmother, her fairy godmother, a pumpkin and a prince.

Designed by Disney artist Dorothea Redmond and crafted by mosaicist Hanns-Joachim Scharff, the palettes contain a million pieces of Italian glass in some 500 colors—as well as real silver and gold. Even a brief look at the walls reveals many treasures: a glimmering gold jewel in the stepmother's tiara, the striking royal blue of Cinderella's eyes, and columns carved with birds and mice that are making her gown.

Many visitors are disappointed to learn that there's no tour of Cinderella Castle. (A spacious apartment near the top of Cinderella Castle was designed for the Disney family, but no one ever moved in.) There is, however, a way to get "into" this enchanting building: dine at **Cinderella's Royal Table**.

This second-floor dining hall is at the peak of a broad staircase that spirals through silvery castle walls. Elaborately designed, it features a soaring rotunda, Gothic arches and stained-glass windows that dispense fine views of the Magic Kingdom. Hostesses wear long medieval gowns and dramatic French headdresses, and medieval court melodies pour across the room.

Castle fare—a lunch and dinner lineup of prime rib, seafood and fruit salads, fish and chicken dishes—is overpriced and mediocre, but the novelty of being inside a palace keeps people begging for tables. And, to the delight of small children, Cinderella makes frequent appearances during breakfast. Reservations are essential; visit a hostess at the restaurant as soon as the Magic Kingdom opens. ~ 407-939-3463.

Ariel's Grotto ★★★ In a courtyard of soft blues and aquas, small bursts of water leap-frog around the grounds while a statue of the Little Mermaid stands center stage. Inside the cool cave at the back, before a curtain of cascading water, Ariel herself sits upon a rock combing her trademark red tresses with a fork while posing for pictures and signing autographs. Given that Ariel can't walk around the park like other characters, this is a rare opportunity to capture the Little Mermaid on film and in your autograph book. Though the line for a visit can get long, it often dwindles considerably when guests discover they're waiting for a photo opportunity and not an elaborate attraction.

TIPS: Ariel's visitors tend to linger longer here than at other character-greetings, making even a short line last a while. For the quickest trip, stop by either before 10 a.m., during the Main Street SpectroMagic Parade or just before park closing. Even if there is a line, the wait (since you'll mostly be standing directly under the hot sun) will be less agonizing during cooler portions of the day.

▼▼▼▼▼▼▼▼▼▼▼▼▼▼▼
Mickey's Toontown Fair

If you were to design a place from a child's point of view, it could easily be Mickey's Toontown Fair. Like a scene from a Saturday morning cartoon, the street is lined with lilliputian-sized structures splashed in red, green, yellow and purple. Yards are trimmed in little picket fences, and there's even a Mickey-shaped mailbox waiting for the arrival of the animated mail carrier.

Set inside a toon town county fair, the fanciful area opened in 1988 as Mickey's Birthdayland to celebrate the mouse's 60th birthday. The theme was changed shortly after to Mickey's Toontown Fair. But the comic-strip ambience endures.

Much of the action takes place through the backdoors of Mickey's Country House where the Disney star appears in the judging tent throughout the day, greeting guests and signing autographs. Some of Mickey's pals, as well as a few arch villains, hold court at the Toontown Hall of Fame. There's also a quiet park filled with blocks, chalkboards and craft activities that provides children and their parents with a much-needed rest.

◆◆

MAHLER MOUSE

You'll have to come to Disney World to see Mickey's latest flick—**Mickey's PhilharMagic**. The 3D film, opened in 2003, replaces the Legend of The Lion King in Fantasyland, and features Mickey et al projected onto what is purported to be an enormous screen. "In-theater" effects are sure to "involve" the audience, so be prepared for some potential surprises.

The most visible attraction in this three-acre niche is The Barnstormer at Goofy's Wiseacre Farm, a pint-sized roller coaster and the first ride to grace any of Disney World's toon land incarnations. The area remains decidedly small, however, hardly qualifying as a "land" in and of itself. Still, it's a must for visitors with small children, particularly since the arrival of Toon Park, a soft play area just for little ones.

Mickey's Country House ** The outside of Mickey's Country House is everything you would expect of a cartoon character's abode. Framed by a yellow picket fence and lined with loosely shaped balusters, Mickey's home is decorated in bright yellow, red, green and blue, with green shutters and a softly shaped dormer standing rooftop. Stroll up the walkway to the front porch and there's a comfortable swing beckoning visitors to sit and sway in the breeze.

WHAT TO SEE & DO

The inside is a Mickey museum, and each room looks as if the mouse was just there. His clothes are laid out neatly in the bedroom, while in the living room an old-fashioned television plays cartoon reruns starring (who else?) Mickey.

Out back is Mickey's unique Toon garden where all the vegetables sprout mouse ears. To exit Mickey's house, either head to the Judge's Tent where you can wait in line to meet The Big Cheese himself, or amble through the contents of Mickey's garage. Though this is primarily a children's attraction, adults will get a kick out of the architecture and Disney humor.

TIPS: This attraction (the house, at least) is almost never crowded, so visit between 11 a.m. and 4 p.m. when the other attractions have long lines. As for meeting Mickey in the Judge's Tent: this line gets long. You'll do better to meet the Mouse at one of the resort's character meals.

Minnie's Country House **** Walking into the fanciful quarters of Mickey's leading lady is something like stepping across the threshold of every little girl's dream. The colors are all pastels, pinks and purples, with heart shapes and fluff the predominant Toontown motif. Inside, you'll find working materials spread across Minnie's home-office desk (she is, after all, editor of Minnie's *Cartoon Living Magazine*) as well as walls full of awards and framed covers from the magazine's back issues.

Apart from the fanciful look, it's the neat gadgetry that's made Minnie's Country House an all-time kid favorite. Much here is interactive, from the fluffy living room furniture you can actually climb on, to the answering machine that plays Minnie's messages. In the kitchen, open the refrigerator and look into Minnie's stash of staple groceries (assorted cheeses, what else?), and push the oven button to see a cake miraculously rise.

TIPS: Guests lingering with the toys inside tend to make the wait to get into Minnie's House a long one. To cut the wait, plan to visit Minnie early in the morning when lines are shortest.

Toontown Hall of Fame ★★ To many of the million or so visitors who venture to Disney World each year, rides and roller coasters are secondary to the main attraction: character greetings (just ask anyone in guest services). Only at Disney theme parks do these beloved animated icons come to life, and here at the Toontown Hall of Fame is where you'll find one of the largest one-stop-shopping selections. Characters are divided into categories: Mickey's pals (Goofy, Donald, Pluto, etc.), villains (Captain Hook, Prince John) and princesses (Snow White, Cinderella, etc.). Characters rotate regularly, making it a good idea to ask who's on hand before you get in line.

TIPS: During the day, the wait for a visit with one of Mickey's pals can go 45 minutes or more (expect a 15-minute wait from the inside doors). Best times to visit: early in the day, or in the evening during the SpectroMagic Parade.

The Barnstormer ★★★ One five-year-old no doubt spoke for millions of preschoolers when she proclaimed, "I don't like Goofy's roller coaster. I love it!" Adults used to the thrills of Space Mountain and Splash Mountain may well ho-hum their way through this attraction. But daring little ones who've been frustrated by the height requirements of the bumpier, speedier coasters will be thrilled with the Barnstormer: there are no height guidelines, but children must be at least three years old to ride.

Before boarding, guests first wind in line through the Wiseacre gardens where goofy vegetables grow (check out the "bell" peppers). At last, you'll board a 1920s crop-dusting plane that twists and turns, culminating when it bursts through the wall of Goofy's barn.

TIPS: Though The Barnstormer is billed as a kiddie ride, it's still a roller coaster. Children who are wary of the faster versions may be equally uncomfortable on this ride as well.

Donald Duck's Boat, Miss Daisy ★★ Named for his sweetheart, *Miss Daisy*, Donald's steamboat, seems to have lost its way at sea and is now permanently grounded in Mickey's Toontown Fair. Inside, you'll find a map of the Quack Sea, as well as Donald's crucial navigation gear (the steering wheel) and prized audio equipment (the ship's bell). Kids love to enthusiastically ring the bell à la The Hunchback, dangling on the rope and setting off frequent "gongs" throughout the Toontown streets. Outside the boat are a number of interactive fountains and water toys guaranteed to refresh on those steamy Florida days.

Tips: If you don't want to walk around in soggy clothes, watch out for the interactive fountains that can get the unsuspecting very wet.

Tomorrowland

Gone is the old Tomorrowland that foretold the future as stark, geometric and loaded with concrete. Disney's new Tomorrowland is a high-technicolor scene of glass spaceships and spinning purple planets and silvery metal stabbing at the sky. Electric blue, bright yellow and seafoam green are splashed everywhere, rockets twirl high in the sky, and a train glides by overhead.

It's all designed as a "Flash Gordon-ish, Buck Rogers–like neighborhood," according to the Disney folks, and we suspect even Gene Roddenberry would have approved. Gone is the sorely dated (but not sorely missed) attraction Mission to Mars and the excellent but long-playing American Journeys. Their replacements are stellar: the ExtraTERRORestrial Alien Encounter, a scare-you-out-of-your-flip-flops thriller that pits audience against alien; and the The Timekeeper, a "time-travel" attraction with a stunning Circle-Vision film.

Still, many people would say the zenith of the new Tomorrowland is leftover from the old Tomorrowland: Space Mountain. Set along Tomorrowland's eastern edge, it is the only attraction situated outside the Walt Disney World Railroad tracks—the unofficial boundary for the Magic Kingdom. Both in location and thrills, Space Mountain symbolizes the outer limits.

Because Space Mountain is perpetually crowded, other Tomorrowland attractions usually are not. By the time some Space Mountain riders have killed an hour-plus standing in line, they're ready

IT'S CHARACTER TIME

Kids love meeting characters from their favorite Disney films. Look for Mickey inside the Judge's Tent in Toontown—he's always there. Many of his pals stick around at the Toontown Hall of Fame. There are characters aplenty at the Fantasyland Character Festival. Ariel spends her day at her Grotto while Belle makes periodic appearances to tell stories in the Fairytale Garden (both in Fantasyland). Check your entrance map for more locations and times. Characters are always eager to sign autographs and pose for family snapshots. Before you get there, it's good to remind children that characters don't talk but communicate (quite effectively) through body language. Also, they appear much larger in person than in movies or on television, which can sometimes startle a small child.

for some new scenery (or a dash to the restroom). And most of Tomorrowland's less popular rides are designed to handle big crowds. Plan to visit everything *but* Space Mountain during the middle of the day, when the rest of the park is predictably packed.

Space Mountain ★★★★★ Looming 180 feet above the area, this concrete and steel structure resembles a ribbed white cone spiked with icicles. Touted as "Florida's third highest mountain," it is Disney's zenith. It is arguably the fastest, scariest, most imaginative mind trip in the theme park lineup. Its futuristic silhouette is permanently etched in the minds of thousands who worship this attraction as the best in the universe.

This ultimate in state-of-the-art thrills is a roller coaster ride in the dark that feels like a trip through outer space in warp drive. Passengers board fluorescent-striped capsules for what's supposed to be a journey through the depths of the galaxy. During the 2-minute-and-38-second ride, strobe lights flash, tunnels flicker and saucers spin as you probe deeper and deeper into inky blackness. Top speed is only about 28 mph, but there are enough twists and turns and sudden drops to plunge you into euphoria (or nausea, in some cases).

Besides its technology, what sets Space Mountain apart from most rides is its universal appeal. Grandparents queue up as readily as ten-year-olds, and pregnant women will plead with attendants to go on (despite posted warnings against expectant mothers riding). But popularity has its pitfalls, and in the case of Space Mountain, these are long, unrelenting lines. Riding during the morning or late afternoon may reduce your wait from one-and-a-half hours to 30 or 45 minutes. However, Space Mountain groupies know the best strategy is to join the Space Mountain Dash (also called the Rope Drop, as the dash begins when Disney attendants drop a rope). Here's how it works:

Arrive 45 to 60 minutes before the park opens, when Main Street will be open. Walk down Main Street toward Cinderella Castle and hang a right at the Sealtest Ice Cream Parlor. Proceed past the Plaza Restaurant and stop at the sign that says "The Plaza Pavilion Terrace Dining." Here there's a rope (and probably already a small gathering) guarded by a Disney employee. The second the park opens, the employee releases the rope while dozens of people skip, briskly walk and/or run the 100 or so yards to Space Mountain. Employees dread working the rope because of the danger of being trampled by hyped-up visitors, who, incidentally, range from seniors to college students to parents with a slew of children.

The advantage of this spot is that it's about 120 yards closer to Space Mountain than the official starting point, located on the east side of the Magic Kingdom's central hub. Here hundreds of unenlightened people gather for their own dash to "the mountain." Even those who walk from the closer location will easily beat out those who sprint from the hub area.

If the Plaza Pavilion "dash" area is mobbed, head back down Main Street toward Cinderella Castle. When you get to the Castle Forecourt, make your first right toward Tomorrowland. There you will likely see another gathering—the overflow crowd for the Space Mountain Dash.

Visitors who feel apprehensive about racing to a ride may (a) reconsider once they see how long the lines can be, or (b) find it's kind of fun after all. Despite initial repulsion to the idea, this writer found the experience quite comical and wacky, and not a bad way to make quick friends. The only unforeseen drawback was a stomach not fully prepared for a 9 a.m. sprint and roller coaster ride.

> The floor under the Space Mountain track is the cemetery for some visitors' eyeglasses, cameras, wallets—and even false teeth.

If you miss the Space Mountain Dash, try to ride about an hour before the park closes. This is when attendants sometimes "stack" the ride, which means queuing visitors *outside* to clear up long lines *inside*. Stacking makes it seem as if lines are never-ending (counting the supposed lines inside), when in fact what you see is what you get. An honest attendant will tell you if there's stacking. If that fails, try peeking in the ride's front door.

Tips: Children shorter than 44 inches are not allowed to ride. Not recommended for pregnant women and people with weak stomachs or bad backs. If you're indecisive about riding, take the Tomorrowland Transit Authority that tours portions of Space Mountain. The dark surroundings and squeals of Space Mountain riders will either scare you good or make you long to go on. *Not to be missed.*

Tomorrowland Transit Authority ★★★ Disney's prototype of future mass transit, these open-air boxcars provide a great introduction to Tomorrowland as they scoot in and out of buildings on overhead tracks. The five-car trains plunge into the pitch-black belly of Space Mountain (listen for the screams of Space Mountain riders); circle Astro Orbiter, an outdoor rocket ride; and explore Buzz Lightyear's Space Ranger Spin. A recording gives narration, including intriguing facts and figures, on each attraction. Notice that the trains, which move about ten mph, make a smooth, noiseless journey. That's because they're propelled by electromagnets and have no moving parts. And, for all the zipping around they do, they produce no pollution.

Tips: Despite its appearance everywhere, the Tomorrowland Transit Authority is not one of the park's more popular attractions. All for the better: Those who do ride know it as a relaxing, informative experience with rarely a long line. Most appealing to adults, though all ages find the ride entertaining.

The ExtraTERRORestrial Alien Encounter ★★★★★ The key words here are "alien" and "terror." A frightful beast with big wings and even bigger teeth is accidentally "beamed" onto planet Earth and makes his way into—of all places— this particular Disney theater. He mistakes the audience for lunch. He selects an appetizer—you. His breath is hot, and you can feel it on the back of your neck. It's black as tar inside the theater. Your mind races to the scene in *Jurassic Park* where the guy stuck his hand into the monster's cage. Big mistake.

> The opening of ExtraTERRORestrial was delayed six months when Disney CEO Michael Eisner previewed it and said it wasn't scary enough. Publicity stunt? Maybe, but the attraction's a chiller.

Of course, nobody loses a hand or anything else in this 20-minute alien encounter—though the special effects, said to cost close to $100 million, might have you doubting for a millisecond.

TIPS: You must be four feet tall to experience Alien Encounter. Anyone easily frightened by scary movies or the dark may find it unnerving. Most teenagers love it.

The Timekeeper ★★★★ The Timekeeper, a gold-plated, nine-eyed, tinsel-haired robot with the voice of Robin Williams and an equally outrageous sense of humor, is the star of this visually compelling trek through time. Working the controls of his "time travel machine," he transports the audience from the Dark Ages and Renaissance town squares to 1900s Paris and then the future. All the action's on a 360-degree, circle-vision screen surrounding the audience, where a film takes viewers across spectacular tableaux around the world. Along the way you "meet" Leonardo da Vinci, Jules Verne and H. G. Wells, among other historic greats. Even if you don't buy into the time travel theme, you'll love the film's scenery.

TIPS: Too loud and chaotic for most small children. If you do take the little ones, understand that the theater has no seats, which means that small children have to be held up so they can see the screen. Don't be fooled by the crowds at this attraction. The huge theater rarely fills up, so the maximum wait is seldom longer than 18 minutes (the length of the show).

Walt Disney's Carousel of Progress ★★★★ A revolving theater that circles six stationary stages, the carousel offers a nostalgic voyage through the history of technology. Having premiered at the 1964 World's Fair in New York, the show is slightly dated but still entertains through a charming cast of Audio-Animatronics characters and a sentimental tune the audience can't help but sing. The characters are a "typical" American family—father, mother, son, daughter and their trusty dog—who experience 20th-century advances. Each stage is detailed and different, from the late-1800s kitchen with gas lamps to the 21st-century living room of blinking video screens. The show is one of Disney's longest—20 minutes—and allows a comfortable, air-conditioned reprieve.

TIPS: Seniors and adults without children love this show, which does a big repeat business. Children and teenagers sometimes find it boring and long. Though fairly popular, it can accommodate several hundred people and so rarely has a long wait.

Buzz Lightyear's Space Ranger Spin ★★★★ Evil Emperor Zurg, nemesis of Buzz Lightyear, is out to take over the universe. Your mission: rid the galaxy of his little green henchmen. "Planetary Pilots" cruise day-glo spaceships through outer space, gunning for enemy aliens. Each ship comes equipped with two infrared "ray" guns and a joy stick for steering. Points are awarded for each alien you zap. There are obstacles aplenty; however, your biggest stumbling block may be battling your co-pilot over which way to turn (the driver in my car seemed to veer off just as I was taking aim). Small price to pay for preserving the universe.

TIPS: Think of "Buzz" as a life-size arcade game. It's a ton of fun, but you may want to think twice if spinning tends to make you nauseous.

Astro Orbiter ★★★ Kids adore this carnival-style ride, which puts them airborne for two minutes in futuristic jets. The open-cockpit aircraft are poised on the arms of a big rocket and look like flailing limbs every time they lunge through the sky. The trip can be tame or mildly exciting, depending on how often you raise and lower your jet. It also offers nice views into surrounding "lands," a reason why all ages enjoy the flight.

TIPS: Children younger than seven must be accompanied by an adult. The Astro Orbiter is a good place for one parent to take young children while the other rides nearby Space Mountain with older children (children shorter than 44 inches aren't allowed on Space Mountain). This works timewise, too, because both rides usually have considerable waits. The Astro Orbiter can only accommodate about 22 passengers per ride, and it takes some time to ferry people up and down a two-flight elevator.

Tomorrowland Indy Speedway ★★★ This is a typical amusement race with miniature gas-powered cars that thread along a steel track. Though not futuristic, the area is cleverly designed with Grand Prix billboards, twisting roadways and a small bleacher that's frequently packed with race car fanatics. Naturally, kids love the excitement of piloting a set of (seemingly) souped-up wheels, and parents hate the pervasive smell of fuel and the noise of the cars, which sound like a horde of angry invading bees.

Unfortunately, the four-foot, four-inch minimum height requirement for drivers eliminates many children who would be big fans (though they can still ride with an adult). Worse yet, the entire ride involves much waiting: waiting to get on the raceway (30 to 60 minutes), waiting for your car to pull up (one to two minutes), then waiting to bring your car back (two to three minutes). For this writer, that's too much waiting for a three-minute ride where top speed is only seven miles per hour and you're not even allowed to bump the car in front of you.

TIPS: A very popular ride where the wait averages an hour during the park's busy season. Unless the kids are relentless about riding, don't waste your time on this one.

ANOTHER HINT: If you and two small children are sharing one car, you can ride the course twice through (without waiting on line in between) to give each child a turn to drive. Ask one of the ride operators about the policy before you board.

THREE

Epcot

Epcot was Walt Disney's lifelong dream. Everything else—Mickey Mouse, the stunning animated films, Disneyland—were just stopovers on the way to his futuristic world of peace and happiness. At Epcot, nations exist in harmony and the future appears a not-so-distant place of prosperity. Half the park is like a permanent world's fair, a skein of striking architecture depicting various countries. The other half features space-age buildings that explore the bounds of technology.

Epcot stands for Experimental Prototype Community of Tomorrow—words that sound too academic for a theme park. Yet Epcot takes the academic subjects of laboratories and museums and serves them up theme-park style. For lovers of knowledge and culture, Epcot has all the right stuff: exhibits that inspire thought and a sense of adventure; rides and movies that inform and amuse; and buildings seasoned with history and design flair.

Theoretically, Epcot began in Disneyland. There, during the 1950s, Walt Disney began to understand that his California theme park, landlocked by development, could never expand. He vowed to start again, this time creating a community with enough room to expand for centuries, an idealistic, futuristic place where people worked and lived.

Although his initial ideas have undergone a few changes (no one actually lives at Epcot), most of Disney's dream has been played out. Major industries sponsor many attractions and make them testing grounds for cutting-edge ideas. Nations from around the globe contribute money, materials and expertise to create attractions that exult in each country's beauty. Environmentally ahead of its time, much of the park is fueled by solar energy. Rainwater is collected from buildings and funneled into ponds and lagoons. And gardens grow without the aid of pesticides or fertilizer.

Epcot is adult. Sophisticated. Even cerebral. A place that suggests and explains, yet always entertains. Carved from 260 acres of central Florida pine and palmetto, this billion-dollar "community" explores space and energy, transportation and biology, communication and agriculture—and people. The park is divided into two vastly different sections: World Showcase and Future World.

The heart of World Showcase is a sea-green lagoon speckled with ferry boats and verdant clumps of islands. Eleven "pavilions," each representing a different country, fan out around the lagoon in a repertoire of architectural styles spanning over a thousand years. From Tudor, Gothic and colonial styles to Aztec, Japanese and Moroccan, World Showcase is like a pie whose slices are all different flavors. Enjoyed individually, they are invigorating; when savored as a whole, they are intoxicating.

Walt Disney's city of countries is a world of peace and happiness. There is no talk of poverty at the Mexico pavilion, no hint of political unrest in China, no mention of recession in America. They are, as one Epcot guide put it, "countries as Americans perceive them."

Indeed, it is virtually impossible to explore a "country" without being overwhelmed by its beauty and intrigue. As visitors exit the pavilions, many ask the same question: "How can I go to this country?"

Details are duplicated with astounding accuracy in each pavilion, from the chimney pots on Parisian rooftops to the hieroglyphics of Mexico's Aztec Calendar. Restaurant menus offer ethnic flair, and shops employ native artists and craftspeople. And not only does each country's native foliage thrive across the pavilion, it changes with each season, just like back home.

Sprawled below the dynamic scenery of World Showcase, Future World looks like a galactic landscape. Silvery metal and glass buildings shaped like pieces of a jigsaw puzzle bear names such as Universe of Energy and Innoventions East and West. Near one cone-shaped building, a metal DNA molecule pirouettes; at another, water spouts do an aerial jig.

Eclipsing the entire area is Spaceship Earth. Coated in aluminum and propped up by steel beams, it resembles a huge silver golf ball. All day long, a conveyor belt delivers a stream of people inside for a journey through the center of the earth.

Future World's intellectual subjects and World Showcase's limited number of rides can make Epcot tiresome for small children. Over the years, the Disney company has introduced more attractions that appeal to kids, including character meals and shows. Still, in most children's minds, the Magic Kingdom is tops.

In fact, when Epcot opened in 1982, some adults received it curiously, if not cautiously. Not everyone was ready for such futuristic themes, at least not after the fantasy of the Magic Kingdom.

But over time skeptics have embraced Epcot, lured by its sophistication, its ability to inspire and its three-dimensional approach. Every year, more people tune into this place that combines fun with thought. A place that, in Walt Disney's words, "will never be completed, but will always be introducing and testing and demonstrating. . . ." A multicultural, cosmic experience poised on its prophetic launchpad.

▼▼▼▼▼▼▼▼▼
Nuts & Bolts

ARRIVAL

From the Contemporary, Polynesian or Grand Floridian Beach resorts: Take the hotel monorail to the Ticket and Transportation Center, then transfer to the Epcot monorail. From the Magic Kingdom: Take the express monorail to the Ticket and Transportation Center; transfer to the Epcot monorail.

From Disney–MGM Studios or Disney's Animal Kingdom: Take a Disney bus directly to Epcot.

From Downtown Disney, Blizzard Beach, Pleasure Island, Typhoon Lagoon, Port Orleans, Dixie Landings Resort, Caribbean Beach Resort or the All-Star Sports, Music and Movies resorts: Take a Disney bus directly to Epcot.

From Fort Wilderness or the Wilderness Lodge: Take a Disney bus to the Ticket and Transportation Center, then transfer to the Epcot monorail.

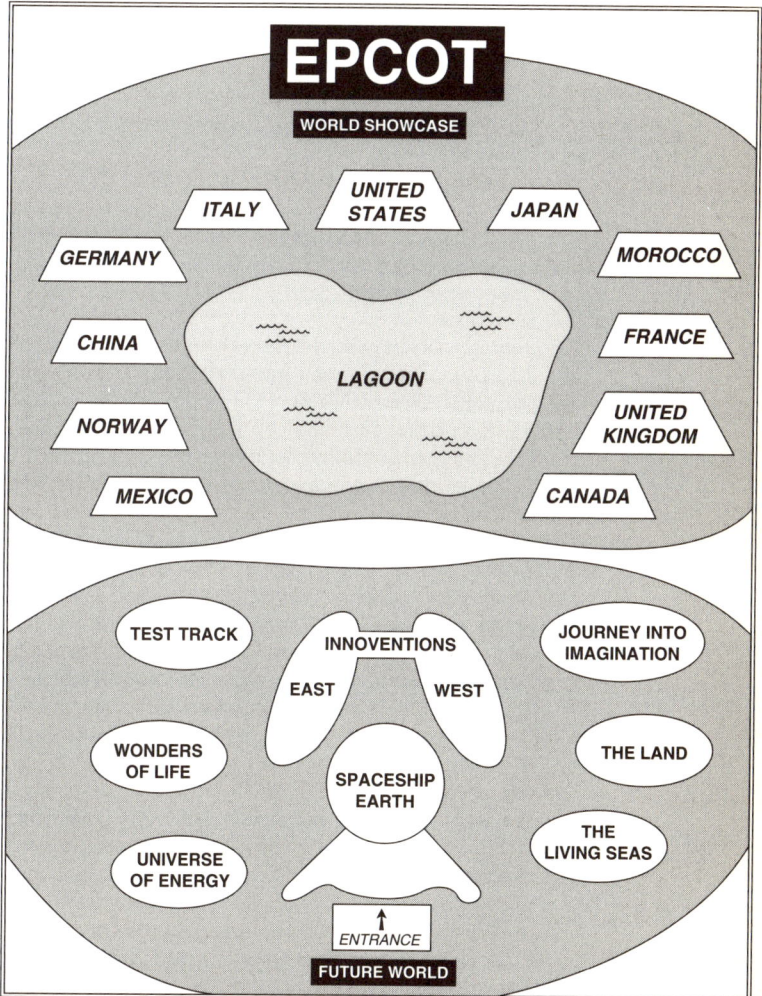

From the Swan, Dolphin, Yacht Club Resort or Beach Club Resort: Take the hotel tram or ferry to Epcot's World Showcase entrance, which is much less crowded than Epcot's main entrance in Future World.

From area hotels not in Disney World: Most hotels provide shuttle buses to and from Epcot. However, shuttles often run only on the hour or every two or three hours. In this case, it's better to drive.

By Car: From Route 4, Epcot has its own exit, located about halfway between the exits for Route 192 and Route 535. Epcot is about one and a half miles from Route 4.

After paying a $7 parking fee (free for guests of Disney World hotels), you'll park in one of 9000 spaces on what seems like a concrete wasteland. Trams will deliver you to Epcot's main entrance.

> If it's raining, notice that no water falls from Spaceship Earth. Instead, it's collected within the globe and funneled into World Showcase Lagoon.

Unlike the Magic Kingdom's parking lot, the lot at Epcot rarely fills to capacity. However, because early arrivers save hours of standing in line, it's critical to get there one to two hours before the advertised opening time. Trams and monorails usually operate two hours prior to opening.

GAME PLAN When plotting your Epcot strategy, it's vital to know that Spaceship Earth, Guest Relations and the surrounding area open 30 minutes to an hour before the rest of Future World. Here you can get a head start on the competition by picking up maps and touring information; renting strollers, lockers or wheelchairs; and riding Spaceship Earth, one of the park's most popular attractions. At Guest Relations, you can make lunch and dinner reservations for one of the World Showcase restaurants, avoiding that distressing phrase so often heard after 10 a.m.: "We're all booked."

On Wednesday during the summer, holidays and other busy times, Disney sometimes opens all of Epcot for resort guests as early as an hour before the advertised opening time. There's no way to know when this will happen, though you can call 407-824-4321 the day before for the park's "official" hours.

World Showcase opens late in the morning, usually at 11 a.m., so you'll spend the first half of your day in Future World. You'll want to hit the most popular Future World attractions—Test Track, The Land and the Wonders of Life—first, since they fill up midday and stay that way through early evening.

Then spend late afternoon and evening at World Showcase. The pavilions here are so self-contained that it's best to see *all* of one country before moving on to the next. Once you've made the one-and-one-third-mile trek around the lagoon (and the sun is beating down), you won't want to backtrack. The only exception is when you dine at a pavilion. If you're coming from Future World, you can save steps by boarding a ferry across the lagoon to Germany (on the southeast corner) or Morocco (on the southwest corner). Double-decker buses do transport visitors around the promenade, but bus lines are usually so long (and buses so crowded) that it's easier and quicker to walk.

All Epcot attractions do close promptly at the advertised time (8 or 9 p.m. most of the year), but most of its restaurants take reservations for times right up until closing. If you don't mind dining late—and missing the IllumiNations laser and fireworks show—take the late reservation. (Or, in most cases, you can show up without a reservation.) You can catch part of IllumiNations from a windowside table at the Chefs de France restaurant at the France pavilion.

Stroller and Wheelchair Rentals   Available at the base of Spaceship Earth (on the east side) and at International Gateway in World Showcase. For replacement strollers and wheelchairs, take your receipt to the Germany pavilion or International Gateway.

GUEST SERVICES

Baby Services   Located at the Odyssey Complex in Future World, on the east side of the bridge to World Showcase. Services include changing tables and comfortable rockers for nursing. Diapers, formula and other baby needs are also available.

Lockers   Available on the west side of the Entrance Plaza near Spaceship Earth and at International Gateway. Additional lockers are located outside the main entrance at the bus station; however, these are inconvenient if you plan on retrieving items during the day. Lockers cost $5 to $7 per day plus $2 refundable deposit for unlimited use.

Pets   Pets are not allowed in Epcot; however, you can board them for $6 per day at the kennels located on the east side of the Entrance Plaza. Boarding your pets overnight costs $11 if you're visiting for the day and $9 if you're staying at a Disney resort.

Lost Children   Report lost children at Guest Relations in Innoventions East or Baby Services in Future World.

Package Pickup   If you plan on doing some serious shopping, this free service comes in handy. Simply have the Epcot store clerks forward your purchases to Package Pickup, located just west of the Entrance Plaza. One drawback: If you're leaving during rush hour (5 to 6 p.m., or the few minutes before closing), you may face a lengthy line at the pickup counter.

Lost & Found   Located on the west side of the Entrance Plaza.

Banking   There are ATM machines at Epcot, one on the east side of the Entrance Plaza, inside the park one at the bridge between World Showcase and Future World and one at the American Adventure near the restrooms.

GETTING AROUND

Sprawled across 260 acres and the largest of Disney theme parks, Epcot is justifiably nicknamed "Every Person Comes Out Tired." If it's your first visit, know this fact: You can't see it all in one day. (Or three days, for that matter.) But that's really good news. After more than a dozen visits, this writer found Epcot so layered with information, entertainment and details that it was impossible to tire of the place.

Despite its exhausting size, Epcot is relatively easy to navigate. The park is split into two distinct "worlds": Future World and World Showcase. The main entrance is in front of Spaceship Earth in Future World. Guest Relations located in Innoventions East is a good place to meet if someone in your party gets lost.

Future World forms an almost perfect circle that's ringed with six sightseeing pavilions. Traveling clockwise, you'll encounter Universe of Energy, Wonders of Life, World of Motion, Journey Into Imagination, The Land and The Living Seas. At the circle's north end is Spaceship Earth; at its center are two crescent-shaped buildings, Innoventions East and Innoventions West.

World Showcase rests south of Future World across a scenic bridge and opens later in the morning, usually at 11 a.m. Eleven "minicountries" border a promenade around the 40-acre World Showcase Lagoon. Traveling clockwise, you'll see Mexico, Norway, China, Germany, Italy, the United States, Japan, Morocco, France, the United Kingdom and Canada. In between France and the United Kingdom is the International Gateway, which serves as Epcot's rear entrance. Here you can rent strollers and wheelchairs and have film developed in less than two hours.

▼ ▼ ▼ ▼ ▼ ▼ ▼ ▼ ▼
Future World

Epcot begins in the future. Here in Future World, plants are pod-shaped, walkways are angled and umbrellas resemble spaceships. Concrete extends for miles, and the slant-nose monorail coils overhead. Buildings of steel and glass reflect the sun's rays and aim for the heavens. Polishing this lunar look are twisted metal sculptures and fountains that mirror crisp white architecture. Spaceship Earth, a silvery sphere that towers overhead, is Future World's punctuation mark.

Future World's attractions delve into the subjects of travel, transportation, communication, biology, agriculture, sea life, energy and the human imagination. The challenge for Disney, of course, is to make these topics so interesting and entertaining that people keep coming back for more. For the most part, Future World more than succeeds.

Unlike the Magic Kingdom's Tomorrowland, which takes just a cursory (and not always accurate) look at what lies ahead, Future World offers forecasts that are comprehensive and believable. Indeed, many attractions combine the best of Disney's best: fantastic special effects, state-of-the-art motion pictures and set work, fascinating hands-on exhibits, and Audio-Animatronics figures so lifelike you're constantly doing a double take. And there are plenty of rides. Not fast rides, but clever ones that often last nearly 15 minutes. The Universe of Energy has a theater that travels from room to room, The Land offers a cruise through hydroponic gardens, and Spaceship Earth sends you forward *and* backward through the world's biggest manmade sphere.

Future World's complexity makes it impossible to see everything here in one day. Certain attractions should be on your must-see list, including Spaceship Earth, Wonders of Life and The Land, though you may choose to tour only one or two features within these attractions.

Above all, don't rush through Future World. Much of the area's appeal lies in its fine tuning and details. The more you absorb and enjoy those details, the more you're likely to say: "Learning never felt so good."

Spaceship Earth ★★★★★ Rising some 18 stories and spanning 180 feet, this space-age spectacle seems dipped in aluminum and marbled with thousands of ridges. From far away—it is visible from an airplane on either Florida coast—the million-pound globe appears otherworldly. Up close, as you stand in its vast shadow, it is overwhelming. Engineers call it "the world's largest geodesic sphere" (the steel beams supporting Spaceship Earth extend some 185 feet underground). Admirers call it "the big silver golf ball." Like Cinderella Castle in the Magic Kingdom, Spaceship Earth is Epcot's chief symbol, recognizable worldwide. By day it reflects the cerulean blue sky and chalky clouds; by night, it mirrors the very planets it emulates.

Inside Spaceship Earth is another world. Continuous moving trams, called "time machines," transport visitors through dim tunnels, fog and light and surrounds them with remarkable projected images and Audio-Animatronics figures. Sponsored by AT&T, the ride is an odyssey tracing the history of human communication.

WHAT TO SEE & DO

IT'S THE REAL THING!

Disney has really outdone itself with authentic details inside Spaceship Earth. Words dictated by the pharaoh are straight from the letter of an ancient Egyptian ruler. The scribble on the wall of Pompeii perfectly matches the wall's original graffiti. Gutenberg's press really is working, and the page it prints is identical to one from his original Bible. And that sleeping monk hunched over his desk appears to be breathing.

You slowly spiral higher and higher into Spaceship Earth, then at the globe's crown you pivot around for a backward descent. All the while, smells and sights and songs are fueling your senses.

During the 14-minute trip, Walter Cronkite talks in your ear (via a recording) and guides you through the days of cavemen, Egyptian hieroglyphics, Phoenician merchants, Roman theater, Gutenberg's printing press, Ed Sullivan and Beaver Cleaver, and finally to an executive at her computer. Along the way you smell the mustiness of ancient caves and the smoke from burning Rome, and hear a monk—quill pen in hand—snoring loudly in the abbey. In one impressive scene, Michelangelo puts the final touches on a Sistine Chapel fresco. Just as spectacular is the view at the top, where you plunge through a jet-black sky peppered with millions of stars. The new ending, narrated by Jeremy Irons, stresses the shrinking of the global village.

TIPS: Everyone seems to love Spaceship Earth. Parents enjoy the fabulous special effects, while children are mesmerized by all the colors, movement and music. Unfortunately, immense popularity means big-time lines. You can, however, avoid long waits by riding between 8:30 and 9 a.m. or after 7 p.m. *Not to be missed.*

Mission Space ★★★★ Enquiring minds have wanted to know about this spiffy new attraction ever since EPCOT starting touting it a few years back. The simulated rocket launch seems like a stretch (a computer screen and some special effects can only take you so far). But this rocket ride to Mars is pretty darned authentic—the closest most of us will ever get to actual outer space.

Mission Space crews buckle into four-person pods where everybody gets a job: navigator, pilot, engineer or commander. It all seems like a standard-issue arcade game until the countdown begins, the launch hatch (really a TV monitor) "opens up" to end-

CELEBRATE DISNEY

The Millennium may have come and gone, but the party at Disney World lives on. **IllumiNations: Reflections of Earth** is a spectacular pyrotechnics-and-music show with astounding sights and catchy tunes—things you don't want to miss. Unfortunately, getting a prime viewing spot requires showing up hours ahead. Another option is to reserve stellar seating aboard a pontoon boat; cost for the boat, driver and up to 12 passengers is $120—more if you add food. You can make similar arrangements for fireworks shows at the Magic Kingdom. Reserve early (as much as 90 days ahead for peak season) and dress warmly in the off-season as the night air can get surprisingly chilly. Call the recreation line (407-939-7529) and ask for Fireworks or Specialty Cruises.

less blue sky, and the rocket lifts off. That's when the little space craft begins to bounce around and inexplicable G-forces bear down.

Actual NASA astronauts have given Mission Space the thumbs up, which should give you an idea of how realistic it is. There are genuine thrills—and more than a few beads of sweat—as the engines fire up and you feel like you're being blasted out of the stratosphere. All that, and Gary Sinese, too (the actor appears on video as your interplanetary guide).

Still, the whole virtual thing isn't thrilling to everyone. In exit polls (my own, strictly unscientific research), adults emerge ecstatic and completely pumped for a second ride; kids, slightly less so, perhaps the side-effects from overexposure to high-tech gizmos since birth. Some folks need their thrills to include the actual motion that you get on a roller coaster. That's not to say Mission Space is quite stationary. Most people are surprised to learn that the pods were spinning furiously through much of the ride—the trick that creates those aforementioned G-forces.

TIPS: The spinning motion isn't evident when you're on board, but your stomach may know anyway. The ride is more forgiving to the sensitive of stomach than, say, the Tilt-a-Whirl. My stomach and I can't even consider the Tea Cups, but I managed Mission Space with minimal nausea that went away the moment I got off. My co-riders claimed not to feel it at all. That said, the ride *does* spin, and supersensitive stomachs might want to think twice. My co-pilot was green for the rest of the day. Either way, definitely not a ride for right after lunch. Claustrophobics, too, take heed, as the "ship" is a mighty tight fit.

Universe of Energy ******** Shaped like a lopsided triangle, this mirrored building is sheathed in 80,000 tiny solar collectors that suck up sun rays and transform them into energy. Inside is a den of lifelike dinosaurs, forests and oversized greenery destined to make even the most skeptical visitors feel they have stepped back into prehistoric time.

Once this attraction's special-effects outshone everything else about it, leaving guests squirming in their seats during the accompanying dry and too-long educational film. But today's Universe of Energy has taken the original concept and improved upon it, providing a film and special effects event that is as much entertaining as it is informative.

The centerpiece of Ellen's Energy Adventure is a film starring comedian Ellen DeGeneres. As a contestant in a *Jeopardy* round where all the categories are about energy, DeGeneres fails miserably until Bill Nye the Science Guy comes to her rescue, taking her on a trip through time to unearth the origins of energy.

At this point, the attraction takes a surprising turn as chunks of theater rows break away and head for the door. These clever, 97-passenger "traveling theaters" take a 300-million-year time trip through spooky forests veiled in mist. (Powered by solar energy, the traveling theater is nicknamed "The Ride on Sunshine.") Here, disarmingly realistic snorting brontosaurs hover over the theater cars (causing some passengers to recoil) while a menacing *T. rex* battles an oversized rival nearby. There's even an animatron Ellen who fends for herself against menacing prehistoric beasts.

Afterward, the film gradually brings DeGeneres and Nye back to the future, comically explaining the ins and outs of energy production.

While not a belly laugher, the film is quick witted and well intentioned, and a good deal more entertaining than its predecessor. Even the dinosaurs, unquestionably still the highlight of the show and alone worth the visit, have been updated to reflect modern scientific views.

TIPS: Some scenes may frighten small kids. Don't be discouraged by long lines: Every 15 minutes, about 600 new people are ushered in.

Wonders of Life—Sponsored by MetLife, this immensely popular place is a study in informative fun. Housed under a vast gold-crowned dome, it brims with dozens of games and gadgets that whiz, whirl, bleep and blink. Kids beg to spend hours here in this "Fitness Fairground," where they can test their tennis and golf prowess; zoom across the world on stationary bikes (while watching travel scenery); and fiddle around in the Sensory Funhouse, which has a "Room with a Skew." Every exhibit has health messages, but they're relayed so playfully it's tough to realize you're learning. In "Goofy About Health," a stressed-out Goofy gives up smoking and starts exercising, snoozing regularly and eating nutritious vittles. The eight-minute show, held in a small open theater, headlines great vintage Goofy cartoons and clever set work, with buildings such as Phast Pharmacy and Goofco store. In another open theater, the Anacomical Players deliver a corny, hilarious improv on human anatomy. Besides all this, Wonders of Life offers three splendid attractions:

Body Wars ★★★★★ The swiftest, rowdiest ride at Epcot, Body Wars is a mind trip through the human body. Using the same technology that propelled Star Tours to Disney–MGM fame, Body Wars takes place in a simulator much like those used to train military pilots. The idea is that you've been miniaturized and "shot" into a patient's arm to rescue a scientist who's trying to pluck out a splinter. From here, the entire room starts rockin' and rollin' as the scientist gets sucked into the patient's circulation system. You plunge in after her, dodging blood cells, lungs and ribs and rebounding off artery walls. Together with terrific body images, the special effects and frenzied pace make this ride an ingenious psychological thriller.

TIPS: Expectant mothers and children under three are not allowed to ride. Some children old enough to ride will find it rough and frightening. Not recommended for people with bad backs or weak stomachs. Epcot's fastest ride, it's also the most popular. The only way to avoid a 45-minute-plus wait here is to arrive as soon as the park opens or during the hour before it closes. Lines sometimes dwindle between 6 and 7 p.m., the peak dinnertime for World Showcase restaurants. *Not to be missed.*

Cranium Command ★★★★ This delightful, highly entertaining attraction is Epcot's best-kept secret. Tucked in the back of Wonders of Life, the show is smashing, with newfangled effects and a witty script delivered by some of America's best-loved comedians. Set in a 200-seat theater, it combines a fast-paced movie with elaborate set work. The show's star is the Audio-Animatronics robot Buzzy, a bumbling, bigger-than-life kid who pilots the brain of a 12-year-old boy for a day. Somehow, Buzzy puts the boy's biological clock off kilter: He dashes off to school without getting dressed, forgets to eat breakfast or lunch and wilts in the presence of a certain pretty female classmate. Along the way, Buzzy has quite a time figuring out which brain part controls what. Body parts are played hilariously by familiar television characters, including *Saturday Night Live*'s (pump YOU up) Hans and Franz as the heart pumpers and *Cheers*' barfly Norm as the stomach.

TIPS: Don't miss the preshow cartoon, which sets the scene for the main presentation. This engaging show is still largely undiscovered, so lines are rarely longer than 20 minutes. See it in the middle of the day.

DANCING WATERS

At the **Fountains of Nations Water Ballet Show**, giant water spouts rise and fall, torrents rocket into blue air, and shapely showers pirouette to powerful music. This liquid symphony, which takes place every 15 minutes, ends with an explosion, like invisible fireworks going off. ~ Future World courtyard between Innoventions East and Innoventions West. There are more whimsical waters outside the Journey Into Imagination Pavilion. Here, **The Dancing Waters** play to big crowds. Tubes of water leap from one pond to another. Glistening water beads do the twist around a shrub sculpture. The Serpentine Fountains form temporary water bridges between gardens. The Dancing Waters rank as one of Disney's most inventive inventions. As Tigger might say, it's absolute imaginationimity!

Test Track ★★★★ Now here's an attraction that really makes Disney World guests look like dummies—crash test dummies, that is. Strap in and get a passenger's eye view of the torture chamber that a car goes through before becoming road worthy. Wild skids, high-speed curves and break tests are all on the menu. A good paint job has to endure extreme temperatures, so prepare to run hot and cold. The best part is the fly around the outside track at a top speed of 60 miles per hour.

TIPS: This ride easily ranks as one of the longest (and slowest) lines in all of Disney. Do yourself a favor and take advantage of the fast pass system.

Journey Into Imagination with Figment—A playful ride, a 3D movie and oodles of nifty electronic games make this place the hands-down Epcot favorite of many children. The building itself, composed of two slightly crooked glass pyramids, is wonderfully illusionary. All day long, the sun's rays wink across the glass and lure visitors to these geometric top hats. Inside the Kodak-sponsored building, you'll find three attractions with imagination gone wild:

Journey Into Your Imagination ★★ Just how imaginative are you? That's what the folks at the fictitious Imagination Institute (the place that recognizes Wayne Szalinski's work in "Honey, I Shrunk the Audience" next door) want to find out. Board this ride, an adaptation of the old Journey into the Imagination ride, and you'll first be tested for your IQ, which in this case stands for Imagination Quotient. Most of us appear sorely lacking at the beginning, a fact illustrated by the puffs of empty steam appearing to emanate from our heads in the mirror. After journeying through the attraction's slightly cockeyed rooms—in one spot everything is upside down, another features sound and no light—we've been reformed. Our IQ at the ride's end is off the charts.

TOURING THE LAND

If you enjoyed the Living with the Land boat ride, don't miss the attraction's 45-minute **"Behind the Seeds" Greenhouse Tour**. A guide provides details on The Land's experimental growing techniques, taking you through the hydroponic garden, tropical and desert farms, and the garden with simulated lunar soil. The tour explores what's covered during the boat trip, but in much greater depth. Best of all, it allows visitors the chance to ask questions. Greenhouse Tours are offered every hour throughout the day. Reservations must be made the day you plan to tour; stop by the Guided Tour Waiting Area just outside the Green Thumb Emporium on The Land's first floor. Tours cost $8 for adults, $3 for kids.

Those who recall the previous Imagination ride will find this a huge improvement over its insipid predecessor. Some of the illusions are truly mind boggling—exactly how did they make that bird appear in the cage?!

TIPS: Imagination is still a kids' ride, but there are a few effects that may startle little ones, especially an "explosion" of light at the very end and a train that whizzes right by you out of the blackness. Those who are afraid of the dark—and we're talking pitch dark here—may want to avoid it entirely.

Honey, I Shrunk the Audience ★★★★★ No doubt about it: This 3D show has some brilliant special effects. Disney plays with the audience not only through visual trickery but also through physical sensation. (In other words, when the mice are unleashed in the movie, you feel them scrambling up your legs.) Wayne Szalinski, the doddering professor from the film *Honey, I Shrunk the Kids*, is back on screen with his shrinking machine—only this time he zaps you, the audience. With your 3D glasses on and your perception warped, you feel lilliputian. And vulnerable. Dogs and tennis shoes tower over you, and a monster king cobra strikes at your face—creepy. Don't be surprised if you find yourself shrieking, screaming and jumping up out of your seat. Everyone does.

TIPS: Too frightening and loud for most small children (the five year old sitting beside me sobbed through the whole show). Otherwise, this is one not to miss.

The Image Works: The Kodak "What If" Labs ★★★ When it comes to fantastically clever stuff, few attractions parallel The Image Works. Filled with electronic wizardry, this place has "the works": all kinds of devices for toying with light, sound, color, images and time. In one station, you can "morph" your face into that of a cartoon character and send it via e-mail to your friends. Another lets you create sounds with the wave of your hand. An Electronic Mirror offers a high-tech version of the funhouse variety. I played the Stepping Tones—where jumping up and down on the carpet creates light, music and psychedelic colors—so long one night I was politely kicked out at closing time. For children, the place inspires creative expression. For adults, it's a reminder that, in our fast-paced world, daydreaming really is a lot of fun. Perhaps the best part, though, is that there's never a line to get in. Midday crowds do create short waits at individual stations, but there's always an activity without any line.

TIPS: There's a separate entrance for those who are just visiting The Image Works.

The Land—This tremendous building, shaped like a galactic greenhouse fused with sunlight, overflows with earthly delights. Colorful food counters line the first floor, dispensing homemade pastries, baked potatoes, barbecue, frosty ice cream, gourmet coffees, chocolatey desserts and bread so fresh it warms your hand. This initial scene is so heady and the aromas so overwhelming that it's impossible to take just a "quick peek" at The Land. And that's good, because the food-themed attraction takes an engrossing and often amusing look at our body's fuel. Three very good and very different attractions, presented by Nestlé U.S.A., are featured:

Living with the Land ***** One of few Epcot attractions with a live narrator, this enlightening boat trip delves into the history and future of farming. The crew first winds through a simulated rain forest, desert, prairie and old-fashioned barnyard, then journeys through actual thriving farms. There's a miniature tropical farm with papayas so fleshy you long to reach out and pluck them. There's a fascinating hydroponic garden and a seafood farm brimming with colorful paddlefish and freshwater shrimp. At the prolific Desert Farm, a computer delivers water to the roots of cotton, sunflowers, buffalo gourds, sorghum and cucumbers. Fascinating trivia delivered by the boat captain and smooth sailing make this an informative and relaxing 14-minute cruise.

TIPS: Much of the information is too academic for preschoolers, though they usually love the scenery and the idea of being in a boat. *Not to be missed.*

Food Rocks **** A delightful tribute to nutrition, this theater show headlines a zany cast of rock-and-roll foodies who sing, dance and pun their way through the kitchen. The many memorable Audio-Animatronics characters include Neil Moussaka, Chubby Cheddar and Fud Wrapper (a real rapper). The Peachboys sing about "Good, Good, Good . . . Good Nutrition!" while The Refrigerator Police remind us of that pesky '80s tune with "Every Bite You Take. . . ." If you enjoy the lighthearted humor of the Magic Kingdom's Country Bear Jamboree, you'll love this show.

TIPS: This is one Epcot attraction that's not popular but should be. All for the better: There's rarely more than a 15-minute wait, so go between 11 a.m and 3 p.m. No matter what time you go, the show offers a cool, dark reprieve from the sun and walking.

The Circle of Life *** This beautiful film shown at the big, comfortable Harvest Theater tugs at your environmental heart strings. Simba the Lion King narrates the picture, trying to persuade his forest buddies not to dam a river and build a tourist resort. He takes them (and the audience) on a visual tour of world destruction: putrid streams, ravaged rain forests, oil-drowned seabirds, gaseous big-city traffic and garbage dumps—all caused by too many people, too much development and too little concern for the earth. The moral of the story, of course, is that everyone should get together and help save the earth. Meanwhile . . . Disney has leveled the Central Florida woods to make way for (among other things) a $2.5 billion residential and cultural center and "mega-mall." The name: Celebration.

TIPS: This film is for all ages, though toddlers tend to use the dark, quiet space for a quick (20-minute) nap, while parents use it to rest tired feet. Rarely a long wait.

The Living Seas ★★★ Water lashes at imitation boulders outside this wavy building trimmed in swimming-pool blue. Sponsored by United Technologies, The Living Seas is one of Epcot's most ambitious attractions—and sadly one of its most overrated. Even hard-core sea lovers find the attraction sorely lacking. The preshow movie on the origin of the seas is dramatic but bookish, and the **Living Seas Ride** ★ —the attraction's main event— seems over before it begins. Too bad, because the idea for the ride is marvelous: You literally cruise through the world's largest manmade saltwater aquarium (some 5000 sea creatures thrive here). Moving trams take visitors through an acrylic-lined cylinder in the center of the aquarium. The 5.7-million-gallon tank, some 27 feet deep and 200 feet in diameter, is chock-full of fascinating sealife such as barracudas, dolphins, sea lions, stingrays, parrot fish and yes, sharks. Scuba divers roam the tank, testing new dive gear, training dolphins and talking to observers via wireless radios. Unfortunately, no sooner are you engrossed in all this than the three-minute ride is over.

> The World Showcase Lagoon could submerge 85 football fields.

The best part of The Living Seas comes after the ride, when visitors can peruse two floors of interesting marine exhibits. Kids go nuts over this area, called **Sea Base Alpha** ★★★ , where they can play ocean-themed video games and slip into an atmospheric dive suit. Numerous aquariums feature some unusual life forms, including camouflage fish, kelp forests and minuscule zooplankton.

TIPS: The Living Seas draws big crowds from about 9:30 a.m. to 6 p.m. If there's more than a 20-minute wait, skip it. Orlando's Sea World, an entire theme park devoted to marine life, is more extensive and entertaining—and less crowded.

Innoventions ★★★ Now that we've officially arrived at the new millennium, Disney wants to show you what the world is going to look like—at least from a technology standpoint. The newest incarnation of Innoventions heralds gizmos and gadgets of the future for home, hospital and office. Look for Dick Tracy–like wrist telephones, robotic pets, and a smart house featuring a refrigerator that keeps track of its contents and automatically catalogues your grocery list (whether or not it can countermand the family members who return the milk with only a drop is anybody's guess).

A complete overhaul, the new Innoventions is decidedly more streamlined than its predecessor, with a loose "road map" guiding you through. There are plenty of detours along the way, and technophiles could easily get caught up in here for hours. Game lovers will get a taste of their favorite sport (we loved Toon Tag, where you get to become a cartoon character) and there are even a couple of freebies, such as the chance to send a video "D-mail" to friends back home.

TIPS: Rarely crowded so browse any time.

World Showcase

The scenic bridge from Future World to World Showcase seems to create a time warp: On one side lies Future World's metal and mirror scenery, on the other, a skyline etched with ancient pyramids, painted pagodas and the Eiffel Tower. There is something comforting about these old buildings that at once captivate and stimulate. Time and space compress. A thousand years ago seems as today.

Flowers frame the paths that wend though World Showcase's 11 pavilions, each claimed by a different country. Like bustling town squares, the pavilions celebrate the architecture and customs born of different cultures throughout history.

Castles and temples, clock towers and stone churches reflect the beauty and lore of places such as Italy, Morocco, Norway, Germany, Japan and China. Gushing fountains, punctuated by sculpture, are sprinkled across plazas. Musicians and actors perform in the streets, providing a taste of their country's artistry. Quaint and exclusive shops peddle the specialties of each region, and some 24 eateries serve up native cuisine.

From the beginning, World Showcase was designed, as one Epcot guide noted, "so that no one country would stand above the others." In fact, the American pavilion, originally planned as a sleek high-rise on stilts, was scaled down to a more modest colonial brick style so as not to outshine the others.

EPCOT'S PEOPLES

If the World Showcase employees seem like true representatives of their countries, that's because they are. Each pavilion employs people native to its host country, providing a cultural cornucopia of accents, costumes and traditions. The employees, who are mostly in their 20s, work in Epcot for one year as part of a World Fellowship exchange program. All the nationals live together in dormitories just outside the park. Cultural exchange is integral to the World Showcase experience, and visitors are encouraged to ask questions at each pavilion. In fact, many employees are so enthusiastic that they're disappointed if you don't inquire about their homelands.

Now, this vast cultural apron, gathered around a 40-acre lagoon, is so collectively stunning that it's difficult to know where to start or how to see it all. Unlike any other Disney theme park, World Showcase is not a place to hop rides or play games or even participate in shows. Instead, it's a place for exploring and listening, or just sitting on a bench and absorbing the surroundings. In fact, to get the true World Showcase experience, all you have to do is *be there*.

The best way to see each "country" is to walk, and walk. Then walk some more. Start by strolling the streets, taking the time to notice each building's design details. Then peruse the shops. More than just stores, they reflect the history, architectural styles and craftsmanship of an entire nation.

Restaurants, too, provide cultural insight. If you don't plan to dine at a country's restaurants, ask to see them anyway. Several pavilions have fine minimuseums, and five show excellent movies. Two countries, Mexico and Norway, have tame but very enjoyable boat rides. And every pavilion has employees who are anxious to answer questions about their native lands.

One of the true joys of World Showcase is its **street performers**. Each country has its own brand of show, from Mexico's hunky mariachi men crowned with boleros to Canada's kilt-clad bagpipe players. Entertainers usually appear every 15 to 45 minutes, bursting out in song, dance or even quirky theater. The United Kingdom's Olde Globe Players, for instance, do a farce where audience members act amusing (and somewhat embarrassing) parts. Morocco has a procession where performers, clothed in caftans, play darbukas (drums), nfirs (trumpets) and uds (lutes). And China presents a miniature but elaborate version of a Chinese New Year celebration. To find out who's playing and when, pick up an entertainment schedule at Guest Relations in Innoventions East.

If you want to get the real scoop on World Showcase, sign up for a behind-the-scenes tour. The three-hour excursion, called **Hidden Treasures of World Showcase,** is led by knowledgeable Disney employees who detail each pavilion's intricacies. From the architectural styles and singular design of each place to the country's music and history, the topics intrigue and inform. You'll also get inside the Epcot wardrobe—big as a city block—and learn all sorts of trivia (such as the number of bricks in the American pavilion—110,000!). Tours, which are for adults 16 and older, are held on Tuesday and Thursday, and start at 9 a.m. The cost is $59 (plus Epcot admission). Reservations should be made at least three weeks in advance by calling 407-939-8687.

A rose is a rose is a rose, right? Wrong, at least in World Showcase, where an astonishing 10,100 rosebushes in 40 varieties shape and color the scenery. That's just some of the "plantese" you'll learn on the **Gardens of the World** tour. Led by a Disney horti-culturist, it delves into the vast variety of flora across World Show-case. Tour members also learn some Disney growing secrets, such as that every plant and tree have several replacements in a mam-moth nursery behind Epcot. Tours, open to those 16 and over, are offered every Tuesday and Thursday from 9 a.m. to 12 noon. There is an additional $49 fee for this tour; reservations should be made at least three weeks in advance by calling 407-939-8687.

WHAT TO SEE & DO

Mexico ★★★★ A spectacular pre-Columbian pyramid, flanked by giant serpents' heads and somber sculptures of Toltec warriors, gives this pavilion a mystic aura. But the spectacle gives no clue to what's inside: a hillside town veiled in twilight. Fashioned af-ter the Mexican village Taxco, the plaza is scattered with canopied carts where you can buy sombreros, flowers or sandals. Stores gather around the plaza, showing off their tile roofs, wrought-iron balconies and window boxes draped with flowers. A mari-achi band strolls and strums, lending festivity. Down below, visi-tors dine by candlelight along a riverfront terrace.

The Mexico pavilion offers two formal attractions, an art ex-hibit and a boat ride. The exhibit, called **Reign of Glory**, possesses a splendid collection of pre-Columbian art, including clay vessels, masks and vases. You can peruse the display before or after the boat ride.

El Rio del Tiempo: The River of Time ★★★ This slow, peace-ful journey is like a nighttime cruise that encounters ancient pyr-amids, rocky caverns and elaborate carvings. Flavored with Mayan, Toltec and Aztec scenes and artifacts, it spans thousands of years of Mexican history. Kids love this colorful, leisurely trip and its beautifully costumed dolls, reminiscent of those at the Magic Kingdom's It's A Small World. Scenes of Mexican life (including cliff divers, flying dancers and speed boats) are interspersed everywhere, giving the ride an interesting travelogue edge. The finale—a dazzling fiber-optics fireworks show—is extra special.

TIPS: Arrive first thing to avoid crowds. If you miss the morn-ing, try again after 7 p.m.

Norway ★★★★ Perhaps one of the most extraordinary World Showcase pavilions, Norway is rugged, complex and stunning. Certainly, the singular beauty of the Land of the Midnight Sun shines through in these cobbled streets, rocky waterfalls, red-tiled cottages and a 14th-century stone castle. The focal point, though, is a wood stave church, modeled after one built in 1250 A.D., with thick shingles and stylized carvings. Notice the dragons that jut out from the eaves: They were added in case the villagers reverted back to paganism.

Maelstrom ★★★★ Despite the ride's scary name and its encounters with grisly trolls, it's really very tame. A favorite of children and adults, it's an indoor glide in dragon-headed longboats just like the one Eric the Red sailed a thousand years ago. The vessels navigate around Viking villages, beautiful fjords and forests, and the slightly tumultuous North Sea. There's one steep but easy plunge, and a nearly backward tumble down a waterfall that's so gentle riders in the front sometimes miss it. After the ride, a five-minute film provides a quick but dramatic look at Norway's breathtaking landscape.

TIPS: A provocative pavilion, Norway usually gets very crowded by midafternoon.

China ★★★★★ China's inspiring panorama seems architecturally spiritual. True to Chinese design and lore, the pavilion is a visual feast woven with symbols of life, death, virtue and the environment. As you pass through the Gate of the Golden Sun, you're greeted with an exquisite replica of Beijing's opulent Temple of Heaven, built in 1420 during the Ming dynasty. Coated in glimmering red (which stands for joy) and gold (imperialism), it is a three-tiered gem with delicate geometric patterns. The temple is edged by a meditation garden where soft tufts of grass and Chinese corkscrew willows invite contemplation. The Hall of Prayer, the temple's main wing, is where emperors prayed for good harvests. Outside, 12 columns represent the 12 months; inside, four columns symbolize four seasons.

> At China's Temple of Heaven, the circular beams represent heaven while the square patterns stand for earth.

The sights here are so detailed it would take several hours to see everything. It's best to try this on your second or third day at Epcot, and only after you've seen the pavilion's stellar movie:

Reflections of China ★★★★★ Rarely does a visitor witness this compelling film without yearning to visit China. For 19 minutes the movie soars across stone forests, rice terraces, cloud-tipped mountains and the Great Wall that's stamped across the forehead of this vast land. From the hustle of modern Shanghai to the awesome silence of the Gobi Desert, it's all dramatically portrayed on a 360-degree Circle-Vision screen.

TIPS: Despite the sensational subject and film work, the theater has one drawback: no chairs. Instead, lean rails are provided while viewers stand. For parents with small children, this may spell disaster. Toddlers can't see the screen unless they're held, and infants must also be held because strollers aren't allowed. Possible solutions: If there are several adults in your group, they can take turns holding young ones. Or one parent can take the kids on Norway's boat ride next door while the other parent enjoys *Reflections of*

China. Unfortunately, the Canada pavilion also has a theater without seats.

Also, China may be World Showcase's most popular, and most crowded, attraction. Try to see it before 1 p.m. or after 7 p.m. *Not to be missed.*

Germany ★★★★ This jovial alcove is a smorgasbord of ginger-bread houses, turrets and wooden balconies, toy shops, beer gardens and blond men yodeling in the street. Modeled after no place in particular, the pavilion combines dashes of architecture, art and costumes from all across Germany. The result is like a fairy tale. In the middle of town square, called St. Georgsplatz, stands a sculpture of St. George slaying a dragon. The patron saint of soldiers, George was said to have slain the dragon during a trek to the Middle East. Nearby is Der Bücherwurm, a bookstore modeled after a *kaufhaus* (merchant hall) in Freiburg, Germany. Notice the facade bears statues of the emperors Ferdinand, Charles and Philip. The original *kaufhaus* includes a fourth emperor, Maximilian, but there wasn't enough room for him on Disney's version of the building. Disney employees like to jest that "Max got the ax."

> Take a good look at the American pavilion's clock tower: The Roman numeral four incorrectly reads IIII to distinguish it from the number V.

TIPS: Because Germany has no formal attractions, you can visit here anytime.

Italy ★★★★ While the "historic" buildings of most other World Showcase countries seem fairly new, Italy's facades look marvelously cracked and weathered. It only adds to the authenticity of this place that emulates the Western world's longtime seat of art and thought. A 105-foot bell tower, or campanile, casts a slender silhouette across the broad piazza, a re-creation of St. Mark's Square in Venice. A nearby replica of the 1309 Doge's Palace is, like the real building, a study in architectural styles. As different doges came and went, they would leave their signatures: Roman-esque columns here, Byzantine mosaics there, even a few Gothic arches. Also notice that the columns have no base. That's because the palace's Venice counterpart has none, a victim of flood erosion that has plagued the sinking islands for decades. Italy's genuineness spills across the World Showcase promenade to a tiny island where gondolas are hitched to moorings painted like barber poles. Olive and kumquat trees flutter in the wind, reminiscent of a Mediterranean vista.

TIPS: It takes at least an hour to absorb all the architectural and historic intricacies here. You can visit any time; Italy is rarely overcrowded.

United States ★★★★★ Despite the heavy patriotic tones here, it's tough not to get caught up in this red, white and blue panorama.

Graced by fragrant southern magnolias and palettes of blooming flowers, the pavilion features a replica of Philadelphia's Liberty Hall. All things considered, it's pretty incredible. The grand five-story building, crowned with a mansard roof and Liberty Bell, is coated in red mason bricks handmade from Georgia clay. The host pavilion of World Showcase, it sits smack in the middle of all the countries. From across the lagoon, it appears so familiar and inviting that it "acts as a carrot to draw people around the promenade," explains a Disney guide. Inside the building is a vast rotunda and a big, comfortable, air-conditioned theater where you'll see a film appropriately called:

The American Adventure ★★★★ Truly a Disney great, this much-talked-about show—which has been revised more than a thousand times—combines superb set work and films with Audio-Animatronics characters so lifelike you feel you know them. Here the Disney imagineers took the technology of the Magic Kingdom's Hall of Presidents and went all out. Not only are characters' expressions, movements and voices realistic, but so are their personalities. Ben Franklin reveals characteristic insight and optimism, while cigar-puffing Mark Twain brandishes his wry humor. The pair narrate the 26-minute nostalgic adventure, which recounts major events such as the Boston Tea Party, the Civil War, the nuclear desolation of Hiroshima and man's first step on the moon. It also delves into the legacies of many notables, including a blond named Marilyn and a cowboy named John Wayne. In one folksy post-Depression scene, several men shoot the breeze on the porch of a country general store. One strums a banjo, another presses a bottle of Coke to his lips, and a third laments the price of gas (18 cents a gallon). Many of the show's sets are mounted on a carriage that moves about underneath the stage. Called the "war wagon," it weighs 175 tons, spans 65-by-35-by-14 feet and is supported by posts planted 300 feet into the ground. As John Wayne might have said, "That's some fancy rig ya got there!"

TIPS: The bad news is this pavilion is usually thronged with people. Now for the good news: The American Adventure seats so many there's rarely more than a 20-minute wait, and that's in a beautiful air-conditioned rotunda. Preschoolers bored by the show often end up using the cool, dark theater for a quick doze. *Not to be missed.*

Japan **★★★★** First-time visitors to this attraction usually do the same thing: They stroll up to the pavilion and—stare. Little wonder, because the swell of winged pagoda roofs—painted so brilliantly blue they gleam like glass—is something to marvel at. Looming above the entrance is the mystic-looking goju-no-to, or five-story pagoda, inspired by the 8th-century Horyuji pagoda in Nara. Each of its five levels represents a different element—earth, water, fire, wind or sky—and at night they glow as one big beautiful Japanese lantern. The pagoda is set against a hill sketched with pebbled streams, arched bridges and tightly cropped shrubs. Blue-tiled buildings gather around this serene knoll, and the sound of wind chimes drifts across the air.

TIPS: Toward the back, a superb replica of the 18th-century *Shirasagi-Jo* feudal castle houses the fine Bijutsu-kan Gallery. Here changing exhibits display the delicate art of Japan and objects that have inspired its people.

Morocco ★★★★ Arguably Epcot's most exotic and romantic pavilion, Morocco is a cluster of fantastic fortresses, castles and prayer towers layered with stucco and carved wood and swirled by glimmering mosaics. Narrow, dusty streets wend through stuccoed archways and keyhole passages to a marketplace scattered with baskets, brass, horns and woven rugs. Moroccan men wear tasseled fezzes and women wear burkas as they stroll the plaza. If it all seems strangely real, it should: Most of the pavilion was a gift from the Kingdom of Morocco, which sent nine tons of hand-cut tiles and 23 artisans to install them. All construction followed the rules of the Islamic religion. Notice that every tile has some small crack or other imperfection, and no tile depicts any living creature. That's because Muslims believe only Allah is allowed to create perfection and life. Much of Moroccan belief and custom is beautifully depicted in the Gallery of Arts and History, which has frequently changing exhibits. Take time, too, to step inside the exquisitely tiled Restaurant Marrakesh.

TIPS: Morocco offers guided tours of the pavilion on request. Check with any pavilion employee.

France ★★★★★ Who, at least once in his or her life, has not longed to visit Paris? Keeping that in mind, you'll understand why this is one very popular (and very crowded) pavilion. The setting is turn-of-the-20th-century France during *La Belle Epoque*, or beautiful time, when architecture took on a delicate, romantic flavor. Buildings boast mansard roofs, minarets, dormer windows and ribbonlike wrought-iron facades. A footbridge, modeled after the Pont des Arts, crosses an inlet of the World Showcase Lagoon meant to mimic the river Seine. Near the back of the pavilion lies an ornate facsimile of the barrel-roofed Les Halles Marketplace, built in Paris during the 1200s and later moved to the country. There's also a marvelous pastry shop and the requisite sidewalk café where the food smells so heavenly it commands perpetual lines. The Eiffel Tower, mounted atop the pavilion's theater, is built to one-tenth the scale of the real tower so visitors can see it from across World

Ironically, the Eiffel Tower can be seen from anywhere in World Showcase except the France pavilion.

Showcase. After admiring it from afar, many people are disappointed to learn they can't get close to it. However, that underlying theater, the art nouveau Palais du Cinema, is where you can see an enlightening film called:

Impressions de France ★★★★★ This 18-minute flick takes a melodic, often whimsical journey across France. Shown on five screens spanning 200 degrees, it courses hills smothered in vineyards, sidewalks brimming with flower carts and castle estates so stunning you're ready to buy a plane ticket. There are dozens of other compelling scenes, including the serene French Alps, the sensual Mediterranean coast and gilded Versailles. And all seen in a cool theater with comfortable seats for resting tired bones. Not to be missed.

TIPS: Known for long lines. Arrive when it opens and you'll cut the wait to ten minutes or less.

United Kingdom ★★★ A waterfront pub, roving comedians and buildings representing over a thousand years of British history make this a jolly cultural experience. A brick street is lined with shops that range from neoclassical to Tudor to Georgian to Victorian—all in the course of 300 feet: A thatched cottage with plaster walls and stone floors leads to a wood house with plank floors and lead-glass windows. Next door, the polished Queen Anne room has tongue-and-groove floors and wainscotting. Outside lie a lush herb garden, rose garden and radiant flower beds skirted by wrought iron. It's so much fun to explore the detail-rich structures here that you don't even notice there's no main attraction.

TIPS: Be sure to watch for the Olde Globe Players and their colorful antics.

Canada ★★★★ Flanked by a totem pole and profuse gardens and topped by stony mountains, Canada is romantic and rugged.

Copper-colored boulders reminiscent of the Canadian Rockies form a backdrop of gushing waterfalls, trickling streams and drop-off canyons. Willow, birch and plum trees are sprinkled across gentler slopes that clone Victoria's Butchart Gardens. Here close-cropped hedges, blooming flowers and vines marble the landscape. Towering above the area is Hotel du Canada, a striking French Gothic brownstone with spires, turrets and a mansard roof.

A keen inspection, however, will reveal the hotel only *appears* to tower: It looks six stories tall but is actually only two-and-a-half. This is because of a technique, called "forced perspective," which involves making the bricks and windows smaller as they get higher. There's more visual trickery here, too: The trees that seem to "grow" out of the Canadian Rockies are really hidden in big pots. The trees are fed water and nutrients via a hidden tube.

And the Rockies themselves are little more than painted concrete and chicken wire mounted on a platform similar to a parade float. One honest-to-goodness attraction here is a film called:

O Canada! ★★★★ The Royal Canadian Mounted Police seem to envelope you as they circle the screen at the start of this film. It's just a prelude to the smashing visual effects of this 360-degree film that rushes down waterfalls, across canyons and plains, and along straight and jagged shores. Canada's savoir faire shines through in scenes from artsy Montreal and sophisticated Toronto, and its wildness is evident in clips of bobcats, bears, bison, reindeer and eagles. The superb filmmaking puts you mentally right in the scenes. Indeed, several scenes were shot by a camera dangling from a helicopter.

Tips: Like China's film presentation, *O Canada!* is a standing-only attraction. This is bad news for parents with small children, who have to be held for 18 minutes to be able to see the show. Infants must also be held because strollers aren't allowed. As an option, one parent could take the kids for a snack at Canada's Le Cellier cafeteria while the other sees the film. The restaurant has plenty of moderately priced food kids like and is rarely crowded.

FOUR

Disney–MGM Studios

When Disney–MGM Studios originally opened, it was hailed, at least in Florida, as nothing short of a world event. Here for the first time was a vehicle for attracting—indeed, *guaranteeing*—big-time movie and television productions while at the same time giving the public a close-up look at the entertainment industry. To a state long thirsty for a taste of Hollywood, it was intoxicating.

Disney, too, was spanning new horizons. Though the company had for years been making movies and running theme parks, the two had never been joined in the same spot. Also, by bringing Metro-Goldwyn-Mayer into the plan, Disney secured a lock on one of the biggest names in the motion picture business.

Built at a cost of $300 million, the 154-acre park is modeled after Southern California's highly successful Universal Studios tour. Despite its size, Disney–MGM at first view seems small and intimate because nearly two-thirds of the area is given over to motion picture and television production centers, where a behind-the-scenes tour is offered. The rest features rides, audience-participation attractions and movie stunt shows that capture virtually every facet of Hollywood-brand entertainment.

Like a movie set out of the 1930s or 1940s, the park is a colorful and nostalgic blend of art deco architecture, kitschy billboards, pop art, sculptured gardens, trendy restaurants, funky diners and curio shops. The whole area is easily walked in less than two hours.

Headlining Disney–MGM is palm-lined Hollywood Boulevard, with its street actors, zany stores and ethereal pastel-colored buildings. To the east is the park's newest area, Sunset Boulevard, and the monstrously popular ride The Twilight Zone Tower of Terror. Just off Sunset Boulevard to the right is Animation Courtyard, home of Disney's animation facilities. Here—for the first time in Disney history—visitors can see the company's cartoon artists at work on vintage and new characters. Along the park's northeast elbow is the Sound Stages/Backlot, a jumble of tin-roofed warehouses and faux neighborhoods that form the vast production centers of Disney–MGM. Here the special effects and production tour provides glimpses of the moviemaking business. Running along the western side of the park is New York Street, where the must-see Jim Henson's Muppet Vision 3D is located. To the south is Echo Lake and its smoke-spewing Gertie, a life-size "dinosaur" that doubles as an ice cream shop. This area draws thousands of visitors every hour to ride Star Tours.

Unlike the Magic Kingdom or Epcot, Disney–MGM Studios is neither imposing nor overwhelming. There are only 15 major attractions, compared to 43 in the Magic Kingdom and 17 in Epcot. This means you can see the entire park (at a fairly leisurely pace) in a single day, even during busy times. This should continue to be true until Disney proceeds with plans to double the size of the place in the next decade.

Much of the park's beauty lies in the design subtleties and the fine tuning so typical of Disney attractions: streams of colors that unify the park, building facades so realistic visitors try to open the front door, out-of-work actors (playing out-of-work actors) who pitch pennies in the streets. Indeed, every place fits the Hollywood bill, from the ABC Commissary and Starring Rolls Bakery to the Backlot Express and Cover Story photo studio.

With few exceptions, each attraction is pumped with action, special effects and oddities that intrigue and delight anyone even remotely interested in the film industry. Sights, too, are more complex. As Disney learned that visitors often want more than just a "quick ride," it developed attractions that combine films, skits, educational narrative and rides.

Disney has also ensured that attractions here offer something for people of every age. While parents, teenagers and young children may often disagree on rides at Disney's other parks, here everyone should concur. In fact, the question won't be *which* attractions the family should see but *how many* it can experience in a day.

Of course, all the attractions symbolize the ultimate illusion. For if Hollywood is just one big act, then Disney–MGM is an act within an act. Every sight, sound and smell plays out the fantasies of Tinsel Town. The park, in effect, is the looking glass inside the looking glass.

▼ ▼ ▼ ▼ ▼ ▼ ▼ ▼ ▼
Nuts & Bolts

ARRIVAL

From the Contemporary, Polynesian and Grand Floridian Beach resorts: Take a Disney bus directly to Disney–MGM Studios.

From the Magic Kingdom, Epcot and the Animal Kingdom: Take a Disney bus directly to Disney–MGM Studios.

From Downtown Disney, Pleasure Island, Typhoon Lagoon, Blizzard Beach or Fort Wilderness: Take a Disney bus directly to Disney–MGM.

From the Wilderness Lodge and the Caribbean Beach, Port Orleans, Dixie Landings and All-Star Sports, Music and Movie resorts: Take a Disney bus directly to Disney–MGM.

By Ferry: Ferries provide scenic shuttles for guests of the Yacht Club or Beach Club resorts.

From area hotels outside Disney World: Most hotels offer shuttle service to Disney–MGM Studios. However, shuttles often run only on the hour or every two or three hours. In this case, it's more convenient to drive.

By Car: From Route 4, take the exit for the Caribbean Beach Resort, Disney–MGM Studios and Downtown Disney. The Studios are about a half mile from Route 4.

Anyone who is intimidated by the complex arrival system of the Magic Kingdom will rejoice when he sees Disney–MGM Studios. The 4500-space parking lot here seems minuscule compared to the Magic Kingdom's. Also, the Disney–MGM lot is lo-

DISNEY–MGM STUDIOS

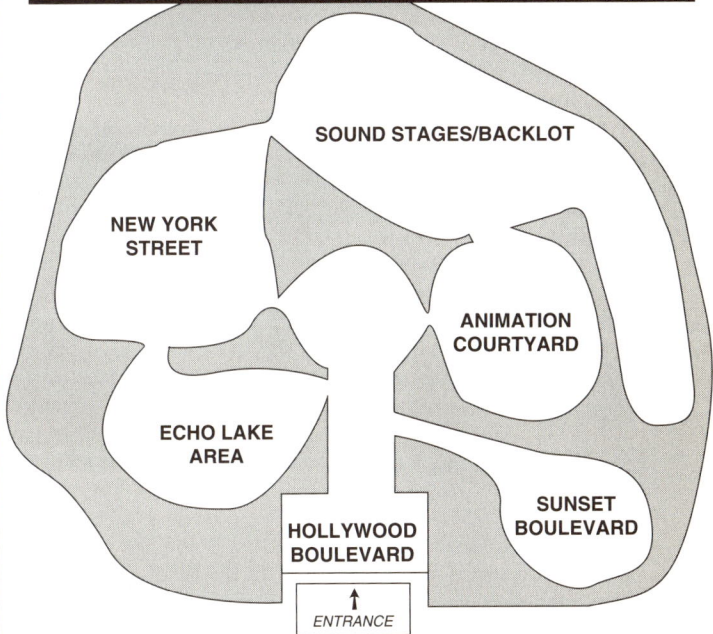

SOUND STAGES/BACKLOT

NEW YORK STREET

ANIMATION COURTYARD

ECHO LAKE AREA

SUNSET BOULEVARD

HOLLYWOOD BOULEVARD

↑
ENTRANCE

HOLLYWOOD BOULEVARD
The Great Movie Ride
Disney Stars and Motor Cars

ECHO LAKE
Indiana Jones Epic Stunt Spectacular
Sounds Dangerous
Star Tours

NEW YORK STREET
"Honey, I Shrunk the Kids" Movie Set Adventure
Jim Henson's Muppet Vision 3D

SOUND STAGES/BACKLOT
Disney–MGM Studios Backlot Tour
Who Wants To Be a Millionaire? Play It!

ANIMATION COURTYARD
The Magic of Disney Animation
Playhouse Disney
Voyage of the Little Mermaid

SUNSET BOULEVARD
Beauty and the Beast—Live on Stage
Rock 'n' Roller Coaster
The Twilight Zone Tower of Terror

cated right at the park's entrance—no monorails or ferry boats to slow you down.

There's a $7 parking fee (free for guests of Disney World hotels) and trams that whisk you from your car to the entrance, though many parking spots are within walking distance. It's crucial to *write down* your parking row number or you might not be able to find your car at day's end.

GAME PLAN   Disney—MGM Studios is rarely so jammed with visitors that it closes its gates. That's not to say it doesn't experience the occasional crowd crush, particularly during the summer and holidays. Thus, it's always best to arrive a *half-hour to an hour* before the park's "official" opening time. During the busy season, Disney sometimes opens the park before the advertised time, though there's no way to know when this will happen. You can, however, call 407-824-4321 the day before to find out the official opening time.

Just as important, Hollywood Boulevard, a sort of Main Street area, always opens a half-hour to an hour before the rest of the park. Here you can have coffee and pastries, get maps, brochures and entertainment schedules, and rent strollers, lockers and wheelchairs—before the hordes arrive. You can also be one of the first in line for the most popular rides—Star Tours, The Great Movie Ride and The Twilight Zone Tower of Terror.

By the same token, Hollywood Boulevard stays open a half-hour to an hour after the rest of the park closes. The official closing time, however, is rarely extended for the rest of the park.

The best news here: It's easy to sightsee at Disney—MGM Studios. Unlike the Magic Kingdom, Epcot and most other theme parks, the Disney Studios are so easily navigated that it's okay to skip attractions in one area and backtrack later. This will provide you with an opportunity to see everything without having to come up with an elaborate strategy. Depending on when you visit Disney—MGM, you may see the filming of a movie or television show. Check at the Guest Services window just inside the park entrance.

If you are concerned about seeing the best rides early, look through this chapter and pick out the four- and five-star attractions that interest you the most. Plan on seeing these after you've ridden Star Tours, The Great Movie Ride and The Twilight Zone Tower of Terror. Then it shouldn't be any problem getting on the less popular rides.

GUEST SERVICES   **Stroller and Wheelchair Rentals**   Available at Oscar's Super Service station just inside the main entrance.

Baby Services   Changing tables and nursing facilities are located at Guest Services at the main entrance.

Lockers   Located next to Oscar's Super Service station inside the main entrance. Lockers cost $5 per day plus $2 refundable deposit for unlimited use.

Pets   Pets are not permitted in Disney–MGM Studios, but you can board them for $6 per day at the kennel located next to the Guest Services window.

Lost Children   Report missing children to Guest Services.

Package Pickup   To avoid toting your purchases around all day, ask the Disney–MGM store clerks to forward your packages to Guest Services. You can pick them up on your way out. The service is free.

Lost & Found   Report missing or found items to Guest Services.

Banking   Automatic teller machines are located just outside the main entrance and inside Pizza Planet.

Although Disney–MGM Studios encompasses 110 acres, nearly two-thirds is devoted to television and movie production centers and backlots. Most of these areas are accessible only through guided tram and walking tours or special observation walkways. The rest of the park is the real "walking" area where visitors are free to explore attractions at their leisure.

GETTING AROUND

Shaped like an irregular circle, the park is divided into five sightseeing areas and the mammoth production facilities called Sound Stages/Backlot. Hollywood Boulevard travels up the front spine and is a good place to get oriented. The boulevard unfolds into a breezy brick courtyard that is more or less the center of the park. A place of oak trees and park benches, the courtyard is a good meeting spot if your party decides to split up or if someone gets lost. It's also a prime place to picnic; hot dogs, ice cream and popcorn are available from the vendors that dot the area. This is also a good vantage point for Disney Stars and Motor Cars. Tra-

CHALKBOARD TOURING TIPS

You've just arrived at Disney–MGM Studios, and you can't decide where to start. Not to worry: Help is available at the corner of Hollywood and Sunset boulevards. Here the Disney folks set up a big chalkboard that lists major attractions with their approximate waiting times, and offers suggestions on when to see each one. Two employees regularly update the information and provide visitors with sightseeing tips for that day. I found most of the information accurate, although one attraction listed with a 25-minute wait had a 40-minute wait because the board advised everyone to "See it Now!" On those rare days when business is slow at the park, you won't find a chalkboard, but then, who needs it?

veling counterclockwise from Hollywood Boulevard there's Sunset Boulevard, Animation Courtyard, Sound Stages/Backlot, New York Street and Echo Lake.

Hollywood Boulevard

An ambitious facsimile of movie town's famous main drag, Hollywood Boulevard oozes panache. Streamlined moderne architecture forms a sassy contour of jutting ledges, gentle curves, pulsing neon and shiny chrome. Buildings washed in rose, turquoise, pale yellow and seafoam green thrust pastel palettes against an aqua-blue sky. Glass blocks play catch with the sun's rays, and store windows reflect the faces of mouse-hatted visitors.

Edging the boulevard are old-fashioned street lamps, black-and-white striped stop signs and pole-mounted stop lights that sound a quirky *ding!* when they change colors. Magnificent palms soar upward from the concrete, their spiked fronds performing little twists in the wind. Strains from the soundtrack of *Doctor Zhivago* sift through the sun-warmed air.

Funky shops and businesses crowd along the sidewalk, drawing visitors in with playbills that announce their fortes. Most are great places to browse, even if you don't like to shop, because they paint a rosy portrait of days gone by.

To complete this tinsel-tinged picture, wannabe actors roam the boulevard with painted faces and outrageous costumes. There's creamy-skinned Marilyn Monroe and trench-coated Dick Tracy, as well as some "typical" Hollywood characters—a gum-chewing cabbie, a nosy television reporter and a pesky guy selling maps of movie stars' homes.

Before you stroll Hollywood Boulevard, stop by the **Crossroads of the World** kiosk. It's the first thing you see after entering the park, and it's stocked with guides, maps and schedules of the day's filmings and performances. Disney employees are also here to help you get organized.

If you're touring first thing in the morning, opt for a quick walk down the boulevard and head for attractions that become crowded

HATS OFF TO DISNEY—MGM

The Magic Kingdom has the castle, the Animal Kingdom has the tree, and EPCOT has Spaceship Earth. So it's about time Disney—MGM Studios got its own icon (apparently the mouse-ears water tower wasn't cutting it) and it's fitting it should be a Sorcerer's Hat. The new centerpiece stands in front of the Chinese Theater and, at 122 feet tall, could only fit the ears of one mighty big mouse. Good thing Mickey is one mighty big cheese.

later in the day. I recommend first riding Star Tours and The Twilight Zone Tower of Terror—usually *the* most popular attractions. Then return to Hollywood Boulevard and see it at a leisurely pace while the rest of the park becomes packed.

One place not to miss on Hollywood Boulevard is **Sid Cahuenga's One-of-a-Kind** antiques and curios. The plank-floored shop brims with Hollywood peculiarities and memorabilia: Brenda Vaccaro's shawl, a program from John Belushi's memorial service, Liberace's table napkins, and racks of original playbills and autographed stars' photos. Look for Sid on the porch, rocking in his wooden chair and spreading Hollywood gossip.

Nearby, a 1947 grape-colored Buick has pulled up to **Oscar's Classic Car Souvenirs & Super Service Station**. Vintage auto buffs will love this service station-cum-museum and shop, which is lined with fuel pump bubble-gum machines and photos of great antique cars. Moms and dads will love the "real" service here: stroller and locker rentals, as well as infant goodies (for sale) such as bottles and diapers. Wheelchairs are also for rent.

Feeling famous? Step into **Cover Story**, where friendly Disney employees will doll you up, snap your picture and put it on the cover of your favorite popular magazine (for a fee, of course). Kids love this place.

Hollywood Boulevard offers two headline attractions:

WHAT TO SEE & DO

Disney Stars and Motor Cars ★★ Consider this rolling extravaganza one-stop shopping for Disney's contemporary characters. The Little Mermaid, Lilo and Stitch, Hercules, Aladdin, not to mention the Big Cheese (Mickey) himself, are among those who make appearances, all perched atop Golden Age–styled motor cars. A live MC caters to the crowd and gets everyone involved. I'm not a huge parade fan myself, but this one is kind of cute.

TIPS: The parade route runs from Star Tours, goes to the right of Echo Lake and then turns right on Hollywood Boulevard, clogging up a large portion of the park's west side. The good news: this clears out attractions in Animation Courtyard and those off of Sunset Boulevard, making it a perfect time to visit those areas.

The Great Movie Ride ★★★★★ This ride easily ranks as "great," but what truly sets it apart is its building—a superb replica of the gorgeous Mann's Chinese Theatre. Situated at the crown of Hollywood Boulevard, the 95,000-square-foot theater boasts spectacular pagoda roofs and an ornate facade with glossy red columns and stone carvings. Scattered across its plaza are foot and hand prints of some Hollywood stars: Bob Hope, Jim Henson, Susan Sarandon, Danny DeVito and Rhea Perlman, among others. Through the threshold are soaring ceilings, elaborate painted panels and massive Chinese lanterns. And that's only the beginning.

The lobby, which is really a massive queue area, features a minimuseum with goodies such as a space suit from the movie *Alien,* ruby slippers worn by Judy Garland in *The Wizard of Oz* and the tiny piano played by Sam in *Casablanca.* If lines aren't long (which is rare), visitors tend to hurry through the lobby and miss all the treasures. Take my advice: Relax and enjoy the exhibits—these are worth seeing.

◆◆◆◆◆◆◆◆◆◆◆◆◆◆◆◆◆◆◆◆◆◆◆

Gene Kelly personally inspected his robot look-alike for The Great Movie Ride.

Once inside, visitors board open-air box cars and are immediately plunged into the spirit of movie-making. Murals of the 1930s Hollywood Hills paint a nostalgic picture with cascading hillside villas and an original "Hollywoodland" sign lit by the sunset. Most of the 20-minute ride, though, uses sound stages to provide a dazzling, dynamic and incredibly realistic trek through Hollywood's most celebrated films. Rain streams down on Gene Kelly in *Singin' in the Rain,* Mary Poppins floats with her magical umbrella to the lyrics of "Chim Chim Cheree" and *Public Enemy*'s James Cagney turns on his throaty drawl to tell a gangster, "Oh, you dirty, double crossing. . . ."

One of the most powerful scenes is a gangster shootout (using pop guns) where visitors get stuck in the line of fire. Amazingly, it's tough to tell the difference between the Audio-Animatronics robots and the real Disney employees in this gunfight. Just around the corner, poker-faced Clint Eastwood is waiting at the Monarch Saloon and rifle-toting John Wayne is astride his horse on a sun-washed prairie. Wayne is after some bank robbers who blow up a safe and send flames hurtling from the building. Visitors can feel the fire's warmth in their box cars.

In one eerie movie snapshot, the *Alien* monster drips goo while smoke pours through metal chambers; in another, Indiana Jones struggles to remove the Lost Ark in a snake-filled tomb. (Warning: Both scenes can frighten young children.) But perhaps the most fantastic scene is from *The Wizard of Oz,* featuring hundreds of lovable munchkins, Dorothy and her crew of quirky friends, and the beastly wicked witch.

Each scene enthralls with intricate costumes, visual details and Audio-Animatronics figures whose features and mannerisms are remarkably real. Indeed, with few exceptions, every figure, ensemble and prop was designed *precisely* as its real-life counterpart, down to the witch's spindly broom and John Wayne's horse and rifle.

TIPS: One of Disney–MGM's most popular rides and therefore the most crowded. A hint for estimating length of wait: When the inside queues are full, there's at least a 25-minute wait. If lines are spilling outside onto Hollywood Boulevard, you're talking an hour or more. Also, posted waiting times usually *overestimate* the wait by 10 to 15 minutes. For instance, if a sign says

"Approximate wait from this point: 40 minutes," it's more likely to be 30 minutes. One exception: Sometimes, particularly toward the end of the day, Disney employees will "stack" this ride, which means queuing visitors *outside* to clear up lines *inside*. So before you let long lines outside scare you off, check for inside lines. *Not to be missed.*

ANOTHER IMPORTANT NOTE: Although this ride will appeal to people of all ages, it has several scenes that sometimes frighten small children.

Sunset Boulevard

Disney–MGM's newest boulevard oozes art deco. Neon tubes race around buildings, eyebrows edge out over windows, and theater lights sparkle from marquees. Elaborate metal fretwork traces facades of pink and yellow and seafoam green. Signs, like the one at Beverly Sunset Gallery, tempt visitors to enter through swank doors.

Most of it's all show. There are a couple of "real" shops here, both selling Disney souvenirs, but everything else is fantasy setwork. You can look, but you can't go inside. You can, however, stand in line for Mickey Mouse's autograph or join the sidewalk disco dancing that rarely quits (follow your ears to the small dance crowd) throughout the day and night. Mickey usually calls it a day around 5:30 p.m.

WHAT TO SEE & DO

Sunset Boulevard offers three attractions:

Beauty and the Beast—Live on Stage ★★★★ No one who loved the movie will want to miss this attraction at the Theater of the Stars. Featuring the animated classic's top songs—"Be Our Guest," "Something There," "The Mob Song" and "Beauty and the Beast"—this show retells the timeless love story of Belle and the motley but huggable castle-dwelling Beast. The show includes all the dancing and singing housewares—clock, candelabra, teapot and cup—and the finale uses onstage fireworks and a bevy of live doves (which are actually white pigeons) to finish the act in high style.

TIPS: The show itself is only 25 minutes long but takes place only five times a day. It's extremely popular and was moved to this theater to accommodate larger audiences. You should, nonetheless, try to get to the Theater of the Stars early—about 30 minutes before showtime.

The Twilight Zone Tower of Terror ★★★★★ Looming eerily at the end of Sunset Boulevard, indeed casting a pall over all of Disney–MGM, is the Hollywood Tower Hotel. Spidery cracks climb its coral facade, balconies teeter, live human screams emanate regularly from its jagged windows. Naturally, visitors here are rushing to get inside. Through the cobwebbed lobby where dead flowers repose, into a "service elevator" and up to the "boiler room," visitors wait their way through a maze of rooms meticulously detailed with Disney special effects. You hear Rod Serling's voice pushing you farther, ever farther into the Twilight Zone.

The ride is in a cage elevator. You take a seat in one of several rows, and a safety bar clamps down across your lap. The elevator climbs up its shaft. The doors open. There are ghostly figures and eyeballs (holograms). Your "cage" car cruises around a spooky room, then gets back in the elevator shaft. You glide higher in the hotel. Then you drop. Lots of screams. Most everyone recovers, smiles at each other, waits to get off the ride. Then the car climbs back up the elevator shaft, to the top of the hotel. And drops you again.

TIPS: These are the longest lines at Disney–MGM, so ride first thing in the morning or at the end of the day. On the plus side, the waiting areas offer fascinating scenery. Children shorter than 40 inches are not allowed to ride.

Rock 'n' Roller Coaster ★★★★★ Imagine the loops and spirals of your favorite roller coaster. Now imagine the loops and spirals inside, in the dark.

That's Rock 'n' Roller Coaster, Disney's latest, and in my opinion, greatest addition in the thrill ride department. Riders board "limos" in an alley behind Aerosmith's recording studio. Your mission: to race through Los Angeles' streets in time for the group's concert at the Civic Center. Cars peel out of the alley going from zero to 60 in 2.8 seconds, and the ride never slows down from there. Along the way, music blasts, street signs whiz by, and you're hurled upside down and sideways until at last you arrive at the VIP entrance (you've got backstage passes, after all) of the concert hall.

The ride itself is a blast, but the theme is half the fun. Rock 'n' Roller Coaster has Aerosmith written all over it (the group actually consulted on its creation); you can actually picture these guys taking to the streets in this fashion. And anyone who's driven the real versions of these West Coast thoroughfares will appreciate the side perk—traveling L.A. without traffic.

TIPS: The Rock 'n' Roller Coaster is a popular ride. Fast Pass will get you on without a wait; otherwise, try boarding during the Disney Stars and Motor Cars parade when prospective riders may be occupied.

▼▼▼▼▼▼▼▼▼▼▼▼▼▼

Animation Courtyard

A short stretch of concrete courtyard northeast of Sunset Boulevard is an art deco enclave with buildings washed in turquoise, yellow and rose. It's usually thronged with people waiting to get into The Magic of Disney Animation or Voyage of the Little Mermaid.

The Magic of Disney Animation ★★★★★ Housed in a piano-shaped building, this multifaceted tour provides the first-ever look at Disney's animation process. One of the park's most popular sights, it ranks as one of the best attractions in all of Disney World. From the history and techniques of animation to a look at working artists, the tour is truly a nostalgic and enlightening voyage.

The prelude is a gallery lined with original cels, or frames, from some of Disney's best-loved films, including 1937's *Snow White* and 1953's *Peter Pan*. There are also papier-mâché, wood and plaster models of characters from *Pinocchio, Beauty and the Beast* and *The Little Mermaid*. The room's centerpieces, though, are glistening reproductions of Disney's many animation Oscars.

From the gallery, visitors enter a cool theater for a delightful eight-minute film on animation. Called *Back to Neverland,* the crowd-pleaser stars maniacal Robin Williams and straight-faced Walter Cronkite. Williams is drawn into *Peter Pan* as a cartoon character, survives a skirmish with Captain Hook and the alligator, and gets rescued by Tinkerbell. Between Williams' hilarious one-liners and Cronkite's constant admonishing, you learn about cel making, layout artists, background artists, sound effects and much more.

Next is a stroll through studios where you watch Disney animators at their drafting tables. Particularly for first-timers, it's a fascinating sight: Headphones turned up and funky artwork everywhere, the artists sketch cels of familiar and yet-to-come cartoon characters. The tour progresses through each phase of animation, from clean-up (where rough sketches become line drawings) to effects (lightning, water, fire) and backgrounds (backdrops for the characters). To create a 24-minute film, the park's 70-plus animators must produce 34,650 drawings with at least 300 background scenes. For those worried about missing the animators on Saturdays and Sundays, there's always a group pulling the weekend shift.

The Animation Tour's hilarious film starring Walter Cronkite and Robin Williams was tough to film because Cronkite kept cracking up.

The tour's finale is a dynamic, sentimental vignette of Disney's premier animated films. Shown in the plush Disney Classic Theater, the movie features great scenes from *Bambi, Snow White, Cinderella, Lady and the Tramp* and many others. Anyone who has ever enjoyed those enduring classics can't helped but be moved by this film.

TIPS: If at all possible, take this tour before 10:30 a.m. After that, the wait is rarely under 45 minutes. Lines do typically shorten after 5 p.m.—but by then most of the animators have gone home. *This tour is not to be missed.*

Voyage of the Little Mermaid ★★★★ This is yet another Disney movie transformed into a stage show. Dive into this ersatz underwater grotto theater and be delighted by the submerged show featuring a waterfall curtain, floating bubbles and a 12-foot by 10-foot Audio-Animatronics villainess. The story, for those who haven't seen the movie, pits humongous villain Ursula against frail mermaid Ariel as Ursula plots to steal Ariel's melodious voice and succeeds, temporarily. The ending (a happy one, if there was any question) combines animation, live action, puppetry and special effects including lasers into a grand finale that will leave your head spinning.

TIPS: First thing in the morning and after six o'clock in the evening are the best times to beat the crowd here. During the day the line builds up and stays that way. The show runs every 30 minutes, however, so if the line looks shorter than two theaters full, jump in; it's worth the wait.

Playhouse Disney ★★★ The best part of this show—a live version of the Disney Channel shows packaged under the Playhouse Disney banner—is the audience. Preschoolers who've spent many a morning watching their favorite characters on TV (Bear in the Big Blue House, Rolie Polie Olie, Pooh and Stanley) are absolutely agog at seeing their heroes in the flesh (or fur, as it were). The phrase "too cute" comes to mind. Even better, all the festivities bring a rare mode of utter cooperation to the crowd—these little ones don't need even a little coaxing to sing and dance along.

TIPS: You know those kiddie attractions that you'd visit whether of not you actually had a kid with you? This isn't one of them. Oh, it's cute—but only if you're under six.

ANOTHER TIP: Unlike continuous action shows (like the Little Mermaid), Playhouse runs on a schedule, and lines to get in are often clogged with stroller-toting families intent on making their little ones happy. If this is a must-see during your visit, be sure to hit one of the earlier shows, arriving 15 minutes early; that way, being closed out doesn't close you out of the day.

▼▼▼▼▼▼▼▼▼▼▼▼▼▼▼
Sound Stages/Backlot

This vast piece of property forms the nitty gritty of Disney's Florida-turned-Hollywood: soundstages that change faces every day; backlots strewn with old cars and airplanes; fake skylines and fake neighborhoods; and warehouses jammed with bizarre props and costumes.

The backlot production facilities make up the East Coast counterpart to Disney Studios in Burbank, California. They're also the "working" part of Disney—the only place where visitors can regularly witness dozens of employees in action. Virtually every day a camera is rolling somewhere. Television commercials are shot, movies filmed, game shows played out. In between all the filming, costumes and props are created, styrofoam buildings are thrown up and extras are gleaned from throngs of hopefuls. Most of the backlot area is accessible only through the special effects and production tour.

Disney–MGM Studios Backlot Tour **** This tour's expansive queue area can seem formidable, and it should. If it's packed with people (which is likely), you're facing a minimum 45-minute wait. There is, however, plenty to entertain you along the way, including Disney movie memorabilia and video clips of Clint Eastwood films and the making of *Jaws*.

Visitors board canopied shuttles, which resemble pastel caterpillars as they coil around tall buildings and backlots. Affable and sometimes humorous guides season the ride with anecdotes and notable details. At the greenery department, there's the faux tree trunk used in *Honey, I Shrunk the Kids*. At the prop warehouse are roadsters from *Dick Tracy*. And in the costume warehouse—home to over two million garments—there are outfits worn by Madonna and Warren Beatty in *Dick Tracy,* Bette Midler in *Big Business* and Julie Andrews in *Mary Poppins*. (Between its theme parks and movie costumes, Walt Disney World boasts the largest working wardrobe in the world.) Here, through big windows, visitors can also watch seamstresses at work on costumes for upcoming movies.

Warning: Restrooms are available only at the start of the Disney–MGM Studios Backlot Tour.

Next is the scenic shop, where sets are built, and the camera and lighting departments. The former are labyrinths of high-tech equipment, blinking lights and tangles of cords. Interestingly, the equipment is so state-of-the-art that it's used by visiting camera crews to film the space shuttle launches some 75 miles away.

The shuttle also winds along what could be termed Hollywood's "Street of Dreams"—a road lined with make-believe houses. From the front you see trimmed lawns and pretty facades; from the back, the buildings are hollow. Notice the midwestern-style home where Vern lived in *Ernest Saves Christmas* and the pink Cadillac used in *Tin Men* parked in a driveway. Down the way is a "boneyard," eternal resting grounds for rusty airplanes, crushed cars, airplanes and other *objets d'Hollywood*. There's an orange-and-red Pacific Electric trolley car from *Who Framed Roger Rabbit?*, spaceship modules from *E.T.* and Mother Goose's house.

From here it's all wet and woolly—at least for passengers sitting on the shuttle's left side. As the driver pulls into a barren cavern called Catastrophe Canyon, passengers witness exciting special effects. An oil tanker explodes, the road splits and a deluge of water comes hurdling toward the tram. The fallout is a lot of shimmying, a lot of soaked people and a few screams of "Let's-get-the-hell-out-of-here." The idea, of course, is a simultaneous simulation of a fire, thunderstorm, earthquake and flash flood.

Later, passengers learn that the "canyon" is actually a mammoth steel coop wrapped in copper-colored cement. The water—all 70,000 gallons—is recycled over 100 times a day, or every three-and-a-half minutes for each shuttle group.

Catastrophe Canyon's flash flood is created by air cannons that blow 25,000 gallons of water over 100 feet.

Desert scenes soon give way to urban ones as the shuttle veers down simulated New York City streets. Brownstones merge with red brick, marble and stained glass in a remarkable illusion of the Big Apple. Look closely and you'll see that the buildings are merely facades of fiberglass and styrofoam that have been expertly painted. Notice that, at the end of the street, the Empire State and Chrysler buildings are two-dimensional painted flats. Both buildings, by the way, can be removed if film crews want to portray a different U.S. city.

TIPS: Though the tour appeals to all ages, some preschool children may be frightened by special effects at Catastrophe Canyon. The best time to visit is after 3 p.m., but note that the tour closes at dusk.

Who Wants To Be a Millionaire? Play It! ★★★★★ It looks the same, sounds the same and feels the same as the one on TV . . . but there's no Regis and you can't actually win a million dollars—congenial stand-in hosts do quite nicely and you'll have to settle for a million points instead. But that doesn't get in the way of even one iota of the fun at this interactive version where contestants take the hot seat and vie for prizes from collectible trinkets to the top award, a trip for two to a taping of the real thing.

The dramatic set is a twin of the original, hot seat and all. The "Fastest Finger" seats are here, but don't fret if you don't snag one for the game. They may look cool, but every seat in the audience is armed for play, meaning each and every guest has the same opportunity to land in the chair of honor. Two of the "Lifelines" are familiar: "Ask the Audience" and "50/50." Since odds are you haven't stationed some knowledgeable person at a nearby phone for the "Phone a Friend" option, the last "Lifeline" is the less-encouraging "Phone a Complete Stranger," where another Disney guest picks up your call from elsewhere in the park. Don't think the upper-award-level questions are any easier than those posed by Regis. During my recent foray, even the Fastest Finger question was a doozy: "Put these actresses in order of their conversion to Judaism, starting with the most recent." Even if you don't answer a single question correctly, you'll have an absolute ball.

TIPS: Shows are generally performed every hour on the half-hour, but check the schedule on the way in so you don't miss it.

Fiery Fantasmic

Fireworks explode, water sprays and music thunders—and that's just the beginning of Fantasmic. Disney's packed so much into its 25-minute nighttime spectacle, they had to build a whole island just to stage it.

Like the original Fantasmic still playing in Anaheim at Disneyland, Disney World's version tells the story of Mickey's dream of a battle between good and evil. Virtually all the classic and contemporary characters make an appearance, good guys (Snow White, Prince Charming, et al.) and bad guys (Malificent, Ursula, Radcliff). Scenes from various films are acted out, and the whole shebang climaxes with a flaming river, a skyfull of pyrotechnics and a group appearance—en boat—of what seems like every Disney character ever drawn.

Disney improved on the California theme by creating a theater to house this spectacular (those who've seen the Disneyland version will recall standing shoulder-to-shoulder with thousands in New Orleans Square). On the other hand, the "bigger is better" philosophy doesn't always apply—the original still stands as the best. Even so, this is an entirely entertaining display—and a popular one.

The theater may be large but you'll want to arrive early to get a good seat. Street performers and vendors will be happy to keep you busy while you wait.

People start lining up for this show as much as 90 minutes before it starts. If you'd like to be more productive with your time, try the Fantasmic Dinner plan. Eat dinner at the Hollywood Brown Derby, Hollywood & Vine or Mama Melrose's Ristorante Italiano and get a voucher for entrance. This option is a much more relaxed way to enjoy the show.

Early performances tend to be on the quiet side; later ones often fill to capacity, closing hopeful guests out. To up your odds of getting in—as well as getting into the hot seat—come to one of the first two shows of the day.

ANOTHER TIP: The 12 Fastest Finger seats don't have any benefits over the rest of the stage—except that they're really cool to sit in. If you want to snag one, be sure to arrive plenty early—even if you're holding a Fast Pass for the show—and put on your best colorful behavior.

▼▼▼▼▼▼▼▼▼▼▼▼
New York Street

Anyone with a passion for detail will particularly enjoy New York Street. Check out the old Smith-Corona behind the dusty window of Sal's Pawn, and the 1950s hair nets and foam curlers in the Rexall window. A rusty old stamp machine on the street corner is out of stamps—but will keep your coins.

WHAT TO SEE & DO

"Honey, I Shrunk the Kids" Movie Set Adventure ★★★ Based on the popular 1990 Disney movie, this area is a giant playpen of distortions. As you wander through a family's yard, blades of grass loom two stories above you and a lawn sprinkler seems like a menacing spaceship. Kids love scaling the 40-foot bumble bee and other colossal insects that tower everywhere.

TIPS: This is a fantasyland for all ages, but because it's tucked away, this attraction has minimal lines. However, as more visitors find out about it, I predict it will become a very popular place.

Jim Henson's Muppet Vision 3D ★★★★★ The Muppets meet Disney at Jim Henson's Muppet Vision 3D, a rambunctious Muppets' adventure with an astonishing array of special effects. Combining Disney's Audio-Animatronics techniques, cutting-edge 3D technology and a boisterous band of Muppets, the movie is wild and wonderful. Other 3D films may fool your eyes, but this one will blow your hat off, spray water in your face, send cannonballs

◆◆

ANIMATED CONVERSATION

Got cartoonish questions you simply have to ask? This is the place. Several days a week, two to ten lucky guests break bread at MGM's Hollywood Brown Derby with someone from the ranks of the Disney art department. It's expensive ($60.99 ages 11 and up; $34.99 for kids). But true fans (or aspiring artists) will find it worth the tab. If the insider information isn't enough, you'll also get to raid the dinner table: all guests take home a souvenir plate. For those with other interests, the restaurant offers a similar program with an Imagineer. Reserve up to 30 days ahead. Call 407-939-3463.

crashing through the walls of the theater and create general mayhem. In an unprecedented display of Muppet high jinks, a Muppet actually flies off the screen and into the audience.

"What we wanted to do," the late Jim Henson once said, "was dream up all the 3D gimmicks that we could and then figure out a way to put them all into one short film." Nevertheless, Kermit promises as the show begins that "At no time will we be stooping to cheap 3D tricks."

And what a show it is. Miss Piggy pushes her musical talents to the limit and Fozzie Bear takes a pie in the face. The tour of a top-secret research lab brings audience members face-to-face with Waldo C. Graphic, a computer-generated character who can transform himself into anything he desires—a taxicab or a sky-rocket, for example. He even talks to each audience member individually and has fun bouncing on people's heads.

The theater effects are more spectacular than ever, and since the characters are aware that they're in 3D, they're not a bit shy about leaning out over the audience and taking advantage of their 3D situation. To establish the ideal setting, the creators designed a theater that brings the show directly into the audience. By combining the authentic Muppet-theater atmosphere with live and animated Muppet characters, advanced 3D technology and special effects, they make the audience part of the show and give new meaning to the phrase "living theater."

Before the theater explodes in a grand finale, you'll experience a series of effects that include squirting boutonnieres, bubble showers, high winds, musket fire, cannon blasts and a patriotic fiber-optics fireworks "Salute to All Nations But Mostly America." As the Great Gonzo sees it, "Now *this* is entertainment."

TIPS: Be prepared to get wet, though it's only a light mist that's added to the special effects to enhance the show. *Not to be missed.*

Echo Lake

Stashed off the west side of Hollywood Boulevard, Echo Lake is Disney's vision of California Cool: trendy restaurants splashed with pink and aqua and trimmed in chrome, lounges and cafés where TVs outnumber waitresses, and a shop where most souvenirs sport the face of a star.

On one side of the lake rests Min and Bill's Dockside Diner, a Disneyesque freighter that serves fast food. On the other side is Gertie, a funky-looking reproduction of a dinosaur. Gertie serves ice cream and Disney souvenirs, and occasionally sends up a puff of smoke.

From here, you'll find a range of attractions scattered throughout the southwest section of the park, from the amusing audience-participation show SuperStar Television to the heart-stopping, simulated space journey Star Tours, the park's most popular "ride."

WHAT TO SEE & DO

Star Tours ★★★★★ This is one fast and furious ride where you—quite literally—take a trip and never leave the room.

Technically, it's a ride in a flight simulator like the ones used to train military and airline pilots. Realistically, it's the ultimate trick on the senses: Your mind says you're not whirling through space, yet your eyes, ears, fingers and pounding heart say you are.

Using themes and scenes from the movie *Star Wars,* the ride features several small rooms, called StarSpeeders, where you are belted into a seat. Eyes planted on a video screen, you plunge through space at lightning speed, dodging planets and ice crystals and battling laser fighters. All the while, your seat is turning, your stomach is churning, and the whole room seems to float.

Piloted by the bumbling but lovable *Star Wars* characters R2D2 and C3P0, the ride is supposed to be a leisurely voyage to Endor Moon. Things quickly go awry, though, when the novice pilots veer off course. After seven minutes of spins and loops and near misses, everyone is returned safely (but shakily) home.

Designed very much like Epcot's Body Wars ride, Star Tours uses spectacular video images and other high-tech effects to induce sensations that most first-time riders have never felt before. Unlike a roller coaster, you don't "go" anywhere; unlike a standard 3D film show, you do get tossed around. Put simply, there's nothing else like it.

TIPS: Pregnant women and children younger than three are not allowed to ride. Some youngsters old enough to ride will find Star Tours rough and frightening. Not recommended for people with bad backs or weak stomachs.

One of the park's most popular rides, Star Tours is plagued by long lines (40 to 60 minutes) virtually all day. Try to ride during the first half-hour after the park opens or shortly before it closes. Like the Great Movie Ride, Star Tours is often "stacked" to clear lines inside (for more on stacking, see "The Great Movie Ride"). *Not to be missed.*

There are a couple of things to remember here: Rule No. 1: If there's a short line at Star Tours, GO FOR IT! Rule No. 2: If the stunt show has just finished, DO NOT attempt to ride Star Tours. Most of the stunt show crowd (up to 2000 people) will be heading for the ride, so you should not. And, because the stunt show holds so many people, you can see it nearly any time.

Sounds Dangerous ★★★★ Drew Carey is a hapless private eye investigating a smuggling ring at a snow-globe company. Working under cover, he's been wired with a mini camera that feeds video of his activities to the "live" show on the theater screen. When the camera breaks, the audience is left to follow the action by sound instead of sight.

In complete darkness, headset-wearing guests are assailed by sound effects. Hairdryers whirr, scissors snip and bees buzz seemingly inches from your ear. The 3D effect is jostling, sometimes startling—more than a few people around me began errantly swatting the phantom bugs. I swore I felt the breath of those people whispering in my ear.

> At Movie Mimics in SoundWorks, you can dub your voice over Mickey Mouse, Roger Rabbit and other Disney heroes.

Interestingly, this attraction draws extreme responses from the audience—you either love it or you hate it. As I was raving about it, a woman ahead of me declared it a complete waste of time. Much of that probably boils down to how much you are affected by what you hear. My husband absolutely hated this—no big surprise since he never listens to anything.

After the presentation, guests are treated to splendid hands-on exhibits called SoundWorks. Filled with all sorts of gadgets that go squeak, creak, bonk and buzz, the place is a child's dreamland, There are panels you touch to go "boing," a drum and knob you push so your voice will sound like a gargoyle's. Eerie Encounters lets you create flying saucer sounds for a scene from a 1956 flick *Forbidden Planet* and Touchtoons lets you re-create gallop sounds in a scene from *The Legend of Sleepy Hollow*. There's a sound-proof booth where you'll get yet another demonstration of the magic of sound.

TIPS: Don't mistake this sound show for one of the earlier kid-friendly versions. If you have a child who's afraid of loud noises or darkness, skip this one. The good news is that anyone who gets too rattled can just flip off the headphones and—silence. Of course, then you're just sitting in the dark, which can be another issue entirely.

ANOTHER TIP: The show's small (270-seat) theater can sometimes make for long waits, much of it in the hot sun. Unless you're visiting during a really quiet time, try to see the show about an hour before the park closes.

Indiana Jones Epic Stunt Spectacular ★★★ This fast-paced, special effects escapade takes place in a 2200-seat amphitheater that seems hunkered beneath the jungle. In traditional *Raiders of the Lost Ark* style, the 25-minute show reels off a series of near-death encounters in an ancient Mayan temple: Indiana plummets from the ceiling, drops in a hidden hole, dodges spears and flames, and barely avoids being squashed by a gargantuan boulder.

In the middle of all the blazes and rumbles, the set crew calls time out and casually wheels away the entire stage. Behind is a re-creation of a busy Cairo plaza where tumblers and acrobats, dressed as Egyptians, frolic along the street. A bunch of Nazis soon show up looking for Indy, and a riot ensues. During the fist fighting and falling, vehicles buzz around and a Nazi airplane roars up. There's one terrific scene where a truck gets blown up and flipped, its flames warming the first few rows of the audience.

Directed by Glenn Randall, stunt coordinator for the Indiana Jones films as well as *Poltergeist* and *E.T.*, the show also provides some insight into the filming of stunt scenes. Professional stunt actors demonstrate using doubles for dangerous scenes, how cameras are tucked behind imitation rocks, and how "pickup" action shots are filmed. Some of these shots are done with audience guests who are randomly chosen about ten minutes before the show. Watch carefully, though, because some participants are actually stunt men *playing audience guests*.

TIPS: This quick-moving presentation captures the interest of all ages. The eight to ten daily shows often fill up well before showtime. Your best bets are the first two and last two shows of the day. These almost never fill up.

ANOTHER IMPORTANT TIP: The Disney people will tell you it's mandatory to line up (in the blazing sun) at least 30 minutes before showtime. This is not necessary. Be at the show ten minutes early, and you should be able to walk right into the theater. If it's full, return for a later show. Make sure you check the *side aisles in the very front*. These seats often fill up last.

FIVE

Disney's Animal Kingdom

With its long shadow in the entertainment world, Disney—or at least Mickey—has often been considered the mouse that roars. But with the addition of 250 species of wildlife in the Animal Kingdom, the newest theme park in the vast and still growing Walt Disney World, the roar is no longer just philosophical.

Disney's Animal Kingdom, the fourth in Disney's Florida theme-park empire, lands wildlife center stage, and it's fitting that animals should be the subject of choice. Walt, after all, made his fortune bringing animals to life, albeit in animated form (save for a series of programs produced in the late 1940s).

But unlike their predecessors, residents of this theme park (most of them, anyway) are the genuine article—the living, breathing, grunting, squealing, snorting, pooping wild-kingdom counterparts to the walking-talking characters to whom we've already been introduced.

Of course that doesn't make them any less, er, animated. On the contrary. The absence of remote control poses intriguing possibilities. Where Fantasyland critters move at the whim of a corporate bigwig (or at least a computer programmer), Disney's Animal Kingdom characters have minds of their own. And when giraffes stand in the road and back up the caravan of safari trucks for a while (as they did the last time I visited), well, that's half the adventure.

All of this can make it a little like a preschool ballet recital: what you see depends on just how the performers are feeling that day. But what you can count on is more than 1500 animals with exotic names like the African jacana, racquet-tailed roller and cotton-top tamarin. Attractions are sprawled across the 500-acre park in seven lands depicting Africa, Asia, The Oasis, Discovery Island, DinoLand U.S.A., Camp Minnie-Mickey and Rafiki's Planet Watch, all punctuated by the 145-foot-tall Tree of Life in the middle. The scenery—colorful African decor—sets the mood, with lush greenery, thatched roofs, worn walls and carefully weathered pavement. It's vaguely reminiscent of a giant Adventureland.

There are roughly 15 attractions and shows here, but actual "rides" are in somewhat short supply—about five if you count the train to Rafiki's Planet Watch and the rip-roaring It's Tough to be a Bug! 3D show. That may surprise some, perhaps even disappoint others.

But the Animal Kingdom's focus is clearly different than at sibling theme parks. Enjoyment is the goal, but whiz-bang thrills are a side note. With lots of self-guided tours, there's no question that you'll spend more time on your feet than in some ride vehicle. But as one Disney World veteran pointed out, the shady trails and leisurely pace are a welcome relief from the ride-to-ride frenzy characteristic of other park visits.

Still, while it's all amply entertaining—and let's face it, none of us would be forking over $52 (yikes!) for the day if it weren't—this is interactive rather than passive entertainment. You'll actually have to do some work (reading the information plaques and such) to get the full effect. And the creators would like to feel that they actually taught you something during your stay.

To that end, caretakers—a dedicated and knowledgeable lot—are on-hand everywhere to answer questions and give pointers, and even to protect the animals from unseemly human behavior (please don't feed the animals!). But in this venue, animal education—or more accurately, animal conservation—is much more colorful than it may sound. The Disney treatment includes a remarkably realistic jungle safari (it even manages to get in a bit of Disney shtick), and a tiger habitat that lets you appreciate the "ruins" of a glorious maharajah's hunting lodge.

Habitats, in fact, are the lions' share of the Animal Kingdom's strength—the place where Disney has really worked its magic. As at Epcot, where "countries" in the World Showcase are reproduced in fine detail, animal homes here are accurate down to the last tree. Native plants and shrubs were imported from Africa and termite mounds were fashioned out of cement. When you're in the "jungle," you'll feel extraordinarily removed from the rest of the park. Cross into the jungle's "Africa" and you'll swear you've left Disney and ventured into the Serengeti.

Certainly, the company's lofty undertaking created some unusual problems for designers. Horticulturalists had to dress up local trees (such as the Southern oak) to masquerade as African arbors (such as the acacia). And landscapers trained in carefully manicured designs had to shift gears to allow for the birth of wild and overgrown jungles. Challenges impacted other departments as well. Costumers had to sew embroidered name patches on employee shirts (animals were likely to grab at the traditional plastic pin-on kind), and concessions had to do away with disposable drink straws and lids (potential choking hazard to animals). Suddenly, feeding the average burger-gobbling park guest didn't seem so hard once elephants started demanding 125 pounds of food per day.

Despite the adjustments, the Animal Kingdom is still Disney, and theme-park trappings are everywhere. Signs of its corporate progenitor are amply evident, if not in the attractions themselves, then in the availability of corporate-logo merchandise inevitably for sale. The most obvious Disney presence is at Camp Minnie-Mickey—a don't-miss for little adventurers—where autograph seekers can get up close and personal with the big cheese and his friends. And pure theme-park kitsch is at least part of what you'll find in DinoLand U.S.A. where one of the features

DISNEY'S ANIMAL KINGDOM

RAFIKI'S PLANET WATCH
(accessible by train)

ASIA
Flights of Wonder
Kali River Rapids
Maharajah Jungle Trek

DINOLAND U.S.A.
The Boneyard
Cretaceous Trail
DINOSAUR
Primeval Whirl
Tarzan Rocks!
TriceraTop Spin

AFRICA
Express train to Rafiki's Planet Watch
Kilimanjaro Safaris
Pangani Forest Exploration Trail

DISCOVERY ISLAND
Discovery Island Trails
It's Tough to be a Bug!
The Tree of Life

THE OASIS

ENTRANCE

CAMP MINNIE-MICKEY
Character Greeting Trails
Festival of the Lion King
Pocahontas and Her Forest Friends

is a hold-on-to-your-hats thrill ride back to the big bang. For pure entertainment value, shows here (and there are many) are among the best the Disney theme parks have to offer, particularly the absolutely wonderful Festival of the Lion King.

So the sum total of Disney's Animal Kingdom experience is as much whimsy as it is wilderness. And perhaps that's the great good fortune of this particular brand of Disney magic—that you might walk away a bit wiser, without realizing that you ever went to school.

▼▼▼▼▼▼▼▼▼
Nuts & Bolts

ARRIVAL

From the Contemporary, Polynesian and Grand Floridian Beach resorts: Take a Disney bus directly to Disney's Animal Kingdom.

From the Magic Kingdom and Epcot: Take a Disney bus directly to Disney's Animal Kingdom.

From the Downtown Disney Marketplace, Pleasure Island, the West Side, Typhoon Lagoon, Blizzard Beach or Fort Wilderness: Take a Disney bus directly to Disney's Animal Kingdom.

From the Wilderness Lodge and the Caribbean Beach, Port Orleans, Dixie Lands, and All-Star Sports, Music and Movie resorts: Take a Disney bus directly to Disney's Animal Kingdom.

From the Beach Club, Yacht Club and Boardwalk resorts: Take a Disney bus directly to Disney's Animal Kingdom.

From area hotels outside Disney World: Most hotels offer shuttle service to Disney–MGM Studios. However, shuttles often run only on the hour or every two or three hours. In this case, it's more convenient to drive.

By Car: Take Route 4 to exit 25B (192 West); follow signs to Blizzard Beach/All-Star Resort to Osceola Parkway West and look for signs for Disney's Animal Kingdom and follow these to the main entrance.

Happily, the parking lot here isn't nearly as vast as at the Magic Kingdom. Often you can leave your car within walking distance to the park entrance, and there are always trams rolling about to transport guests from far-off parking spaces. And remember: rental cars tend to look alike. Make sure to write down the row and number of your space or your last adventure of the day may be spent in a security vehicle hunting for your car.

GAME PLAN

Planning your visit to Disney's Animal Kingdom is a bit different than planning for other theme parks, in that you'll have to work around the schedule of the animals. Time of day often impacts the level of activity of the different species, and even on the long days of summer, attractions here are among the earliest in Disney World to close, primarily because it takes time to settle the animals for the night. The most significant illustration of this is the Safari, which closes at least a half-hour before the rest of the park.

Because Disney's Animal Kingdom opens before all other parks (ostensibly to get in the most daylight hours), there are no early admission perks for guests of official Disney hotels. At the very least, though, arriving a half-hour ahead will net you the chance to purchase your ticket early (ticket office people arrive 30 minutes before park opening) and perhaps give you a jump on those rare days during busy season when gates open early. Even if attractions aren't open, you can use some early hours to grab your map, check show times and plot strategies for your visit.

In the absence of a central event such as a major parade (for obvious reasons, Disney's Animal Kingdom does not have nighttime fireworks displays), there are no "off-peak" times to sneak out to popular attractions. Instead, the best strategy is to head early to flagship rides like the Kilimanjaro Safaris, It's Tough to be a Bug!, Kali River Rapids, the train to Rafiki's Planet Watch, and DINOSAUR where queues fill up early and only get more crowded as the day wears on. Crowds are not as much of a factor in self-guided attractions such as the Pangani Forest Exploration Trail and the Tree of Life. Your best bet is to plan those visits around show times, a schedule of which can be found on the map you get at the entrance.

> Animal Kingdom's 500 acres are home to nearly 1500 animals and more than 4000 varieties of trees and plants.

How long you spend here will depend largely on the size of the crowds. With the people factor at a minimum, it is indeed possible to see the entire Animal Kingdom in a day. That's at a pretty brisk pace, however, and you'll probably want more time to appreciate all the intricacies, as well as to ride the Safari—a ride that never gets tired—over and over again.

GUEST SERVICES

Stroller and Wheelchair Rentals   Available at Garden Gate Gifts just to the right inside the Main Entrance.

Baby Services   Changing tables and nursing facilities are located behind the Creature Comforts shop on Discovery Island.

Lockers   Located just outside the park near the kennel, and inside near Guest Relations. Note: Lockers cost $5 for the day ($2 deposit).

Pets   Pets are not permitted in Disney's Animal Kingdom, but you can board them for $6 per pet per day at the kennel located outside the park to the right of the entrance.

Lost Children   Report missing children to Guest Services and pick them up behind Creature Comforts in Discovery Island.

Package Pickup   To avoid toting your purchases around all day, ask the Disney's Animal Kingdom store clerks to forward your packages to Guest Services. You can pick them up on your way out; if you're staying at a Disney property, you can have packages sent to your hotel (not, however, on the day of your departure). The service is free.

Lost & Found   Report missing or found items to Guest Services.

Banking There's no bank at the Animal Kingdom; however, an automatic teller machine is located outside the park to the right of the main entrance.

GETTING AROUND One of the most apparent differences between the Animal Kingdom and other Disney parks is organization. The wilderness theme has been so authentically achieved, you might occasionally feel you need a compass to get around (I did, anyway).

Though much of the 500 acres is inhabited by animals, there are plenty of human foot paths as well. To find your way, the important thing to remember is the position of the Tree of Life. The gargantuan arbor—symbolically referred to as the Animal Kingdom's "Castle"—is on an island at the center of the park, with all other lands connected across the Discovery River by bridges. Cross the Oasis bridge and you'll come face-to-face with the tree. Turn left on the main path and you'll travel in a circle around the tree, first encountering Camp Minnie-Mickey, then Africa, Asia, DinoLand U.S.A. and finally back to The Oasis. The train to the Rafiki's Planet Watch lies just off of Africa. Though many people keep tabs on each other these days with two-way radios and cell phones (not a bad idea, really) low-tech methods still apply: the Guest Relations office at the entrance is a good place to meet (or leave messages) if your party becomes separated.

> Pity the poor souls who had to hand-affix all 103,000 leaves to the Tree of Life!

The Oasis

The Magic Kingdom has Main Street U.S.A., MGM has Hollywood Boulevard and Disney's Animal Kingdom has The Oasis.

Setting the mood for the adventure at hand, this opening stretch of the Animal Kingdom is a matrix of lush greenery winding along streams, waterfalls and miniature meadows. Unlike the main drags at other Disney parks, however, The Oasis isn't a retail and dining mecca (save for the Rainforest Cafe located beside a gushing waterfall to the left of the park entrance). Rather, it's the place to get your first glimpse of a dozen-or-so habitats housing gentle creatures such as iguanas, macaws and sloths.

Interestingly, many people fly through this under-appreciated section as if they're going from the gate to baggage claim, making it one of the most blissfully quiet places in the park. It's often only on the way to the park exit, when visitors are slowed down by a reluctance to let the day end (sort of what happens at park closing on Main Street U.S.A.), that they realize the area is overflowing with furry and feathered critters of its own. The rewards for straying along these tropical paths are unusual sights such as the colorful (and loud!) macaws who playfully, and sometimes not so playfully, duel each other for a space on their tree.

Disney likes to think of its Discovery Island as an African artist's colony. The colorful vista is punctuated by one giant-sized piece of art—the 14-story

Discovery Island

Tree of Life. On it are carvings depicting hundreds of animals found in this Animal Kingdom and beyond.

It's fitting that the sprawling Tree of Life, icon for the park, should take up residence on Discovery Island, the focal point for the entire Animal Kingdom, where all "lands" connect. You will find the lions' share of the parks shops and restaurants here.

Discovery Island Trails ★★★ The first thing you're likely to see as you come near the Animal Kingdom is the towering Tree of Life. The focal point of the 500-acre park, the tree rises 145 feet high, with thousands of leaves swaying in the breeze.

WHAT TO SEE & DO

Height and girth aside, what may be most surprising about this natural wonder is that it isn't a natural wonder at all. Like many of the landmarks in the overall Disney World landscape, the Tree of Life is a Disney invention. The enormous trunk—extending 50 feet wide with roots stretching 170 feet around—had to be built outside the park and brought in piece by piece; fully assembled, it's large enough to camouflage an entire 430-seat theater beneath it. And if you think stringing Christmas lights is a challenge, consider that these tree trimmers had to attach all 8000 branches by hand, each with high-tech joints to allow them to authentically sway in that rare-but-welcome southern Florida breeze.

Apart from marveling at the accomplishment itself, the attraction of the tree is the chance to see more animals. Fashioned out of the behemoth's root system is a maze of paths that wind along habitats for about a dozen inhabitants including flamingos, lemurs and tortoises.

But what's most amazing—and certainly most fun—about adventuring here is the trunk itself. While it may at first look like simply a mass of "bark," a closer inspection reveals hundreds of engraved animal images, making the canvas the equivalent of a giant hidden-picture book. Just when you think you've found them all, another image seems to appear before your eyes. There are 325 "carvings" in all—some of the more spectacular include a bald eagle and a very large snake.

TIPS: Paths along the tree are rarely crowded, and are best taken when you've had your fill of some of the more energizing theme park fare (you may turn some kids off if you start here and let them believe it's going to be a day of art gazing). Besides, in addition to a cool cave or two, the walkways are sprinkled with a few benches—the perfect shady spot to rest those aching dogs.

It's Tough to be a Bug! ★★★★★ After centuries dodging tennis shoes and being maligned as one of the planet's greatest nuisances, the creepy crawly critters of the world have united to explain their plight. Animated masters of ceremony resembling the folks from *A Bug's Life* (the attraction's movie was actually based on the feature film) detail the atrocities of bug treatment and set out to demonstrate the perils of being the size of a thumbtack.

What follows is pure hysterical fun—undoubtedly one of the high points of a visit here (opening day, Drew Carey pointed this one out as his very favorite, if that means anything). Without giving too much away (and that would definitely ruin the fun here), brilliant special effects creep out, startle and, thanks to motion mechanisms in the seats, literally shake up all 430 audience members who laugh, squirm, squeal, and more than occasionally leap to their feet. It's all in good fun—unless you happen to be a self-confessed creepy-crawly-phobe, in which case you might want to reconsider. On the other hand, you may never swipe at mosquitos the same way again.

Creators of this attraction anticipated long lines (sometimes really long lines) and wisely wound the queue around the Tree of Life's roots where you can divert yourself from the long wait by deciphering the trunk's animal images and observing real animals in their habitats. There's also some pre-show silliness, such as the faux posters (my favorite was the one for the "Dung Brothers" act), as well as appropriate bug music ("Beauty and the Bees," and songs from "Antie").

TIPS: Loud noises, all-too-real special effects, and larger-than-life "bugs" make this one way too frightening for many children. Some brave little ones (mostly over age eight) do actually enjoy it, but more often the whimpering starts as soon as the first bugs appear.

ANOTHER NOTE: The first time I visited Disney's Animal Kingdom, I missed out on this entomological (so to speak) attraction because it was hidden within the roots of the Tree of Life. My advice to others venturing here—don't make the same mistake. This 3D/live action spectacle is an absolute hoot—that is, assuming you don't mind being "flattened" by a giant fly swatter.

Africa

It took more than imagination for Disney to come up with the look for its African village.

To construct the characteristic thatched roofs, the company had to go to the experts—in this case, Zulu craftsmen—who assembled the roofs from truck loads of Berg thatch from Africa.

The finished product is a tribute to their hard work. The scene appears authentic, with "Africa's" port village of Harambe replete with a bustling marketplace formed of white-coral walls and Bantu-inspired architecture.

The feature attraction here is the Kilimanjaro Safaris, an event that seems perfectly at home in this well-crafted departure point. But be sure to take time to appreciate the carefully assembled landscape. It would be a shame to miss out on the charms of this Africa by spending all your time waiting in line.

Kilimanjaro Safaris ★★★★★ Authenticity has reached new heights at this remarkable attraction, the largest (110 acres) and uncontested star of Disney's Animal Kingdom.

WHAT TO SEE & DO

Riders will sense they're in for something completely different the moment they board the Safari truck. Open-air vehicles aren't on a track—they're actually controlled by drivers who navigate authentic (and authentically bumpy) dirt roads (be sure to use the storage nets in front of you).

Scenery that begins with some overgrown brush eventually opens up to a magnificent panorama of the "savannah." Disney deserves a giant pat on the back for this alone. The landscape of acacia trees and baobabs is truly amazing; it looks like a place that could only exist in Africa.

Animal sightings start almost immediately, usually something along the lines of an impala, inevitably eliciting gasps and grabs for the cameras (fortunately, we heeded our guide's wise warning to "try not to use all your film on the first animal—there will be more"). Dozens of subsequent sightings include lions lazing on their rocks, tree-grazing giraffes, swimming elephants, cheetahs, as well as rhinos, warthogs and hippos. They all seem to roam together, but they're actually cordoned off by imperceptible boundaries, an arrangement no doubt set up to prevent unscheduled demonstrations of the food chain. Still, gentler animals are free to wander near the tourist trucks, creating memorable moments when wildlife literally stops traffic.

> Keep in mind that the Safari starts shutting down a bit before the rest of the park closes.

Unlike the Magic Kingdom's Jungle Cruise, guides here don't seem to have a script—they're left instead to narrate at least somewhat at will (although it's hard to imagine Disney didn't lay out some sort of guidelines). The down side is that not all guides are created equal. All, however, point out sights as you go, and charts on the backs of all seats help with identification.

This being a theme park, creators couldn't play it 100-percent straight. The static-heavy tour bus radio crackles with communications with local game wardens; and there's even a a bit of shtick about a perilous dash across a collapsing bridge and a chase to nab some ivory poachers. All of this either adds to or detracts from the experience, depending on your age and disposition. Still, not all the flair is unwelcome. That trucks seem to blow no exhaust—or at least none that we were aware of—must be another bit of Disney magic.

TIPS: Because animals don't follow scripts, the wildlife content will vary every time you take the tour. There are no guarantees as to exactly what you'll see and when, but some say that animals are most active during the early morning hours.

Pangani Forest Exploration Trail ★★★★ At the end of the Kilimanjaro Safari, the road leads to the entrance of the Pangani Forest Exploration Trail. While arrival admittedly feels a little anticlimactic after the Safari, it gets better as you go along. Once you're deep in the "jungle," you'll be hard-pressed to believe the Magic Kingdom isn't several continents away.

Apart from a walk through some lush and leafy trails, hiking here will give you a more sustained look at some of the animals you may have merely glimpsed while in the "savannah." Small animals, such as the okapi (a zebra-looking animal that is actually related to the giraffe), inhabit these forest trails. Among the more dramatic attractions is the giant picture window into the hippo pool. This underwater hippo ballet (they're just swimming, but surprisingly gracefully) is pretty much your only chance to see these big guys' full girth; their tendency to spend most hours underwater limits the safari view to about the ears up.

Midway through the trail, a "research station" offers a look at some naked mole rats (trust me, the name suits their appearance), as well as some hands-on activities, including a headset playing all-too-real animal sounds you definitely don't want to hear in the wild (the lion roar actually made the hair on the back of my neck stand up).

By far, the climax of this adventure, of the whole park, perhaps, is the gorilla family—majestic, all-too-human silverbacks and babies. These huge, hairy beasts live in a remarkably real jungle, and are visible from an open suspension bridge. The effect is that they appear to be able to swing right up to you; but don't worry, they can't.

Throughout your journey, carefully stationed animal handlers are happy to answer questions, and infuse a little humor ("Ask me anything," ribbed one. "If I don't know the answer, I'll make it up and you won't know the difference.")

TIPS: Something about the imposing gorillas brings out the primate in humans who jump around and screech, ostensibly to get a gorilla-sized reaction. Be careful what you wish for. "Too much noise can upset the animals," explained a handler. In gorilla-speak, "upset," can translate into throwing, er, unmentionables.

Rafiki's Planet Watch ★★★ When you've had enough time on your feet, hop on a vintage-feeling locomotive that transports you to this interactive education center where you can learn a bit more about how the animals who live here are cared for. The observation window into the veterinary station lets you watch the animals as they're being tended to. If you're tired of being separated by glass, the Affection Section outside features all the usual petting-zoo suspects. When you're done, hop the train again for the return trip back "home."

TIPS: Save this one for the middle of the day. The leisurely stroll here will temporarily remove you from the hustle-bustle outside.

DinoLand U.S.A.

You can't miss the entrance to this paleontological wonderland—it's marked by the presence of some very large dino bones, the assembled remains of a brachiasaur.

Fact and fiction co-exist rather peacefully in this prehistoria. During a day trip, you're just as likely to time travel to the big bang as to encounter real-life paleontologists assembling the remains of a deceased *T. rex*. Not everything of prehistoric interest comes in fossil form, however. Gardens and habitats along the Cretaceous Trail feature living specimens—plants and animals directly descended from animals and plants who lived and grew on the earth millions of years ago.

DINOSAUR **** In the hallowed halls of the Animal Kingdom's starched white research facility, "investigators" at the Dino Institute offer an irresistible adventure: a quick trip in a time machine to take a gander at some dinosaurs in the wild. But a radical scientist programs your Time Rover to pick up a coveted iguanadon. The catch: the pickup occurs only milliseconds before a dreaded meteor comes to wipe out all life one earth.

Hydraulically controlled cars and fiery special effects whiz by as vehicles zoom back to the "big bang" where you're menaced by some toothy dinosaurs. It's dark, loud and bumpy enough to swoop hats and loose articles right off the bodies of their owners (those bins in front of you are there for a good reason!). Twisting and turning aside, the real scream here is apprehension: you know some humongous, big-fanged beasts are going to pop out at you at some point—you just don't know when and where.

WALK THE WALK

Not everything featured in DinoLand U.S.A. is extinct . . . exactly. The **Cretaceous Trail**, designated by markers near DINOSAUR, features plant and animal life, some species that are direct descendants of prehistoric ancestors, others that actually survived the Cretaceous period. Many of the latter (such as crocodiles and alligators) look much the same as they did millions of years ago.

The good news/bad news here is the line: it's almost always long, but once once inside the research facility, you'll enjoy the queue in blissful air-conditioned comfort.

TIPS: Though it's got its share of action, DINOSAUR may disappoint lovers of true heart-stopping thrills. One rider lamented that the effects were more simple jostling around than creative thrills. By all means, don't skip it. But to up the excitement factor at least a little, try out the back seat that, for my money, offers the best effect.

Primeval Whirl* It's not as fast as Space Mountain or as wild as Rockin' Rollercoaster. But the thing that makes this ride interesting is that it's a double threat: a roller coaster that spins like a teacup (which, depending on your disposition, means you might exit shaken up *and* nauseous). Ride cars seat up to four people and zip around steep drops and sharp corners, often spinning wildly along the way. It's a hoot—the novelty alone had my family laughing all the way through. And, surprisingly, it was actually a lot more thrilling that it appeared from the ground.

TIPS: Primal Whirl wins honors as one of the longest waits in the entire Disney World resort. Do yourself a favor and skip the "Standby" line—get a Fastpass instead.

TriceraTop Spin ** Dumbo, but on a dino—need I say more?

TIPS: Being the only true kiddie ride in the park, lines here tend to be long. Alas, there is no FastPass. Your best bet is to arrive first thing, or very late.

Tarzan Rocks!* You'd expect to find the ape-man in this musical revue based on the popular animated film. But it's the rock band that blasts the tunes penned by Phil Collins that really swings.

Tarzan Rocks appropriately blasts the soundtrack of the film in a lively show. The seven-member band includes bassist, electric guitar, drummer, bongos, lead singer and sultry backup vocalists. There's even a bit of X-games thrown in, with rollerbladers careening around in a flashy display of acrobatics. Kids in the au-

DINORIFFIC

Disney apparently listened to folks who reasoned that the Animal Kingdom didn't have enough actual rides. So in 2002, they opened this latest area, Chester & Hester's Dino-Rama. A part of Dino-Land, the area gives visitors a taste of traditional theme park fare with a roller coaster (albeit a rather tame one) and a kiddie ride. It's all rather cute, though the carnival-style games where you can win stuffed animals, are a little too traditional for my taste.

dience love it when Turk (Tarzan's mischievous ape friend) leads the audience in a rendition of the Crashing the Camp song.

The scantily-clad muscle man (the pecs are real, the dreadlocks are not) appears about halfway through, swinging dramatically on a vine with Jane in tow. The performance maintains its "G" rating thanks to a loincloth that, as in the film, defies gravity.

TIPS: Theater in the Wild is a big arena, but Tarzan is a popular show—one you don't want to miss. Scope out the performance schedule on your entrance map and make sure to arrive 15 to 30 minutes early. If you're in the audience ahead of time, you'll at least get to enjoy some of the entertaining pre-show shenanigans.

The Boneyard ★★★ Consider the Boneyard the *Tyrannosaurus rex* of playgrounds—a playground extraordinaire. Like the Honey I Shrunk the Kids Playground in Disney–MGM Studios, the Boneyard is a jungle gym with a theme, in this case, that of a deserted paleontological dig site. Look for excavation vehicles, dino bones and lots of rocks for climbing and crawling; you can even stick your head into the teeth of a "triceratops" and scramble around on an actual *T. rex* skeleton. Adventurous grown-ups can have some fun here, too, particularly in the upper levels of the climbing sculpture where a steep incline (steep enough to require a rope to haul yourself up) challenges young and old alike. When you're done climbing, you can start digging at the full-sized sandpit complete with uncoverable fossil.

TIPS: If you've got kids, plan to hang around here for a while. The climbing stuff alone is intoxicating; paired with the dino-theme, it's an attraction the kids simply won't want to leave.

Asia

A colorful swimming dragon and a stone bridge flanked by peaked columns greet you as you cross into the Animal Kingdom's newest continent, Asia. The sixth and final "land" to be added, Asia is where you'll find such adventures as a whitewater rafting expedition and a footpath through a remarkable palace. The rural "village" here is stocked with authentic artifacts. Look closely at the colorful junk floating in the water at Asia's entrance—the ship, full of supplies, helps camouflage the fact that it's really stocked with cases of Coke.

WHAT TO SEE & DO

Flights of Wonder ★★★★ If someone says "duck" at this live presentation about birds, they're not flagging you to the onstage appearance of a particular breed of fowl. Rather, they're signaling the approach of a low-flying bird.

Hair-skimming flights are one highlight of this ornithological performance where several times during the show enormous owls and hawks glide so close overhead, you'll actually feel the air whizzing by. Other feathered friends enact a few tricks. A couple of lucky audience members even get to join the crew on stage, one tossing up a grape for a bird to retrieve mid-flight. Ever wonder about your kids' table manners? Check out the seriema that "tenderizes" (or rather terrorizes!) its food by banging it against a rock. Don't worry; in this case, the "food" is a rubber alligator.

TIPS: To fully appreciate the performance, make sure to arrive early and grab a seat in one of the front sections. Those in the bleachers will miss out on low-flying creatures, and hosts often (but not always) look to those in the front rows for onstage volunteers.

Maharajah Jungle Trek ★★★★ Deep in the heart of Asia is the mythical village of Anandapur and the remains of what was once a spectacular maharajah's palace.

The palace, as created by Disney, is still spectacular despite the fact that it's in ruins. Spread upon the sprawling property—you'll swear you're in another country—are tigers who laze around as if royalty (and who would argue with them?). These felines are amazing for their size and abilities—that they can jump from the upper level to the water below is astounding. Another spectacle here: the giant fruit bats, some of whose wings can spread to six feet may have faces only a mother could love, but these upside down sleepers are intriguing. I must say I was happy for the one-inch slats that were too narrow to let the creepy critters escape. You'll be equally fascinated by the Komodo dragon and the spectacular aviary.

TIPS: Done right, with enough time to fully appreciate it, the self-guided trek might take you a while. Since you can't bring food in with you (one woman had to toss a luscious-looking ice cream after only a few meager bites), make sure no one's stomach is growling before you go.

Kali River Rapids ★★★ What's the best way to cool off after a day in Disney's Animal Kingdom? How about a trip down the Chakranadi River?

Oversized rubber rafts launch you straight on into rapids in the middle of the jungle where you'll be besieged by the requisite splashes, spins and near dunks. How wet will you get? Just observe the wringing-out being done by exiting riders.

The camaraderie born of getting collectively drenched brings the 12 otherwise strangers on the boat together. But don't be surprised if at least some of your raftmates begin rooting for you to get dunked. There's no exact science for who'll be squeegeeing pants on the way out (your shoes and cameras, at least, can be saved by the water-tight bin in the center of the raft); on my trip, those who sat down facing forward on the raft's right side paid the biggest price.

If you're not busy wiping water out of your eyes, you might catch some of the scenery along the way—temple ruins and such.

But don't worry if you miss it. You probably had plenty of time to take in the large collection of artifacts in the queue area.

TIPS: The long lines at this popular ride are only half the challenge; the fact that you'll spend most of that time in direct sunlight is the other. To minimize the swelter (and wait) factor, plan your water ride early in the day. Or go at the end of the day, after the worst of the midday heat had passed (though the lines are likely to be longer than in the morning).

▼▼▼▼▼▼▼▼▼▼▼▼▼▼

Camp Minnie-Mickey

The most Disneyfied of the lands in the Animal Kingdom is also the one occupied by the big cheese himself—Mickey Mouse. Designed like an Adirondack summer camp, Camp Minnie-Mickey is primarily the place for catching autographs. But don't bypass it just because your group lacks John Hancock–seekers. The land is also home to the Festival of the Lion King, one of the best (if not the best) shows Disney has to offer.

WHAT TO SEE & DO

Character Greeting Trails ★★ You've seen the warthog and gazed at the meercat. Now it's time to meet the real thing—the real Disney characters, anyway. Mickey, Minnie and a rotating crew of their buddies can be encountered throughout the day here, all dressed up in safari garb and ready to sign autographs and snap pictures with bold Animal Kingdom adventurers. Pick your trail in this Adirondack summer camp and find your favorite (ask before setting out).

TIPS: People don't often equate character greetings with Disney's Animal Kingdom (for that, they go to the Magic Kingdom). For this reason, the lines to greet these animated folks usually tend toward the short side.

Festival of the Lion King ★★★★★ Taking its cue from the mega-success of the Lion King on Broadway, this lively 25-minute stage show brings together colorful costumes, exhilarating music, and performers with voices that will knock your socks off.

Unlike other Disney stage shows, the Lion King is not simply a retelling of the feature film. Simba, Pumba and Timon are here (some are on floats that look like they're recycled from the Lion King parade), but in more of a superfluous role. It's the other performers who steal the show; dramatic fire-twirlers, trampoline-jumping monkeys, aerial acrobats and jungle animals with attitude, all performing to tunes from the film. Four excellent singers in tribal robes keep the pace lively. Even the audience gets in on the act, with each of the four seating sections assigned an all-important animal sound—elephant, lion, giraffe (anyone know what sound that animal makes?) or warthog (parents take note: your children will love snorting the sound of the warthog and will repeat it throughout the rest of the day). Some lucky kids are also chosen to dance with the troupe during the last number. Sure it's a little shmaltzy. But if you're not completely caught up in the very grand grande finale—a rousing rendition of Simba's jungle anthem, "The Circle of Life"—you'll be the exception.

TIPS: With room for 1000 people, crowds are well accommodated. But this is a very popular show, and it can be closed out. To be safe, show up 15 to 30 minutes ahead.

Pocahontas and Her Forest Friends ★★★ The story of Pocahontas is a fitting way to tell the story about native animals of North America. The heroine of the eponymous film enchants little ones with the "Colors of the Wind" ballad and confers with Grandmother Willow about how to save the forest and its creatures. Kids will like the bunnies, raccoons and other small wildlife here, and the turkey that struts across the stage at the beginning is sure to get a laugh. Overall, though, the theme and enactment are directed at small children. If you don't have any, you could probably skip it.

TIPS: Animals in this performance are small, and the theater rows don't have a very steep grade. For little ones to get the best view, arrive a few minutes early and seat them in the special area up front for kids roughly ten and under.

SIX

The Rest of the World

Some people say the rest of Disney World is the best in the world. Considering what "the rest" is, who could argue?

You have thick pine forests for pitching a tent and broad, clear lakes for taking a plunge. There are big and brassy night-clubs and tranquil rivers, drop-off water slides and one of the biggest swimming pools in Florida. And there's more: whimsical shops and backwoods hayrides, even an island for a zoo, a place so pristine and remote it's overlooked by most visitors.

There's so much to see and do you could easily spend a whole week taking in these seven themed attractions that are truly the icing on the Disney cake. Spanning over 800 acres "the rest of the world" boasts Fort Wilderness, a vast, forested campground and outdoor playground. Nearby is Typhoon Lagoon. Fashioned like a sand and palm tree paradise, the lagoon is a water-slide fantasyland. And at Blizzard Beach, a "snowy" version of Typhoon Lagoon, you'll find Disney's fastest water slide. Then there's Pleasure Island, a pulsing pad of nightclubs, restaurants and shops on the edge. Next door, Downtown Disney offers a lake-side menagerie of more shops and restaurants.

No doubt, the Disney Company has added these attractions over the years to capture even more of your time and money. But really, they give you more (and sometimes better) options. After an exhausting day at the Magic Kingdom or Epcot, you can decompress at one of the smaller parks the next day. Many places put you out-of-doors and away from the computerized attractions of the big theme parks. And at three places, you get to wear your swimsuit. These minor parks also cost less than the big parks and—with the exception of Typhoon Lagoon and Blizzard Beach—don't stick you in long lines.

This easy-on-the-mind-and-wallet approach has attracted many locals who rarely venture into the big parks. Like them, once you discover the flip side of Disney World, you won't want to miss "the rest."

▼ ▼ ▼ ▼ ▼ ▼ ▼ ▼ ▼ ▼ ▼

Fort Wilderness

Spread across 740 acres, ribboned with streams and canals, teeming with small animals and places to swim, bike, run and hide, this wooded wonderland is the best. Here at Fort Wilderness, fences are made of pine poles, bus stops are wood shingled, and trash cans look like tree stumps. Paved lanes, with names like Possum Path and Cottontail Curl, cut through miles of campsites surrounded by spidery slash pines. All the lanes lead to Bay Lake, where still, picturesque waters are rimmed in cypress trees and marshy reeds.

Fort Wilderness is the only attraction that looks a lot like it did when Disney bought it three decades ago. Unfortunately, the only reminders of the forest's first settlers, Seminole Indians, are a few totem poles outside a trading post. Inside the post, youngsters can buy coonskin caps and toy rifles. Fort Wilderness bus drivers add to the backwoods mood by talking with a twang and cracking corny camping jokes.

For families on a budget or who love the outdoors, the campground is a perfect place to stay (see Chapter Eight). Even if you don't camp here, be sure to visit. There are many activities for kids and spots where parents can take it easy. And everything is tuned to nature, from horseback riding and canoeing to just beaching it along the lake.

ARRIVAL

Whether you arrive by Disney bus or in your own car, it takes some time to get to the heart of Fort Wilderness. Driving a car, however, is the fastest and easiest way to go. Here are the various ways of getting there:

From the Magic Kingdom and Contemporary Resort: Take the scenic, 30-minute boat launch. Or, take the monorail to the

◆ ◆

THE TREE THAT TAMED THE LAWN MOWER

At the foot of a spiraling pine tree, not far from the Fort Wilderness Marina, rests a bizarre poem:

> *Too long did Billy Bowlegs*
> *Park his reel slow mower*
> *Alas, one warm and sunny day*
> *Aside a real fast grower*

Beside the poem, the rusted blades of a lawn mower are entwined in the trunk of the pine tree. It's a strange sight, for sure, but even stranger is that no one knows how the tree and mower got that way. Some cynics speculate that when Walt Disney bought the forest, the tree—fearing it would be bulldozed to make way for a theme park—snared the offensive machinery.

Ticket and Transportation Center, then catch a Disney bus to Fort Wilderness. The monorail-bus trip takes around 40 to 50 minutes.

From Epcot and the Polynesian and Grand Floridian Beach resorts: Take the monorail to the Ticket and Transportation Center, then ride the Disney bus to Fort Wilderness. Traveling time: 40 to 50 minutes.

From Disney's Animal Kingdom: Take the 15-minute bus ride here. Or, bus to the Magic Kingdom and catch the 30-minute boat ride.

From all other Disney World locations: Take a Disney bus to the Ticket and Transportation Center, then transfer to the Fort Wilderness bus. From the Ticket and Transportation Center, the ride is 30 to 40 minutes.

From area hotels not in Disney World: Most hotels provide a shuttle to the Ticket and Transportation Center. From there, take the bus.

By Car: From Route 4, take the exit for the Magic Kingdom (also Route 192) and follow the signs to Magic Kingdom. As soon as you pass through the Magic Kingdom toll plaza (and pay the $7 parking fee), bear to the right. From here, you can follow the signs.

GAME PLAN Now that you're out in the woods, you might as well stay awhile. Stop by Fort Wilderness Lodge (407-824-3200) for maps, schedules and touring information. From here you'll take a bus to the main sights. It's about a ten-minute ride through the woods, with frequent stops for camping loops. Fort Wilderness is never really crowded, so you can enjoy the activities in any order at your leisure. Two musts for families are the petting farm and the horse stables, where you can join a trail ride. A few events (Hoop-Dee-Doo Revue, hayrides, campfires, etc.) are scheduled each day, so check the times before you go. Campfires are open only to guests of Disney World resorts.

GUEST SERVICES

Baby Services Changing tables are located at the Pioneer Hall restrooms. Diapers, formula and other baby supplies are available at the Meadow and Settlement trading posts. Strollers are *not* available, so bring your own.

Babysitting Available at the fort's Kinder Care Learning Center. For reservations, call 407-827-5437.

Pets Not allowed except in a few campsites. However, you can leave yours at the kennel at the Fort Wilderness parking lot.

Lost Children/Lost & Found Report lost children and lost and found articles to the Fort Wilderness Lodge.

WHAT TO SEE & DO

FORT WILDERNESS BEACH   A swath of silvery white sand edged with tall pine and oak trees, this is one of the prettiest spots in Disney World. The view of Space Mountain and the Contemporary Hotel across the water is spectacular. There's a shallow, sandy swimming area, playground and picnic area and shady hammocks for taking a snooze.

MARINA   Right off the beach, here's where you hire a bass fishing guide or rent boats.

PETTING FARM   Children can't get enough of these barnyard animals. All day, you'll see them chasing goats, ducks and peacocks, dirt and grass flying everywhere, until their little legs give out (the kids' legs, that is). Nestled under broad shade trees, the petting farm also features pony rides.

TRI-CIRCLE-D RANCH   You know those neat horses that pull the streetcars down Main Street U.S.A.? They live here in a stable surrounded by pastures. A smithy, or blacksmith, cares for over a hundred Percheron and Belgian Draft horses and lets visitors take pictures while he works.

HORSEBACK RIDING, BICYCLING AND CANOEING   All three activities make great family excursions. If your children are at least nine years old, you can take the Fort Wilderness Trail Ride, a 45-minute guided walk through the woods. For reservations, stop by the Fort Wilderness Kennel or call 407-824-2832.

Fort Wilderness has super bike paths. You can rent bicycles by the day or hour from the Bike Barn, located behind the Meadow Trading Post. If you're looking for an easy ride, rent an electric golf cart (reservations are required; call 407-824-2742). The Bike Barn also offers canoes for those anxious to explore Fort Wilderness' vast labyrinth of canals and streams.

HAYRIDES   A long, hay-stacked wagon, pulled by a pair of black Percherons, winds through the woods twice each night. It's the quintessential family outing, where kids bound around in the hay and parents share the day's ups and downs. At the end of the one-hour ride, you've made good friends.

▼ ▼ ▼ ▼ ▼ ▼ ▼ ▼ ▼ ▼ ▼ ▼

Typhoon Lagoon

On a typical day at Typhoon Lagoon, you will drift along a slow river and whirl down a twisting, turning slide. You will bodysurf some waves and snorkel with sharks, then dry out on a palmy beach. You will climb a mountain called Mayday and ride a slide called Humunga Kowabunga. This will scare the smithereens out of you, but you will insist on riding again. You will climb many steps and wait in many lines. And you will get tired, very tired.

And so it goes at Typhoon Lagoon, whose tranquil setting belies its frenetic activity. The Disney-proclaimed "world's ultimate water park" is truly the ultimate, certainly when it comes to fast slides, wet times and lovely surroundings. The 38 acres are a glorious oasis of jungly hills, sugar white sand, thatched huts, wooden bridges, meandering creeks and swimming pools that could cover two football fields. Add to that the seemingly endless special effects, right down to the thunderous whitecaps created by wave machines. And then there are the slides: corkscrew slides and whitewater slides, storm slides and speed slides that put you airborne at 30 mph.

The idea behind Typhoon Lagoon is that the island is recovering from a terrible storm. Surfboards poke through palm trees, buildings are half-cocked, and a shrimp boat named *Miss Tilly* is impaled on a volcano. The ragged boat and the 85-foot "volcano," called Mount Mayday, form the showpiece of the lagoon. Every half-hour Mayday releases a torrent of water, supposedly trying to eject ole Tilly.

There is a terrific energy at Typhoon Lagoon. The whitewater rapids and heaving waves, shrieks of children and pound of steel

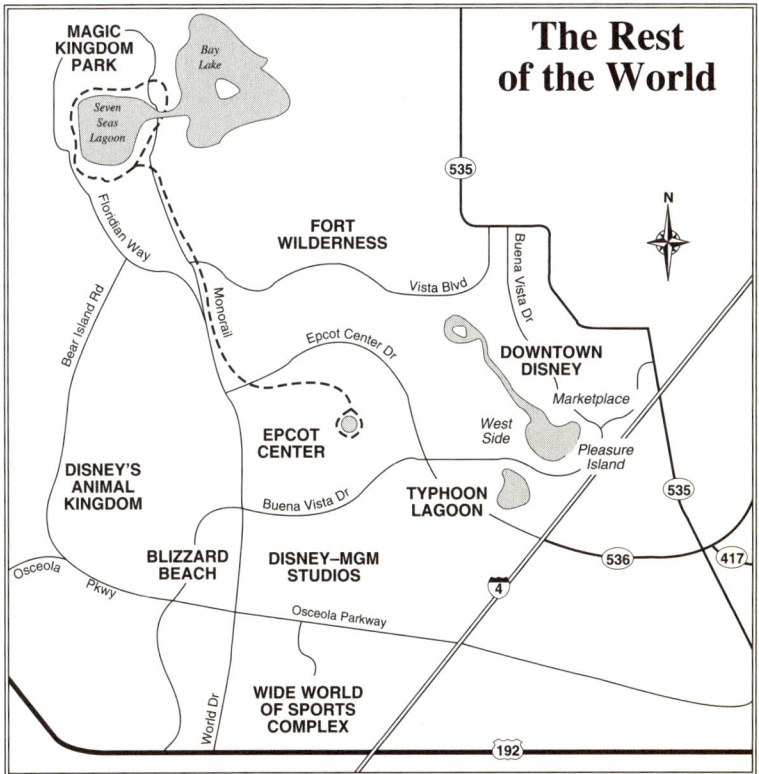

The Rest of the World

MAGIC KINGDOM PARK

Bay Lake

Seven Seas Lagoon

Floridan Way

Bear Island Rd

Monorail

535

FORT WILDERNESS

Vista Blvd

Buena Vista Dr

Epcot Center Dr

DOWNTOWN DISNEY

Marketplace

EPCOT CENTER

West Side

Pleasure Island

DISNEY'S ANIMAL KINGDOM

Buena Vista Dr

TYPHOON LAGOON

535

Osceola Pkwy

BLIZZARD BEACH

DISNEY–MGM STUDIOS

Osceola Parkway

536

417

4

World Dr

WIDE WORLD OF SPORTS COMPLEX

192

N

drums, and screams of surfers and sliders create a maelstrom of constant activity. Of course, whether you choose to roar down a slide at breakneck speed or toast on the beach and swill a drink is completely up to you.

ARRIVAL　If at all possible, drive to Typhoon Lagoon. It's much faster and easier than Disney transportation, and parking is free.

From the Magic Kingdom, Epcot, Wilderness Lodge, or the Contemporary, Polynesian or Grand Floridian Beach resorts: Take the monorail to the Ticket and Transportation Center, then transfer to a bus going directly to Typhoon Lagoon.

From Fort Wilderness or the Caribbean Beach Resort: Take a bus directly to Typhoon Lagoon.

From any other Disney World location: Take a Disney bus to the Ticket and Transportation Center, then transfer to the bus to Typhoon Lagoon.

By Car: From Route 4, take the exit for Epcot. Follow the signs to Typhoon Lagoon. The park is about half a mile from Route 4.

GAME PLAN　Typhoon Lagoon is easy to navigate, once you pick up a map. The real problem is that Typhoon Lagoon gets unbearably crowded. To me, rubbing elbows in a water park is the pits. The best time to go is the spring or fall, or on Mondays during the summer. Sunday mornings, when locals are at church, is also crowdless. If you must go on a summer weekend, arrive 30 minutes before opening time. This gives you time to park, buy tickets and rent an inner tube before mass water mania starts. And for the first hour, slides and other rides have minimal lines. You should also know that, during summer and holidays, Typhoon Lagoon often reaches capacity (4500) and closes by mid-morning. When this happens, lines at all the slides and raft rides have an hour-plus wait.

Once you're there, set up camp. If you have toddlers, the beach near Ketchakiddee Creek children's area is best. For a mix of sun and shade, seek out the grassy areas around Getaway Glen. The glen is fairly quiet and has picnic tables. If you're into people-watching, plant yourself front and center of the surf pool. With teenagers and grandparents competing for body surfing action, you'll get quite a show.

Your first Typhoon Lagoon ride should be Castaway Creek. The inner-tube cruise rambles around the park, providing an excellent orientation. After Castaway Creek, you can enjoy the pools and rides in any order.

GUEST SERVICES　**Baby Services**　Restrooms throughout are equipped with changing tables. Strollers are not provided, so bring your own.

Wheelchairs　Wheelchairs are available, free for the day, at Guest Relations.

Towels and Life Jackets   You can bring your own towel, but it's more convenient to rent one. After paying over $20 to get in, I say towels should be free. If you're not a good swimmer, life jackets are provided free (there is a refundable deposit).

Showers, Dressing Rooms and Lockers   I love the showers here; they're under a thatched roof. So are the dressing rooms and lockers; lockers can be rented.

Shoes   Even if you don't have tender feet, it's a good idea to wear shoes. There's a lot of concrete inside the park, and some of the footpaths are rough on the soles. Flip-flops will do just fine.

Coolers   Bring a cooler filled with thirst quenchers and eats (sliced fruit tastes great when you first come from the water). Glass containers and alcoholic beverages not permitted. However, beer and frozen rum drinks are sold at several spots.

Inner Tubes   Tubes are provided free of charge for all the raft rides. To avoid long lines, be at the rental counter first thing in the morning. You cannot bring your own tube into Typhoon Lagoon.

Pets   Not allowed.

CASTAWAY CREEK   Parents, this inner-tube ride is for you. A long, slow float along a picturesque creek, it's relaxation at its best. The water is three feet deep and crystal clear, and the scenery is imaginative. You'll wind through caverns and tropical greenery, bypass shipwrecks, barrels and abandoned coolers (from the typhoon, remember?) and cruise right under two waterfalls. Along the way, you'll get a great overview of Typhoon Lagoon. There are several spots where you can bail out for a break, then get back in again. Without any stops, the trip takes about 30 minutes.

WHAT TO SEE & DO

Typhoon Lagoon's surf and wave pools hold 2.75 million gallons of water.

SURF AND WAVE POOLS   Sprawled across the heart of Typhoon Lagoon, these swimming pools are where the action is. Technically, there are three pools: (1) Typhoon Lagoon, a surf pool that sits right in the middle; (2) Blustery Bay, a wave pool on the left of the lagoon (as you face Mount Mayday); and (3) Whitecap Cove wave pool, to the right of the lagoon. Serious surfers hang out in Typhoon Lagoon, waiting for the six-footers that come barreling out every 90 seconds (no surfboards allowed—it's bodysurfing only). For those who like their waves less ferocious, Blustery Bay and Whitecap Cove offer four-foot swells where you can swim or bob in an inner tube.

KETCHAKIDDEE CREEK   A water version of a schoolyard playground, Ketchakiddee has dozens of places to romp and get wet. Children can climb barrels, explore damp caves, slide down a whale (he even toots water from his spout) and ride baby inner tubes down baby rapids. A favorite spot is the bubbling sand ponds, where kids can sit in gurgling waters. Children must be four feet or shorter and accompanied by an adult.

HUMUNGA KOWABUNGA When people talk about Typhoon Lagoon, the first thing they mention is Humunga Kowabunga. Little wonder, since these three speed slides are meant to scare the living daylights out of you. Situated side by side, they each plummet from Mount Mayday, a vertical fall through caves and into the deep blue yonder. Average speed is 30 mph. And average length of ride? Three seconds. To ride, you must be at least four feet tall and not be pregnant.

Magic Linkdom? That's the title for the 99 holes that make Disney World one of the largest golf resorts in the country. For information on all six courses, call 407-939-4653.

STORM SLIDES What great names these three slides have: Jib Jammer, Rudder Buster and Stern Burner. Designed for the chickens who won't go on Humunga Kowabunga, they offer a sinuous journey through caves, under waterfalls and around boulders. Each 300-foot ride is fairly fast—20 mph—and offers some nice scenery.

RAFT RIDES These are incredibly fun. All three raft rides—Gangplank Falls, Mayday Falls and Keelhaul Falls—corkscrew down the face of Mount Mayday and send you swishing and twirling through caves and around rocks and trees. None are really scary, though Mayday has the most twists and turns. Mayday and Keelhaul are one-person inner-tube rides, while Gangplank is a three- to four-person ride in inflatable rafts. Gangplank is ideal for families, though if you don't have enough people, the attendants will pair you with other riders. You must be four feet tall to ride Mayday and Keelhaul; Gangplank has no height restrictions. Pregnant women are prohibited from all three rides.

SHARK REEF SNORKELING TANK What a drag this place is. First you have to wait in a crummy line, and then be rushed through a tank swarming with other snorkelers (the attendants practically time your swim). On rare occasions when Shark Reef is not crowded, it's worth a dive. The reef is fake, but the thousands of colorful fish—including small leopard and nurse sharks—are very real. With no lines, you can spend as long as you like chasing the fish and exploring the pool's sunken tanker. Landlubbers can view the pool from porthole windows inside the tanker.

Special notes: Free snorkeling gear is furnished; you can bring your own mask (must be tempered glass) and snorkel, but no fins. Attendants provide a quick snorkeling lesson. For those who want proof of their dive, underwater cameras are available for sale. To keep the algae out, Shark Reef is kept at a chilly 72 degrees—18 degrees colder than the rest of Typhoon Lagoon's waters. The Reef is usually closed from November through April.

One might be tempted to think that if Disney opened yet a third water park, one suspiciously similar to its own Typhoon Lagoon (as far as slides and rides and layout), that somewhere, somehow, the crowds might ease up.

Blizzard Beach

No way. Both Blizzard Beach and Typhoon Lagoon are packed nearly every day, with speed slide lines approaching one-and-a-half hours and the mid-morning scramble for lounge chairs as healthy as ever.

The 66-acre Blizzard Beach feels very much like Typhoon Lagoon, a "snowy" version of the lagoon, with imitation snow (painted concrete) oozing everywhere, skis and poles stuck all around, and a mini chairlift gliding to the top of Mt. Gushmore. The premise: A freak snowstorm roared into Central Florida, dumping heavy snow on the west side of Disney World, where Disney folks promptly opened Florida's first ski resort. Out came the Florida sun, melting much of the snow, and turning the ski slopes into water slides. Disney's fastest water slide, and supposedly the world's fastest, is here at Blizzard Beach.

The fastest, easiest way to Blizzard Beach is to drive. Parking is free, and you don't have to wait around for Disney buses. If you'd rather take the bus, all Disney resorts offer direct service to Blizzard Beach. There are bus links with all other Disney World locations, as well.

ARRIVAL

By Car: From Route 4, take Route 192 west to World Drive, then go north on World Drive.

It's easy to get around Blizzard Beach. Orient yourself first with a map, available at Ticket Sales or Guest Relations. Then head for the nearest lounge chair and set up camp. I like the chairs parked in the sand along Melt Away Bay, a great big swimming pool with gentle, machine-made waves. Parents with young children like the scene around the kiddie pool called Tike's Peak, while teenagers check out the chairs near Ski Patrol Training Camp. No matter where you settle down, you'll be with a crowd: most chairs are squeezed cheek-to-jowl.

GAME PLAN

Next, ride Summit Plummet speed slide, fastest water slide around and the most popular. Then go on Snow Stormers and Toboggan Racer. The long lines for all these slides will tire you out (and eat up a good chunk of your morning), so take a break and relax. You can enjoy most other slides and water pursuits at your leisure.

Bring a picnic (coolers are permitted) to avoid waiting in yet another line for lunch. If you do decide to eat at Blizzard Beach, go early or late to avoid the noontime crowd crush.

Blizzard Beach fills up fast, so arrive early, preferably when the park opens. If you plan a midday arrival, call before you go, as the park often closes its gates by late morning. Guests of Disney resorts are usually still admitted after the park closes, provided they take a Disney bus.

**GUEST
SERVICES**

Baby Services Restrooms throughout Blizzard Beach are equipped with changing tables. There are no stroller rentals, so bring your own.

Wheelchairs Free wheelchairs are available from the Guest Relations office.

Towels and Life Jackets You can bring your own towels, but you'll end up lugging them, wet, back to your hotel room. It's easier to rent them, available for $1 each. (After paying $25 admission to Blizzard Beach, I think towels should be free.) If you're not a good swimmer, life jackets are provided free (there is a refundable deposit).

Showers, Dressing Rooms and Lockers Locker rentals, showers and dressing rooms are located near the entrance to Blizzard Beach.

Shoes The concrete walkways heat up and burn your feet, so wear shoes. Sturdy flip-flops are ideal.

Coolers Pack a cooler with a picnic and your favorite thirst quenchers (alcoholic beverages and glass containers aren't permitted). Sliced fruit, particularly watermelon, tastes great when you first get out of the water. Beer and wine coolers are sold in the park.

Inner Tubes A limited number of inner tubes are provided for certain rides. After riding, you pass your inner tube off to the next rider (some stingy souls try to keep their tubes, causing a ruckus in the slide lines). You cannot bring inner tubes into Blizzard Beach.

Pets Not allowed.

**WHAT TO
SEE & DO**

CROSS COUNTRY CREEK The creek winds long and slow around the perimeter of Blizzard Beach, offering a fine overview of the park. You can drift peacefully in an inner tube along its waters, taking in tropical landscaped scenery and listening to the happy screams of children riding nearby slides. Fountains chilled to 38 degrees threaten at intervals, and here there is a great push by kids to put their parents under the frosty falls. You can enter or exit the creek at several points along its 2900-foot length.

MELT AWAY BAY This vast pool of see-through blue sits at the foot of Mt. Gushmore and has a tame wave machine that sends folds of water across its surface. Disney's trademark "boulders" edge the far side of the bay, and waterfalls gush down from their tops. Position yourself under the falls for a back massage, or float on an inner tube across bay waters.

CHAIR LIFT   Fashioned as an old-time ski lift, with wood slats for seats (but with modern, lengthy lift lines), this ride can fool you. At first glance, it appears you can wait for the chair lift (usually 20 to 30 minutes), then ride right up Mt. Gushmore to the slides at Summit Plummet, Slush Gusher and Teamboat Springs. Actually, you ride right up to *the lines* at those slides. Better to walk up to the slide lines and skip the chair lift line.

SUMMIT PLUMMET   Ever freefall 60 mph down a water slide? It's a little frightening, great fun—and over in four seconds. As one slider said, "You beat the water to the bottom of the slide." The plummet down the face of Mt. Gushmore is 120 feet, and if you look before you slide you may chicken out. (It's the fastest speed slide at Disney World, and said to be the fastest in the world.) Teenagers worship it, waiting in its gruelingly long lines over and over to ride. It can get super hot up here, thanks to all the white concrete (imitation snow) which reflects sun. I can't fathom waiting an hour-and-a-half in the brutal sun for a four-second splash down. Ride first thing in the morning, and save line time. To ride, you must be at least four feet tall and not be pregnant.

> Wanna go really fast on a water slide? Lay flat and cross your ankles, then cross your arms over your chest and arch your back. Happy flying!

SLUSH GUSHER   A longer, tamer trip down Mt. Gushmore with shorter lines, the "gusher" is where you ride, stomach down and face first, on a rubber mat with handles. You zip along a curlicued water course, swishing high on the banks of the slide and landing in a pool of cool water. The setting is supposedly a snowbound mountain gully.

TOBOGGAN RACER   Remember those big, multilane slides at the state fair? This is it, only with water and mats. You lay on your stomach on the mat, and cruise down one of eight lanes that gently dip down the face of Mt. Gushmore. Not very scary, but fun.

TEAMBOAT SPRINGS   Here the family hops onto a six-person raft and careens down 1200 feet of rushing, swirling waters— something like a wet bumper-car ride. It's not Colorado whitewater, but its Florida's best whitewater. Sadly, the springs are plagued by long lines, so ride early or late in the day.

RUNOFF RAPIDS   A tamer, shorter, one-person version of Teamboat Springs, these rapids are ridden in an inner tube. You careen down one of three flumes along the back of Mt. Gushmore—an easy, breezy, wet trip that puts you in the dark for a few seconds.

SNOW STORMERS   Blizzard Beach's answer to a slalom ski course, these three flumes take a switchback course down the back of Mt. Gushmore. Racing flags and markers zip by as you careen down on a mat.

SKI PATROL TRAINING CAMP Tin slides and T-bars and giant, floating "icebergs" that you can walk across—that's what you'll find at this summer camp gone water crazy. Designed for pre-teens and teens, it's perpetually swarmed with young bodies climbing, sliding and splashing down into clear blue water.

TIKE'S PEAK A teeny person's camp, with shallow pools, water toys, short and easy slides, and mini inner tubes, Tike's Peak is a real parent pleaser. No one over four feet tall is allowed in the pool.

Wide World of Sports Complex

Disney World has indeed fashioned a field of dreams with its mammoth-sized Wide World of Sports Complex. This is no backyard ball field. Facilities here can accommodate nearly three dozen amateur, pro, senior and scholastic sporting events from archery to tae kwon do.

Set on 200 acres, the complex features a 7500-seat ballpark, softball fields and a track-and-field stadium, not to mention all the courts: basketball, beach volleyball and tennis. Several professional sports teams will call the Complex home, including the Atlanta Braves, who use the place for spring training; and the Orlando Magic, who practice on one of the facility's many basketball courts.

Some of the past and present events include Globetrotter's basketball games, a professional football exhibition, national collegiate track and field meets and a men's professional beach volleyball tour. But this is an armchair quarterback's paradise as well, with plenty of seating to accommodate the accompanying throngs of screaming fans. After all that cheerleading, head on over to the Official All Star Cafe, a sport-themed family restaurant owned by Andre Agassi, Wayne Gretzky, Ken Griffey, Jr., Joe Montana, Shaquille O'Neal and Monica Seles.

Tickets are available through Ticketmaster outlets or at the door. Prices vary, depending on your seats and the event. For details about upcoming events, call Disney's Wide World of Sports Information Line at 407-939-1500.

ARRIVAL Take resort busses to Blizzard Beach and transfer for Wide World of Sports.

If you're driving, take Route 4 to Disney exit 25B (192 West). Go to first exit (World Drive). From World Drive, take first exit (Osceola Parkway). Turn right at first traffic light.

Downtown Disney

More than a quarter of a century after it first opened, Disney World has emerged not only as an entertainment mecca, but as virtually an independent city with its own restaurants, hotels and even its own zip code.

Now Disney World even has its very own downtown: Downtown Disney. Made up of the Marketplace, Pleasure Island and the fashionable West Side, Downtown Disney is a mammoth complex of 120 lagoon-side acres featuring shopping, eating, playing, entertainment and nightlife.

PLEASURE ISLAND   Pleasure Island is where you go to get wild—at night, anyway. Come 7 o'clock, it cranks with rib-rattling music, brilliant lights and a sea of people jammin' in the streets. A mod mix of painted metal, brick streets, neon signs and trendy dressers, Pleasure Island is Disney's hip zone, its outer edge. The place boasts eight nightclubs, three restaurants and nine shops.

One of the best things about Pleasure Island nightlife is that there's just as much happening outside as inside. Waiters sling drinks at curbside bars, and street vendors hawk outrageous gifts. Rock-and-roll bands and lithe dancers—wearing next to nothing—perform on outdoor stages. Here's where locals and tourists really mix—the high schoolers and grandparents and yuppies. And here's where nightly New Year's Eve street parties are held. Fireworks blast above the island, confetti fills the air and laser strobes sear the night sky, sending flying colors for miles around. For further information, see Chapter Eight.

Although there are no rules against it, Pleasure Island at night is no place for kids. Those 18 and older are allowed in all the clubs except Mannequins Dance Palace and BET Soundstage Club, but you must be 21 to drink. Clubs do permit those under 18 to enter if they are accompanied by an adult, but there is no discounted children's admission.

WEST SIDE   West Side is no doubt the trendiest thing to happen to Disney World since Planet Hollywood. Part of the 120 la-

LIFE IN THE FAST LANE

Until now, the Magic Kingdom parking lot has only seemed like a raceway. Now it's got the real thing. At the **Richard Petty Driving Experience**, located in the speedway in the center of the Magic Kingdom's parking lot, novice drivers get behind the wheel of two-passenger stock cars and burn up the track at speeds of up to 145 miles per hour. Driving suits and helmets are provided. All you need is a driver's license, a working knowledge of standard-transmission operation and a constitution of iron. While there are no fitness requirements, these cars have no doors; only 15-inch windows you must be agile enough to get in and out of. Drivers must be 18 and older (those ages 16 and 17 can ride as passengers, but must be accompanied by an adult). Prices vary by the number of laps. ~ 1-800-BE-PETTY.

goon-side acres that make up the whole Downtown Disney complex, the West Side features live music, entertainment, food, shopping and the largest movie complex (5390 seats) in Florida.

A few of the "hip and happening" hot spots include Bongos Cuban Cafe (owned by singing superstar Gloria Estefan), House of Blues (owned by Dan Aykroyd, Jim Belushi, John Goodman and members of Aerosmith) and the Wolfgang Puck Cafe. Bongos and House of Blues both have live entertainment. There's also a Virgin Megastore, the largest music and entertainment store in Florida, with outdoor stage, live deejay booths, 300 CD listening stations and 20 video viewing stations. New additions include Disney Quest, with a slew of virtual reality "rides," and Cirque du Soleil.

MARKETPLACE   I hope you're not going to Disney World just to shop. But for those who can't resist a quick spree, there's the Marketplace. Next to Pleasure Island, it's a fanciful place with wood-shingled buildings draped along a lake. Little speedboats zip across the water, and lyrical music floods the whole area.

Repeat Marketplace customers will immediately sense the changes brought by the creation of Downtown Disney. The 26 shops (some of them new, some of them old) still feature a slew of items from pricey toys and Christmas decor to surfing duds, but most have been revved up. One store, The World of Disney, houses an awe-inspiring collection of Disney paraphernalia. You can also be professionally photographed with Mickey or some of your other favorite characters.

Even if you're not a shopper, the market is a good place to relax. During midday when the theme parks are most crowded, it's quiet here (although the Rainforest Cafe seems to be constantly busy). You can window-shop, have a cocktail along the lake or rest on a waterfront bench.

To help you explore, pick up a map and directory at any shop.

BOATING, ANYONE?

No one should come to Florida without getting in a boat, and Disney World has plenty of 'em. Most cruise the 200-acre Seven Seas Lagoon (the one you see from the monorail) and the lovely 450-acre Bay Lake, which borders Fort Wilderness. Motorized pontoon boats (flotebotes) are ideal for families. They are easy to drive and have bench seats and a canopy for shady, relaxing sightseeing. Boats are rented by the half-hour or hour and are available at several locations. Fort Wilderness Marina and Downtown Disney Marketplace Marina have water sprites, flotebotes and pedalboats. Fort Wilderness also rents sailboats. In addition, several Disney resorts rent boats. ~ Information, 407-828-2204.

By car, it's easy to get to Downtown Disney. There's plenty of free **ARRIVAL** parking, but it's a hike from your car to the main gate. From Route 4, take the exit for Epcot and follow the signs for Downtown Disney. If you're arriving by Disney bus, allow at least 30 minutes from your Disney hotel. Good news for those driving to the West Side: Disney is preparing for the additional crowds brought by the new eateries by adding 7300 spaces on site, with 2500 nearby overflow need. Parking is free.

By taxi, contact Yellow Cab Taxi Service at 407-422-4455 to schedule a pick-up.

From the Magic Kingdom and Epcot: Take the monorail to the Ticket and Transportation Center, then transfer to a bus going directly to Pleasure Island, the West Side and the Disney Marketplace.

From Disney resorts: Take a bus directly to Pleasure Island, the West Side and the Marketplace.

From any other Disney World location: Take a Disney bus to the Ticket and Transportation Center, then transfer to the bus to Pleasure Island, the West Side and the Marketplace.

The whole Downtown Disney complex lines one long stretch of **GAME PLAN** Lake Buena Vista Boulevard, and though quite a hike from end to end, is fairly well laid out. Pick up a map at the ticket window or from any club, shop or restaurant.

The fee to amble Pleasure Island is $19.95 and it gets you into all the nightclubs, so you can come and go as you like. Shopping is available from 7 p.m. through 1 a.m., and nightclubs stay open until 2 a.m.

Across the bridge from Pleasure Island on the West Side there's no such overall cover, but some individual establishments (such as House of Blues) charge for live entertainment. Most of the West Side is open for lunch and dinner, the exception being the upstairs dining room at the Wolfgang Puck Café.

SEVEN

Universal Studios

With a cast of characters such as Mickey Mouse, Cinderella and Shamu the killer whale, it was only logical that Orlando would eventually go Hollywood. Disney–MGM Studios got the film rolling when it opened in 1989, but it was Universal Studios that a year later staged the savviest movie coup outside Tinsel Town.

In classic Hollywood style, the film giant scooped up a patch of Orlando pasture and sand pits and cast it with mythical characters and places and electrifying scenes from great American movies. Sprawled across these 110 acres is a $650-million movie mecca of imitation earthquakes, cartoon capers and time travels all reeled into one sizzling special-effects bonanza.

If Hollywood is one big fantasy, Universal Studios is one big set within the fantasy. For here virtually everything happens on a set. There's the seaside town straight from *Jaws*, the damp forests roamed by E.T., L.A.'s chic Rodeo Drive and the streets of San Francisco.

More than four times the size of Disney–MGM Studios, Universal Studios houses the largest motion picture and television studio outside Hollywood. It boasts 38 elaborate set streets, 9 sound stages, 31 rides, shows and other attractions, 17 eateries and 22 shops.

Technically, the park is split into six different theme or backlot areas, though to the eye they appear as a single fluid stroke of an artist's brush. The glass blocks, buff-colored stucco and gilded marble of Hollywood mix with the painted metal, circus-style canopies and grand palms at the adjacent World Expo. The Expo buildings rim a Pacific-blue lagoon shared by San Francisco's floating tin shacks and weathered wharfs. The City by the Bay spills into the New England seaside town of Amity, dotted with shuttered cottages and carnival vendors.

Sea scenes easily give way to a New York cityscape of brownstone walkups, Broadway billboards and high-toned shops. A nearby warehouse district, called Production Central, is a minimalist's vision of blank streets and slate-gray buildings with cinema billboards parked on the front. Around the corner is The Front

Lot, a parade of pastel-washed facades, art deco curves and arches and glass-front eateries that welcome visitors to Universal Studios.

Snazzier and slightly bigger than its Hollywood counterpart, Universal Studios owes at least some of its sparkle to moviemaking genius Steven Spielberg. As the studios' creative consultant, Spielberg helped craft rides fueled with action, shows offering insight into moviemaking, and a landscape shaded with surrealism. Universal owes most of its kid appeal to Nickelodeon, the children's television network that moved its headquarters here in 1990. All day every day, the network produces clever and zany kids' shows and offers peeks at its state-of-the-art facility.

Ever since Universal Studios opened, its rides have become notorious for their long lines. But anyone who has felt the mystique of *E.T.*, the wackiness of Yogi Bear, or the white-knuckle thrill of *Back to the Future* knows Universal's rides are worth the wait. And though the rides and shows are the main events here, it's the street sets that prove to be the true flights of fantasy. Like Hollywood footprints, they offer a nostalgic journey from one film to the next.

Universal's magical street sets put visitors behind and in front of the camera. Virtually every day, it's possible to witness a motion picture or television show being filmed somewhere in the park. It's also possible (though not as probable) to land a role as an extra or an audience guest. For most people, though, simply absorbing all the Hollywood imagery and nuances is truly intoxicating enough. There's a certain excitement, a childlike elation, in knowing that the line between illusion and reality runs very thin here indeed.

Nuts & Bolts

ARRIVAL

From area hotels: Most hotels provide shuttle service to Universal Studios, either on the hour or every two or three hours. Disney World hotels, naturally, don't offer this service. However, **Mears Transportation** (407-423-5566) will take you there from any Disney resort. Universal Studios is about ten miles northeast of Disney World.

By Car: Universal Studios is just east of the intersection of Route 4 and Florida's Turnpike. From Route 4, take exit 29 or exit 30B. The studios' main entrance is off Kirkman Road.

You'll pay a parking fee and be directed to a parking garage. From here, a people mover moving walkway will take you through CityWalk. Bear right towards the scenic main gate marked by an archway and a giant Universal Studios globe.

Because of its mammoth size, Universal Studios is rarely so crowded that it closes its doors. Still, getting there early can save several hours standing in line. It's best to arrive 30 minutes before the park's scheduled opening time so you can park your car, purchase tickets (if you don't already have them) and pick up maps and brochures. This will put you in perfect position to see Universal's most popular attractions as soon as the park opens.

GAME PLAN

In an ideal touring situation, you would leisurely enter Universal Studios and linger along the picturesque Front Lot, then stroll down Hollywood Boulevard. But such is not reality in the jungle of theme-park ride warfare. If you're going to avoid megalines, you have to get there early, hightail it past all the scenic stuff, and catch a few rides right away. Based on popular appeal and location of each attraction, I recommend riding in the following order:

(1) Back to the Future
(2) E.T. Adventure
(3) Jaws
(4) Jimmy Neutron's Nicktoon Blast

If you ride these four before 10:30 a.m., pat yourself on the back: You've just saved two to three hours standing in line. Now you can relax and explore the rest of Universal, including Terminator 2-3D where lines are shorter in the afternoon.

To save valuable time, decide where you want to eat lunch and be there by 11:30 a.m. Likewise, plan to eat dinner at 4:30 p.m. in order to miss the 5:30 dinner traffic jam. If you plan to dine at Lombard's Landing, Universal's most popular restaurant, make reservations early in the day either at Guest Services or the restaurant itself. Or you can call 407-363-8000 up to several days in advance. Monsters Café does not take reservations.

It's best to see all of one area (Hollywood, New York, etc.) before moving on to the next. The park is so big you won't want to backtrack, particularly with small kids and a stroller in tow.

GUEST SERVICES

Stroller and Wheelchair Rentals   Available just inside the main entrance on the left hand side.

Baby Services   Located at Guest Services, just inside the main entrance, and at First Aid, behind Louie's Italian Restaurant between New York and San Francisco. Diaper changing tables are available in every restroom.

Lockers   There are two sets of lockers: inside the park next to the exit area and outside the park next to the group entrance. Lockers cost $7 to $10 for day-long unlimited access.

Pets   Pets are not allowed in Universal Studios. However, for a daily fee of $10 you can board them at the kennels just outside the main entrance, next to the parking toll plaza.

Lost Children   Report lost children to Guest Services, located just inside the main entrance.

Package Pickup   Purchases made in the park can be sent to On Location to be picked up later in the day.

Shows and Showtimes   Check the *Preview* brochure/map you're given upon entering the park for up-to-date listings.

Lost & Found   Located at Guest Services.

Banking   Wachovia Bank, located just inside the main entrance, provides credit-card cash advances, traveler's-check services and currency exchange. You'll also find an ATM. Banking hours fluctuate seasonally and reflect the park's opening and closing times.

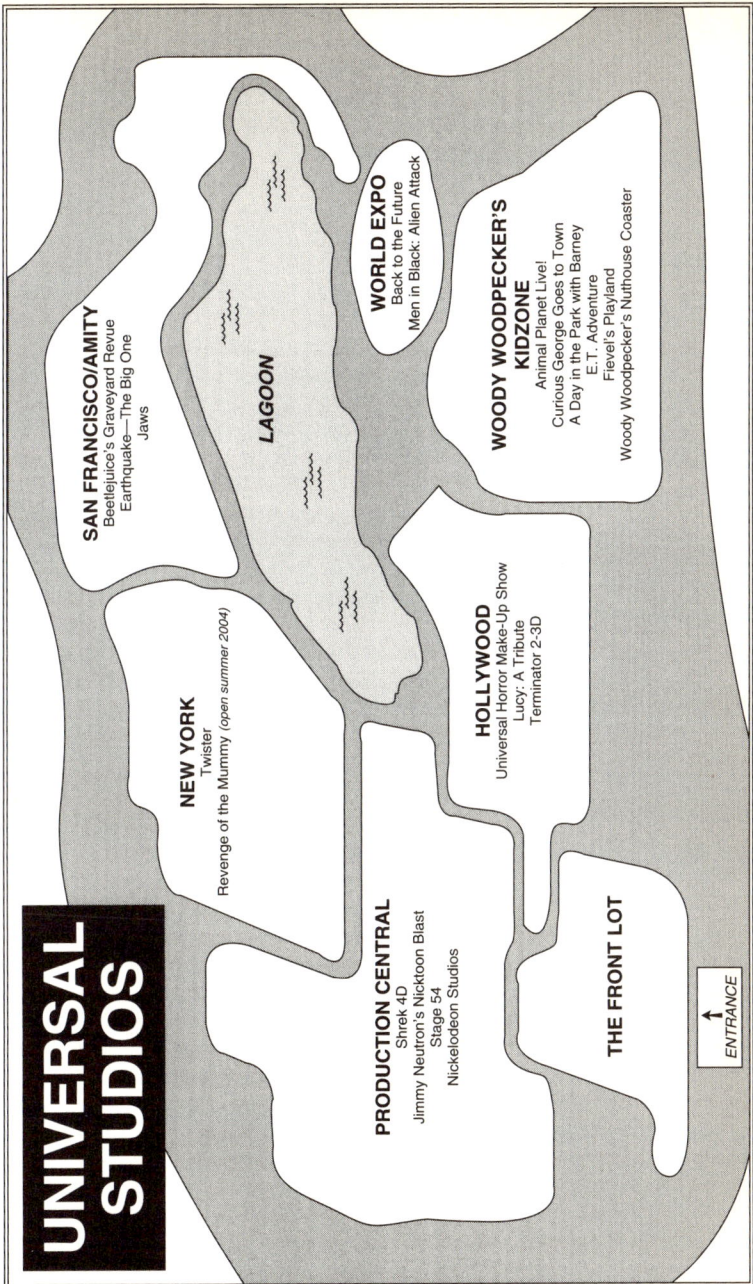

UNIVERSAL STUDIOS

PRODUCTION CENTRAL
Shrek 4D
Jimmy Neutron's Nicktoon Blast
Stage 54
Nickelodeon Studios

NEW YORK
Twister
Revenge of the Mummy *(open summer 2004)*

SAN FRANCISCO/AMITY
Beetlejuice's Graveyard Revue
Earthquake—The Big One
Jaws

LAGOON

WORLD EXPO
Back to the Future
Men in Black: Alien Attack

HOLLYWOOD
Universal Horror Make-Up Show
Lucy: A Tribute
Terminator 2-3D

WOODY WOODPECKER'S KIDZONE
Animal Planet Live!
Curious George Goes to Town
A Day in the Park with Barney
E.T. Adventure
Fievel's Playland
Woody Woodpecker's Nuthouse Coaster

THE FRONT LOT

↑
ENTRANCE

GETTING AROUND

By far the largest individual Florida theme park, Universal Studios sprawls. Even during low season when lines are minimal, it takes at least two days to see everything these 110 acres have to offer. Unlike Disney–MGM Studios, where two-thirds of the park is accessible to visitors only by guided tour, nearly all of Universal can be explored at leisure.

On a map, Universal Studios looks like a boxy letter C getting ready to take a gulp of water. The water is The Lagoon, and the C is made up of six different theme areas that gather around The Lagoon. At the bottom crook of the C is The Front Lot, punctuated by the palm-lined main entrance with its grand Universal Studios archway. The bottom of the C curves out into Hollywood and then the World Expo. Along the back of the C is Production Central, where vast buildings house movie and television production stages and rides. New York and San Francisco/Amity make up the top of the C.

It's a good idea to establish a meeting place in case your party gets split up. The best spot is in front of Mel's Drive-In, a flashy art deco eatery on a corner of Hollywood Boulevard in (where else?) Hollywood.

The Front Lot

What better way to dive into film fantasy than through rose-colored scenery? This small but sassy place offers a host of chrome and glass block, crimson balloon awnings, bleached gray buildings and ledges that snake across facades. Straddling a street corner, the Beverly Hills Boulangerie alfresco café tempts passersby with whiffs of espresso and fresh-baked

ERASING LINES

You have to love anything that speeds you through theme park lines. **Universal Express** does just that. Put your pass into the attraction kiosk, get your ticket with ride time, return within the designated window and wait no more than a few minutes to get on. Regular Express tickets are free, but limited to one every two hours. An extra $25 per park ticket buys you an Express Plus pass, good for one line-free ride on each of the applicable attractions; the benefit is no time restrictions and no worries about Express Passes running out (as they often do). Is it worth the money? If you're short on time, the answer is an absolute "Yes." On a day during which the line for Shrek ran as much as two hours, our Plus passes got us through five major attractions (including Shrek) in just a couple of hours. You can still get an Express Pass if you'd like to go on a ride a second time. To move extra fast (assuming money's no object), sign up for a VIP Tour, which, for $100 per person, nets you a personal guide who gets you front-of-line privileges on at least eight attractions.

croissants. At the nearby Fudge Shoppe, women in pinafores stir huge vats of gooey chocolate and advertise "variety platters" of the sweet stuff.

But behind all the niceties, The Front Lot is mostly business. There are no attractions here; rather, the place is a catch-all for visitor affairs such as stroller, wheelchair and locker rentals, lost and found, foreign-language interpretation and banking. Before you start touring, be sure to stop by Guest Services for brochures, maps and schedules of the day's entertainment and filmings.

Hollywood

From The Front Lot, Hollywood Boulevard angles off into dreamland. Here in this fantasy factory called Hollywood are star-studded sidewalks, hat-shaped shops, posters of cheeky movie stars and elaborate facades that seem styled by a magician. Soaring palm trees cast leafy shadows across the rosy pavement, and strollers step in tune to the street music.

Many Southern California trademarks have been dreamily reproduced here, including the Beaux Arts–style Beverly Wilshire Hotel and Schwab's soda fountain with its timeworn penny scale parked out front. From the legendary Sunset Strip there's Ciro's nightclub and the Garden of Allah, a tranquil cluster of red-tiled stucco buildings rimmed in silky soft grass and flowers in fat clay pots. Chic shops boast names such as Studio Styles, and the spaceship-shaped Mel's Drive-In boasts a slew of gleaming '50s "cruisin' " cars. All day long, family members take snapshots in front of these snazzy locales.

Of all Universal's street scenes, Hollywood's seem to evoke the most passion and intrigue. It's not unusual to hear comments such as "Is it really like this?" or "Take a long look—this is as close as *you'll* ever get to Hollywood!" Maybe it's the human psyche reveling in the ultimate world of make-believe. Or perhaps it's because everyone—regardless of age or background—wants a piece of the camera.

Unfortunately, the attractions in Hollywood are Universal's worst. My advice is to explore Hollywood's street sets, skip the duds and head over to the World Expo.

WHAT TO SEE & DO

Terminator 2-3D ★★★★ It's probably hard to imagine a *Terminator* flick that could be more of a white-knuckler than the original two films. Well, this is it: the ultimate Terminator experience. If the movies set your heart racing, this elaborate attraction will make the old pump go double time as you "ride" your way through this "virtual" experience.

Much of the action explodes from a film projected off of three 23-by-50-foot movie screens at the front of the theater. The 12-minute movie, shot just for the attraction, stars Arnold Schwarzenegger and other original cast members. With special effects that seem to burst from the screen, the film literally rocks you in your seat as it ping-pongs the whole audience from present-day Orlando to the year 2029 where Arnold and company wage war on Cyberdyne's sinister defense system.

Most amazing is the way stage actors seem to materialize in and out of the film. In one stunning moment, a live actor rides his motorcycle into the room, onto the stage and into the screen where his road ride continues seamlessly on footage.

Like other Universal attractions, Terminator 2-3D effectively perpetuates its theme from start to finish. The premise—that you've arrived at Cyberdyne's corporate headquarters for a classified defense presentation that goes awry—is carried out with characteristic panache. You know it's only a show, but it's hard to avoid trepidation as the ersatz demonstration unfolds.

> Each year, the Horror Make-Up Show uses about 365 straight-edge razors, 912 quarts of stage blood and 547 gallons of blood and guts (employing a secret recipe that mixes shrimp sauce, oatmeal and red dye).

Although not five-star from start to finish, Terminator 2-3D is a must-see. The finale alone is worth the whole shebang. Not for young kids.

TIPS: Terminator 2-3D is one of the first attractions you'll encounter as you enter the park, and is most crowded early in the day when waits of an hour or more are common. Try it out after 3 p.m.

Lucy: A Tribute ★★ Graceland it's not, but if your heart belongs to this red, white and blue-blooded American icon stop in at Lucy: A Tribute. Having done for the television sit-com what Elvis did for rock-and-roll, Lucille Ball earned the honor of being commemorated in true theme-park style and Universal Studios has done just that. This Lucy "museum" is filled with an extensive array of costumes, props and memorabilia, including fan letters from former presidents Hoover, Eisenhower and Nixon. The attraction also features home movies and slides of the Arnaz family, a scale model of the *I Love Lucy* sound stage and an interactive trivia game for those television wiseacres.

TIPS: If you don't love Lucy, chances are you'll find a lot more excitement rummaging through your own memorabilia in the far reaches of your bedroom closet.

Universal Horror Make-Up Show ★★ Guts and gore have always had a way with American filmgoers, so you'd expect this to be a hit attraction. Sadly, unless you're between 8 and 18 and love gross-outs, this show is less entertaining than a B horror flick. Presented in a comfortable theater and hosted by a zealous Universal employee, the show aims to imaginatively divulge the special effects in some of Hollywood's grisliest scenes. Instead, it offers a dull and disjointed series of failed shock-attempts: wrist slashings, bullet hits, torsoless heads and headless torsos. You learn how an actor's mouth became a roach motel in the movie *Creepshow*, how heads spun 360 degrees in *The Exorcist*, and how man became wolf in *An American Werewolf in London*. The best parts of the show are the classic clips from these movies and others such as *Gorillas in the Mist* and *The Fly*. And, though it all sounds rude and crude, most of the demonstrations are done in cornball fashion.

TIPS: Some preschoolers are frightened by the show's gory details, while older kids love this gross stuff. For infants, the cool, dark theater is a good place to take a quick snooze.

World Expo

This brilliant, bubbling place is a vision of vast metal buildings with candy-cane stripes, circus-style canopies, thick stands of palms and fat columns painted like barber's poles. Despite its moniker, the area's only real reference to a World's Fair Exposition is a strand of international flags and a food bazaar peddling Greek gyros alongside Asian egg rolls and German bratwurst. Most of the scenery here looks colorfully futuristic, though some sights are a study in contrasts. The broken-down Psycho House, for instance, broods atop a spooky hill right next to the flashy, guitar-shaped Hard Rock Cafe. At night, heavy metal music pours through the pitch-black house tainted by memories of Hollywood-brand murders.

WHAT TO SEE & DO

Back to the Future ★★★★★ This flight simulator–style ride is a super symphony of speed, fantasy, terror and mind-blowing special effects. When it's over, your throat aches because you've unwittingly screamed so long and hard. It's the kind of ride where 12-year-olds do high-fives at the end, then turn to Mom and announce: "We're going again!"

Based on the *Back to the Future* smash-hit trilogy, the four-minute journey hurls you through centuries at supersonic speed. The action begins in a briefing room where bug-eyed scientist Doc Brown tells guests that Biff (the movie's bully) has come back from the past. As a "time-travel volunteer," you must find him and send him back to 1955. Biff dares you, his big-oaf face filling a video screen and taunting: "What are you looking at, butt head!" Eight riders then climb into a fancy DeLorean Time Machine, which spews liquid-nitrogen fog that looks like ice on fire. (Before you hop into your DeLorean, notice the license plate: It reads "Outatime.") Your car eerily floats out of its garage, and suddenly you're enveloped by a room-size video screen that takes you on a brain-blasting visual trip: You tumble down waterfalls, soar off cliffs, ricochet around caverns and canyons, and get chomped and spit out by a growling *Tyrannosaurus rex*. In the meantime, you're getting bounced around the car and desperately trying to focus on the person next to you.

What Universal did here was take the state-of-the-art simulators used in Disney's Star Tours and Body Wars—and turn up the juice. The sounds, feelings and visuals are all more intense, almost like a fourth dimension. Much of this 4D realism is created with a 70mm film that's projected on seven-story "hemispherical" screens around each DeLorean. The ride's electrifying soundtrack comes from a "multichannel surround-sound" system, and the DeLorean's perfectly timed jolts are fueled by hydraulics. The Back to the Future building itself—a crazy crisscross of orange, aqua and mustard-color metal—is a real piece of work.

TIPS: Signs outside Back to the Future call it a "dynamically aggressive ride simulating aerial acrobatics," a convoluted way of saying this is a *very* rough ride! Children shorter than 40 inches are not allowed to ride. Not recommended for expectant mothers, people prone to nausea or claustrophobia, or those with bad backs. Take it from me: If you have even a slightly queasy stomach, think twice about riding.

Just about everyone who visits Universal wants to ride Back to the Future (even those masochists with queasy stomachs and bad backs). Given this fact, know that unless you ride *as soon as the park opens*, you'll face a wait of 45 minutes to (incredibly) two hours. In this writer's opinion, no ride no place is worth a two-hour stint in a boring line.

Men in Black: Alien Attack ★★★ Creepy crawlies are out to take over the world and it's your job to stop them. Modeled after the feature film of the same name, this life-sized arcade-style ride sends unwitting journeyers out in six-person vehicles to hunt down alien life forms. "Streets" are rife with multi-limbed beasts who jump out at you from all corners. With laser gun in hand, riders aim, shoot and score, racking up points for the number of aliens done away with.

This silly-but-fun ride is a lot less ominous than you might expect—a little bit edgier than the Buzz Lightyear ride at the Magic Kingdom. The scariest part: it spins a lot, meaning a post-lunch

WHAT SHOULD WE RIDE NEXT?

It's midday, and you've ridden Back to the Future, Jaws, E.T. and Nicktoon Blast. What next? To find out which attractions have the shortest (and longest) lines, check the information stations located throughout the park. The marquees list each Universal Studios attraction with its approximate waiting time and advice on when to see it. I found that several posted times underestimated the real waits by five to ten minutes, though in all fairness it's tough to keep up when line lengths can change drastically in a matter of seconds.

ride could get messy. That probably makes it extra appealing to kids—particularly boys. Be warned, however: there is a moment of darkness and loud sounds at the end that can be creepy to even the bravest small soldiers.

Tips: The ride is neatly nestled next to one of the other big lines in the park at the Back to the Future ride. Beeline for both of them first thing in the morning as they're bound to get more crowded as the day wears on.

It used to be that kids visiting Universal Studios had just an area to play in; now they get a whole zone.

Woody Woodpecker's KidZone

Woody Woodpecker's KidZone pays homage to the fact that kids are theme-park enthusiasts, too. Much of what's here is from the old setup: the purple dinosaur is still singing about how much he loves you ("A Day in the Park with Barney"), E.T.'s still trying to phone home ("E.T. Adventure") and Fievel's still looking around the New York drain system for his family ("Fievel's Playland").

But there's new material here, too. Welcome additions include a kid-sized coaster à la Woody Woodpecker ("Woody Woodpecker's Nuthouse Coaster") and an interactive play area ("Curious George Goes to Town") with bells, whistles and water to spare. Stop here first and you may never even make it to Amity.

WHAT TO SEE & DO

E.T. Adventure ★★★★ Steven Spielberg's celebrated and wildly successful film sets the scene for this airborne bicycle tour through misty redwood forests and to faraway planets. The story line closely follows the movie, with E.T. stranded on Earth three million light years from his beloved Green Planet. E.T. (actually his computer image) hops aboard your bicycle for a trip back home, where he must save his planet from ruin. City lights sparkle below as you pedal away from Earth and across showers of stars. On the Green Planet you encounter enchanted waters, rainbow colors, dancing baby E.T.s and plants that seem right from the pages of a fairy tale. No doubt the most endearing moment comes at the ride's end, when E.T. bids you goodbye by your first name!

Tips: E.T. gets my vote for having the best waiting area of any ride in the universe: a cool, dim forest where tree trunks are broader than cars and the air is scented with evergreen. As you inch toward the front of the line, a lifelike E.T. glows atop a knoll and speaks to you. Considering these surroundings, the typical 45-minute wait for this ride isn't so bad after all.

Animal Planet Live! ★★★ After all its success out in the wilds of cable television, it's fitting that the little channel that could is getting its due via this eponymously named show. There's no Steve Irving, but you'll be plenty entertained by the colorful assortment of critters Universal has assembled for the performance. Essentially, the new moniker marks a repackaging of the previous occupant of the theater, the now-defunct Animal Actors Show. Not that that's a bad thing. Animals of all shapes and sizes—particularly those looking cute, talented or even goofy as they muff their "lines" and make their trainers look like stooges—are guaranteed kid pleasers. Sure, the 20-minute show does have some slow moments, and it's not exactly high-brow humor, but my daughters belly-laughed all the way through—who could ask for more?

> Truly an elaborate special-effects feat, E.T. features 80 animated figures, 558 simulated trees and bushes and 306 dancing plants. The sprawling Earth city has 3340 miniature buildings, 1000 streetlights and 250 cars, while its galactic ceiling boasts 4400 stars.

TIPS: Staged in a big theater, this show rarely has long waits—arriving ten minutes before the show is usually plenty. If you see it between 10 a.m. and 4 p.m., you'll not only get a respite from the other attractions' long lines, but you'll get a nice breather as well.

Fievel's Playland ★★★ It's probably too much to hope for, but Fievel's Playland may be the only place you'll find where your young kids can be dropped off, let go and forgotten for a short while. That's because inside the mouse-size world of this attraction is an unrestricted play area where children have free run of giant props re-created from the two *American Tail* movies. The problem in coming here to relax is that you're certain to be intrigued by Tiger, the 16-foot "cinebotic" cat and archenemy of Fievel, who talks to all passersby with Dom Deluise's voice. You're also sure to be dragged to the "sardine-can sewer ride," a water slide excursion deeper into Fievel's world. So much for relaxing, but then you knew a rest was too good to be true.

TIPS: Not popular with children over the age of ten.

A Day in the Park with Barney ★★★ Universal Studios opened this family-themed attraction in honor of every preschooler's favorite purple dinosaur. This is an "edutaining" visit with the melodic reptile in a newly designed environment for kids and families.

Inside the Barney Theater, a theater-in-the-round holding only 350 people, special effects make the audience feel like the weather is magically changing and that day is quickly turning into night. Joined by his best friend, Baby Bop, and her big brother, BJ, Barney leads the throng through beloved chantalongs like "If You're Happy and You Know It" and "I Love You."

After the show, the audience funnels into Barney's Backyard, full of interactive delights like a velcro wall mural that children can rearrange, and rocks that emit musical tones and silly barnyard-animal noises when stepped on. Kids especially like exploring Barney's treehouse with its slides and tunnels.

TIPS: To avoid long lines, plan on being here when Universal opens.

Curious George Goes to Town ★★★★★ Judging by the name of this attraction, I thought it was going to be for kids—little kids. And it is. But that doesn't stop big kids—and their children—from going to town here as well.

The brightly colored miniature city looks right out of the pages of the H. A. Rey books. You can climb around both levels, and George himself is mischievously perched atop a fountain of water. Water, in fact, is the overriding theme here since virtually everything is designed to get you, well, drenched. Booby traps are everywhere (that old-time telephone looks so innocent!) and when the fire bell rings, watch out—we're talking waterfall here, folks. Out back is Universal's take on a ball pool—a roomful of about 13,000 foam balls that fire off (literally, since there are ball cannons available to guests) from every direction.

TIPS: There are but two pieces of advice I can give you for this riotous attraction: visit on a hot day and wear a bathing suit.

Woody Woodpecker's Nuthouse Coaster ★★★ They've watched older family members career around some of the park's daredevil rides; now kids have a coaster of their own. Climb aboard this pint-sized thrill ride and take a tour of Woody's factory of gadgets and gizmos. On a mere 800 feet of track with a top speed of 22 mph, this ride nevertheless takes a few sharp turns—tame next to some of the bigger guns, but a bit sharper than I expected. At only one minute and thirty seconds, it's so short most kids won't have time to get too bent out of shape.

TIPS: Though most definitely a kiddy coaster, the ride picks up a bit more speed than you might expect. That's not to say your budding coaster enthusiasts should forego it: just don't oversell the "it's a slow ride" approach, lest they be unpleasantly surprised.

San Francisco/Amity

In all of Universal Studios, no place is so inviting as San Francisco/Amity. These two towns converge along a rippling lagoon lined with boulders and dotted with sloops and soot-covered tugboats. This is a festive maritime place, with tin warehouses, street jugglers, ruddy brick buildings, carnival vendors, shingled cottages, banjo and trumpet players, and lighthouses all tossed into one vibrant, merry cultural collage.

It's tough to know just where San Francisco ends and Amity begins, though naturally each place maintains its own flavor. San Francisco has stone streets, wood-plank buildings, old gas pumps and D. Ghirardelli Co., the trademark brick chocolate factory near Fisherman's Wharf. Docks are piled with lobster traps and fish nets, and cable-car tracks cut through the middle of the street (though there's no car in sight). Details here are so precise that even the rusty "No Fishing" signs are written in Chinese.

Farther along the waterfront, Amity smells and looks like a carnival. This New England seaside village, meant to imitate the town victimized in *Jaws*, is a jumble of popcorn and ice cream vendors, street artists, Cape Cod–style homes and game stalls strung with stuffed animals. A suntanned man with a ponytail does "salty sketches," while a burly woman clutching a microphone will guess your age or weight. The big guy himself, a 24-foot great white shark with spiked teeth, dangles from a rack in the middle of town.

WHAT TO SEE & DO

Jaws ★★★★★ In the wake of Earthquake and other horror movie greats comes Jaws. Not the lackluster shark-o-matic you may have seen at Universal Studios in Los Angeles. No, this is the real thing. Well, almost. Spread over an awe-inspiring seven-and-a-half acres and featuring a five-million-gallon lagoon, this attraction is one of the most popular ever at Universal. Thrill seekers board one of eight tour boats that chug unsuspectingly around the quaint, ill-fated New England town of Amity. Suddenly terror erupts in the form of a 32-foot, three-ton killer great white moving at 20 feet per second toward your wallowing tour boat. Again and again the shark attacks, making for over five minutes of white-knuckled suspense culminating in explosions, walls of flames and the delicious scent of charred shark flesh.

TIPS: This ride is sure to be jam-packed, even into the evening hours. See it as early in the day as possible. Those people with a fear of water should think twice before riding.

Earthquake—The Big One ★★★★ The subway train is packed with people when the first tremor hits. Slowly, the mild earth twitch escalates to full-blown shaking so violent you can't get your grip. Lights blow and it's pitch black. The burning city above comes tumbling down as flower pots and chunks of roadway land near your train. A propane tanker slips through the crack in the earth and explodes, the heat warming your face. But the fire is instantly doused by a tidal wave that surges toward you. You're saying your "Hail Marys" when suddenly a man yells: Cut! Then—like a videotape being rewound—the whole scene strangely goes back to normal. Your subway train continues on, as if nothing happened.

Universal's masterful earth-quaking, stomach-shaking ride does register on the Richter Scale—at a sobering 8.3. Based on the movie *Earthquake* and narrated by Charlton Heston, the attraction offers a fascinating insider look into catastrophe filming. A pre-ride movie reveals how miniature sets, matte painting, blue screen and stunt actors can make something so fake seem so real. Universal hired special-effects ace John Dykstra to design the dramatic film

Stars on the Streets

What could be more exciting to a child than bumping into Fred Flintstone and Barney Rubble? The nutty buddies usually hang out at Universal Studios' main entrance, posing for photos and signing autographs. Other favorite cartoon characters show up, too, including Popeye, Olive Oyl, *MIB* agents, and Wilma Flintstone and her pal Betty Rubble.

Children should know that characters don't talk but communicate through body language. Also, they often seem larger in "real life" than on television, which can sometimes startle unprepared toddlers.

Larger than life at all times are the **street performers** that appear throughout the park. You'll spot amazing celebrity look-alikes of famous Universal entertainers, including the Marx Brothers and Lucy and Ricky Ricardo. Some celebrities have their own turf—look for Marilyn Monroe vamping it up along New York's Upper East Side or the Blues Brothers performing on Delancey Street—while others will surprise you just about anywhere.

For showtimes, pick up a schedule from Guest Services or any Universal Studios store.

sequence. Many props are the real McCoys, including the 20-ton subway train (purchased from the city of San Francisco) that holds 200 passengers and the falling roadway slab that tips: the scale at 45,000 pounds. Near the exit, a place called Amazing Pictures will put your photo on the cover of a well-known magazine.

TIPS: Not recommended for young children. Some older ones may be frightened by the special effects. Not recommended for those with a low fright threshold.

Beetlejuice's Graveyard Revue ★★★★ This revue is best described as a live version of the classic rock-and-roll creep song, "Monster Mash." The live performance is led by film and cartoon star Beetlejuice and features a cross section of the greater undead including Dracula, Wolfman, Frankenstein and his lovely bride. The monsters dance, sing and play through a medley of reggae, rock, soul and rhythm-and-blues hits while special effects light up the stage.

TIPS: This show is not frightening for kids unless they tremble at the sight of actors in monster make-up. For more atmosphere, come to a night show at this covered (but not indoor) theater.

New York

At Universal Studios, all that separates San Francisco from New York is 50 feet. In this short stroll, salty bay scenes give way to wall-to-wall brownstones, silvery brick streets, ornate theaters and roadside fruit boxes piled with the orangest oranges and reddest apples. A rusted barber pole punctuates a narrow alley lined with crinkled metal signs and filmy store windows crammed with cheap merchandise.

There's a certain charisma, a saucy veneer, about this place that emulates the East Coast's cultural dynamo. Billboards flash the latest on Broadway, and carved facades paint a swanky picture of the Upper East Side. Just outside Macy's, a Marilyn Monroe look-alike leans against a cab, her image reflecting across the glassy yellow hood. Wrapped in a clingy gold dress and sapphire feather boa, she aims her painted lips at passersby and coos demurely. A man in a zoot suit and spats stops in front of her, checks his gold pocket watch and continues down the street.

Some famous Big Apple addresses have been nostalgically duplicated, including Gramercy Park, a residential street of brownstones and the Queensboro Bridge. There's a Coney Island arcade, a faux thrift shop called Second Hand Rose and a real Italian restaurant named Louie's.

WHAT TO SEE & DO

Twister ★★★★★ Though the name—Twister—sounds like some kind of newfangled roller coaster, the attraction is actually a special effects show. It is, nevertheless, a "ride."

Following a bit of footage about twisters (hosted by Helen Hunt and Bill Paxton, stars of the film), guests are led along the remains of "Aunt Meg's" home before reaching the drive-in that was flattened in the film. Then the soundstage twister begins. Jet-engine-strength winds howl, water sprays, fire erupts; just when you think it couldn't get any more intense—boom—a flying cow.

TIPS: To say the least, Twister is loud and intense. Many adults—myself included—recoiled during the worst of the "storm." "What's that screaming?" I asked a Universal employee as I waited on line. "Oh, that's just the pre-show," he replied. Definitely not a place for skittish kids—or adults, for that matter.

▼ ▼ ▼ ▼ ▼ ▼ ▼ ▼ ▼ ▼ ▼ ▼
Production Central

Like a warehouse district that's been spit-shined, Production Central is a maze of mammoth, unadorned buildings laid out in neat rows. These are Universal's muscles, its production pad of sound stages, technical equipment, wardrobes and props.

One exception to this spartan setting is Nickelodeon Studios, the children's television network. The area is sprinkled with cardboard castles for picture taking and park benches shaped like hands making an okey-dokey sign.

Unlike San Francisco, New York or other theme areas, Production Central has no street sets. Instead, sights here are concentrated inside five attractions that delve into both new and fabled Hollywood productions.

Nickelodeon Studios **** This must be Universal's happiest place, where kids get to lose themselves in some of their favorite television programs. Everything seems like one big game, right down to the building—a post-modern design with yellow stairwells, red triangles, black squiggles and blue amoebas. Just outside the front door, Nickelodeon's trademark Green Slime spews out of showerheads. A sign explains that the slime, used on shows

WHAT TO SEE & DO

◆ ◆

TRICK PHOTOGRAPHY

If you've ever wanted to shoot some movie-style trick photography, here's your chance. Using miniature cardboard sets and distorted glass, you can make your subjects look like they're in the Hollywood hills or bustling Manhattan—or like the crew of a NASA shuttle. Here's what you do: Go to one of the three special-effects photo spots located in Hollywood, New York and San Francisco/Amity. Position your subjects underneath the cardboard set, put your camera on the adjacent metal stand, line up your lens with the distorted glass, and shoot! (If you get stuck, follow the directions on nearby panels.) For best results, shoot between 1 and 6 p.m.

like Double Dare 2000, is "purified" until "only the slimiest parts remain." Inside the building, guests get a tour of the world's only television network designed especially for kids. The majority of Nickelodeon's shows are shot here on two sound stages, so guests frequently get peeks of a taping. At the very least, you'll get to see the actual sets where some of your favorite shows take place.

The tour culminates (where else?) in a room filled with elated children and even-more-elated parents: the Nickelodeon Studios Game Lab. Kids (and some very good-natured parents) participate in all kinds of wacky games in which the luckiest kid of all might get a chance to actually get slimed.

The details don't stop at the featured attractions. If you visit the bathrooms outside Nickelodeon Studios, you'll find that they have green slime soap, Nickelodeon toilet paper and sound effects, like locomotives and jet planes, piped in.

If you're lucky enough to visit when a show is in production, you might be able to see a taping; check with the ticket booth on the way in for same-day tickets. To get information about the studios, call Nickelodeon's automated line. ~ 407-363-8586.

TIPS: Television tapings such as Slimetime Live are a hoot, but they'll take longer than you think. You'll also be expected to cheer and clap A LOT! It's a whole lot of fun, as long as you budget for time *and* enthusiasm.

Stage 54 ★★ It's always a kick to see some of the things that went into the making of a favorite movie. Visit this relatively new area and look for props and costumes from the Universal movie of the moment. Past exhibits have included *The Grinch* and *The Mummy*.

TIPS: A rarely crowded, quick-visit self-guided tour. Visit any time.

Shrek 4D ★★★★ My first look at the Shrek theater made me wonder what kind of tricks Universal had up its sleeve: the enormous seats looked wired for something diabolical. My daughter, only half in jest, kept looking on the side for the "eject" button. There wasn't one. But the fact that they called the auditorium Lord Farquaad's Torture Chamber didn't help, either. Nobody

COMING ATTRACTIONS

Scheduled to make its debut in summer 2004, **Revenge of the Mummy** promises to deliver an exciting blend of pyrotechnics, cutting-edge robotics and—always a crowd pleaser—roller coasters. Banking on the success of *Mummy* films past and present, Universal will subject thrillseekers to a wild ride through tombs, Egyptian sets, chambers and secret passageways. The experience from each car will vary, ensuring a different experience with each ride.

gets catapulted, but in keeping with the tradition of "4D," there's plenty of bumps and "flying" to involve everybody in the action. A few of the surprises may literally jolt you out of your seat.

The green one and his donkey pal have returned for this made-for-theme-park movie sequel in which the evil Lord Farquaad comes back from the dead to menace the fairytale world. Though the film (starring Mike Myers and the rest of the original cast) is the feature attraction, we especially enjoyed the pre-show in the lobby where the live host shows off Universal's brand of irreverent humor, including a few blatant (and hysterical) jabs at the theme park across town. The film that follows is great fun, if not quite the laugh-fest I'd hoped for. To be fair, though, *Shrek* the theatrical release (a personal favorite of mine) is a tough act to follow. Nevertheless, if you're a true ogre fan, this is a definite don't-miss.

TIPS: At press time, Shrek was the most popular ride in the park, with waits during peak time stretching into hours. Do yourself a favor and skip the standby line and use Express Passes instead. Make sure to get yours early in the day as Express Passes are limited and often "sell" out for this attraction. To guarantee line-free passage, spend the $25 at the park gate and buy an Express Plus.

ANOTHER TIP: My 12-year-old daughter's words to the wise: the attraction is dark, loud and bumpy. Though it's based on a kid's movie, parents with young children may want to think twice.

Jimmy Neutron's Nicktoon Blast ★★★ Halfway through this flight-simulator ride, my husband and I looked at each other in total confusion. Neither of us had any idea what was going on. We were vaguely aware of catapulting around "in" a rocket. But apart from the familiar presence of Spongebob, Angelica and a few other Nickelodeon personalities, we were lost.

No matter—the ride was a lot of fun, and the whole Jimmy Neutron phenomenon doesn't seem to be meant for us parents anyway ("Mo-mmm," chided a small passenger behind me to his mother, "can't you tell that guy's Ooblar?!"). The animated flick is really just a good excuse to strap everybody into the theater's moving seats and fly, soar and "crash" along with Jimmy. The effects are pretty convincing, and it was enjoyable, even if I didn't know what was going on.

TIPS: The ultra-kid-friendly subject matter and the large-scale theater (it's not a small pod, as in Back to the Future) make this a great introductory flight-simulator ride for kids.

ANOTHER TIP: Unique to Jimmy Neutron is the stationary front row, meaning motion-sensitive guests can still experience it. Those who prefer their cartoons a little less realistic should put in a request for such a seat with the attraction host.

EIGHT

Universal Islands of Adventure

Up until Universal Orlando opened its second theme park, the King Kong of Central Florida attractions was merely a day-trip on your average week-long itinerary.

With Islands of Adventure, Universal became a bonafide vacation. The unveiling of this whiz-bang theme park, in fact, marked a reinvention of the Florida movie-making mecca from a pitstop into a self-contained destination. Now collectively known as Universal Orlando, the place suddenly became one-stop shopping for theme parks (two), lodging (three ultra-deluxe hotels) and a boatload of themed restaurants (NBA City and Jimmy Buffet's Margaritaville to name two)—not to mention bigger competition for you-know-who.

That this second Universal park is about unapologetic thrills (as opposed to movie illusion) becomes completely apparent the moment you enter. Hunks of colorful steel have been artfully bent into the manna of the roller-coaster-enthusiast diet, namely gravity defying loops, corkscrew spirals and nearly vertical dives. The theme-park soundtrack might well be described as a duet of piped in music and happily terrified shrieks. If the motto of the original Universal is to "ride the movies," the credo here seems to be simply just to ride.

Concocting the landscape took the wizardry of some mega-geniuses (Steven Spielberg was named as a consultant) who actually had to design the technology to make it all run. It must have been some pretty imaginative engineers who stayed up nights to come up with this list of theme-park "firsts" including a rollercoaster that catapults *up*; a flume ride that goes below water level; and a dual-track roller-coaster that careens so close together (within 12 inches according to park spin) that riders with a free hand may be penning (or at least mentally concocting) their last will and testament.

While "state-of-the-art" in this age of instantly obsolescent technology is only momentarily descriptive (no doubt already passe by the time this makes it to print), all that innovation nevertheless makes Islands of Adventure a blast—literally, since you'll spend a good portion of your time here soaring up or catapulting down some death-defying cliff or other.

Not that you have to be Evel Kneivel to have fun here. Colorful landscapes from mythology, cartoons and Sunday funnies can engage the mere spectator, and the most faint-hearted can at least enjoy a turn on the carousel or a seat in a stunt show. And for pure humor quotient, you can't beat the sight of comrades exiting a thrill ride, their faces locked in the smile/grimace of someone who's just experienced zero G.

There are five islands here (six if you count Port of Entry)—Seuss Landing, The Lost Continent, Toon Lagoon, Jurassic Park and Marvel Super Hero Island—encompassing about 18 shows and rides. Unlike the flowing decor of Universal Studios, each section here is independent enough to be, well, an island. Designers took a page from their movie-magic counterparts, creating scenic backdrops that tell a story, involving visitors just by their presence. Among the ruins of the Lost Continent, you'll feel as if you're in a forgotten city. Even music has been tailored, with original scores (such as the notes by John Williams for the *Jurassic* films) written for all. Apart from setting the mood, the differentiation helps navigate, since there's absolutely no mistaking the change in scenery when you cross from, say, the comic-strip goofiness of Toon Lagoon into the playfully ominous Jurassic Park.

That little family members can get in on the act here is a big plus. Universal wisely realized that families are doing theme parks en masse these days and designed accordingly. Nearly every Island has something that's little-kid appropriate—more so now that they've added a small roller coaster and a spinning ride. Better yet, most of the attractions are the kind mom and dad can actually enjoy instead of just tolerate. No wimpy mini-choo-choo trains here. Instead, there's a dino discovery center where you can watch the hatching of a "baby raptor," and a climbing sculpture that beats all. The nostalgia-factor of Seuss Landing goes a long way to entertaining the grownups in your party. Even those who wouldn't be caught dead on a typical carousel horse can't help but be endeared of the creatures on the Caro-Seuss-el.

Still, extreme thrills are the hallmark, the place where Universal really struts its stuff. Most rides take guests to the limits. That goes double for the water rides, which all but submerge you during the experience. Your best bet is to visit in clothes you won't mind getting wet. Better yet, wear a bathing suit (at least in summer) and give in to the inevitable.

Cowabunga.

Nuts & Bolts

ARRIVAL

From Portofino Bay Hotel: Take buses or the water shuttle directly to the theme parks.

From area hotels: Most hotels provide shuttle service to Universal Orlando, either on the hour or every two or three hours. Disney World hotels, naturally, don't offer this service. However, Mears Transportation (407-423-5566) will take you from any Disney resort to Universal Orlando, which is about ten miles northeast of Disney World.

By Car: Islands of Adventure is just east of the intersection of Route 4 and Florida's Turnpike. From Route 4, take exit 29 or exit 30B. The park's main entrance is off Kirkman Road.

You'll pay a parking fee and be directed to a space in the studios' immense parking lot. From here, a moving walkway will carry you toward the main gate. It is a long way, however, since you'll have to go through CityWalk before you get to the main gate.

GAME PLAN Though it's roughly the same size as its sibling, Universal Studios, Islands of Adventure doesn't feel quite as unwieldy. With Islands laid out in a symmetrical ring, there's at least a bit of rhyme and reason to the plot plan.

Still, there's a lot of area to cover—and a lot of lines to wait on.

Doing it all even on a line-free visit (an as-yet unfulfilled theme-park fantasy of mine) would be exhausting, too exhausting to really be fun. To best enjoy the park, you'll want at least two days. Otherwise, you can almost count on leaving at least some of the attractions for a return visit.

Early birds will want to start with at least one of the flagship rides. The Amazing Adventures of Spider-Man isn't the first one you'll come to (that would be the Hulk Coaster), but with arguably the longest line in the park, one that only gets longer as the day wears on, starting here will give you the biggest advantage. In addition to these two attractions, other flagship rides include Dueling Dragons, Dudley Do-Right's Ripsaw Falls, Popeye & Bluto's Bilge-Rat Barges and the Jurassic Park River Adventure.

You could island-hop from thrill ride to thrill ride. But the downside of this approach is that you'll miss a lot and log a lot of foot miles backtracking later. Also, think carefully before launching on the water rides first thing. Sure, you may beat the lines this way. But you'll have to weigh that against the near certainty that you'll spend the day splashing around in soaking (and I do mean soaking!) wet clothes.

Whatever your approach, do leave time for a meal that's more than a burger on the run. Islands of Adventure has the unique distinction of being one of the few (if only) theme parks where not-your-run-of-the-mill restaurant fare is the kind you'll actually want to sit down for.

GUEST SERVICES **Stroller and Wheelchair Rentals** Available just inside the main entrance on the left side.

Baby Services Located at Guest Services inside the main entrance, to the right.

Lockers All-day lockers are available at the front of the park, $7 to $10 per day. Short-term lockers at the foot of the Hulk and Dueling Dragon coasters allow you to store loose items while you ride; the first 45 to 90 minutes are free, then you'll have to pay $2 per hour.

UNIVERSAL ISLANDS OF ADVENTURE

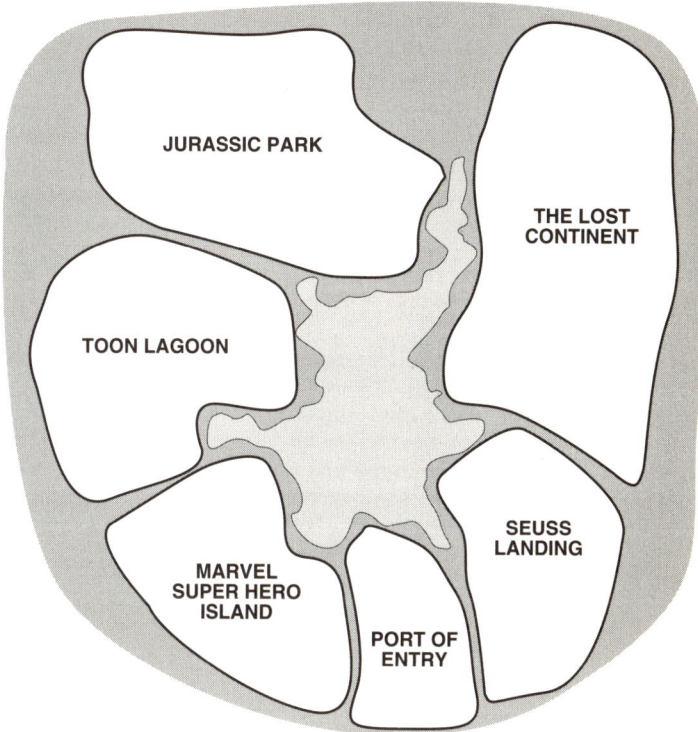

JURASSIC PARK

THE LOST CONTINENT

TOON LAGOON

SEUSS LANDING

MARVEL SUPER HERO ISLAND

PORT OF ENTRY

↑
ENTRANCE

MARVEL SUPER HERO ISLAND
The Amazing Adventures of Spider-Man
Doctor Doom's Fearfall
The Incredible Hulk Coaster
Stormforce Accelatron

TOON LAGOON
Dudley Do-Right's Ripsaw Falls
Me Ship, The Olive
Popeye & Bluto's Bilge-Rat Barges

JURASSIC PARK
Camp Jurassic
Jurassic Park Discovery Center
Jurassic Park River Adventure
Pteranodon Flyers
Triceratops Encounter

THE LOST CONTINENT
Dueling Dragons
The Eighth Voyage of Sindbad
Poseidon's Fury
Flying Unicorn

SEUSS LANDING
Caro-Seuss-el
The Cat in the Hat
If I Ran the Zoo
One Fish Two Fish Red Fish Blue Fish

Pets   Pets are not allowed in Islands of Adventure. However, for a daily fee of $10 per pet, you can board them at the kennels next to the parking toll plaza.

Lost Children   Report lost children to Guest Services, located just inside the main entrance.

Package Pickup   Purchases made in the park can be sent to Silk Road Clothiers to be picked up at the end of the day.

Shows and Showtimes   Check the Preview brochure/map you're given upon entering the park for up-to-date listings.

Lost & Found   Located at Guest Services.

Banking   Wachovia Bank, located just outside the main gate to Universal Studios, provides credit-card cash advances, traveler's-check services and currency exchange. You'll also find an ATM outside the gate at Islands of Adventure. Banking hours fluctuate seasonally and reflect the park's opening and closing times.

GETTING AROUND   In addition to being technologically advanced, Islands of Adventure has to be one of the easiest theme parks to navigate. The lakeside landing at the Port of Entry gives you a clear vista of the entire landscape. This makes it easy to not only get your bearings, but also to plot your visit strategy.

The islands are arranged in a circle around the lake: turn right from Port of Entry to reach first Seuss Landing and then the Lost Continent; turn left for Marvel Super Hero Island and then Toon Lagoon. Jurassic Park is farthest from the entrance (across the lake, directly opposite Port of Entry), meaning you can travel the same distance in either direction to reach it.

The mazes within each island can be a little trickier. If you get lost, heading away from the lake should bring you back to the main drag. Still, in a place this big it's not hard for groups to get separated. Make sure to designate a meeting spot; the Guest Services window inside the front gate is always a dependable place for regrouping.

LOCK, STOCK AND STORE IT

The average theme park Lost & Found is a storeroom of articles cast off during thrill rides—hats, keys, even video cameras—they're all here. While some theme park lockers are too out of the way to make them useful, Universal has thoughtfully placed short-term use lockers at the entrance of some of the wilder rides such as Hulk Coaster and Dueling Dragons. They're free for the first 45 to 90 minutes (they're meant to be used only when you're riding). So stow your stuff (hats, sunglasses and anything that might catapult off mid-scream) and ride with the confidence of someone who knows she will have car keys at the end of the day.

Any good adventure has to have a place to start. At Islands of Adventure, Port of Entry is the place, the spot to get your gear (film, suntan lotion, water) on the way in, and of

Port of Entry

course to stock up on those all-important, last-minute souvenirs on the way out.

Designers sent an adventurous prop man all over the world to gather paraphernalia for the exotic land. Apart from his mementos, the place is decked out like a faraway marketplace with adobe-like walls and canopied vendor stands. The well-traveled look is furthered by the trash bins designed à la war-torn travel trunks. And check out the stores here—more than just your average theme park stuff—you'll find coffees, international food fixings and exotic spices. Stow your superfluous gear in the lockers marked "Storage" and rent alternate modes of transportation. In addition to providing wheelchairs and strollers, the sign at Reliable Rentals says its provides transport by dogsled, submersible and velocipede. Alas, the last three have been permanently hired.

Sure, you could spend the day living on the edge of those hold-on-to-your-shorts rides. But for those who simply would not, could not, there is Seuss Landing.

Seuss Landing

This imaginative realization of the Seuss legacy, fashioned with the blessing of Theodor Geisel's widow, looks just like the pages of the famed Doctor's books. Loopy, off-kilter buildings (there doesn't seem to be a square edge in sight here) form the skyline, curled lampposts light the street and green stars (the Sneetches' perhaps?) punctuate the colorful walkways. The top-off—a giant Cat in the Hat chapeau. Rain or shine, you can count on the mischievous feline to make guest appearances here. The Grinch, Horton, the "Things" and Sam I Am visit as well; you can also grab a plate of Sam's delicacy at the Green Eggs and Ham Café.

The Cat In The Hat ★★ If you have young children, you'll probably find yourself reciting verbatim lines from the book ("The Sun did not shine, it was too wet to play . . .") as you meander through this realization of the classic book. Under a familiar big top—a tall, sagging red and white hat just like the one you-know-who wears—travelers *en couch* (a six-passenger couch-mobile, really) roll through the living pages of this Dr. Seuss classic while the cat and company cause bedlam all around. Characters literally spring to life, with animatronic Things (that would be Thing 1 and Thing 2) and the sourpuss fish popping up intermittently and a hundred or so effects appearing from all sides.

WHAT TO SEE & DO

TIPS: Not a bad ride, really, but truly made for little ones. Kids will love it, adults will merely tolerate it.

ANOTHER NOTE: One surprise was the amount of twirling action throughout. If spinning makes anyone in your party nauseous, skip it.

One Fish Two Fish Red Fish Blue Fish ★★★★ Leave it to the folks at Universal to install a little diabolical mischief into what might otherwise have been a pretty ordinary ride. Riders board red, yellow or blue "flying" fish-planes that look just like the ones in the books (except for the fact that they fly). Fishy vehicles circle around in the air, each one equipped with levers for controlling up and down motion. The catch: You have to raise and lower your fish in accordance with the rhyme playing overhead, or risk being doused by squirters mounted on encircling 18-foot posts. In the words of the sign here: "Yes some are red and some are blue, some are wet and so are you!"

TIPS: Though it looks like a little-kid ride, you'll see lots of big kids (and their children) riding this one and having a ball. The squirters really do make the difference between ho-hum and hysterical. Do prepare little ones in advance for the strong possibility of getting wet—particularly if you're challenged in the hand-eye coordination department.

Caro-Seuss-el ★★★ You wouldn't expect an ordinary carousel here, would you? Universal's take on this theme-park standard is utterly adorable, with seven Seussian characters (hoofing in for carousel horses) circling around under a lopsided pink canopy. The more recognizable of the mounts include elephant-birds from *Horton Hatches the Egg*, and twin camels from *One Fish Two Fish Red Fish Blue Fish*. Other ride-on characters are of the floppy, Seussian cute-but-unrecognizable breed (they all look like some kind of dog/bear to me), but you'll know them instantly as the Doctor's. Apart from the kick of riding, you'll get to work a bunch of gizmos that work eyes, heads and other vehicle contraptions.

TIPS: All the characters have different gizmos. Some blink their eyes; others move their heads. Scope out the crew of "horses" and what they do in advance if you care.

If I Ran the Zoo ★★★ From the pages of the eponymous book, If I Ran the Zoo tells the story of Gerald McGrew's idea of the perfect animal farm. The interactive play place is a collection of gizmos you can tweak, push and step on, each pretty much guaranteed to make little ones giggle. A stair climber makes a charming "thhp" sound that's sure to be a hit; pump hard enough, and you'll be rewarded with a surprise. There are caves to climb through, a kooky doorbell to ring and a climb-on caterpillar. This is still Islands of Adventure, however, so look for plenty of opportunities to get wet, including a couple of fountain areas, and a Scraggle Foot Mulligatawny with a cold (watch out when he sneezes).

Tips: This self-guided attraction is rarely crowded, but you might want to save it for later in the day. Little ones who spend time here have a tendency to come out very wet.

Thatched roofs and flaming lanterns indicate your arrival into another era. In the Lost Continent, buildings look out of some Arthurian Leg

The Lost Continent

end, with decaying pavement, royal banners hanging from golden posts, and the sounds of Celtic music intermingling with the fragrant aroma of incense.

Universal worked overtime infusing its forgotten island with trappings of mythology. The old-time marketplace features canopied tents sheltering palm readers and purveyors of mystic arts. Broken statues are strewn about (the enormous remaining arm of Poseidon reminded me of the broken Statue of Liberty in the last scene of *Planet of the Apes*) and carefully crumbling buildings look like they've weathered at least a few millennia worth of elements. Look for the camouflaged image of Merlin embedded in the enormous Enchanted Oak tree; he's particularly vivid at night.

Poseidon's Fury ★★★ An archeological dig has gone miserably awry. Thanks to a bumbling guide, the evil "Dark One" has been reawakened, trapping your group of unwitting tourists in an underground cavern about to be flooded. Thankfully, Greek God Poseidon is there to smooth the way. A godly battle unfolds in an impressive spectacle of film, flame and live special effects. At one point, travelers must journey through a 42-foot tunnel encircled by 17,500 gallons of churning, gravity-defying water. The climax of the event includes fireballs, water explosions and a shroud of darkness.

WHAT TO SEE & DO

Involvement in the presentation begins the moment you get in line. Queues weave through a well-created palace where stone walls feel appropriately dank, and dimly glowing sconce lights recreate the flickering of candles. How completely involved you become may well depend on where you stand during the show;

FOUNTAIN OF KNOWLEDGE

Some fountains just dispense water—others, at least if you're at a theme park, dispense advice. Check out the sage inhabiting the fountain in front of the Eighth Voyage of Sindbad. Ask it anything, and it will answer—often with attitude. But beware: the wisecracking water vessel can not only talk back, it can squirt back, too—with a vengeance!

those standing in the front rows near the water bursts are likely to get very, shall we say, involved.

TIPS: While a lot of fun, this attraction leans toward the long side; from queue to end, you'll be standing for at least 30 minutes. Make sure to embark on this one when you're awake and well fed enough to not mind the walk.

ANOTHER NOTE: Poseidon's Fury is a fairly dramatic presentation. Loud sounds and darkness may make this one inappropriate for some young children.

The Eighth Voyage of Sindbad ★★★ After adventuring across the seven seas, Sindbad has come back once more, ostensibly for adventure number eight. It seems Sindbad's girlfriend, Amoura, is in the clutches of the nasty Queen Miseria. In this 17-minute stunt show, the legendary traveler dodges fire and other calamitous forces of nature, not to mention boatloads of bad guys, in order to save her.

TIPS: In typical stunt-show fashion, Sindbad is loud. Your view in the enormous, 1700-seat stadium will be unobstructed no matter where you sit, but skittish little ones may appreciate a seat set back a bit from the roaring flames and thundering effects.

Dueling Dragons ★★★★★ The sense of foreboding emerges the moment you approach this ride. Or as my husband so accurately surmised when we surveyed the intertwined mazes of twisted metal, "This is no ordinary roller coaster." Terrifying and heart-stopping, this roller coaster is also a ton of fun—one you absolutely don't want to miss.

Riders are strapped into ride cars inverted-style, meaning your upper body is harnessed but your feet are left to dangle. The crawl up that first 125-foot peak is excruciating as you wait for the ensuing 60-mph plummet.

Half the zing of the inverted ride is the disorientation. With loops and turns galore, you'll rarely be able to tell whether you're right-side up or upside down. But Dueling Dragons has an added twist, namely a second car of victims . . . er, riders, appearing to

◆◆

FRONT ROW SEATS

Universal has very wisely done away with the "play-the-odds" method of getting those coveted head-of-the-car roller coaster seats by designating separate lines for the front row. The wait may take a bit longer this way, but if you're a real thrill rider, the rewards will be worth it. This goes double for Dragons, where the unobstructed vantage point will enable you to fully appreciate the near misses with the other car—that is, if you dare.

careen directly at you for a head-on collision. Only at the last second do cars veer off in different directions, leaving all on board to ponder whatever "If I survive this" deal they just made with the Almighty. In case you wonder exactly what "near miss" is, the folks at Universal tell us that some of these in-ride encounters come within 12 inches of each other.

Universal put immense effort into creating a story behind this attraction, namely the feud between two dragons (one breathes fire, the other ice) dueling for supremacy. At one point, you'll have to choose your path based on whether you prefer your demise by fire or frost. The queue takes you through an enchanted forest where elaborate props and strewn "bodies" reveal the fate of those who have traveled before. While all the hoopla is impressive, it is ultimately lost in the spectacle that is the ride itself.

TIPS: My sheltered, inside seat kept me mercifully unaware of the near collisions outside. However, the truly brave may want to opt for outside or front-row seats, both of which have the best, if you'll pardon the expression, impact.

ANOTHER NOTE: Those who fear queasiness on this ride may be in for a surprise. Although I had been warned that inverted coasters can sometimes be nauseating, I experienced nothing but exhilaration. Nevertheless, ride this one *before* you eat.

Flying Unicorn ★★ There's no question that Universal set new standards with its selection of wild thrill rides. But for kids (and adults) who regard the Dueling Dragon coaster as torture of mythical proportions, there is the Flying Unicorn. Riding behind a fully-armored unicorn, riders happily experience the mini thrills of this mini-thrill ride. In the tradition of the park, the ride has a little more edge than your typical kiddie ride. Not that that's a bad thing. You'll just want to make sure the kids are prepared.

TIPS: The ride is super short—maybe a minute long. That, however, means the lines run fairly swiftly so don't be intimidated by a long line.

The notes of John Williams' dramatic movie score play as you enter the immense gateway to this prehistoric Island.

Jurassic Park

If one kind of fantasy world involves princesses and fairies, this prehistoric land is the other—an imaginative creation based on the movie of the same name, and the stuff of every dino lover's dreams.

Those who have been to Universal's theme park in California—where the original Jurassic Park River Adventure was built—might be willing to write this off as just a "Been there, done that" on the menu of attractions. But where California's Jurassic Park is but one ride, Florida's version is a whole island. "Ancient" stone pathways bear the remains of eons gone by, "pteranadons" fly overhead, and overgrown greenery makes you feel lilliputian in this prehistoric world. You'll hear the voices of menacing dinos coming from every direction (thanks to an effective soundtrack). But don't worry: the carnivores are safely caged behind "electric fences."

WHAT TO SEE & DO

Jurassic Park River Adventure ★★★★ It's a typical day in your average dinosaur preserve and you're invited to go for a tour. Boats cruise lazily along while you scope out some beloved favorites in the vegetarian dinosaur world. But something goes wrong and suddenly you're drifting along helplessly amid the dreaded meat eaters.

All of this dramatic setup is just an excuse to catapult you down a heart-stopping plummet over an 85-foot fall (for anyone who's interested, that's about 30 feet longer than what you experienced on Disney's Splash Mountain). All along, dinosaurs snatch at and drool on you, culminating with a big, toothy beast who lashes out right before you tumble down. The fact that you know it's coming only makes your heart pound harder as you approach the plummet.

TIPS: Rumor has it that Universal toned down the soak-factor after riders in California came out completely drenched. Still, you're going to get wet. To minimize the damage, try to find a seat in the back on the right-hand side.

Triceratops Encounter ★★ Jurassic Park has a genuine triceratops and you're about to meet him. After a stroll through the laboratories of resident paleontologists, visitors are led into one of three pens to visit with these gentle giants.

Universal definitely scores points here for realism. The animatronic behemoths look remarkably authentic, even if they do seem a little like rhinos in dino clothing. The nose runs, the head moves and the eyes blink and seem to look right at you. The "vets" even coddle these creatures as if they were the real thing.

Recently, the wise theme-park-powers-that-be altered the attraction from a "show" into a constant-flowing walk-through. That's good news because while there is a moment of awe at the initial sighting, the novelty wears off pretty quickly. Apart from demonstrating various bodily functions that toddlers are bound to find endlessly amusing (I'll let you imagine what we're talking about), the triceratops doesn't really do much. Vets encourage you (beg you, actually) to ask questions about eating and sleeping habits. But it all feels kind of contrived when you know "sleep" is a function achieved with the flick of an "off" switch.

TIPS: The new attraction format means lines move fairly quickly. Still, the best times of day to visit remain either early morning or late in the day.

Pteranodon Flyers ★ With the wings of a bird and the face of a dino, this flying contraption is sure to call to every kid who sees it. Flyers sit two to a bird, gliding high up on a slow lap around the outskirts of Camp Jurassic below.

The Flyers create a nice effect in the prehistoric land, as if humongous birds were actually circling overhead. But spectators get the better end of the deal. Not that it's a bad ride. But you won't get a whole lot of time to enjoy it—the sum total from takeoff to landing is a whopping 80 seconds.

TIPS: Veterans of Disney World will recognize this as Universal's version of Dumbo. The brief ride attracts some of the longest lines in the park (the day I visited saw short lines virtually everywhere except here where the wait was a constant 45 minutes) and will be an absolute must-do on every kids' list. My advice? Try and hit it as early as you can. Otherwise, simply accept the inevitable.

Camp Jurassic ★★★ There's no doubt about it—this "research-camp"-cum-climbing-maze is about the best play sculpture ever invented. Need proof? I came here without my kids and I still had a ball (think of me what you will).

Rustic structures of wood and rope crisscross the camp with bridges, nets, treehouses and caves. There's no exact area measure, but stacks of places to explore seem to go on forever. Just when you think you've found the end, there's a whole new avenue to consider. Adventurous kids who reach the top will be rewarded with a hideout they'll wish they could have at home. Gadgetry includes some dino prints (step on them and hear the corresponding dino roar) and some mounted viewers to let you scope out activity below. Spooky caves are equipped with "amber" and what would an Islands of Adventure attraction be without a couple of water cannons to douse your friends? Just watch out for the "electrified" fences.

SAY CHEESE

A picture's worth a thousand words—or at least two or three. Ingenious Toon Lagoon photo opportunities let you stand beneath a bunch of different dialogue bubbles and show what's on your mind. Another favorite picture spot is behind mammoth mutt Marmaduke. Pose by reaching up and grabbing the dog's tail, then turn the developed photo sideways; you'll look like you're careening in Marmaduke's wake. For the full effect, make sure to flail those arms and legs and grimace accordingly.

TIPS: The good news is your kids will love it here; the bad news is you'll have to follow them. If you have older kids, this might be a good place to put those walkie talkies into action. The place is large and there's more than one way to get in and out (I counted at least two). To keep an eye on your clan, you'll either have to brave the maze yourself or station a grownup by each exit.

Jurassic Park Discovery Center ★★★★ The last time I visited this truly inspired attraction, I got to witness a reversal of a theme as a parent tugged a rapt child's arm and whined, "Can we go yet?"

Once you bring kids to this fantastical "education" universe, expect to stay a while. Where else can you see a raptor nursery? Incubators here are full of future dinosaurs, with raptor eggs "hatching" regularly. The births are utterly realistic—you'll swear there's a little raptor in there just waiting to spit acid in your face (cute little guys, aren't they?).

Fans of the original Steven Spielberg epic will recognize the setting as a twin of the film's ill-fated welcome center. There's no peril here, just lots of cool activities such as a chance to look through special viewers to experience infrared dino vision. If you really want to live on the edge, you can splice your DNA with a dinosaur's (okay, not really—but it's a great gimmick) and see what kind of prehistoric creature you can create.

TIPS: Raptor hatchings are not on a schedule, but they're worth seeing if you can. If you're really determined, you might want to check back while in Jurassic Park to see if the blessed event is near.

Toon Lagoon You simply have to love a place that heralds Wimpy Burgers and Dagwood Sandwiches as mainstays of its cuisine. Everything about this animated island comes from some comic strip or other, from the Sunday-funnies colors to the lop-sided ramshackle buildings seemingly concocted from staples and two-by-fours. Big-lettered signs advertise bad-guy "Hideouts," restaurant marquees dictate "No #*@#!" and snowcapped "mountains" look like marshmallow fluff on ice cream sundaes.

BABY SWAPPING

No, the term doesn't mean trading children (although that might occasionally seem like a bonus). For parents of little ones who don't make the height (or fright) requirements, it's actually a ride convenience. One parent rides while the other watches the kids, and then swap—all without having to wait in line twice. Comfortable waiting areas are located alongside the points of departure, making the whole concept particularly feasible.

It's fitting that visitors here suffer cartoonish indignities such as splashes, squirts and encounters with "explosives"—there are, thankfully, no pies in the face. Residents of the comic strips—Betty Boop, Blondie, Beetle Bailey, et al.—make appearances throughout the day, and every couple of hours a trolley zips by with the likes of Popeye, Olive Oyl and a leggy Betty Boop doing a song and soft shoe. Animated folk aside, it's the water rides here you'll remember the most—particularly since you may well spend the day wringing out your pants!

Popeye & Bluto's Bilge-Rat Barges ★★★★★ You absolutely don't want to miss this wildly funny ride with that spinach-guzzling sailor—unless the label on your clothes reads "dry clean only," that is.

WHAT TO SEE & DO

Multi-person rafts on this twisting, turning river ride speed over bumps, dousing occupants as the ride progresses. Thinking we might avoid the fate of drenching, my compatriots and I went as far as to conduct exit polls to determine which seat might get the fewest splashes. That hope was, well, washed away when we realized the diabolical raft designers had left gaps at the seats for water to flow *up* under our bottoms.

Suffice it to say, this ride is utterly determined to leave no shirt un-soaked. If the splashes don't get you, the pass through the "Boat Wash" will. Other cartoon-like indignities include an encounter with a fully-loaded octopus. On the off chance you're not already sitting in a puddle, Universal stacked the odds by arming guests (mostly kids) with high-powered water cannons mounted on the deck of the *Olive*. If you think these young uns will show mercy because they don't know you—think again! Remember those faces (that is if you can see your way through the water in your eyes) and exact your revenge later.

Tips: In case I haven't said it enough, this ride will get you very wet. If you don't want to splosh around all day in squishy sneaks, be sure to deposit your shoes in the water-tight bins at the center of each raft.

Me Ship, The Olive ★★★ If you've come with little kids, save this cute little tugboat until the end or you may spend most of your afternoon right here. Named for Popeye's goilfriend, Olive, the attraction is a ship-full of gadgets, with everything on board meant to be pushed, pulled or tinkered with for some kind of special effect. Bells ring, whistles blow, and water spurts—there's even a working piano to plunk on. And diabolical youngsters will love the squirt-gun batteries in Cargo Crane: the high-powered cannons are mounted for accuracy, allowing a straight shot at hapless passers-by on Popeye & Bluto's Bilge-Rat Barges.

TIPS: Kids will love it here; however, parents may be unnerved by the frenetic pace of keeping little ones in sight. If you can enlist help, your best bet may lie in teamwork—one follows the little one while the other stands guard between the two doors.

Dudley Do-Right's Ripsaw Falls ★★★★★ After designing the tracks for Jurassic Park and Popeye & Bluto's Bilge Barges, the folks at Universal were apparently not satisfied with just getting the riders wet; now they had to dampen unwary spectators, too.

Of course, while bystanders can step right or left to avoid the spray, those on board the four-person logs are destined for a drenching. But don't worry: you'll be having way too much fun to care.

The buildup for the monumental plummet takes you through the fictional town of Ripsaw Falls where Nell (girlfriend of Canadian Mounty Dudley) has fallen into the clutches of the evil Snidely Whiplash. The course has lots of entertaining scenery, not to mention numerous well-executed false-starts that leave you convinced you've reached the end. When you finally do career over the falls, you'll be certain you're heading straight through the roof of Snidely's dynamite shack.

Ingenious designers created a track that tunnels beneath the 400,000 gallon water tank: just when you think the fall is over, you drop down another 15 feet. The mist that settles over the entire boat assures that no one emerges unscathed.

TIPS: The decision you'll have to make here is whether to ride early and risk being soaked all day, or ride late and risk waiting in a long, long line. Much will depend on how hot a day it is, and how much your patience can stand.

Marvel Super Hero Island

▼ ▼ ▼ ▼ ▼ ▼ ▼ ▼ ▼ ▼ ▼ ▼

This futuristic metropolis is everything you'd ever expect of a superhero comic. Even if you don't catch the image of the giant Spider-Man on the outside of the Daily Bugle building (home of the rag where Peter Parker, a.k.a. Spider-Man, has his day job), the imprint on the skyline is unmistakable, with pointed, otherworldly buildings painted in purple, silver, red and green.

Everything about this energetic environment is designed to jostle the senses, from the larger-than-life superhero images to the loud electric guitar music that serenades you throughout. You almost expect to see dialogue bubbles exclaiming "Bam" and "Oof." It's not surprising, then, that there's not a single tame adventure in the lot.

WHAT TO SEE & DO

The Amazing Adventures of Spider-Man ★★★★★ Think what you will about the webbed one, this attraction truly is amazing. When 3D film interacts with flight simulators and actual special effects, the lines between fiction and fantasy are unbelievably blurred.

The story: the Statue of Liberty has been stolen by the arch enemies of Spider-Man and your job is to help him get it back.

Visitors board cars that catapult you through the adventure. Animation and special effects weave together in mindboggling ways. When cartoon Spider-Man lands on your car, you'll feel certain he's flesh and blood. Cars feels as though they're spinning wildly out of control (whether they actually spin at all is anybody's guess) and the sense of foreboding is palpable when you're suddenly whisked to the peak of a skyscraper. When Doctor Octopus (Doc Ock for short) at last takes aim with his Anti-Gravity ray gun, you'll experience every bit of the 400-foot plummet that follows. Half your time on the ride, in fact, is spent anticipating that drop. Says one fellow rider: "When it happens, it's every bit as good as you thought it would be."

Tips: An absolute don't miss—our favorite ride in the park. The sensation of dropping is real, so beware if you have a fear of heights. On the other hand, you can always close your eyes, as this experience is only virtual.

Stormforce Accelatron ★★ X-Men fans, now's your chance to come to the aid of your superheroes. Archvillain Magneto is up to no good, and on the Accelatron you can help defeat him.

All of this is just a grand excuse to board saucer-shaped vehicles and twirl until your innards are hanging out. That, of course, makes it a favorite among superhero wannabes, especially since this whirling dervish is a mite faster than the typical teacup-style contraption.

Tips: Hidden away in a corner of Marvel Super Hero Island, you might miss it if you're not looking. Then again, if you're not in the park with the little kids for whom this ride was created, that might not be such a bad thing.

Doctor Doom's Fearfall ★★ Nasty Doctor Doom, enemy of the good guys the Fantastic Four, has a plan. The vile villain of comic-book fame plans to extract all the frightful thoughts from

MAN'S BEST FRIEND

What would a vacation be without Fido or Fluffy? You'll never have to find out. Not only does Universal include pet-friendly rooms at their on-site hotels, they also offer pet sitting and walking (for fee) and a special vegetarian Pet Room Service menu. We humans should only have it so good.

his victims (that would be you), subjecting you to his dastardly contraption designed to suck the fear juice right out of you (what he plans to do with it is anybody's guess).

All of this is just a grand excuse to strap you into a launchable seat and fire you up one of the doctor's two 200-foot towers. The adrenaline rush fires right along with the launch, but it's the free-fall back down that really pumps the ticker. The soaring attraction has kind of a comedic effect on the landscape of the Marvel Island below. Spectators posed in an upward gaze at their catapulting cronies look as if to say, "Look, up in the sky . . . ."

I must admit that the very thought of this kind of free-fall to doom terrified me: the only way anyone could convince me to get on was to remind me it was part of my job (strange job, I know). Surprisingly enough, the anticipation proved much more fearsome than the actual ride. I can hardly believe I'm saying this, but it actually ended way too soon, concluding with a fluffy "thud" after a surprisingly abbreviated free fall (rumor has it the ride was toned down from the original). The result: Fans of this type of attraction may be disappointed.

TIPS: With only a couple of riders launched at a time, the line for this can be long. If you hit it early, you'll not only limit the line factor, but you'll get a great daytime panorama of the islands when you fly (assuming you keep your eyes open!).

The Incredible Hulk Coaster ★★★★★ This monster-green hulk of a coaster is indeed incredible, especially if you've ever wondered what it would feel like to be shot from a cannon. In fact, it shoots you from zero to forty in two seconds—and upside down—with the same force as an F-16 fighter jet.

Prospective riders wind through the lab of Bruce Banner (a.k.a. big green superhero) learning about his special gamma-ray accelerator tests. Once on board, the ride starts ordinarily enough with an agonizing "click-clack" up the opening incline. Just as you're anticipating that inevitable decline, "phoooom," the ride catapults you *up* through a 150-foot tube. What follows is a nonstop concoction of loops, banks and turns. Taken at a top speed of 60 miles per hour, the Hulk is bound to leave you catching your breath, as well as to do in your good hair day. Up the hairraise quotient by joining the special line for the front seat.

TIPS: There is absolutely no place to stash your belongings once you're strapped in the car. Save yourself some running around and use the short-term lockers available on your way in.

NINE

SeaWorld Adventure Park

It's only fitting that a state virtually surrounded by water should harbor an artificial aquatic wonderland. Covering more than 200 acres, SeaWorld is a mere drop in the ocean, yet it packs a gulf-size dose of shows, exhibits and attractions that probes the puzzles of the deep.

The 20,000 creatures who call SeaWorld home hail from as close as Tampa Bay and as far as Antarctica. Here at the best-known oceanarium on earth are house-size whales and toe-size clownfish, slick black seals and pink-fringed invertebrates. There are playful dolphins and endearing penguins, whiskered sea lions and mischievous otters. There are less familiar characters, too, such as puffins and buffleheads, unicorn fish and slithering eels.

Many of the critters hang out in big, blue swimming pools that dot SeaWorld's lush landscape. Every day thousands of people file into stadiums around these pools to watch the fascinating animals play while they work: whales who whistle and do jumps, seals who slap each other on the back, and dolphins who swim the backstroke.

Amphibious actors (plus a few human performers) steal the shows that have made SeaWorld world-famous. But this place is much more than shows. The multimillion-dollar theme park and research center boasts over 30 major shows and attractions that dive into underwater mysteries. From the mammoth coral reef aquarium and snow-filled house of penguins to the den of scary sharks, they paint a poignant portrait of the sea.

Outside the exhibits, the park looks like a seaside painting in motion. Seagulls shriek overhead, and salty breezes shift across lawns of soft grass. Rock ponds weave through palmy gardens, and bubblegum-colored flamingos make claw-prints on patches of sand. Speedboats roar across a rambling lagoon earmarked by the 400-foot SkyTower. SeaWorld's frame of reference, the tower resembles a blue needle pricking the shore.

Within this briny setting you can watch swivel-hipped Polynesian dancers or lounge on the lagoon beach—frozen rum drink in hand.

If this sounds like quintessential Florida tourism, it is. Since SeaWorld opened in 1973, it has offered marine life education with a kick-back-and-take-your-shoes-off attitude.

Still, it is no longer just the kinder, gentler theme park. In this age of bigger, better or bust, the theme park, now owned by Anheuser-Busch, is arming itself to compete. The burst of capitalism can be felt in the park's new name—it's now SeaWorld Adventure Park—as well as in the addition of a splashy new entrance and some whiz-bang new rides. Journey to Atlantis and the massive Kraken roller coaster provide thrills, while the adjacent Discovery Cove features face-time with dolphins, stingrays and other sea creatures.

Nevertheless, while it is being revamped and revitalized, SeaWorld remains a place where you can downshift into flow gear and think about what happens below sea level. It's a destination that, for many people, is the only real thread to the strange, liquid cosmos.

Nuts & Bolts

ARRIVAL Hurray! SeaWorld is easy to find. It's located right next to the intersection of Route 4 and the Bee Line Expressway, about ten miles south of downtown Orlando. From Route 4, take the SeaWorld exit and follow the signs to the main entrance. You'll park and board a boxy tram that ferries visitors to the front gate. Remember to *make a note of where you park* so you'll be able to find your way back to the car at the end of the day.

GAME PLAN As a first-time visitor, you may expect the same crowd craze faced at Disney World and Universal Orlando. Don't. SeaWorld rarely has gridlock and is so well-planned it hardly ever has lines. The main thing to know is that most attractions are shows, so you should plan your day around showtimes. You can't see every single one, but you can see the majority.

SeaWorld helps you decide what to see and when to see it with an up-to-the-minute **Map and Show Schedule** that varies everyday. No matter what the schedule says, don't miss the shows at the Sea Lion & Otter Stadium and at Shamu Stadium.

Allow at least 45 minutes between shows. This gives time for restroom stops and for enjoying smaller, "walk-through" exhibits such as the Tropical Reef and Penguin Encounter. It also lets you arrive 15 minutes early for each show so you get a seat. Some shows fill up fast, particularly during midday. If you have small children, take a seat near an aisle so you can easily make restroom or other emergency trips during the shows.

Parents also will want to schedule a midday stop at Shamu's Happy Harbor. Children love all the nifty activities, and you'll love taking a break in the shade. Above all, don't rush. Half the joy of SeaWorld is taking the leisurely way around.

GUEST SERVICES **Stroller and Wheelchair Rentals** Both are available at the Stroller Gift Shop just inside the main entrance.

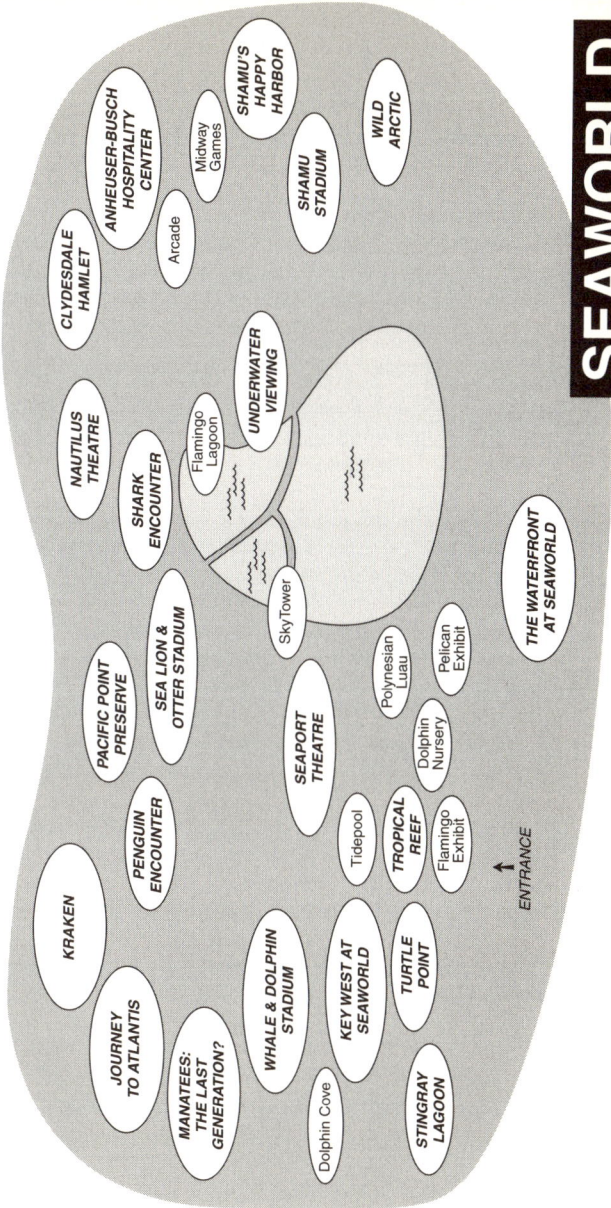

SEAWORLD
ADVENTURE PARK

SHAMU'S HAPPY HARBOR
WILD ARCTIC
Midway Games
SHAMU STADIUM
ANHEUSER-BUSCH HOSPITALITY CENTER
Arcade
CLYDESDALE HAMLET
NAUTILUS THEATRE
SHARK ENCOUNTER
Flamingo Lagoon
UNDERWATER VIEWING
PACIFIC POINT PRESERVE
SEA LION & OTTER STADIUM
SkyTower
Polynesian Luau
Pelican Exhibit
THE WATERFRONT AT SEAWORLD
Dolphin Nursery
SEAPORT THEATRE
PENGUIN ENCOUNTER
KRAKEN
Tidepool
TROPICAL REEF
Flamingo Exhibit
ENTRANCE
JOURNEY TO ATLANTIS
MANATEES: THE LAST GENERATION?
WHALE & DOLPHIN STADIUM
KEY WEST AT SEAWORLD
TURTLE POINT
Dolphin Cove
STINGRAY LAGOON

Baby Services Nursing facilities are next to the Friends of the Wild Gift Shop near the Penguin Encounter. Changing tables are provided inside or next to most restrooms.

Lockers Located near the exit area. Lockers cost $1.00 to $1.50 each time you open them.

Pets Not allowed. However, there is an air-conditioned kennel to the right of the front gate; boarding costs $6 a day.

Lost Children Report lost children to the Information Center inside the main entrance.

Package Pickup This free service lets you shop without having to tote the bags around all day. Just inform any SeaWorld store clerk you want package pickup, and they'll send your purchases to Shamu's Emporium. You can pick them up there on your way out of the park.

Lost & Found Located just inside Guest Services.

Banking ATMs are located at the main gate and throughout the park. To exchange foreign currency, visit the Guest Relations window at the main gate from 9 a.m. to 3 p.m.

GETTING AROUND

SeaWorld is a breeze. Just think of it as a lopsided doughnut. The doughnut's hole is a lagoon bridged by a Y-shaped walkway. Just off the lagoon are shops and eateries, small marine life pools and the SeaWorld Theatre. Along the doughnut's outer edge are 14 major shows and attractions. Traveling clockwise they are Key West at SeaWorld; Whale & Dolphin Stadium; Manatees: The Last Generation?; Journey To Atlantis; Kraken; Penguin Encounter; Pacific Point Preserve; Sea Lion & Otter Stadium; Shark Encounter; Nautilus Theatre; Anheuser-Busch Hospitality Center; Shamu's Happy Harbor; Shamu Stadium; Underwater Viewing; and Wild Arctic.

If you're in a wheelchair, SeaWorld is easy to navigate. Walkways are broad, and ramps are abundant and gently sloped. Stadiums and theaters offer plenty of wheelchair seating (often front-row) that's a snap to get in and out of.

▼ ▼ ▼ ▼ ▼ ▼ ▼ ▼ ▼ ▼ ▼ ▼ ▼

Shows & Attractions

WHAT TO SEE & DO

Whale & Dolphin Stadium **★★★★** Remember that SeaWorld television commercial where the dolphin rockets into the air and does a really great triple flip? It was a teaser for this "Key West Dolphin Fest" show that reveals just how athletic and agile dolphins can be. For 25 minutes the jovial creatures perform gracefully on command, doing flips, twists and even the limbo. The crowd oohs and aahs at just the right times, like when a child from the audience does a flipper shake with a dolphin.

TIPS: If you'd like to be an audience participant, be there 30 minutes before showtime and go to the front of the stadium.

There is, of course, no guarantee you'll be chosen, but this gives you a big head start.

Key West at SeaWorld ★★★ Colorful architecture, quaint shops, entertaining street shows and Calypso music set the scene for Key West at SeaWorld. Here you'll find some great opportunities for getting up close with some of SeaWorld's most colorful residents: sea turtles, dolphins and stingrays.

The most popular spot here is Dolphin Cove. On the surface of the two-acre habitat, you can feed, touch and interact with these playful mammals. Walk down and around the pool and you'll find an oversized window with a panoramic view of the Cove's underwater world. Trainers are on hand regularly to answer questions, and daily dolphin performances take place at the Key West Dolphin Fest nearby.

Apart from the animals, Key West is a welcome antidote to the typical theme park frenzy. Instead of rushing around, enjoy one of the area's street performers—jugglers, mimes or faux tour guides—or settle in and listen to a jazz band.

TIPS: Dolphins are most receptive to humans early in the day. To really get to know these guys, arrive as close as you can to park opening when the dolphins are eager to meet and greet.

Manatees: The Last Generation? ★★★★ It's hard not to be affected by the teddy-bear looks of a manatee. Bulbous and benevolent, these denizens of warm shallow waters are facing extinction at the hands of developers and unwary boaters. This three-and-a-half acre attraction features a 300,000-gallon naturalistic habitat and a circular theater where visitors are treated to an engrossing manatee's eye view of the world projected on the walls and ceiling. The exhibit is both heart-warming and heartwrenching as you learn about these mysterious and imperiled creatures.

TO THE RESCUE

Orphaned manatee calves. Injured sea turtles. Beached sea lions. Those are but some of the animals SeaWorld has taken under its wing of late, offering them refuge from the wild, rehabilitation and then a return home. The undertaking is enormous, with more than 5000 sea animals coming under SeaWorld's care in the last ten years alone. Visitors can take a closer look at such rescue efforts via SeaWorld's **To the Rescue Tour**. The one-hour guided walk (separate admission required) includes a look at rescue vehicles and rehabilitation pools, as well as accounts of what it takes to recover a 2000-pound manatee from the wild. Other information details efforts aimed at saving from extinction some species such as manatees and sea turtles.

TIPS: Allow yourself at least a half-hour to see and appreciate these wonderful mammals. Also, don't miss the 126-foot underwater viewing window.

Journey To Atlantis ***** SeaWorld may be known as a haven for docile entertainment, but the theme park has proven itself thrill-worthy with this flume/roller coaster ride. Lyrical music accompanies you as you tour the starlit interior of this elaborate palace before climbing up toward the inevitable decline.

One of the most ominous parts of this ride is the ascent. While other flume rides take you up gradually, Atlantis carries you along what seems an unthinkable incline . . . and then take you up some more. By the time you reach the top, the ride down seems unimaginable. The final twist (which I won't disclose for fear of ruining it) makes the ride truly unique.

TIPS: The sign says "You will get soaked." Believe it—and leave your perishables in the nearby lockers ($1–$1.50 each).

Kraken **** Shamu isn't the only thing that's killer at SeaWorld. The theme park known for its tranquil naturalist attractions now has some killer attractions, too.

The park's second thrill ride (Atlantis was the first) takes guests on a twisting, turning inverted journey on the back of the mythical creature, Kraken. Riders travel to heights of 15 stories strapped into bottomless contraptions that travel up to 65 miles per hour. Ride it if you dare.

TIPS: Beware the inverted ride—the kind where your feet dangle. Bonafide thrill aficionados have called the setup nauseating, but I (one who's instantly seasick in the bathtub) was unfazed by the experience. Still, it's worth noting. If you're worried at all, save this one until late in the day—that way you won't ruin your whole stay, and you'll get the benefit of shorter, later-day lines.

Penguin Encounter **** SeaWorld's most charming creatures live here in a den of snow-capped rocks, icy waters and blustery breezes. As visitors drift by on a 120-foot moving beltway, the little guys waddle across the floor, dive into their seapool and zoom around underwater. Occasionally, they cock their heads at you through the viewing window as if to say, "What's the big deal?" To many people, the Penguin Encounter *is* a big deal. The simulated polar world—six thousand pounds of manmade snow falls here every day—is the largest penguin home away from home. Hundreds of the flightless birds live here, where the light changes with the time of year to reflect seasonal Antarctic sunlight and the air is a penguin-comfy 30 degrees. Next door in a similar room are dozens of alcids, arctic birds who look like a cross between a parrot and a duck. Unrelated to penguins, alcids have wonderfully bizarre names such as buffleheads, puffins, smews

Getting Up Close and Personal

Do you want to get close to SeaWorld's animals? Just feed them. Buy a box of herring or smelt and head over to the **Stingray Lagoon, Dolphin Cove at Key West at SeaWorld** or the **Pacific Point Preserve**. The stingrays and dolphins will eat right out of your hand, and you can even pet them. The sea lions and seals put on a real show, barking for food and rolling on their backs. Get there late in the day and you'll see the whiskered fellows all fat and happy and snoozing in a big heap.

Get your hands dirty at the **Trainer for a Day** program, which includes a moment of glory as a guest trainer at the Shamu show. Submerge yourself with either sharks or false killer whales. Or get to know some of the park's rescued animal residents. A number of one-hour behind-the-scenes tours, as well as a six-hour "Adventure Express" tour that includes front-of-line privileges to some attractions, are also available. Tours and experiences can get pricey, and space is limited. The $399 price tag (for ages 13 and up) lets you work side by side with the pros, feeding, training and playing. ~ 407-370-1382.

If you'd like a truly personal interaction with a dolphin or other sea creature, consider a visit to **Discovery Cove**, which offers guests the opportunity to get in and splash around with some of their flippered friends. At $219 per person, it is pricey—especially if you're traveling with the family. But the cost includes some unique elements, like a swim with a dolphin, as well as all of your equipment, from wet suit to snorkel (the latter is yours to keep) and lunch. You'll also get a seven-day pass to go next door to SeaWorld. In addition to dolphins, park features include explorable reefs, shipwrecks, waterfalls, a free-flight aviary and a stingray lagoon at which you can actually feed those slimy guys. The best part: with admissions limited to 1000 per day, the place is virtually line-free, making it a remarkably relaxed experience. Don't feel like swimming? Grab some zzz's on a beach-side lounge chair. For the budget-conscious, a $119 per-person entry option offers access to everything but the dolphin swim. Guests of all age are welcome, but you must be over age 6 to swim with the dolphins. ~ 877-434-7268.

SeaWorld adventures don't all end at closing time. Spending a night in Shamu's house is now possible thanks to **SeaWorld Sleepovers**. Offered a couple of times a year, the sleepovers include special activities and a night in one of the animal habitat attractions (sadly, the Shamu tank is not an option). Sleepovers are just one of myriad programs allowing guests to experience the park, backstage style. ~ 866-479-2267.

and murres. If you have small children, take them to the alcids: they'll love seeing the strange creatures and learning to pronounce their names.

TIPS: After stepping off the beltway, guests can take longer looks at the alcids from a separate viewing area. There's also a Learning Hall where exhibits and videos detail penguin research and exploration.

Pacific Point Preserve **★★★★** This two-and-a-half acre, 450,000-gallon pinniped habitat is a meticulous re-creation of California's north coast. Here, California sea lions, harbor seals and fur seals cavort in a chilly saltwater environment complete with wave-making machine. Featuring below- and above-water viewing areas, Pacific Point provides perfect vistas for watching the graceful acrobatics of these marine mammals.

TIPS: Avoid the preserve after a show at the Sea Lion & Otter Stadium, when you'll have to fight the crowds.

Clyde and Seamore Take Pirate Island **★★★** Pirates, a pirate ship and treasure—what could be better? Only in this pirate adventure, performed at the Sea Lion & Otter Stadium, the heroes are sea lions Clyde and Seamore. The goofy but adorable performance tracks the escapades of a ship full of "maties" as they take to the high seas. The talented sea animals walk on their hands, slide around on deck, and take part in a whole boat load of silly stunts. Kids will go nuts for it, and most adults can't resist the adorable quotient.

TIPS: Arrive early to get the best seat. This is particularly important if you want to sit beyond the Splash Zone (the first few rows). Getting wet is great for the kids, but not so great for grownups with video cameras.

◆◆

MISCHIEVOUS MIMES

The pot-bellied man from Idaho never had a chance. No sooner had he wandered into the stadium than a mime was tailing him, mimicking the man's jelly belly. Every time poor Idaho took a step, the mime would shake his gut in perfect unison. The crowd in the stands erupted with laughter and Boise glanced around, confused. SeaWorld's mimes poke fun at unsuspecting guests who come to see the show at Sea Lion & Otter Stadium. The mimes' forte is picking out the tacky in tourists: sun-scorched legs in pink socks, long-eared Goofy caps, high heels and shorts up to here. To see the mimes, be at the stadium 15 minutes before showtime. And don't forget to look behind you.

Shark Encounter **** There's nothing too terrifying about this exhibit, except for the toothy barracuda, prickly pufferfish and six-foot sharks that slink around you. And oh, did I mention the surgeonfish whose scalpel-sharp barb can saw right through a wetsuit? These sea scaries and more prowl the aquariums in this large exhibit that is all the more fascinating because you view it from a tunnel—with the demons and 500 tons of seawater *above you*. Traveling on a moving walkway, you are very much the stranger in this watery Oz of deadly underwater creatures. Many are immediately intimidating, but others are more subtle. The gorgeous lionfish, for instance, injects a venom that kills a human in six hours. And camouflaged scorpionfish are nicknamed "three steppers" because, after walking across the fish, victims take three steps before recoiling in pain. Ready for a quick swim?

TIPS: Children of all ages give this attraction high marks because, as one eight year old said, "It's like being inside a big aquarium." They also like being able to easily walk through again . . . and again . . . and again. . . .

Odyssea **** Nothing about this show in the Nautilus Theatre is what you'd expect—particularly since it's performed entirely by humans and with nary an aquatic theme to be found. Nevertheless, it is entertaining, a mix of the exotic—penguin characters, aerial performers and a contortionist. Good views can be had from virtually anywhere you sit.

TIPS: The show is fun, but the preshow is even better. Plan to arrive at least 15 minutes early to fully appreciate the hysterical mime who becomes part of the main act later on. But beware: those not on their guard may be mercilessly toyed with.

Anheuser-Busch Hospitality Center ** A partnership between SeaWorld and its parent company, Anheuser-Busch, is the reason for the nonaquatic sights here: a turn-of-the-20th-century brew kettle, an old-fashioned beechwood chipmaker and a Clydesdale stable. The Anheuser-Busch Hospitality Center, where it all happens, is a two-building complex surrounded by lawns, waterfalls, and gardens. Tour the Hospitality House to learn about Anheuser-Busch's history and the beechwood aging process or just relax on the building's terrace and take in the scenery. Next door, the **Clydesdale Hamlet** offers an opportunity to become acquainted with some of the brewer's world-famous horses. Or, catch a look at the previously behind-the-scenes hitching barn.

TIPS: This area, though not an engrossing attraction, is an ideal place to enjoy your lunch. A great photo opportunity, albeit an incongruous one, awaits at the Clydesdale Hamlet where you can pose with a two-ton equine.

Shamu's Happy Harbor **** "I wish you hadn't shown them this. I'll never get them out," lamented one mom after dad brought the kids here. Getting small fry to leave is a common problem, and little wonder: It's filled with stuff kids love. There are tunnels to roam and water muskets to fire, bells to clang and wheels to turn. There are shallow pools and net ladders, and rooms where children can wade thigh-high in plastic balls. All day, jubilant kids pour across the three-acre playground, testing one gadget after another. The crowd favorite is the 55-foot Funship Schooner with zillions of places to run, climb and hide. For parents, there's a sheltered area with good views of the kids and (yes!) plenty of seats for resting aching feet.

TIPS: Open from 10 a.m. until an hour before closing. At Shamu's Happy Harbor, there is an area for even the smallest tykes.

Shamu Stadium ***** Outside the Disney domain, no theme-park character has gotten more hype than Shamu the killer whale. Not to worry: Everything you've heard is true. SeaWorld's best-loved mammal—all 11,000 pounds of him—lives up to his reputation in this splendid attraction called "The Shamu Adventure." Black and white and glossy all over, the big guy does a graceful underwater ballet and waves to the crowd with his tail, then sends a mini tidal wave over the first 15 rows. The action is captured on state-of-the-art cameras that broadcast Shamu's feats (and the crowd's reactions) on a 15-by-20-foot video screen above his pool. In one exhilarating scene, a trainer straddles Shamu as he barrels full-speed toward an underwater camera. Just before impact, the pair soar out of the water, separate and dive back into the pool.

TIPS: Unless you want to get wet, and I mean *soaked*, sit in row 15 or higher. This is the only attraction that regularly fills up well before showtime. Check the information center just inside the entrance for showtimes and plan to get there 30 minutes early. If you must see one of the midday shows (between 11:30 a.m. and 2:30 p.m.), arrive at least 45 minutes ahead of time. *Not to be missed.*

Underwater Viewing *** This attraction, a 1.7-million-gallon underwater habitat located next to Shamu Stadium, allows visitors a chance to see killer whales between showtimes. From the safety of three eight-foot underwater windows, you can enjoy front-row views of the majestic creatures without fear of getting drenched. Kids love to watch the baby whales frolicking in their new surroundings.

TIPS: To avoid the crowds, see this attraction at least one hour before or after a show at Shamu Stadium.

Wild Arctic **** SeaWorld's simulated helicopter ride transports you to the icy ends of the world, to the land of night and dim daytime skies, of polar bears and beluga whales, of jagged-edge glaciers and thunderous avalanches. It's a rambunctious ride aboard a flight simulator (remember Disney's Star Tours and Body Wars?) that's meant to resemble a helicopter en route to Base Station Wild Arctic research center. You get waylaid—dodging glacial mountains, soaring through solid ice canyons, and careening down valleys. The scenery would be spectacular if the simulator screen weren't a little fuzzy. People who choose not to ride the simulator can walk through to the Arctic exhibit.

When you finally "land" at the Base Station, you leave the simulator for a walk through cool hollows. Here, behind big walls of glass, you can look at polar bears roaming their simulated Arctic dens and beluga whales and walruses swimming through enormous tanks where the water is cooled to 50 degrees.

TIPS: Children shorter than 42 inches are not allowed. Wild Arctic has SeaWorld's longest lines—but they're rarely more than 30 minutes.

The SkyTower ★★★ Often called "the needle in the sky," this ink-blue tower rises a skinny 400 feet from the lip of SeaWorld's lagoon. A round, windowed elevator ferries people back and forth to the summit and looks like a top in slow motion spiraling up and down a string. It's the only attraction that costs extra ($3 per person). The 15-minute vertical voyage is quiet, leisurely and scenic, and the view from the top is enough to make your day. Whether it's worth the extra bucks is, of course, a matter of opinion. Frankly, I think the scene from the top of Disney's Contemporary Resort is just as stirring—and it's free.

TIPS: Some preschoolers are frightened when they see the ground start to shrink below. Older kids, however, think it's the greatest thing since Shamu.

ON THE WATERFRONT

SeaWorld's latest addition is a bit removed from the animal education the park is known for. Still, the departure is a nice diversion for folks who like a little more "theme" with their park visit. And the ambitious **Waterfront** delivers. On five acres, the lively area is designed in the image of a seaport fishing village. The ambling walkways and quaint architecture seem to be a message from designers to slow down and soak it up. Look for colorful characters telling stories, "local" merchants selling items billed as "wares from around the world," and street shows like Kat 'n' Kaboodle featuring actual felines. But the mainstay of the area is the food served up with gusto. Both ends of the 400-foot Tower have been salvaged as well, with the top offering stellar views of the park and the bottom morphing into an alfresco pub featuring appetizers as well as ale.

Pets Ahoy! ★★★ You can't help smiling through this old-time show that showcases some of SeaWorld's non-aquatic animals. Cats roll over, dogs play sick, and a donkey smiles for the dentist. Then there's the pig who totes signs proclaiming the injustices to swine-kind ("stop makin' bacon" was my favorite). Sure it's fairly predictable. But kids won't be able to resist the furry critters, and parents won't want to miss their reactions; that it's indoors and air conditioned ought to appeal to everyone. The fact that these talented kitties and pups were all adopted from local animal shelters sends a nice side message. In short: Vaudeville never looked so cute.

TIPS: Be sure to stick around after the show when kids can get up close and fur-sonal with some of the show's star performers.

Tropical Reef ★★★★ A stroll-through aquarium swarming with weird and wonderful creatures, Tropical Reef is truly a walk on the watery wild side. Unlike the sunny outdoor settings of most attractions, this exhibit offers pitch-black hollows ignited by neon coral the size of a semi-truck. The coral looms inside a 160,000-gallon tank, the nation's largest South Pacific coral aquarium. More than 1000 oddities thrive here, including moray eels and raccoon butterflyfish, surgeonfish and giant lobsters. Bright-orange clownfish flutter against underwater waves, and purple anemones do a silent ballet on the sandy aquarium floor. Preschoolers line up along the bottom of the tank, pressing their faces against the floor-to-ceiling glass. Smaller tanks are sprinkled everywhere, each home to some peculiar brand of sealife.

TIPS: One of my favorite things about this attraction is the big, luminous signs that point out various sealife and help explain the riddles of the ocean.

TEN

Staying, Eating and Playing

Among the many tough decisions Disney vacationers face is where to sleep and eat. To help you make good choices, this chapter provides lodging and restaurant suggestions inside Disney World and just outside Disney's boundaries. The "Playing" part of the chapter takes you sightseeing and shopping in the Disney area, and also offers prime nighttime spots.

Lodging

Ever since Mickey Mouse came to town, hotels have sprouted more profusely than orange blossoms. Disney World alone boasts over 21,500 hotel rooms and campsites. Just outside Disney's door are some of Florida's most luxurious accommodations, as well as motel rows that stretch into distant cow pastures. These chain lodgings were slapped up so fast it has taken awhile for the demand to catch up. Consequently, you can find some deals here, especially in the off-season (May 1 to December 15).

Perhaps the most-asked lodging question is the toughest to answer: Should we stay inside Disney World? Staying at a Disney resort is one of your most expensive options, but it's *the* most convenient. And when it comes to a Disney vacation, convenience cannot be stressed enough. Particularly for families with young children, proximity to the theme parks and Disney transportation can save *hours* of travel time (and aggravation) every day.

If your budget prohibits Disney resorts (or they're all booked up), consider staying at Disney's Fort Wilderness campground or one of the several campgrounds nearby. If you prefer a motel or family-style apartments, stick to those within a few miles of Disney. You may save money at a motel out in the boonies, but you'll likely spend hours fighting traffic to and from the Disney World area. No matter where the accommodations are, most let children stay free with parents.

If your children are older and you have plenty of time and money, I recommend staying at the Hyatt Regency Grand Cypress or Marriott's Orlando World Center. Located about five minutes from Disney World, they both offer superb Florida lodging experiences.

◆◆◆◆◆◆◆◆◆◆◆◆◆◆◆◆◆◆◆◆◆◆

For discount hotel packages near Disney World, check the Sunday travel section of almost any major newspaper.

Unless otherwise noted, the following price categories include two adults and two children under 18 staying in a room. *Budget* hotels are generally less than $80 per night; *moderately* priced hotels run $80 to $120; *deluxe* hotels are between $120 and $200; and *ultra-deluxe* facilities price above $200.

DISNEY WORLD   Certainly one of the biggest benefits of staying on Disney property is that you can put away your car keys as long as you're here. Monorails, ferries and buses provide free transportation to all the Disney sights, restaurants, shops and nightclubs. You also can take midday breaks from the theme parks, retreating to your hotel for an afternoon swim or nap—a big plus if you're traveling with children.

But that is only the beginning, particularly if you have kids. Most resorts here were designed with families in mind. Sleeping in Disney's world means Mouseketeer Clubs, teen programs, cartoon wallpaper and Mickey Mouse roaming the lobby. Also, there are a host of other advantages, such as being able to make Disney restaurant reservations up to three days in advance. And since imagination is at the heart of Disney World, it is only natural that this extends to the accommodations (including camping!) as well. From elegant to zany, Polynesian to New England, each Disney resort has a style all its own. When finding a place, you really can wish upon a star.

Does all this sound swell? Well, join the crowd. So many people want to stay inside Disney World that reservations are needed several months in advance. In season, booking a year ahead of time is not uncommon. Reservations at all Disney properties can be made through the **Walt Disney World Central Reservations Office**. ~ Box 10100, Lake Buena Vista, FL 32830-0100; 407-934-7639, fax 407-354-2192; www.disneyworld.com.

A giant "Tramp" holds court over Disney's newest "value" hotel, the **Pop Century Resort**. The oversized dog isn't the only big thing about the hotel—the property is HUGE, with more than five-thousand (yes, 5-0-0-0!) rooms. Opened in December 2003, the brightly colored hotel will entertain kids with its purple façade and adorable icons. The price is nice for on-property, but, as at the All Stars, you'll feel a bit like you're living in a dorm. ~ 1050 Century Drive; 407-938-4000, fax 407-938-4040. MODERATE.

The **Contemporary Resort** is the most faceless of the Disney properties. Meant to look futuristic with a monorail through the

4th floor, lots of glass and an 11-story atrium housing guest rooms, shops and restaurants, the concrete ziggurat comes off as stark and sterile. But the lobby portrays stylish flowers, trees, birds and one five-legged goat (can you find the goat?). Of its 1053 spacious rooms, those facing the Magic Kingdom offer the best view. For an additional charge there's the Mouseketeer Club for children featuring activities from 4:30 p.m. to midnight. Teenagers gravitate to the Fiesta Fun Center, a mammoth video gameroom just off the lobby. ~ 4600 North World Drive; 407-824-1000. ULTRA-DELUXE.

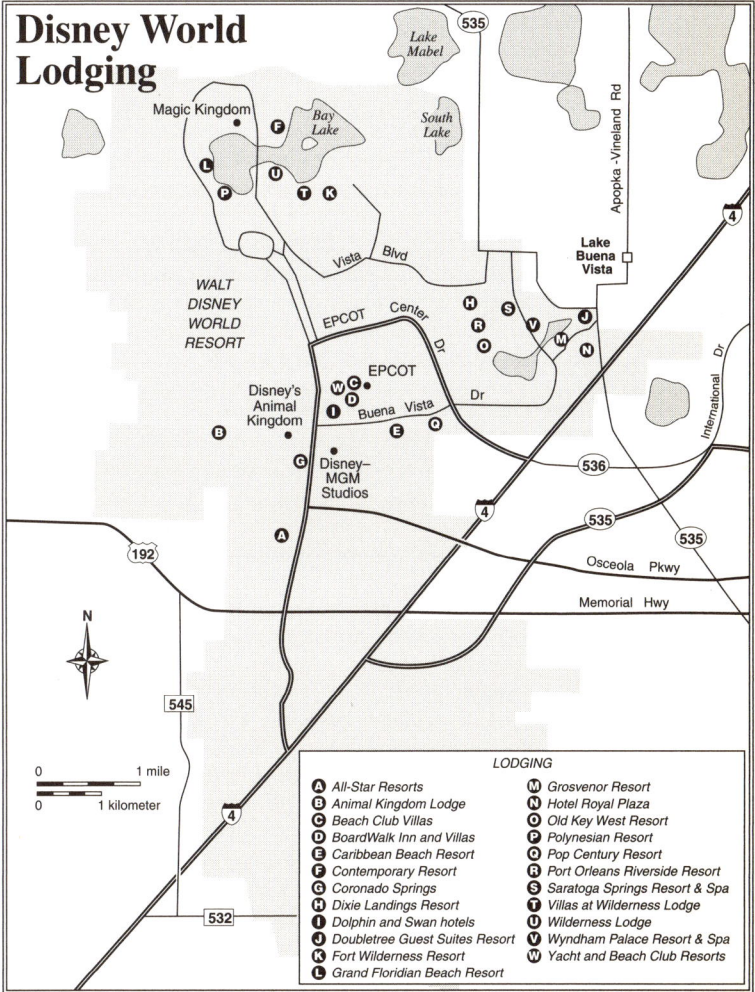

Disney World Lodging

Lake Mabel
535
Magic Kingdom
Bay Lake
South Lake
Apopka - Vineland Rd
4
F
L
P
U T K
Vista Blvd
Lake Buena Vista
WALT DISNEY WORLD RESORT
EPCOT Center Dr
H S V J
R
O M N
International Dr
EPCOT
W C
D
I Buena Vista Dr
Disney's Animal Kingdom
B
E Q
536
G Disney—MGM Studios
A
535 535
192
Osceola Pkwy
Memorial Hwy
N
545
0 1 mile
0 1 kilometer
4
532

LODGING

- **A** All-Star Resorts
- **B** Animal Kingdom Lodge
- **C** Beach Club Villas
- **D** BoardWalk Inn and Villas
- **E** Caribbean Beach Resort
- **F** Contemporary Resort
- **G** Coronado Springs
- **H** Dixie Landings Resort
- **I** Dolphin and Swan hotels
- **J** Doubletree Guest Suites Resort
- **K** Fort Wilderness Resort
- **L** Grand Floridian Beach Resort
- **M** Grosvenor Resort
- **N** Hotel Royal Plaza
- **O** Old Key West Resort
- **P** Polynesian Resort
- **Q** Pop Century Resort
- **R** Port Orleans Riverside Resort
- **S** Saratoga Springs Resort & Spa
- **T** Villas at Wilderness Lodge
- **U** Wilderness Lodge
- **V** Wyndham Palace Resort & Spa
- **W** Yacht and Beach Club Resorts

The **Grand Floridian Beach Resort** is the *grande dame* of the Disney resort area, with the look and feel of elegance enjoyed by the 19th-century privileged class. Victorian verandas, red gabled roofs, brick chimneys and delicate gingerbread lend the exterior a grand appearance. In the lobby are stained-glass domes, crystal chandeliers and ornate balustrades. The 867 guest rooms are dreamily decorated with Victorian wallpaper, plush carpets, armoires and marble vanities. Parents who want a night out alone can make use of the in-room babysitting service or let the kids join the Mouseketeer Club (for a fee, of course). The Grand Floridian also has an opulent spa and health club. ~ 4401 Floridian Way; 407-824-3000, fax 407-824-3186. ULTRA-DELUXE.

One of the first Disney World resorts, **Polynesian Resort** creates a South Pacific ambience. The two- and three-story longhouses lie on South Seas Lagoon and its sandy, palm tree–strewn beaches. In typical Disney fashion, the public areas feature a bit of manufactured Polynesia, complete with volcanic rock fountains and gardens thick with banana trees, orchids and sweetsmelling gardenias. Of the Polynesian's two jungle-like swimming pools, the one near the beach is the absolute favorite of kids. Here they can duck under waterfalls and zoom down water slides that cut through boulders. For toddlers, there are shallow areas in both pools and a good-sized playground nearby. There's also the Neverland Club, which offers supervised activities for children at night (for a fee). The resort's 855 guest rooms accommodate up to five people each (or a sixth under three years old). ~ 1600 Seas Drive; 407-824-2000, fax 407-824-3174. ULTRA-DELUXE.

People either love or hate the **Dolphin** and **Swan** hotels. Inside and out, the coral and turquoise resorts look like they were dreamed up by a Disney animator. Seahorses dangle from chandeliers, lamps resemble birds, and hall carpets have painted-on beach blankets and palm trees. Headboards zigzag, pineapples and bananas are sketched throughout the resort. To admirers, this is imagination gone wonderfully wild. To critics, it's decorator overload, tacky city. Designed by architect Michael Graves as prototypes of "entertainment architecture," the whimsically flamboyant hotels face each other along a lake and are connected by a flower-lined cord of pavement. Nearly twice the size of the Swan, the pyramid-shaped Dolphin has 1509 rooms and a vast lobby rotunda draped with ballooning canvas. Water plunges down the face of the Dolphin, cascading into terraced scallop shells for a crowd-ahhing effect. Smaller but certainly not subdued, the 758-room Swan is fashioned like a gentle arch painted with aqua waves. Both places boast sprawling swimming pool areas, fitness centers, gamerooms, *beaucoup* restaurants and bars, and afternoon and evening camps for

Notice that the Dolphin hotel's fish statues aren't dolphins; rather, they resemble the fish from *The Little Mermaid.*

children ages 4 to 12. ~ Dolphin, 1500 Epcot Resort Boulevard, 407-934-4000, 800-227-1500; Swan, 1200 Epcot Resort Boulevard, 407-934-3000. ULTRA-DELUXE.

In recent years, Disney has taken pity on the poor souls who can't afford $200-a-night hotel rooms. The result: **Caribbean Beach Resort** and **Port Orleans Riverside Resort**. Both cost about half as much as the other Disney resorts but still offer the advantages of staying "on property." Villages at the Caribbean Beach Resort are named and color-coded for different Caribbean islands, such as pale peach for Barbados and ocean blue for Martinique. Each island has its own swimming pool, and each hugs a 45-acre lake rimmed with sand. There's also a lively street market laced with Caribbean food and colorful wares. The Caribbean Beach Resort's 2112 rooms make it one of the largest hotels in the United States. On the downside, most of the hotel restaurants are all fast-food, and they're usually packed. There are, however, a beautiful playground and plenty of water sports. Port Orleans Riverside represents the Disney vision of the Crescent City. Wrought-iron balconies and clapboard shutters decorate the resort's three-story rowhouses perched along the Sassagoula River, an artificial river much cleaner than the real Mississippi. The elaborate pool area, with its Mardi Gras character sculptures and giant sea serpent statue, looks New Orleans funky. Kids like to slide down the serpent's tongue and land in the pool. Like its Caribbean Beach buddy, the 2048-room Port Orleans is extremely popular and should be booked *at least six months* in advance. ~ Caribbean Beach, 900 Cayman Way, 407-934-3400; Port Orleans, 2201 Orleans Drive, 407-934-5000. DELUXE TO ULTRA-DELUXE.

Tile roofs and mosaic accents bring Southwest flair to **Coronado Springs**. The hacienda-style hostelry is large—1921 rooms—but three divisions (Casitas, Ranchos and Cabanas, each section with its own pool) makes navigating more manageable. There's also a full-service restaurant and a central pool featuring a 50-foot Mayan pyramid with a flashy water slide. ~ 1001 West Buena Vista Drive; 407-939-1000, fax 407-939-1001. DELUXE.

Less expensive are Disney's trio of moderate priced hotels: **All-Star Sports Resort, All-Star Music Resort** and **All-Star Movies Resort**. Together, the adjacent properties offer a whopping 5760 rooms in a mind-numbing maze of buildings flanked by seas of parking lots. (Hint: make a note of your parking spot, then use the hotel maps to find it. As one employee said, "I've been here three months and I still get lost.") The "resorts" are more like Disneyesque dorms, with three-story buildings painted glaring colors, trimmed in metal railings and decorated with gargantuan basketballs, hoops and tennis rackets (at the Sports Resort), giant amplifiers, microphones and jukeboxes (at the Music Resort) and oversized Dalmatians, Buzz Lightyear and Woody (at the Movies Resort). The swimming pools swarm with screaming kids (remember: there are nearly 6000 rooms). Small rooms can't accommodate more than four, but larger parties can get two rooms here for just a little more than the cost of a more deluxe Disney hotel. The ambience may be less than luxurious, but you do benefit from conveniences such as the Disney bus system (which can save on the cost of a rental car). ~ Sports Resort, 1701 West Buena Vista Drive, 407-939-5000; Music Resort, 1801 West Buena Vista Drive, 407-939-6000; Movies Resort, 1901 West Buena Vista Drive, 407-939-7000. MODERATE.

Two other resorts, the **Yacht Club Resort** and **Beach Club Resort**, re-create New England. The oyster-gray clapboard buildings converge on a 40-acre lake outlined with magnolia and pear trees and punctuated by a lighthouse. The more formal of the two, the Yacht Club boasts a lobby of millwork and brass, Naugahyde sofas and shimmering oak floors. Its 630 guest rooms are navy and white and nautically themed and have French doors that open onto lanais. The Beach Club lobby features white wicker furniture and cool, limestone floors. Jars of seashells garnish its 583 pastel-colored guest rooms. The hotels share Stormalong Bay, a fabulous three-acre water playground with tons of treasures: a life-size shipwreck with water slides (including one that plunges down a broken mast); hot sand baths and a bubble pool; and a kiddie pool that's sunk into a treasure ship. The hotels also offer the Sandcastle Club, which features supervised games for ages four through twelve. ~ Yacht Club, 1700 Epcot Resort Boulevard, 407-934-7000; Beach Club, 1800 Epcot Resort Boulevard, 407-934-8000. ULTRA-DELUXE.

Those who prefer the New England charm but with more space can try out the **Beach Club Villas**. The newest member of the Vacation Club family has apartment-size dwellings with as many as three bedrooms. Larger units have in-room laundry and well-equipped kitchens. The only downside: all Villas are located

NEW YORK STATE OF MIND

More and more visitors to Disney World are actually "homeowners"—members of Disney's growing number of Vacation Clubs. The latest club, set to open in 2004, is the **Saratoga Springs Resort & Spa**. On the site of the Disney Institute (the defunct experiment in Disney learning vacations), Saratoga Springs harks back to turn-of-the-20th-century Upstate New York, with one-, two- or three-bedroom units. The location—overlooking the Downtown Disney complex—is great for lovers of nightlife and shopping. And the Spa is sure to calm the frazzled nerves of parents traveling with overstimulated kids.

at the back of the Beach Club property, meaning you lose out on the Boardwalk views, perhaps making Boardwalk Villas (my personal favorite) a better choice. ~ 1900 Epcot Resorts Boulevard; 407-934-2175, fax 407-934-3850. ULTRA-DELUXE.

After a hot, hectic day at the theme parks, there's nothing like retreating to the cool, shady woods of **Wilderness Lodge**. One of Disney's finest creations, the multistoried, wood-hewn haven is designed like the great national park resorts of the Pacific Northwest. Timber balconies are hinged high around the enormous lobby of stone and glossy wood, where a "geyser" erupts every hour. From the geyser, a rock-bottomed creek winds outside through a hot-springs courtyard, down into the freeform swimming pool with water slide. The 728 rooms (my husband commented that they reminded him of his old Boy Scouts camp) are less magnificent than the public spaces, but the skinny balconies have tranquil views. ~ 901 West Timberline Drive; 407-824-3200, fax 407-824-3232. ULTRA-DELUXE.

Larger units are available at the on-site **Villas at Wilderness Lodge** featuring studio, one and two-bedroom units, all with kitchens or kitchenettes, many with in-room laundry. ~ 801 Timberline Drive; 407-824-3200, fax 407-824-3232. ULTRA-DELUXE.

Across the waters from the Beach and Yacht Club resorts is Disney's "seaside" BoardWalk. The quaint complex of shops and restaurants includes two hotels—the **BoardWalk Inn** and **Board-Walk Villas**. Both do a good job harking back to the mid-Atlantic beach resorts of the early 20th century, with shingled roofs, striped awnings, fan-back chairs and lazy-day balconies. There's even lawn croquet! The inn's 372 rooms are typical deluxe hotel accommodations with either one queen-sized or two double beds. The 520 villas are either studios with kitchenettes, or one-, two- or three-bedroom villas, each with a living room, full kitchen and dining areas. The properties share access to three pools, a health club, a children's club, an arcade and tennis courts. Those worried about nighttime noise might want to choose river or pool views, although upper-floor BoardWalk views are surprisingly quiet. ~ 2101 North Epcot Resorts Boulevard; 407-939-5100 (inn), 407-939-6200 (villas). ULTRA-DELUXE.

Disney's **Dixie Landings Resort** offers two sides of Southern life. Choose from rustic cabins in the bayou or plantation mansions. The various buildings in the Southern-mansion style, with columned facades and shaded verandas, hold clean, modern but rather ordinary-looking hotel rooms. The bayou buildings, however, with tin rooftops and wood siding, look like they came right out of the plains of Louisiana. Inside, the theme continues with unfinished wood bedframes and dressers. ~ 1251 Dixie Drive; 407-934-6000. DELUXE TO ULTRA-DELUXE.

The soft sounds of Jimmy Buffett and calypso music lull you into a state of comfort at the **Old Key West Resort**. The accommodations, larger and more upscale than those at other Disney resorts, are decorated in pastels and have porches where you can sit and enjoy your Key lime pie. You can choose from the deluxe studio, one-, two- and three-bedroom homes; or the Grand Villa that sleeps up to 12. ~ 1510 North Cove Road; 407-827-7700. ULTRA-DELUXE.

Animals roam right outside your door at Disney's **Animal Kingdom Lodge**. Perhaps the park's most elaborately themed property to date, the place has African-inspired furnishings and food, and more than 1000 rooms, most of which overlook the hotel's own private savannah; there's even has a place to enjoy African stories by firelight. ~ 2901 Osceola Parkway; 407-938-3000, fax 407-938-4799. ULTRA-DELUXE.

Several resorts on Disney World property are not owned by the Disney Company and have slightly lower rates. Located in the Walt Disney World Village, these hotels offer free transportation to the theme parks as well as Epcot restaurant reservation privileges. You can reserve rooms through the Walt Disney World Central Reservations Office.

For a taste of old England, try the **Grosvenor Resort**. Its 626 rooms are pleasantly decorated in a modern style with British flair and are equipped with a refrigerator and VCR. Guests have access to a game room, tennis courts, two pools, and an evening kids camp. ~ 1850 Hotel Plaza Boulevard; 407-828-4444, 800-624-4109, fax 407-828-8192; www.grosvenorresort.com, e-mail info@grosvenor.com. DELUXE.

The **Hotel Royal Plaza** plays the other side of the street. Modern with Mediterranean highlights, this 394-room contemporary facility provides amenities such as a restaurant, a lounge, tennis courts, a swimming pool and a sauna. The hotel's boast is its location in the Downtown Disney resort—they offer complimentary transportation to all Disney attractions. ~ 1905 Hotel Plaza Boulevard; 407-828-2828, 800-248-7890, fax 407-828-6338; www.royalplaza.com. MODERATE TO ULTRA-DELUXE.

The **Wyndham Palace Resort & Spa** houses 1014 rooms and features even snazzier decor. Situated on 27 acres, the mega-resort looks like a sleek tower poised on a huge pedestal. The lobby soars sky-high and is crowned with stained glass. Guest rooms are modern affairs with plush carpeting, light oak furniture and private balconies. For families, the adjacent Palace Suites building has spacious one- and two-bedroom accommodations with kitchenettes, living and dining rooms. In between the two buildings are three heated swimming pools, children's wading pools and tennis courts. You'll also find six 18-hole Disney golf courses in the area along with nine restaurants and lounges, including one family-style eatery with quality fast food. ~ 1900 Buena Vista Drive; 407-827-2727, 800-996-3426, fax 407-827-6034; www.wynd hampalaceresort.com. ULTRA-DELUXE.

Doubletree Guest Suites Resort has the distinction of being the only all-suite hotel right on Disney World grounds. That means you get some of the comforts of home (a separate bedroom for the kids and a modest kitchenette) plus the conveniences of staying inside the park system (complimentary bus service, preferred golf-course access, etc.). The 229 suites are modern and spacious,

Orlando Area Lodging

LODGING

Ⓐ The Castle
Ⓑ Fort Summit KOA Campground
Ⓒ Golden Link Motel
Ⓓ Hard Rock Hotel
Ⓔ Holiday Inn Family Suites Resort
Ⓕ Hyatt Regency Grand Cypress
Ⓖ Kissimmee-Orlando KOA
Ⓗ La Quinta Inn Lakeside
Ⓘ Magic Castle Inn and Suites
Ⓙ MainStay Suites Maingate
Ⓚ Marriott Residence Inn Lake Buena Vista

Ⓛ Orlando World Center Marriott
Ⓜ Outdoor Resorts at Orlando
Ⓝ Peabody Orlando
Ⓞ Portofino Bay Hotel
Ⓟ Radisson Hotel Orlando
Ⓠ Renaissance Orlando Resort
Ⓡ Royal Pacific Resort
Ⓢ Sheraton Vistana Resort
Ⓣ Sherwood Forest RV Resort
Ⓤ Summerfield Suites
Ⓥ Thrift Lodge
Ⓧ Tropical Palms Resort

with either one king-sized or two double beds in the bedroom, and a sofa bed and dining area in the accompanying sitting room. Other features include a restaurant, in-room video games, adult and kiddie pools, a hot tub, an exercise room and a game room. ~ 2305 Hotel Plaza Boulevard; 407-934-1000, 800-222-8733, fax 407-934-1101; www.doubletree.com. DELUXE.

JUST OUTSIDE DISNEY WORLD   A mouse hop from Disney's gates are more places than you can possibly, yes, imagine. Most every chain motel known to mankind can be found here—sometimes two or three times in only a few miles. In between are cheap sleeps with high-camp names like Adventure Motel, Viking Motel and Maple Leaf. At the opposite end, several addresses rank as some of the state's finest accommodations.

Lodging services can help you find a room. Visit **Kissimmee–St. Cloud Reservations**. ~ www.floridakiss.com. Or try **Central Reservations Service**. ~ 800-548-3311.

Besides its distinction as one of Florida's largest hotels, **Orlando World Center Marriott** is also one of the most dramatic. The 143,000-square-foot resort rests on 220 acres adorned with swimming pools and fountains, rock grottos and golf greens, and ponds filled with swans. The main building is a series of tiered towers that unite in a dazzling atrium lobby with marble floors, waterfalls and three glass elevators. At night, braids of light trace the hotel's tiers and are striking from miles away. The 2000 guest rooms, decorated in soft pastels, feel relaxed and airy. Included in the myriad of amenities are a health club, five swimming pools (including one indoor), four tennis courts, an 18-hole golf course, nine restaurants and lounges and the All About Kids babysitting service. ~ 8701 World Center Drive, Orlando; 407-239-4200, 800-621-0638, fax 407-238-8777; www.worldcentermarriott.com. DELUXE TO ULTRA-DELUXE.

> After Las Vegas, greater Orlando has more hotel rooms than any other metropolitan area in the country

If I could stay at any hotel in Florida, with money no object, I would choose the **Hyatt Regency Grand Cypress**. Set on 1500 acres, this shimmering tower with tiered roof and spectacular 18-story glass atrium is truly a showplace. The world-outside-Disney World has it all: a half-acre fantasy swimming pool cascading with waterfalls, pretty lakeside beaches, lush hills and bridges, and winding footpaths laced with bronze sculptures and herb gardens. Flowing streams, flourishing tropical flora and stylized artwork accent the lobby. And there's more: a 45-acre Audubon nature preserve, tennis courts, horseback riding, jogging trails, a 45-hole Jack Nicklaus–designed golf course, a smaller-scale pitch-and-putt course, a 21-acre lake with sailing center, a health club and four superb restaurants. The rooms have such special

Two on the World

You want Chilean sea bass, the kids want ... chicken nuggets. What to do when mom and dad need a night away from the offspring? Disney World hotels have a handful of supervised kids' clubs for children age 4 to 12, ranging from the quaint Cub's Den at the Disney Wilderness Lodge to the elaborate Never Land Club (the entrance is through the Darlings' bedroom window) at the Polynesian Resort.

Programs run roughly from late afternoon to late night and often include dinner. Sure, they're kind of expensive—this is Disney, after all—but it's a small price to pay to re-charge for the next day's dozen rides through "It's A Small World." Reservations are required. Call 407-939-3463 for details.

If you're not at a Disney resort, there are a number of bonded child-care services in the area. Try **Super Sitters** (407-382-2558) or **ABC Mothers, Teachers, Nannies and Grannies, Inc.** (407-857-7447); either will send a babysitter to your hotel room. **Kids Nite Out** (407-828-0920, 800-696-8105; www.kidsniteout.com) also offers in-room sitting.

touches as wicker settees, love seats and floral and striped color schemes. There's a children's pool and playground, and children age 3 to 12 can join Camp Hyatt for supervised activities. The Hyatt also offers in-room babysitting and a daycare center. Folks traveling with children can take advantage of a rate plan that provides a second room at a discounted price. ~ 1 Grand Cypress Boulevard, Orlando; 407-239-1234, 800-233-1234, fax 407-239-3800; www.hyattgrandcypress.com. ULTRA-DELUXE.

Visitors enjoying Universal Orlando can escape to the Mediterranean at the Italianate **Portofino Bay Hotel,** Universal's first resort located within the theme-park complex itself. Pretty row house–style buildings harbor 750 luxury rooms, all overlooking the water set with bobbing gondolas. The scene is charming enough, though there is an inexplicable shortage of balconies. If you can't enjoy the view, you can at least placate yourself with butler service (limited availability). ~ 5601 Universal Boulevard, Orlando; 888-322-5541, fax 407-503-1010. ULTRA-DELUXE.

Also a Loews property, the **Hard Rock Hotel** features lots of rock-and-roll memorabilia in the public spaces. All 650 rooms are predictably ultra-plush. One surprise: there are some kid suites to make staying with family more palatable. ~ 5800 Universal Boulevard, Orlando; 407-503-7625, 888-322-5541, fax 407-503-7655; www.usf.com. ULTRA-DELUXE.

The latest of Universal's trio of on-site hotels, the **Royal Pacific Resort** has a tropical theme, right down to its own lagoon (really a swimming pool) and a sandy beach. The rooms are a bit smaller than those of its siblings, but Royal Pacific is also the least expensive of the three. ~ 6300 Hollywood Way, Orlando; 407-503-3000, 888-322-5541, fax 407-503-3010; www.usf.com. ULTRA-DELUXE.

When the **Radisson Hotel Orlando** opened in the mid-1970s, it was the largest convention hotel between Miami and Atlanta. Today, after several renovations, it is only one of many sleek hotels catering to the theme-park visitors. Parked at the main entrance to Universal Orlando, the hotel's double spires house 742 oversized rooms outfitted with wicker furnishings, pastel designs and two queen beds. There's a heated swimming pool, health club and game arcade. ~ 5780 Major Boulevard, Orlando; 407-351-1000, 800-327-2110, fax 407-363-0106; www.orlandoradissonhotel.com. DELUXE TO ULTRA-DELUXE.

From the outside, the **Renaissance Orlando Resort** looks like a stark concrete block painted tan and blue. But inside is the world's largest atrium lobby, a vast and opulent space styled with lush gardens, fish-filled ponds, Victorian aviary and balconies strung with vines. The grandeur continues into 780 oversized rooms where the decor is pastel mauve, and the vanities and bathrooms are marble. Located next door to SeaWorld, the Marriott features an Olympic-sized swimming pool, tennis courts, volleyball court and playground for kids. There is a teen game room and free coffee and newspapers every morning. ~ 6677 Sea Harbor Drive, Orlando; 407-351-5555, 800-228-9290, fax 407-351-9991; www.renaissancehotels.com. DELUXE TO ULTRA-DELUXE.

Parents *and* kids get their own space at **Summerfield Suites**, where the majority of accommodations offer two bedrooms, living room, fully-equipped kitchen, and three TVs and telephones. The remaining suites have one bedroom and a sofa bed in the living room. They're all housed in an apartment-style complex, somewhat generic in architecture and landscaping, but offering a courtyard with heated swimming pool, a laundry room, a grocery and video library (all rooms have VCRS). An extensive continental breakfast (with lots of kiddie eats) is included in the rate. Summerfields is popular with European and Canadian families, who stay two to three weeks. ~ 8480 International Drive, Orlando; 407-352-2400, 800-866-4549, fax 407-352-4631; www.summerfield-orlando.com. ULTRA-DELUXE. If you'd rather be closer to Disney World, stay at the Summerfield Suites in Lake Buena Vista. ~ 8751 Suite-side Drive, at Apopka-Vineland Road, Lake Buena Vista; 407-238-0777, 800-866-4549, fax 407-238-2640. ULTRA-DELUXE.

Splashed with pinks and purples and corals and crowned with soaring storybook spires, **The Castle** looks like something a kid conjured up. Birdsong and medieval music are piped through speakers in this place of whimsy, where seven stories of spacious rooms are "royally" outfitted with purple satin bedspreads and draperies, satin brocade chairs and other medieval-style decor. There are lots of family extras at this Doubletree property, including in-room mini-refrigerators and coffeemakers, a laundry room and a big, round, heated swimming pool with

THE BEST OF BOTH WORLDS

Few hotels anywhere cater to families like the **Holiday Inn Family Suites Resort**. Each of the hotel's 800 accommodations is a suite with two bedrooms (albeit one with a curtain partition as opposed to a door) and a living room; kitchenettes have microwaves and refrigerators. You can choose themed kid suites (featuring bunk beds and video games in the kids' rooms) or more traditional setups. If all that isn't enough, the sprawling pool has tons of toys, and kids under 12 eat free. The location is only a mile from the mouse. ~ 14500 Continental Gateway, Orlando; 407-387-5437, 877-387-5437; www.hifamilysuites.com, e-mail contactus@hifamilysuites.com. DELUXE.

fountain. Two adjoining restaurants offer room service. ~ 8629 International Drive, Orlando; 407-345-1511, 800-952-2785, fax 407-248-8181; www.doubletreecastle.com. DELUXE TO ULTRA-DELUXE.

The luxurious **Peabody Orlando** is distinguished by the profile of a duck on its tower. Inside, five real mallard ducks parade across a red carpet rolled out for their processions to the pond. Guests gather for the twice-daily event in the lobby, an elegant, soaring space filled with sunlight, marble and vigorous plantings of orchids, ferns and bromeliads. There's a Mallard Lounge and the outstanding Dux Restaurant (but no duck on the menu). The hotel's 891 rooms are extra large and plushly adorned; the service, exceptional. On the fourth floor you'll find lighted tennis courts; a heated, double-size Olympic pool; a health club and beauty salon; and a "duck palace" where the feathered guys spend their evenings. ~ 9801 International Drive, Orlando; 407-352-4000, 800-732-2639, fax 407-351-9177; www.peabodyorlando.com. ULTRA-DELUXE.

During recent years, a new brand of family-style lodging has popped up around Disney World. Fashioned like apartment and townhouse complexes, these resorts offer spacious units with full kitchens, bedrooms and washers and dryers. Grocery shopping service is usually available for a small fee, and on-site restaurants cater to young picky eaters. These are three of the best:

Waterfalls decorate the lush landscaping at the **Marriott Residence Inn Lake Buena Vista**. This Caribbean-style lodging features studios and one- and two-bedroom suites. Amenities include a basketball court, an outdoor pool, an exercise room and self-service laundry facilities. There's a complimentary breakfast buffet as well as dinner delivery service from local restaurants. ~ 11450 Marbella Palms Court, Orlando; 407-465-0075, 800-228-9290, fax 407-465-0050; www.residenceinn.com. DELUXE TO ULTRA-DELUXE.

Tennis players with generous vacationing budgets might like **Sheraton Vistana Resort**. The nearly 1000 units can accommo-

LINE-JUMPING

Staying at one of Universal's on-site hotels offers more convenience than you think. Room keys from either hotel get you front-of-the-line privileges at many Universal Studios and Islands of Adventure attractions. Just show your key at the Universal Express entrance and you're in. Certain passes offer limited access to the Universal Express approach. Ask at time of purchase if you qualify.

date large groups in their spacious designer villas and town-houses, all with full kitchens. Thirteen tennis courts are framed in 135 acres of lush landscaping. Seven swimming pools and three fitness centers are other extras. ~ 8800 Vistana Center Drive, Lake Buena Vista; 407-239-3100, 800-877-8787, fax 407-852-4631; www.scanwoodvo.com. ULTRA-DELUXE.

The first thing most people notice about the **MainStay Suites Maingate** is its wood-burning fireplaces (a rarity for a Central Florida hotel). What families should notice are the inn's spacious suites (all with kitchens) and swimming pool, kiddie playground and picnic areas with charcoal grills. They're all nestled in the woods along pretty Lake Cecile, where you can sail, water ski, canoe or fish off a dock. Rates include a generous family-style continental breakfast buffet. ~ 4786 West Route 192, Kissimmee; 407-396-2056, 800-468-3027, fax 407-396-2909; www.choice hotels.com. MODERATE.

Named for their location at Disney World's northern entrance, "Maingate Hotels" are mostly of the generic chain variety and offer lower rates than Disney hotels. A few stand out:

The most reasonable prices near Disney World can be found at the string of chain hotels on Route 192. **La Quinta Inn Lakeside** boasts its own private lake, tucked in a 24-acre throng of pine trees and tropical landscaping. Accommodations have plenty of added touches: three swimming pools plus two kiddie pools, two children's playgrounds, a video gameroom, a fitness center, putt-putt golf, tennis courts and a late-night deli. Herbie's Kids Club hosts nighttime games and meals for children ages 5 through 12. ~ 7769 West Route 192, Kissimmee; 407-396-2222, 800-848-0801, fax 407-239-2650; www.laquintainnlakeside.com, e-mail info@laquintainnlakeside.com. MODERATE.

The two-story, brick-front **Golden Link Motel** sits on Lake Cecile. A heated swimming pool and a fishing pier come with 84 clean and adequate rooms. ~ 4914 West Route 192, Kissimmee; 407-396-0555, 800-654-3957; www.goldenlinkmotel.com, e-mail goldenlinkmotel@cfl.rr.com. BUDGET.

Arches and red-brick trim lend **The Thrift Lodge** a touch of Mediterranean flavor. Large, modern rooms are complemented by a swimming pool. ~ 4624 Route 192, Kissimmee; 407-396-2642, 800-673-2642, fax 407-396-6653; www.thriftlodge.com. BUDGET.

Fresh as a hibiscus, **Magic Castle Inn and Suites** decorates its 114 guest rooms in typical Ramada fashion and offers family convenience. The inn also serves a continental breakfast, and the swimming pool and playground are kid-pleasers. ~ 4559 Route 192, Kissimmee; 407-396-1212, 800-544-5712, fax 407-396-7926. BUDGET.

▼ ▼ ▼ ▼ ▼ ▼ ▼ ▼ ▼
Camping

Few experiences put you closer to the "real" Florida than camping. Dozens of campgrounds, right outside Disney's door, offer sleep among mossy slash pines and palmettos or on wide-open fields dotted with lakes. You can arrive in your own RV or pitch a tent, or rent those provided by many campgrounds. In addition, there is a splendid campground in Disney World itself.

For families, camping can be an ideal alternative to the hotel-motel scene. Children have plenty of room to run (no more zipping down hotel hallways and waking up the neighbors) and myriad other activities. There are hayrides, campfires, canoeing, swimming, bicycling, trees to climb, trails to explore and lakes to fish. Of course, camping is usually cheaper than staying at a hotel. You get to cook your own food and can often bring your pets. And no fancy room service can replace the camaraderie of campers, particularly among families. All in all, a welcome change of pace from theme-park mania.

From vast RV parks and tiny backwoods fish camps to nudist resorts, there is a wide range of ways to camp outside Disney World. When booking a site, check the distance from Disney: It's best to stay within a few miles or you'll waste time getting to and from the theme parks. Most campgrounds will arrange shuttles to the parks (for a fee), though it's more convenient to drive. For an extensive listing of campgrounds, write or call the **Kissimmee–St. Cloud Convention and Visitors Bureau**. Closed weekends. ~ 1925 East Irlo Bronson Memorial Highway, Kissimmee; 407-847-5000, 800-333-5477; fax 407-847-0878; www.florida kiss.com. Or try the **Florida Association of RV Parks and Campgrounds**. ~ 1340 Vickers Road, Tallahassee, FL 32303-3041; 850-562-7151, fax 850-562-7179; www.floridacamping.com, e-mail flaarvc@aol.com.

Some of the prime camping grounds for families are:

The **Tropical Palms Resort** is one of the biggest campgrounds, featuring 600 sites for RVs, pop-up campers and tents. Some sites are right out in the open, while others rest amid the tall oaks and palms that dot the park. There are also 144 "cottages." Only three miles from Disney World, the village is next to the Old Town shopping and entertainment complex. There are two swimming pools and a grocery and some unusual amenities such as cable TV hookups and a guest-services desk that sells Disney tickets. ~ 2650 Holiday Trail, off East Route 192, Kissimmee; 407-396-4595, 800-647-2567, fax 407-396-8938; www.tropicalpalmsrv.com. BUDGET.

Kissimmee-Orlando KOA has 100 RV and tent sites, some in shaded and grassy areas, some on concrete. Amenities include a swimming pool, small playground, coin laundry and grocery. ~ 2644 Happy Camper Place, Kissimmee; 407-396-2400, 800-562-

Camp
Wilderness

Not unexpectedly, Walt Disney World boasts the most elaborate campground. **Fort Wilderness Resort** offers every amenity imaginable, from a nature island and petting zoo to nightly Disney movies and a water theme park. The shower facilities are so complete, says one mother, that "we could get real dressed up for dinner every night." And you can even hear the birds sing. Among the many Disney perks offered are:

❖ Boat shuttles to the Magic Kingdom and bus service to everything else inside Disney World.

❖ Air-conditioned "comfort stations" with restrooms, hot showers, spacious changing areas, ice machines and coin laundry.

❖ Several delis and snack shacks, a moderate-priced restaurant and a tavern.

❖ Riding stables, nature trails, tennis courts, swimming pools, arcades, playgrounds, a picturesque lake with a beach and swimming, canals for canoeing and a marina with sailboat and water ski rentals and bass fishing charters.

❖ Pioneer Hall, home of the Hoop-Dee-Doo Musical Revue.

Despite all this, many people incredibly won't stay at Fort Wilderness because they think they'll be roughing it. What a mistake. The 740-acre wooded retreat has trailer homes that make motel rooms look like closets. Nestled in shady pines, the 407 air-conditioned trailers come with full kitchens and bathrooms, bedroom, televisions, telephones and daily maid service. They're deluxe to ultra-deluxe-priced, but they sleep up to four or six people. Outside, there's a little yard with a picnic table and barbecue grill.

For those who bring their own RV, pop-up camper or tent, Fort Wilderness offers 784 campsites buried in the trees. They all have electrical outlets, picnic tables and charcoal grills, and all provide water and sewer hookup. Most sites are in the budget range year-round; sites with cable TV hookup are moderate.

During the summer, Fort Wilderness is often booked solid by Easter. If you're going in-season, make reservations several months in advance. ~ 407-824-2900. (For more on Fort Wilderness, see Chapter Six.)

7791, fax 407-396-7577; www.kissorlandokoa.com, e-mail kissimmee@koa.net. BUDGET.

Sherwood Forest RV Resort is thick with trees yet has a modern spic-and-span look. Over 500 RV and tent sites are available, as well as a heated swimming pool, miniature golf, tennis courts and a pond. Families frequent the park during summer, but seniors are the primary winter customers. ~ 5300 West Route 192, Kissimmee; 407-396-7431, 800-548-9981, fax 407-396-7239. BUDGET.

The Cadillac of RV camping, **Outdoor Resorts at Orlando** sprawls across 150 beautifully manicured acres. Paved lanes crisscross the park, which boasts 980 RV sites, an executive par-3, nine-hole golf course, tennis courts and huge clubhouse. There's fishing and sailing on a 400-acre lake, and swimming in the Olympic-size pool and children's pool. There's no tent camping, but you can rent an RV on a weekly basis. ~ Route 192 just east of Route 27, Clermont; 863-424-1407, 800-531-3033, fax 863-424-5476; www.oro-orlando.com. BUDGET.

If you prefer to camp in the buff, check out **Cypress Cove Nudist Resort & Spa**. Tucked inside a 260-acre forest, the purist's retreat hosts couples as well as families who have RVs and tents. Most campsites are in the slash pines, while a few additional sites (open only when the rest are full) lie along a 50-acre lake (small boats welcome). There are two swimming pools, two hot tubs, two full-service restaurants and motel villas for those more tuned to life's luxuries. Kids under 12 stay free. ~ 4425 Pleasant Hill Road, Kissimmee; 407-933-5870, 888-683-3130, fax 407-933-3559; www.cypresscoveresort.com, e-mail relax@cypresscoveresort.com. Villas are MODERATE TO DELUXE; campsites are BUDGET.

Among the fun things you'll find at **Fort Summit KOA Campground** are air-conditioned log cabins and bathhouses. The cabins sleep up to four people in their double and bunk beds and have cable TV hookups. There are also 300 RV and tent sites, sprinkled across the flat pastureland, as well as a heated swimming pool and children's wading pool, fenced playground and video gameroom. One drawback: Fort Summit is seven miles from Disney World, though free shuttles are provided. ~ 2525 Frontage Road, Davenport; 863-424-1880, 800-424-1880, fax 863-420-8831; www.fortsummit.com, e-mail info@fortsummit.com. BUDGET.

Lake Toho Resort is farther from Disney World—about 25 miles—but it features idyllic camping along beautiful Lake Tohopekaliga. The 280 RV sites have water, sewer and electric hookups. ~ 4715 Kissimmee Park Road, St. Cloud; 407-892-8795, fax 407-892-3525. BUDGET.

The several hundred restaurants inside Disney World tend to fall into three categories: (1) Lousy, overpriced fast food; (2) Decent, overpriced fast food; and (3) Quality, upscale dining.

Dining

Unfortunately, many fall into the first group, particularly in the Magic Kingdom, where families spend a lot of time. For the convenience of eating on Mickey's turf, you often have long lines and crowded dining. Even at Epcot's four-star restaurants, tables are squeezed together, and diners are sometimes hurried through their meals.

But Disney dining isn't all bad. Indeed, where else do you find elegant restaurants that welcome you, dressed in shorts and sneakers, with your kids and stroller? Even better, most restaurants have good kids' menus (though not always kid-size prices) and special touches such as coloring books and Disney character visits. Dining outside Disney World may lack some of these effects, but you can find some interesting places away from theme-park confines.

A little advance planning will help you avoid long waits for any restaurant. If you're visiting in-season, avoid the Disney rush hours (11:30 a.m. to 1:30 p.m. and 5 to 8 p.m.). Or skip lunch by eating a big breakfast before you go to the parks, then buy a mid-afternoon snack from a vendor. The vendors, located throughout Disney's theme parks, peddle everything from pretzels and hot dogs to baked potatoes and ice cream.

Pluto signs the "o" in his name with a paw print.

Within this chapter, the restaurants are categorized by theme park, with each restaurant entry describing the establishment as budget, moderate, deluxe or ultra-deluxe in price. Dinner entrées at *budget* restaurants usually cost $10 or less; *moderately* priced restaurants range between $10 and $20; *deluxe* establishments tab their entrées above $20; and at *ultra-deluxe* dining rooms, $30 will only get you started.

If you're staying at a Disney resort, you can request priority seating for lunch and dinner at full-service restaurants one to ninety days in advance for most eateries. ~ 407-939-3463. Otherwise, make reservations at the restaurant as early as possible on the day you plan to dine.

MAGIC KINGDOM The fast food at the Magic Kingdom needs no introduction—its reputation for poor taste precedes it. Still, everyone ends up eating it eventually out of necessity. To help you know where to eat, here are my best of the worst:

❖ On Main Street, a cart called **Caffe Italiano** has precisely what you need in the morning: steamy espresso and cappuccino, fruit-studded muffins and bagels, and bottled juice for the kids. Iced cappuccino cools you off in the afternoon.

❖ On Tom Sawyer Island, **Aunt Polly's Dockside Landing** (Frontierland) has peanut-butter-and-jelly sandwiches that are served with an apple as well as a cookie.

❖ The **Columbia Harbour House** (Liberty Square) makes a decent Monte Cristo sandwich (deep-fried, with turkey, ham and cheese) and has good clam chowder.

❖ **Sleepy Hollow** (Liberty Square) is open seasonally and makes the kids happy with brownies, cookie sandwiches and root beer floats.

❖ **Cosmic Ray's Starlight Cafe** (Tomorrowland) does a decent veggie burger and also rotisserie chicken. The caesar and chef salads are "tossed to order," but aren't always the freshest.

Unless you're a glutton for gastronomic abuse, stay away from these places: Tomorrowland's **Launching Pad at Rocket-tower Plaza** (the hamburgers are horrible); Tomorrowland's **Plaza Pavilion** (the hoagies are scary); and any fast-food restaurant in Fantasyland. Besides having bad food, they're the most crowded eateries in the Magic Kingdom.

Five Magic Kingdom restaurants offer full-service dining. One of these, the Crystal Palace, has a good breakfast and, best of all, opens a half-hour before the rest of the park.

Remember the romantic scene in *Lady and the Tramp* where the two dogs smooch over a plate of spaghetti? They were in an Italian joint called Tony's, which has been re-created on Main Street as **Tony's Town Square Restaurant**. Scenes from the movie line the brick walls of the airy Victorian café with polished brass and painted, white iron chairs. Like many Disney eateries, the setting is fancier than the food—standard Italian fare served in heaping platefuls. Children get their own coloring-book menus filled with pictures of Lady and the Tramp (waiters provide the crayons). MODERATE.

> The waffles at Tony's Town Square Restaurant are shaped like the faces of Lady and the Tramp.

The Magic Kingdom's prettiest restaurant, the **Crystal Palace**, is wrapped in French windows and crowned by a sparkling glass dome. Located on Main Street, Crystal Palace is outlined in delicate white filigree and overlooks palm trees and sculpted flower beds. The breakfast, lunch and dinner buffet features appearances by Winnie the Pooh, Tigger and Eeyore. A hearty breakfast selection (bacon, eggs, omelettes, etc.) starts the day. The children's buffets include Mickey waffles for breakfast, and macaroni and cheese, pizza and hot dogs for lunch and dinner. Go for the breakfast buffet, the best in the Magic Kingdom. MODERATE.

The **Plaza Restaurant**, also on Main Street, serves only lunch and dinner. Across from the Sealtest Ice Cream Parlor, it's a breezy place with mirrors and windows and dressed-up fast-food fare.

Kids like the burgers and milkshakes, and parents usually go for the chef's salads, quiche or fancy chicken pot pies. BUDGET.

Little girls adore **Cinderella's Royal Table** because they get to meet Cinderella. The stunning blonde princess, draped in chiffon and crowned with a jeweled tiara, sweeps through several times a day. Another reason to go is that it's the only way to get into the Cinderella Castle in Fantasyland. For lunch there are prime rib sandwiches and a variety of salads; for dinner, you'll find prime rib and seafood and chicken dishes. Unfortunately, the food is only passable. But the fabulous surroundings and excitement of the kids more than makes up for it. DELUXE TO ULTRA-DELUXE.

With its stone hearth, plank floors and Colonial wallpaper, the **Liberty Tree Tavern** feels warm and cozy. Located in Liberty Square, this charming place is an oasis of early Americana. There's an antique spinning wheel, ladder-back chairs and Venetian wood blinds. To match the decor, the lunch menu has such items as the Yankee Peddler (prime rib sandwich), Boston Seafood Melt (seafood combo in wine sauce) and Minuteman Club sandwich. For dinner, there are chicken, steak and seafood, including Maine lobster in season. The service is good and the food better than average. Unless you plan to dine early, reservations are a must here. Make them at the restaurant, anytime after 11 a.m. MODERATE.

EPCOT People go to the Magic Kingdom to dream, but they come to Epcot to eat (at least part of the time). What the Magic Kingdom lacks in decent dining, Epcot more than makes up for with fresh, innovative fare and lovely surroundings. Strangely, even the Epcot vendors seem better than those in the Magic Kingdom. Another big difference: You can't buy alcoholic drinks in the Magic Kingdom, but you can at most of Epcot's sit-down establishments.

Epcot's most popular restaurants (Chefs de France, L'Originale Alfredo di Roma Ristorante and the Coral Reef Restaurant) are difficult to get into. Reservations are highly recommended. If you are staying at a Disney resort, you can request priority seating up to 90 days in advance. ~ 407-939-3463.

Future World Epcot's Future World has two mundane fast-food restaurants and one very good one: **Fountain View Espresso and Bakery** in Innoventions West. Take a seat at the pretty espresso bar for your early-morning wakeup call; choices include cappuccinos, lattes, mochas, croissants and pastries. BUDGET.

For fancier breakfasting, go to the **Garden Grill** at The Land pavilion, the only Epcot restaurant offering table service in the mornings. Character dining is available here where you can pose with Minnie, Mickey and Chip and Dale. Lunch and dinner feature an ever-changing menu filled with herbs, vegetables and fish from the restaurant's own hydroponic garden and fish farm. You might find sautéed trout or tilapia, corn on the cob, mashed potatoes, or barbecue riblets and rotisserie chicken. Diners nestle into cozy booths bordered by sunflower-patterned walls and, as the restaurant revolves, get great views of the rain forest, prairie and other scenes from The Land's boat ride. DELUXE.

Downstairs from the Garden Grill, **Sunshine Season Food Fair** is a lively food court in a huge rotunda hung with miniature hot-air balloons. This colorful space offers a veritable smorgasbord of fresh, healthy, smell-and-taste-good fare. There are steamy spuds and soups, tossed pasta salads, stuffed pita pockets, deli sandwiches and barbecue chicken. Kids gravitate toward the ice cream counter, while parents head for the beverage window that has frozen cocktails and nonalcoholic fruit slushies.

For a quick, healthy meal, stop by **Pure and Simple** in the Wonders of Life pavilion. In keeping with the attraction's "be good to your body" theme, the takeout eatery offers turkey and veggie hot dogs (most kids can't tell the difference), fruit-topped waffles, chili with lean venison and other low-fat fare that tastes good. BUDGET.

The best thing about the Living Seas' **Coral Reef Restaurant** is the sweeping view of a mammoth coral reef aquarium. From dimly lit, tiered rows, diners can watch sharks, dolphins and shrimp—then eat some. The shrimp is simmered with tomatoes, leeks and onions, and the mahimahi broiled and brushed with lemon caper butter. Lunch and dinner menus feature mainly seafood such as sashimi-style tuna and pan-seared swordfish. DELUXE TO ULTRA-DELUXE.

World Showcase Many of the restaurants here are striking replicas of famous restaurants in their respective countries and offer an array of ethnic and Continental cuisine. Waiters and waitresses are natives of their host countries and enjoy talking about their homelands, so don't be afraid to ask questions.

You might expect Epcot's most romantic restaurant to be in the France or Italy pavilions, but it's in Mexico. The **San Angel Inn Restaurante** rests along a dark river actually flowing beneath a simulated night sky sprinkled with stars. The air is cool, and the tables are well-spaced and topped with pink tablecloths and flickering oil lamps. Unfortunately, the ambience is far better than the fare, which is only average and overpriced (typical lunch entrée: $12; average dinner entrée: $18—and we're talking Tex-Mex food here). Expect such dishes as chicken enchiladas, *chiles rellenos* and *cochinita pibil* (pork baked in spice marmalade). However, San Angel is a good place to bring the kids because they can explore the adjacent Mexican market while waiting for the food and while you're waiting for the check. MODERATE TO DELUXE.

Scandinavia has never been known for its culinary achievements, and perhaps that's why many visitors shy away from Norway's **Restaurant Akershus**. For those willing to experiment, the eatery has a hot and cold buffet, or *koldtbord*, piled with smoked salmon and herring dishes, cold roasted chicken, rutabagas, lamb and cabbage and other native eats. For children's palates, there are meatballs and macaroni and cheese. The food was not to my liking, but the restaurant, with its carved wood ceilings, turret rooms and Gothic archways, was positively beautiful. MODERATE TO DELUXE.

Despite the grandeur of the China pavilion, its **Nine Dragons Restaurant** is disappointing. The food, a rendition of American-style Chinese favorites, is mediocre and deluxe-priced. Maybe you pay for the opulent surroundings, a fusion of garnet-red carpets, rosewood dividers and wood tabletops that glimmer. DELUXE. If in the mood for Chinese, stop by the pavilion's **Lotus Blossom Café**, which offers stir-fried beef, egg rolls, sweet-and-sour chicken and red bean ice cream. BUDGET.

Every meal at Germany's **Biergarten** is a party. Strolling accordion players, yodelers and an oom-pah-pah band make merry while diners feast on an all-you-can-eat buffet. The rousing atmosphere is perfect for families, and kids like the cool, castle-like surroundings. Though the food focus is decidedly German, the tasty and robust fare—ranging from sausages to rotisserie chicken—is bound to have something for everyone. MODERATE TO DELUXE.

Italy's **L'Originale Alfredo di Roma Ristorante** is the second-most popular Epcot restaurant. Fine Italian dishes such as fettuccine Alfredo (whose creator the restaurant is named for), veal piccata and plenty of pasta are featured. Kids go for the spaghetti and meatballs and enjoy watching the strolling musicians. One drawback: The tables are way too close, and the place is always crowded. I was seated at a table in the middle of the room and got bumped several times by waiters. Either dine early or late, or go off-season. MODERATE TO DELUXE.

❖❖❖

EPCOT'S FIVE-STAR STREET VENDORS

Epcot's vendor fare goes way beyond traditional street food. Here are my favorites:

- ❖ Warm waffles and cool kaki-gori (fruit ices), in front of Japan's pavilion.
- ❖ Foot-long hot dogs and popcorn (smell it and try to walk by), in front of the United States pavilion.
- ❖ Jumbo baked potatoes (with cheese, please), in front of the United Kingdom pavilion.
- ❖ Creamy bread custard and fresh fruit, outside Canada's pavilion.

How sad that the United States pavilion's signature restaurant is a fast-food joint. (Every other World Showcase country has at least one fine dining establishment, and some have two.) On the plus side, the **Liberty Inn** is a blessing for families. Children love the burgers, hot dogs and chocolate chip cookies (look for the kids wearing cookie on their faces), and the outdoor seating provides plenty of open space. BUDGET.

Before queuing up at a Disney fast-food restaurant, check the line farthest from the door— it's often the shortest.

Ever been to a Benihana's? Then skip the Japan pavilion's **Mitsukoshi Teppan Yaki Dining Room**, which does a great job of imitating the Japanese chain restaurants. Like China's restaurant, Japan's avoids true regional creations and instead offers Americanized versions of teppan table cooking. Japanese cooks do put on a nice show as they slice and sear the meats, chicken and seafood right on your tabletop stove. It's a good place for families because everyone shares tables and the cooks are sociable. DELUXE.

Couscous and bastila are some of the delicious dishes served at the **Restaurant Marrakesh** in the Morocco pavilion. The first consists of tiny pasta grains served with a vegetable stew; the second is spicy almonds, saffron and cinnamon layered with filo. The atmosphere is properly North African, featuring musicians and beautiful belly dancers. If the kids (or dad) want to be part of the show, mention it to a waitress. The dancers enjoy including children. DELUXE TO ULTRA-DELUXE.

Les Chefs De France and the adjoining Petit Cafe in the France pavilion have merged into one dining establishment that offers a full menu inside in the more formal dining area and outside on the sidewalk café. MODERATE TO DELUXE.

I prefer the **Bistro de Paris**, a charming spot with carved ceilings, brass sconces and tabletop bouquets and candles. Cuisine includes roasted fish, seafood casserole and beef tenderloin, all bathed in light cream sauces. The bistro is difficult to book, so plan ahead. DELUXE.

At the United Kingdom pavilion's **Rose & Crown Dining Room**, serving wenches deliver simple English pub fare such as fish and chips, Scotch eggs or steak-and-kidney pie. You can dine indoors amid brass and etched-glass surroundings or on the patio at the edge of the lagoon. MODERATE TO DELUXE.

Le Cellier Steakhouse in Canada is a dependable and consistent full-service eatery featuring steaks, grilled burgers, salads, seafood and pasta. Set inside thick stone walls, this is a medieval-style place with dark, heavy wood, wrought-iron lamps and Naugahyde booths. MODERATE.

DISNEY–MGM STUDIOS   As you might guess, restaurants in The Studios reflect a passion for Hollywood and movies. Unfortunately,

Disney thought and imagination went into the decor but not the menus. Still, most food is at least passable, and the starry surroundings make it worthwhile for most people.

For a light breakfast, **Starring Rolls Bakery** (Hollywood Boulevard) has bagels, muffins and giant bearclaw pastries. It opens a half-hour before the rest of Disney–MGM, so you can get a bite before seeing the sights. Later in the day, stop by for one of the bakery's many decadent desserts.

Hollywood's legendary Brown Derby restaurant is gone, but its copycat is alive and prospering at Disney–MGM. Like its California namesake, the **Hollywood Brown Derby** (Hollywood Boulevard) is classy and clubby and outfitted with teakwood, chandeliers and caricatures of film stars. Included on the lunch and dinner menus are pasta, veal and seafood dishes and the colorful cobb salad. The latter, made famous at the original restaurant, features fresh greens topped with rows of chopped bacon, avocado, tomato, bleu cheese and turkey. The portions are large but the service is slow and the prices high. For families in a hurry or on a budget, the Brown Derby is not a good choice. DELUXE.

The **50's Prime Time Café** (near Echo Lake) is marvelous for families. The setting is a *Leave It to Beaver*–style kitchen where you pull up a vinyl chair to a formica table. A June Cleaver look-alike (please, call her mom) serves, then urges you to clean your plate. (Make sure to keep your elbows off the table and mind your p's and q's lest "Mom" puts you in a corner.) The food comes on those great school lunchroom plates with little compartments and features homey yummies such as meatloaf and mashed potatoes, granny's pot roast, Aunt Selma's chicken salad and alphabet soup. "Mom" brings coloring books and crayons for the kids and checks for dirty fingernails before dinner. MODERATE TO DELUXE.

In addition to the 50's Prime Time Café, there are other restaurants stepping back in time to Hollywood-past. The **ABC Commissary** (located by the Chinese Theater) is a cafeteria-style eatery decorated in 1930s art deco that features seafood bean salad, stir-fried chicken and a banana egg roll dessert. BUDGET.

Next door is the full-service **Sci-Fi Dine-In Theater Restaurant**. The club sandwiches, hamburgers and seafood lean toward the just-passable side, but the setting—an indoor re-creation of an outdoor drive-in theater at twilight—is a hoot. You'll dine in vintage "cars" and get to watch some sci-fi shorts on the big screen. Truly unique. MODERATE TO DELUXE.

A permanently moored steamer with outdoor seating, **Min & Bills Dockside Diner** (on Echo Lake) serves sandwiches, salads, fruit and yogurt. BUDGET. **Hollywood & Vine** (near Echo Lake) is a buffet restaurant done in 1950s-era diner decor that specializes in grilled, broiled or rotisserie steak, fish and chicken. Be sure to ask for a seat with a view of the enormous wall mural depicting Hollywood landmarks. BUDGET TO MODERATE. For dessert, step back in time to **Dinosaur Gertie's Ice Cream of Extinction** (near Echo Lake) for a budget-priced frozen candy bar sold from the belly of a *brachiosaurus*. BUDGET.

Tucked on a side street beyond Star Tours, **Mama Melrose's Ristorante Italiano** is my favorite Disney–MGM eatery. The inside really is reminiscent of a warm, old-time pizzeria—with cozy booths, red-and-white-checkered tablecloths, flickering oil lamps, and heat emanating from the big brick pizza oven. The bubbly, cheesy disks are the dish of choice, though the vegetable lasagna and chicken breasts with basil garlic sauce, topped with mozzarella and parmesan cheeses, are also excellent. Other pluses: a big children's menu and reasonable prices. There's lunch and dinner, though "Mama" usually closes before the park does, so check times. MODERATE.

Disney–MGM also has several fast-food eateries. **Studio Catering Co.** (Disney–MGM Studios Backlot Tour) serves sandwiches and coffee and is so hidden it's rarely crowded. **Backlot Express** (near Star Tours) has decent burgers and dogs, and **Pizza Planet**—The *Toy Story*–themed restaurant (it was named for the restaurant where Woody met the little Martian guys)—has salads and good, gooey pizzas.

DISNEY'S ANIMAL KINGDOM Unlike at other theme parks, dining at the Animal Kingdom is not a major attraction. Restaurants don't have quite the level of, er, character that you'll find at, say, the Magic Kingdom or Epcot. The food isn't bad though—in fact, some of the little coffee shops with baked goods are exceptionally good.

Your only full-service choice in the park is technically outside of the park: the **Rainforest Cafe**. You don't have to pay admission to enjoy it (in fact, you'll need a handstamp to get back in the park if you dine there), but you may have to wait in line just the same. Launched as a vehicle for environmental awareness and entertainment, the restaurant is decidedly authentic, featuring tropical mists (making the restaurant a bad choice if you're counting on a good hair day!), cascading waterfalls, resident parrots (real ones) and tropical flora and fauna. The place even has the exotic smell of a rainforest. This chain restaurant is a hectic place, often featuring waits of an hour or more. The food (hamburgers, ribs, chicken nuggets) isn't bad, and the kids will like the animatronic animals (check out the squirting elephant outside) and periodic thunder storms. MODERATE.

Past the ticket counters, your options are pretty much counter service. In Discovery Island, you'll probably smell the fare of the **Flame Tree Barbecue** before you see it. The aromatic menu of bar-

Where Shall We Eat?

Choosing a restaurant at Disney is no simple affair. There are literally hundreds of eateries here, from the standard fast food at the theme parks to gourmet meals at some of the hotels.

Some of the most coveted tables are at the character meals where kids can grab a bite with Mickey Mouse, Donald Duck and the rest of the Disney gang. The daily galas are most common at breakfast, but some restaurants host character lunches and dinners as well. Perhaps the best part is the chance to get some of those autographs without having to wait in an endless line.

Perhaps the most popular of them all is the **Once Upon a Time** breakfast in Cinderella Castle at the Magic Kingdom. It's not known for the food (it's a fixed menu), but the opportunity to meet and greet the royal cast is unforgettable. Another princess meal is at **Restaurant Akershus** in Epcot's Norway. There are about a dozen character dining opportunities in all, including **Restaurantosaurus** (Donald, et al; breakfast; Animal Kingdom), and the **Crystal Palace** (Pooh and friends; all day; Magic Kingdom). Cupcakes and tea are the whole menu at the **Wonderland Tea Party** (1:30 daily; Magic Kingdom). Look for buffets, including my favorite, at the Grand Floridian's **1900 Park Fare** (Mary Poppins at breakfast; Cinderella at dinner) at which you can stuff yourself silly. Such meals can be booked as much as 90 days out—a good idea if you want to dine with Cinderella at Christmas. Prices are all on the deluxe side.

Grownups, too, need to think ahead. The romantic **Victoria & Albert's** at the Grand Floridian (jacket required) can be booked as much as six months in advance. Reserve your slot at the **Spirit of Aloha Dinner Show**, and the **Hoop-Dee-Doo Musical Revue** as much as two years ahead. Rave reviews at the **California Grill** (the Contemporary), the **Flying Fish Café** (BoardWalk), **Jiko** (Animal Kingdom Lodge) have drawn crowds, so it's best to take advantage of the 90-day booking window. Most other Disney restaurants can be booked 90 days ahead of time.

Call 407-939-3463 for all locations.

becue chicken, ribs, pork and beef are a decidedly tasty alternative to your typical theme-park burger, and you can enjoy it on a comfortable outdoor plaza on the water. MODERATE. Fresh slices are always in the oven at **Pizzafari** where you can also grab a quick salad or a sandwich. MODERATE.

In DinoLand U.S.A., the paleontologically themed **Restaurantosaurus** offers food throughout the day. Breakfast is an all-you-can-eat buffet (Donald's Prehistoric Breakfastosauraus) with the characters. After 11 a.m., the dining spot becomes the place for quick bites of McDonalds. BUDGET. As an alternative, you can get a handle on an oversized turkey leg at the **Dino Diner**. BUDGET.

You won't have to walk far to find a bite in Africa. Food at the **Tusker House Restaurant** runs the gamut from rotisserie to fried chicken, as well as beef sandwiches and salads. MODERATE. If it's sweet treats you're craving, you can find them throughout the park. A couple of favorites include the fresh-baked goodies at Africa's **Kusafiri Coffee Shop & Bakery**, where you can also grab a cup of joe, and the ice cream and cookies at **Chip 'n' Dale's Cookie Cabin** in Camp Minnie-Mickey. BUDGET.

DOWNTOWN DISNEY   Away from the big theme parks, Disney World has even more to offer diners. Some of these eateries play to smaller crowds, particularly during lunch when the theme parks are gorged with visitors, while others are attracting their own mobs, making reservations or creative scheduling a must.

Marketplace   The **Wolfgang Puck Express** serves up fast-food with panache. The colorful eatery, dotted with deco bistro tables, features Puck's signature wood-fired pizzas, as well as tomato gazpacho soup, chinois salad, garlic mashed potatoes and rotisserie chicken caesar sandwiches. BUDGET TO MODERATE.

Under an active volcano at the back of the Marketplace, the **Rainforest Cafe**, a sister eatery of the Disney's Animal Kingdom

DINING WITH ROYALTY

The Earl of Sandwich, the latest addition to the Downtown Disney Marketplace, offers king-sized sandwiches with a dash of pedigree. Opened in fall 2003 by—you guessed it—a descendent of England's very own Earl of Sandwich, the eatery offers hot and cold sandwiches in a space designed after the Sandwich's English estate. What prompted such a chain of events? Apparently, according to the *New York Times*, being an English aristocrat isn't what it used to be. And the sandwich shop, the first in a planned chain, seemed a natural. "Like it or not," Orlando Montagu, son of the current Lord Sandwich, told the *New York Times* in July 2003, "the connection between our family and the food product has turned from being a story to a brand."

restaurant, offers adventure as well as repast. Here, you don't just dine; you go on safari. Inside the dining rooms is a jungle of oversized greenery, wildlife and tropical storms that sweep the room every 20 minutes. Kids will love the animatron gorillas and elephants, not to mention Tracy the talking tree. Sample fare includes Rasta Pasta (bowtie pasta with creamy garlic sauce, grilled chicken and spinach) and Tuscan Chicken (chicken with cucumbers and kalamata olives). All the gimmickry has made for a very popular dining spot, and waits of two hours or more are not unusual. Reservations are suggested. Show up early (before noon for lunch, before 5 p.m. for dinner) to avoid the wait. ~ 407-827-8500; www.rainforestcafe.com. MODERATE TO DELUXE.

If you want a sit-down dinner without the wait, you can make a reservation at **Fulton's Crab House**. Seafood is the featured fare, but meat eaters will find steak and chicken on the menu as well. Children's selections include pasta, hamburgers and hot dogs. The restaurant makes its home on the permanently docked riverboat alongside the Marketplace and lunch and dinner are served daily. ~ 407-934-2628. DELUXE TO ULTRA-DELUXE.

The **Portobello Yacht Club** is a charming Italian eatery that sits waterside and is nautically furnished with rudder ceiling fans, ships' models, wood paneling and shiny brass. Service is impeccable, the atmosphere jovial and the food fresh, tasty and well-priced. There are thin-crusted pizzas, grilled over a wood fire, garlic shrimp and lots of pasta dishes, all cooked in an open kitchen. ~ 407-934-8888. DELUXE TO ULTRA-DELUXE.

Modeled after the Nashville club of the same name, the split-level **Wildhorse Saloon** reflects real Southern hospitality. The only country-and-western establishment in the Disney metropolis, you'll find both food and fun under one roof. Chow down on barbecue—steak, ribs, chicken—as well as catfish, hushpuppies and other down-home standbys. Then tap your toes to the songs of emerging country artists, or learn how to tap them differently with a hot new dance. MODERATE TO DELUXE.

One place where everyone wants to go to eat, drink, be seen or simply breathe the movie star–tinged air, is **Planet Hollywood**, part of the international chain owned by Demi Moore, Bruce Willis, Arnold Schwarzenegger and Sylvester Stallone. Phenomenally popular, with phenomenal lines to match, this big blue ball with a spaceship planted in its side has nightly waits approaching two hours—much of it outside. You can skip the lines by visiting between 2:30 and 4:30 p.m. Forget lunchtime; the wait's at least an hour. Now, about the food and mood: they're good. Very good, indeed, from the far-out, planetoid decor and movie clips blasting from giant screens to the feverish crowds and tasty servings of chicken and fish and wood-grilled pizzas. The bi-level "planet" is big and open and filled with strangeness: glittering gems under glass at the bars, leopard-print carpet and zebra-print tablecloths, a VW beetle and canoe dangling from the ceiling, dozens of movie artifacts encased in glass on the walls, hostesses using their little headset microphones to summon the next lucky diners. MODERATE.

West Side Of course, Planet Hollywood and all the other Pleasure Island dining establishments have gotten a hefty dose of competition as other high-profile eateries have moved into this neighboring area. Bearing the name of the world-famous Spago chef, the **Wolfgang Puck Café** features Puck's own brand of California cuisine, including those famed wood-fired pizzas. You'll also find glorious entrées and soups. Kids are often given dough to make their own pizza at the pizza bar. You can get full service inside, or opt for cafeteria style on the patio. ~ 407-938-9653. MODERATE TO DELUXE.

Live music rocks **House of Blues** on Thursday through Saturday nights. Owned by Dan Aykroyd, Jim Belushi, John Goodman and members of Aerosmith, the restaurant/music center features "Delta-inspired" cuisine such as jambalaya, étouffée and homemade bread pudding. For a lively start to your day, try the Gospel Brunch. This popular breakfast gala, held every Sunday, features live gospel music. ~ 407-934-2583. MODERATE.

If you prefer Latin flavor, head over to **Bongos Cuban Cafe**, owned by singer Gloria Estefan, where you'll find Cuban cuisine served alongside colorful Latin rhythms. MODERATE.

DISNEY RESORTS For back-to-basics, family-style dining, head for the **Trails End Buffet** in Fort Wilderness Campground. The wood cabin restaurant has wagon-wheel chandeliers and all-you-can-eat Southern vittles such as fried chicken and barbecue ribs. The omelette and waffle breakfasts are stomach-stuffers. There's also a pizza bar open 4:30 p.m. to 9:30 p.m. nightly. ~ 407-824-2900. MODERATE. In the same building, **Crockett's Tavern** has ground buffalo burgers, a children's menu, and a serious cocktail called the Gullywhumper. BUDGET.

Poolside snack bars provide the quickest (and often least expensive) meals at Disney World hotels.

Disney World hotels offer several eateries where you can grab a quick, relatively inexpensive meal. The Yacht Club Resort's **Beaches & Cream** is a colorful, fanciful soda fountain that has rich sundaes and the Fenway Park Burger. ~ 407-934-7000. BUDGET. **Tubbi Buffeteria**, in the Dolphin resort, features a cafeteria lineup of hamburgers, grilled chicken, spaghetti and other hot dishes served 24 hours a day. ~ 407-934-4000. BUDGET. Over at the Polynesian Resort, you'll find burgers, fresh fruit platters and coconut hot dogs served 'round the clock at **Captain Cook's Snack and Ice Cream Company**. BUDGET.

Most of the area's best restaurants are found in its resorts. For elite Disney dining with or without the kids, **Victoria & Albert's** does a six-course, fixed-price meal served by folks dressed as queens and kings. Selections change daily, but usually include fish, fowl, veal, beef and lamb dinners, often followed by the restaurant's famous dessert soufflés. For a classy finale, diners are presented with long-stem roses. Dress code. Reservations required. Two seatings nightly. ~ In the Grand Floridian Beach Resort, Lake Buena Vista; 407-824-3000, fax 407-824-0093. ULTRA-DELUXE.

Families like the **Grand Floridian Café** for its casual atmosphere and prices and good, innovative food. Decorated in peach, mint green and cream, the place is sprinkled with marble tables and filled with the clatter of dishes and children. There are chicken, pork, beef and seafood dishes, often with a tropical flavor. Recommended dishes include the barbecue chicken quesadillas (with a mango barbecue sauce) and the Key Largo Pasta (cooked in white wine and garlic). For kids, there are burgers and fries. No dinner. ~ In the Grand Floridian Beach Resort, Lake Buena Vista; 407-824-3000. MODERATE TO DELUXE.

If you're up for a buffet with character, that's exactly what you'll get at **1900 Park Fare** in the Grand Floridian. Oodles of food includes a separate kids' menu, as well as enough desserts to fill you up just by looking at them. No lunch. ~ In the Grand Floridian Beach Resort, Lake Buena Vista; 407-824-3000. ULTRA-DELUXE.

The **Outback** in the Wyndham Palace Resort & Spa takes you down under for dinner. Australian-style food is prepared on grills in the middle of the dining room. Baby back ribs, lobster tail, kangaroo and alligator tail as well as a wide variety of domestic and imported beer are available. To arrive at the restaurant, you ride a glass elevator car through a waterfall. Dinner only. ~ 1900 Buena Vista Drive, Lake Buena Vista; 407-827-3430, fax 407-827-3103; www.wyndampalaceresort.com. DELUXE TO ULTRA-DELUXE.

The Wyndham Palace Resort & Spa's most elegant dining address is **Arthur's 27**, a penthouse restaurant that dazzles with primo cuisine and breathtaking views of the Magic Kingdom in lights. Dinner comes in four- and six-course prix-fixe meals. Look for specialties such as lobster bisque and filet of tenderloin. Dinner only. Closed Sunday. ~ 1900 Buena Vista Drive, Lake Buena Vista; 407-827-3450, fax 407-827-3103; www.wyndam palaceresort.com. DELUXE TO ULTRA-DELUXE.

Nearby, in the Hilton Hotel, **Finn's Grill** serves steaks, seafood and tropical drinks in a Key West setting. You can begin your meal with selections of items from the raw bar, such as oysters and crab. Dinner entrées include a variety of pasta, seafood and game dishes. Dinner only. ~ 1751 Hotel Plaza Boulevard, Lake Buena Vista; 407-827-4000, fax 407-827-6369; www.hilton. com. MODERATE TO DELUXE.

The **California Grill** moves Disney World a little further beyond its image as the hamburger and hot-dog capital. Located on the 15th floor of the Contemporary Resort, the grill offers fresh California cuisine and some of the best views of the Magic Kingdom. The stylish restaurant conveys an image of cool sophistication. The menu changes regularly, but some of the tasty and trendy fare includes Sonoma goat cheese ravioli with shiitake mushrooms, and grilled tofu with stirfry spring vegetable basmati rice. The kids' menu (ranging from macaroni and cheese to oak-roasted chicken breast) is reasonably priced, but the restaurant definitely has the feel of a grown-up's night out. Visit at night for dramatic views of the Magic Kingdom's fireworks. Dress code. ~ 4600 North World Drive, Lake Buena Vista; 407-824-1000. DELUXE TO ULTRA-DELUXE.

The homey touches at cozy **Olivia's Café** are fitting since this restaurant is located at the quaint Old Key West Resort. Pot pie, mashed potatoes and home-style soups are just some of the fixings you'll find. There's kids' fare as well—but skip the hot dogs. ~ In the Old Key West Resort, 1510 North Cove Road, Lake Buena Vista; 407-827-7700. MODERATE TO DELUXE.

Barbecue eats are plentiful and served family style at the Wilderness Lodge's **Whispering Canyon**. Better yet, the lively wait staff makes it an all-around good time. MODERATE TO DELUXE. Also at the Wilderness Lodge is the elegant **Artist's Point**, a Pacific Northwest–style restaurant specializing in fresh seafood and game. No lunch. ~ 901 Timberline Drive, Lake Buena Vista; 407-824-3200. DELUXE TO ULTRA-DELUXE.

If you enjoy big breakfasts, go to the Polynesian Resort's **Kona Cafe** and order Tonga toast. It's made with sourdough bread that's chocked with creamy bananas, quick-fried until puffy, and topped with cinnamon sugar. The no-frills coffeehouse also serves eggs and cereal for breakfast, and stacked sandwiches and jumbo salads for lunch and dinner. One drawback: People have discovered the place (and its fabulous Tonga toast), so it's usually crowded. A children's menu is available. ~ 1600 Seas Drive, Lake Buena Vista; 407-824-2000. MODERATE TO DELUXE.

At the Polynesian Resort's **'Ohana**, you can take part in the festive Polynesian Luau. Grilled seafood, poultry and meat are served on skewers, presented by a waitstaff clad in Hawaiian attire. Part of the show is the 16-foot open-fire pit where the food is prepared. The restaurant serves fixed-priced, family-style dinners with drinks and desserts à la carte—bring a hefty appetite as the food is plentiful. Breakfast is all-American—eggs, pancakes, hash browns and the like. No lunch. ~ 1600 Seas Drive, Lake Buena Vista; 407-824-2000. MODERATE TO ULTRA-DELUXE.

At the BoardWalk, seaside ambience goes hand in hand with eclectic restaurant fare, and there's much to choose from. Warm and relaxing, **Spoodles** embraces the Spanish custom of tapas, serving up Mediterranean dishes meant to be passed around the table. The grilled portobello mushrooms are a treat. Other choices include Moroccan Spiced tuna, charred spicy Tunisian lamb chops and grilled beef rib-eye steak. The food is excellent, but the portions are sometimes small, meaning you'll have to order quite a few selections to satisfy a whole table. For kids, there are the staples: pizza, macaroni and cheese, spaghetti and chicken. ~ 2101 North Epcot Resorts Drive, Lake Buena Vista; 407-939-5100. MODERATE TO DELUXE.

Seafood is the specialty of the BoardWalk's **Flying Fish Cafe** where the ambience is that of a mid-Atlantic pier restaurant. Named for the first car of a 1930s Atlantic City roller coaster, the restaurant is adorned in deep blues with deco fixtures, not to mention a glass ferris wheel and decorative roller coaster. With trendy fare reminiscent of its sister restaurant, the Contemporary Hotel's California Grill, the menu includes Oak grilled salmon filet and potato-wrapped striped bass. Vegetarian and meat dishes are also served. Children's menu includes fish and chips, chicken fingers and hot dogs. Reservations recommended. Dinner only. ~ 2101 North Epcot Resorts Drive, Lake Buena Vista; 407-939-5100. DELUXE.

The **Big River Grill & Brewing Works** at the BoardWalk features good old fashioned pub favorites such as baby back ribs, hot beer pretzels and grilled chicken salad. The children's menu, printed on a coloring page delivered with crayons, is also vintage: hamburger, cheeseburger, hot dog, grilled cheese. ~ 2101 North Epcot Resorts Drive, Lake Buena Vista; 407-939-5100. MODERATE TO DELUXE.

Don't forget to try out some of the home-brewed ales at the Big River Grill & Brewing Works (you can watch the brewing process through floor-to-ceiling windows).

For the armchair quarterback, there's the BoardWalk's ESPN **Club**. With 90 TVs perpetually tuned to sporting events, this is a sports fan's Nirvana. Monday night football season occasionally features celebrity athlete guest stars and live play-by-play commentary. There are seats barside as well as courtside (the main dining is designed to look like a basketball court). Fare here is pure stadium: hot dogs, steak sandwiches, burgers, etc. The food is good and plentiful. ~ 2101 North Epcot Resorts Drive, Lake Buena Vista; 407-939-5100. MODERATE.

Like any good summer strolling grounds, the BoardWalk is also heavy on sweet shops. Homemade fudge, chocolate-covered pretzels and other confections fill the display cases at **Seashore Sweets**, next to the ESPN Club. ~ 407-939-5100. **The Boardwalk Bakers**, with its quaint waterside bistro tables, is a good place to take a breather with a cappuccino and a sticky bun or oversized muffin. ~ 407-939-5100.

JUST OUTSIDE DISNEY WORLD Almost every Florida city has a restaurant named for Ernest Hemingway, and Orlando is no exception. This **Hemingway's** conforms to the Key West style preferred by most of these restaurants, with a casual atmosphere and seafood cuisine. Orlando's version also offers an elevated poolside location and woodsy ambience. The menu swims with grouper, pompano, squid, conch, shrimp and other salty creatures, plus a steak or two. A childrens' menu is available, as are half portions for kids under 12. No lunch. ~ Hyatt Regency Grand Cypress, 1 Cypress Boulevard, Orlando; 407-239-1234, fax 407-239-3800. DELUXE TO ULTRA-DELUXE.

Fashioned as a Spanish artist's loft, with distressed yellow walls, original artwork, and worn wood floors, tables and booths, **Café Tu Tu Tango** offers "food for the starving artist." A branch of the tapas bars in Miami and Atlanta, this restaurant has an uproarious bar but is fine for families; kids can order grilled cheese, spaghetti or chicken fingers while mom and dad enjoy brick-oven pizzas, grilled swordfish, crab empanadas, alligator niblets, and Mediterranean and nouvelle offerings, all served in appetizer portions. ~ 8625 International Drive, adjoining The Castle hotel, Orlando; 407-248-2222, fax 407-352-3696; www.cafetututango.com, e-mail orlando@cafetututango.com. BUDGET TO DELUXE.

For low-priced meals with an exotic flair, check out the international food pavilion at **Mercado Mediterranean Village.** You'll have a choice of fast foods from Latin America, China, Italy and the United States. ~ 8445 South International Drive, Orlando. BUDGET.

Many local folks will point to **Ran-Getsu** as your best bet for authentic Japanese food. The sushi bar whips around like a dragon's tail, and floor tables overlook a bonsai garden and pond. Besides sushi, the restaurant offers sukiyaki, *kushiyaki*, alligator bits and other Japanese-Florida crossbreeds. Dinner only. ~ 8400 International Drive, Orlando; 407-345-0044, fax 407-351-

ALL YOU CAN EAT

One way families can save on food is to eat buffet-style. Numerous restaurants near Disney World specialize in buffets, offering all-you-can-eat smorgasbords at budget and moderate prices. Most places are concentrated along Route 192 and International Drive: **Golden Corral** is a no-frills eatery with all-you-can-eat breakfast, lunch and dinner. ~ 7702 West Route 192, Kissimmee; 407-390-9615. Also, try the following chain restaurants: **Ponderosa Steak House**, **Olive Garden Italian Restaurant** and **Sonny's Barbecue.**

0481; www.rangetsu.com, e-mail rangetsu@prodigy.net. MODER-
ATE TO DELUXE.

For a night away from the kids, **Atlantis** serves elegant Mediterranean cuisine on tables surrounded by nicely appointed furnishings and art. The menu, which emphasizes seafood, contains
such pleasures as yellowfin tuna with soy truffle vinaigrette and
rack of lamb with garlic rosemary sauce. Reservations are
strongly recommended. Dinner only. Closed Sunday and
Monday in summer, Sunday year-round. ~ Renaissance Orlando
Resort, 6677 Sea Harbor Drive, Orlando; 407-351-5555, fax
407-351-9991. DELUXE TO ULTRA-DELUXE.

If you are with the kids, the Renaissance Orlando Resort's
less-formal **Tradewinds** provides coloring book menus. Parents
will find fancy sandwiches and salads and nouvelle preparations
such as sea bass with garlic bread topping and tomato vinaigrette. ~ Renaissance Orlando Resort, 6677 Sea Harbor Drive,
Orlando; 407-351-5555, fax 407-351-9994. MODERATE TO DELUXE.

UNIVERSAL ORLANDO   Universal Orlando has outdone Disney
when it comes to food. From fast food to cultured dining, eateries here stand a notch above standard theme-park fare.

Universal Studios   One of the best spots to get a quick, filling
meal is **Louie's Italian Restaurant** (New York), a rendition of a
Little Italy bistro. Pizza, lasagna and other pasta dishes are served
cafeteria style. On the lighter side, there's minestrone soup and
pasta salads. BUDGET.

Few families can pass up **Mel's Drive-In** (Hollywood). Kids
like the burgers, malts and cherry-red booths with individual jukeboxes, while parents enjoy the blast from the past. Classic '50s
tunes throb through the *American Graffiti*–style joint, decorated
in hot-pink neon and formica and silver metal. BUDGET.

The place at Universal with the elegant atmosphere is **Lombard's Landing** (San Francisco/Amity). Nestled along a lagoon
inside a warehouse, the restaurant is embellished with plank ceilings, shiny teak tables, archways, a bubble-shaped aquarium and
copper fountains. Fresh seafood dishes such as grilled salmon and
Maine lobster headline the menu, though you'll also find prime
rib, chicken dishes and a children's menu. MODERATE.

The Earthquake-themed **Richter's Burger Co.** (San Francisco/
Amity) has a do-it-yourself fixins bar where you top your burger
or grilled chicken sandwich the way you like it. BUDGET.

The atmosphere is positively frightful at **The Classic Monsters Café** (Production Central). Select your food from Frankenstein's laboratory (look for such original fare as Cauldron
Soup, Monster Salads and Mummy's Pasta) and then dine in the
Sci-Fi room, adorned with props from Buck Rogers–era flicks, or
the Crypt rooms, where the ambience is simply, well, to die for.
MODERATE.

There are numerous spots for budget-priced quickie meals. The **Beverly Hills Boulangerie**, located in The Front Lot, has croissants and pastries—made on the premises and served the same day— and stacked sandwiches. Over in World Expo, stop by **Animal Crackers** for burgers, hot dogs and chicken fingers. For international fare (befitting World Expo's theme), stop by the **International Food and Film Festival** and choose from Italian, Chinese, German and Greek cuisine. Throughout the park are **outdoor stands** stocking oranges, apples and other fresh fruit.

Universal CityWalk Apart from the obvious additions to Orlando's crop of nightlife haunts, CityWalk has upped the gourmet quotient as well. New Orleans chef Emeril Lagasse kicks it up a notch at **Emeril's Restaurant Orlando**. DELUXE TO ULTRA-DELUXE. Whether or not you've seen the chef's TV shows, you're bound to appreciate his delectable New Orleans–inspired fare. For Italian flavor, head over to **Pastamoré** where you can dine in the open-air marketplace of the full-service restaurant. BUDGET TO MODERATE. And don't count out all those groovy themed haunts (see "Nightlife") that serve food (standard café fare that it is) as well as atmosphere.

Universal Islands of Adventure Islands serves up theme-park food with an unusual amount of flair. Port of Entry's full-service **Confisco Grill and Backwater Bar** has a menu of pasta, grills and salads amid a roomful of chachkas. Servers play along with the theme—the restaurant's name refers to the items confiscated from unsuspecting adventurers, hence all the stuff on the walls—so expect to be temporarily relieved of some of your possessions. MODERATE. Next door is the **Croissant Moon Bakery,** where you'll be tempted by a display case of baked goodies. Sweets here are large—really large—and delicious. If you can resist, you're a better person than I. BUDGET.

In Seuss Landing, the outdoor **Green Eggs and Ham Café** serves up the namesake dish for those brave enough to partake. If you would not, could not, you can opt for a hamburger or some chicken fingers. BUDGET. Eat under the "big top" in the lively **Circus McGurkus Cafe Stoopendous**. The fried chicken, spaghetti and pizza will appeal to the kids, as will the lively circus atmosphere featuring perpetual high-wire acts. MODERATE.

The smoked fare of the Lost Continent's **Enchanted Oak Tavern,** under Merlin's tree, is a real treat, and you can wash it down with one of 45 beers. MODERATE. Nearby is the culinary highlight of the park, **Mythos Restaurant,** where gods and goddesses take the place of a wait staff. The upscale decor and atmosphere suggests fine dining—theme-park style, meaning you don't have to trade in the T-shirt and shorts for a suit. In addition to table service and some unusually tasty seafood and grilled meats, you'll get a grand view of the entire park. MODERATE TO DELUXE. If you're feeling more carnivorous, **The Burger Digs** in Jurassic Park features enormous hamburgers and other sandwiches to satisfy a dino-sized appetite. BUDGET. There's characteristic fare in Toon Lagoon where giant sandwiches are on the menu at **Blondies: Home of the Dagwood** and you can even get a Wimpy Burger at—where else?—**Wimpy's**. BUDGET.

SEAWORLD   SeaWorld's restaurants are a medley of sit-down places, fast-food eateries and delis with food that's pretty tasty.

The addition of the Waterfront has introduced new options for dining in SeaWorld. There's more than just pizza at **Voyagers Wood Fired Pizzas,** where you'll also find tasty salmon and pasta dishes. The acrobatic pizza tossers are pretty entertaining, too. Also serving schtick and salad is **The SeaFire Inn.** In addition to its little-bit-of-everything-international fare, from stir fry to Greek salads to French sandwiches, the restaurant has Rico and Roza's Musical Feast show. Polynesian takes over at night when SeaFire welcomes the Makahiki Luau. Enjoy appetizers and cocktails at the **SandBar** at the base of The Tower.

Sights

Just outside the bounds of Walt Disney World on Route 192, **Splendid China** is a near-clone of the original Splendid China in Hong Kong. This $100 million outdoor attraction is set on 76 acres behind a big strip shopping center and backing up to an upscale housing development.

The concept seems a little strange: First create miniature replicas of China's most famous sights, including the Great Wall, Imperial City and Stone Forest. Then fasten them to faux cliffs in the Central Florida flatness, and have visitors walk around taking pictures and admiring the teeny setwork. There is the Magao Grotto complex, which re-creates the grotto caves dating to A.D. 492 and discovered in 1900. There is the imitation miniature Midair Temple of Shanxi Province, where more than 40 buildings and palaces appear to float on a cliff side. And there is the 13-story Potala Palace, world's highest palace, though here it has a lilliputian look.

> Despite overdosing on tackiness, the Irlo Bronson Memorial Highway (Spacecoast Parkway) features a slew of family-style fun.

Most kids don't go for this place; there are no rides, no hands-on adventures, no video screens they can get glued to. On the flip side, Splendid China offers a relaxing respite from the hectic haze of Disney parks, an enjoyable walk through attractive gardens of weeping willows, crepe myrtles, rose bushes and lily ponds—though it is a pricey walk. Admission is $28.88 for adults, $18.18 for kids 5 through 12. Kids under five are free. Guided walking tours are an additional $5.35, while golf cart tours are $15.35. There is no parking fee.

Visit Splendid China anytime—it's never crowded. Explored leisurely, with lunch or dinner included, you'll need about four hours. You can, however, see all the sights in an easy two hours. There are two restaurants, one serving fast American food, and one serving fine Chinese fare, and numerous shops selling Chinese souvenirs and pricey furniture, porcelain and jewelry. Various live performances, from acrobatics to magic and folk fashion shows, are presented throughout the day, except on Monday. Admission. ~ 3000 Splendid China Boulevard, at Route 192, one mile west of the Walt Disney World main entrance, three miles west of Route 4, Kissimmee; 407-396-7111, 800-244-6226; www. floridasplendidchina.com, e-mail schina@earthlink.net.

West of Splendid China, Route 192 leads you into downtown **Kissimmee** along a trail of seething traffic, flashing billboards and neon signs with ten-foot letters, all trying to persuade you to see an alligator, watch a medieval joust, get wet, ride an airboat, buy oranges or T-shirts and eat seafood. This is "tourist trap trail," also known as the Irlo Bronson Memorial Highway or Space-coast Parkway.

For information on the area, contact the **Kissimmee–St. Cloud Convention and Visitors Bureau**. Closed Saturday and Sunday. ~ 1925 East Irlo Bronson Memorial Highway, Kissimmee, FL 34742; 407-847-5000; www.floridakiss.com.

One of the first super attractions you will encounter is **Old Town**, a nostalgic extravaganza of shops and restaurants, with a ferris wheel, a carousel, a go-cart track, a roller coaster, a haunted house and cobbled streets. A splendid place for families, the pedestrian mall is rarely crowded during the day and offers plenty of room for the kids to roam. There's also a Kidstown area with rides for small children. Admission is free but there are fees for the rides. ~ 5770 West Route 192, Kissimmee; 407-396-4888, 800-843-4202, fax 407-396-0348; www.old-town.com, e-mail webmaster@old-town.com.

Seven acres of wild animals, reptiles and alligators are the draw at **Jungleland Zoo**, where over 300 exotic animals, including monkeys and tigers, keep the Florida natives company. Admission. ~ 4580 West Route 192, Kissimmee; 407-396-1012; www.thejunglelandzoo.com, e-mail zooinfo@junglelandzoo.com.

Despite its whirlwind tourist reputation, Kissimmee manages to maintain the flavor of its bucolic cattle town beginnings. When you reach this town at the end of the road, you will find a transformation from the maelstrom behind you. Little has changed in the heart of the city since its founding in 1878. Many original buildings remain, including the courthouse and the **Makinson's Hardware Store**, purported to be the Sunshine State's oldest retail hardware store. Closed Sunday. ~ 308 East Broadway, Kissimmee; 407-847-2100, fax 407-847-7969.

Located near the lakefront in downtown Kissimmee, the **Monument of States** is built of stones from every state in the nation,

Splish
Splash

Once upon a time, before Disney ever built its Typhoon Lagoon and Blizzard Beach water parks, there were two places in the area you went for a mix of water and slides: Water Mania and Wet 'n Wild. Today, Typhoon Lagoon and Blizzard Beach lure the most vacationers, but Wet 'n Wild draws locals who want the steepest, fastest, scariest slides. (See Chapter Six for detailed information on Typhoon Lagoon and Blizzard Beach.)

Wet 'n Wild's premier attraction is The Flyer, a four-passenger toboggan ride through 450 feet of exciting curves. Also popular are Bomb Bay, a 76-foot free-fall slide, the Black Hole, a $2 million, space-themed slide where you corkscrew through pitch blackness on a 1000-gallon-a-minute stream of water and the Blast, an exciting ride through a tunnel with visual and sound effects. And the 25-acre Wet 'n Wild has much more: whitewater rapids, a wave pool, a lazy river, kneeboarding and five vertical drops called the Mach 5. It also has a children's water playground with scaled-down versions of the big slides as well as kid-size restaurants. Admission. ~ 6200 International Drive, Orlando; 407-351-3200, fax 407-363-1147, 800-992-9453; www.wetnwild.com, e-mail info@wetnwildorf.com.

Water Mania, on the other hand, is much smaller and offers only a handful of fast slides. It does feature some children's slides, kiddie pools, a waterfall rock climbing wall and a small wooded area perfect for family picnics. Closed November through March. Admission. ~ 6073 West Route 192, Kissimmee; 407-396-2626, 800-527-3092; www.watermania-florida.com.

Of the four water parks, Typhoon Lagoon and Blizzard Beach naturally have far more landscaping and special effects. Water Mania, in fact, is almost all concrete, and Wet 'n Wild has only a minimum of trees and grass. Other factors to consider: The slides at Wet 'n Wild and Water Mania feature easier climbs and—oftentimes—shorter lines than those at Typhoon Lagoon and Blizzard Beach. During spring and fall, Wet 'n Wild and Water Mania are usually less crowded on weekdays than the Disney parks. All four parks cost about the same—there's no more than a dollar difference between them.

plus 21 foreign countries. Built in 1943 by the townspeople, it stands as a 70-foot monument to tourism. Somewhat disheveled in appearance, it appeals to rock-hounds with its impressive gathering of flint, alabaster, coquina, meteors, stalagmites, marble, petrified teeth, lava and other specimens. ~ Monument Avenue, Lakefront Park.

Lakefront Park lies at the end of Monument Avenue. This city park skirts Tohopekaliga Lake (called Lake Toho for short), where fishing, canoeing and bicycling are popular sports.

HIDDEN ▶

Another hint of Kissimmee's uncontrived lifestyle can be found in the 50-mile-long **Kissimmee Chain-of-Lakes** resort area. This string of lakes, of which Lake Toho is the largest, provides secluded activities for families. Houseboating, motorboating, sailing, bass fishing and birdwatching are offered. Follow Route 525 out of Kissimmee for a scenic oak-tunnel drive around the big lake.

Southwest of downtown Kissimmee, kids can spend a day on the farm. The **Green Meadows Petting Farm** offers 40 acres of pretty countryside where children (and adults) can milk a cow, ride a pony, take a hay ride and help feed the goats. A perfect break from theme-park crowds and noise, the quiet retreat is home to over 200 animals. Arrive during October, and you can pick pumpkins. Admission. ~ Poinciana Boulevard, five miles south of Route 192, Kissimmee; 407-846-0770, fax 407-870-8644; www.gmf.com.

North toward Orlando along Route 441, you will find a pair of giant alligator jaws beckoning you to enter **Gatorland**. Here you can see thousands of Florida alligators and crocodiles, along with exotic snakes and birds. Not as much a tourist trap as it sounds, this refuge maintains a natural cypress swamp setting, carpeted with ferns and brightened with orchids. Scenes from *Indiana Jones and the Temple of Doom* were filmed in this jungle atmosphere. If your kids are brave enough (and you don't mind forking over a few extra bucks), they can have their picture taken with a baby alligator or a snake. Admission. ~ Route 441, Orlando; 407-855-5496, 800-393-5297, fax 407-240-9389; www. gatorland.com, e-mail customerservice@gatorland.com.

▼ ▼ ▼ ▼ ▼ ▼ ▼ ▼ ▼ ▼

Shopping

Both at Walt Disney World and outside its confines are many ways to spend your shopping dollars. Within the Magic Kingdom, Epcot, Disney–MGM Studios and Disney's Animal Kingdom, fantasy stores fuse atmosphere into the illusory surroundings. Cinderella Castle, for instance, has a cache of twinkling jewels and medieval-style swords and axes. Shops also carry Disney *everything*, from Mickey sunshades and underwear to Donald Duck cookery. It's easy to spend hours (and megabucks) in the Disney shops, but you'll end up wasting valuable sightseeing time. Unless you're a shopaholic, save the heavy duty shopping for a mall. On the other hand, Disney's best stores include some so unusual they qualify as sightseeing.

MAGIC KINGDOM   On Main Street U.S.A., shops help create the ambience of a charming American town. The fragrant **Main Street Market House** stocks dried herbs, teas and Mickey Mouse cookie cutters. The **Main Street Confectionery** is a wonderful old-time candy store with illuminated shelves of chocolate and fresh peanut brittle.

Adventureland has two covered markets offering exotic treasures. One, **Traders of Timbuktu**, features African jewelry and prints. **Zanzibar Shell Co.** has such tropical goodies as shell jewelry and pirate swords and hats.

Frontierland Trading Post excels in gifts and leather goods in a Western and Mexican vein.

One of my favorite Magic Kingdom shops is Liberty Square's **Yankee Trader**. Like a New England general store, it's brimming with jams and jellies, pretty country furnishings and nifty kitchen gadgets.

Stores in Fantasyland naturally appeal to kids. **Tinker Bell's Treasures** has princess-style gowns for little girls and model cars for boys. Few can resist a peek inside **The King's Gallery**, at the base of Cinderella Castle. With its twinkling blown glass, medieval-style costumes and miniature castles, the place seems magical. **Mickey's Christmas Carol** smells like cinnamon and looks like a yuletide party. Pick up your Mickey tree lights and ornaments here.

Mickey's Toontown Fair and Tomorrowland have little in the way of interesting shops. If you must browse, go to Tomorrowland's **Merchant of Venus** and check out the campy "futuristic" gifts.

EPCOT   The Future World half of Epcot offers a few novel stores. **Green Thumb Emporium** (The Land) has gardening books, seeds and strange jewelry shaped like fried eggs and black olives.

World Showcase shops are part of the Epcot cultural experience. Each pavilion highlights goods native to its host country and

PACKAGE PICKUP

If you're a sucker for Mickey Mouse T-shirts, Goofy caps and other silly souvenirs (don't try to hide it—we know you are), here's good news: You don't have to lug your packages around all day. Any time you make a purchase at a Disney World theme park or SeaWorld, you can have the store clerk forward your bags to Package Pickup. Then you collect them on your way out of the park. For Package Pickup locations inside Disney World, check with Guest Relations at each theme park. Inside SeaWorld, check with the Information Center.

often showcases works from visiting artists and crafters. Store architecture often emulates the beautiful designs of each country, so take time to peruse the buildings.

Fashioned like a town square at night, **Plaza de Los Amigos** (Mexico) is a festive market scattered with baskets, pottery, piñatas, colorful papier-mâché and other south-of-the-border wares.

During medieval times, Scandinavian peasants painted their old furniture to give it style and color. The painted furnishings at Norway's **Puffin's Roost** are done in a method called rosemaling, which uses floral designs and inscriptions. The shop, which also features beautifully painted ceilings and floors, carries Norwegian souvenirs made of pewter and wood.

China's **Yong Feng Shangdian**, or "Bountiful Harvest," is an exquisite gallery of silk tapestries, carved chests, jewelry and other Asian treasures. For children, there are plastic snakes and swords.

The German pavilion boasts no less than nine shops, including the engaging **Glas und Porzellan**. Like many German craft shops, the place has dozens of built-in cabinets and cubbyholes lined with Hummel figurines and Goebel giftware. **Der Teddybär** has toy chests filled to the top with traditional German toys. Cuckoo clocks and beer steins can be found next door at **Volkskunst**.

Chocoholics should visit **Delizie Italiane** (Italy), an oasis of gourmet Italian chocolates. The marble-floored **Il Bel Cristallo** specializes in Armani and alabaster figurines, inlaid wood music boxes and Venetian jewelry.

Kids can get their coonskin caps and Daniel Boone rifles at **Heritage Manor Gifts** (United States). Out front, vendors sell dulcimers and American flags.

In the true spirit of capitalism, Japan's pavilion has its own department store. At **Mitsukoshi Department Store**, you'll find an assortment of elegant Japanese handicrafts, dolls, fine porcelain, jewelry, kimonos and much more.

Merchants at the exotic **Moroccan** pavilion peddle such authentic goods as tasseled fez hats, finger bells, woven rugs and bellows. Horn and drum players stroll while you shop.

France is a wonderful place to shop. The **Plume et Palette** sells crystal and Limoges porcelain, while **La Mode Française** features casual clothing with a French flair. **La Maison du Vin** stocks a good selection of French wine and offers winetasting and **Galerie des Halles** proffers toys, French memorabilia and snacks.

Each United Kingdom shop signifies a different architectural period. **The Tea Caddy**, purveyor of English teas, is fashioned like a thatched cottage from the 1500s. The Tudor-style **Magic of Wales** offers Welsh crafts and mementos, while the Queen Anne–style **Queen's Table** displays Royal Doulton china, porcelain figurines and Toby mugs.

Canadian, Eskimo and tribal crafts are offered at **Northwest Mercantile**, a log cabin in the Canada pavilion.

DISNEY–MGM STUDIOS   The place for Hollywood mementos is **Sid Cahuenga's One-of-a-Kind** (Hollywood Boulevard). You can pore through rare movie and television treasures, as well as autographs of stars such as Al Pacino and Burt Reynolds. Across the street, **Oscar's Classic Car Souvenirs** is lined with fuel pump bubble gum machines and classic car models. Head to Hollywood Boulevard's **Sweet Success** for your candy fix.

Disney Princess Shop (at Voyage of the Little Mermaid) stocks costumes, gifts and sweatshirts from *The Little Mermaid* and other "princess" movies. Some of my favorite Disney plush toys and kids' fashions can be found at **L.A. Prop Cinema Storage**.

DISNEY'S ANIMAL KINGDOM   It must be the naturalist theme that prompted Disney to water down the number of shops in the Animal Kingdom—all told, there are less than a dozen merchants. No matter, merchandise here is often among the most interesting. After Countdown to Extinction, you can plan to spend at least a little time at **Chester and Hester's Dinosaur Treasures**—DINOSAUR drops you right in the DinoLand U.S.A. shop. The place has some cute items—all the essentials for budding paleontologists such as hardhats with spotlights mounted on them. There are exotic wares of another sort at **Mombasa Marketplace** in Africa. Much of the merchandise here hails from Africa. The shop is also stocked with the predictable collection of logo items. In another part of the world (namely Asia), **Mandala Gifts** doles out merchandise with tiger and Asian themes. The most concentrated selection of shops is in Discovery Island. Your little creatures will tug you to **Creature Comforts** and its selection of plush animals and neat toys, or perhaps to the **Beastly Bazaar** where you can collect It's Tough to be a Bug! items. **Island Mercantile** is where you can pick up souvenirs representing any of your favorite lands. At **Disney Outfitters**, look for animal-themed apparel and gifts.

> When mom is shopping at the Marketplace, dad and the kids can rent mini-speedboats at the nearby marina.

THE REST OF THE WORLD   A stroll along Disney's BoardWalk makes for a quaint afternoon or evening retail experience. At the Character Carnival, you'll find general Disney paraphernalia. **Dundy's Sundry Shop** sells traveler essentials alongside Vacation Club and BoardWalk logo merchandise. Those with kitchens in their BoardWalk Villas will find groceries, beer and wine in addition to penny candy and novelty items at **Screen Door General Store**. A few other retail opportunities: the ESPN **The Yard** (sports logo stuff), **Thimbles and Threads** (men's and women's apparel) and **Wylands Gallery** (prints, lithographs and other decorative art). While much of the merchandise here is standard fare, the ambience is charming, a nice way to get away from the hustle and bustle of the theme parks.

Pleasure Island shops have some really out-of-the-mainstream stuff. ~ 407-934-7781. The avant-garde **Changing Attitudes** has leather and lace getups, counterculture T-shirts and mod artwork and jewelry. **SuperStar Studio** makes you a music-video star, where you can lip-synch to your favorite songs. **Avigator's** will outfit you in expedition wear.

In addition to eating and drinking at the West Side, you can put a large-sized dent in your wallet. There are roughly 14 shops here, some in conjunction with food and entertainment franchises (Wildhorse Store, Cirque du Soleil store). Books and records are available aplenty at the elaborate multi-story **Virgin Megastore** that also features a broadcast booth. Stock the outside of your refrigerators at **Magnetron Magnetz**. You can drop a few dollars on treats **Candy Cauldron**, or blow a very large stack of change at **Starabilia's** where you'll find mementos of entertainment and sports celebrities.

> The lakeside gathering of decorative shops and eateries at the Marketplace is a good place to spend a rainy afternoon or a relaxing evening (stores stay open until 11 p.m.—check times during off-season).

The Marketplace was created so you could buy Disney souvenirs without paying theme-park admission. ~ 407-828-3800. One store, the **World of Disney**, boasts the most Disney paraphernalia anywhere; 50,000 square feet of stuffed, ceramic and rhinestone Mickeys, Minnies and Goofys, not to mention toys, collectibles and a costume shop that is every little girl's dream. One of the 12 themed rooms has a 25-foot-high wall of plush toys. The LEGO **Imagination Center**, a good place to buy or browse, features 75 fanciful LEGO models, as well as a three-story construction crane, and LEGO creatures ranging from sea serpents to dinosaurs. Disney cell and art collectors will find what they're looking for at **The Art of Disney**, while team-logo merchandise can be found at **Team Mickey's Athletic Club**. Other stops include **2R's Reading and Riting** for Disney-related books for children and **Disney's Days of Christmas** for Disney-related tree-trimming articles. If you like, you can be professionally photographed with Mickey at **Studio M**, or with some of your other favorite characters at the adjoining **Image Capture**.

JUST OUTSIDE DISNEY WORLD **Old Town** is a tourist-belt shopping center offering specialty wares and trendy items in an old-fashioned ambience. Brick-lined streets re-create a nostalgic atmosphere of nickel colas, merry-go-rounds, ice cream parlors and city squares. They also feature a vintage-car parade every Saturday night. ~ 5770 West Route 192, Kissimmee; 407-396-4888, 800-843-4202; www.old-town.com.

In Old Town, **Tiki Jim's** carries a variety of silly T-shirts and other humorous gifts. At **The Old Town Pet Palace** you'll find gifts for Fluffy as well as animal-themed items that range from cute to kitsch. **The General Store** corners the market on old-fashioned funky stuff, with antique phones and old Coca-Cola and Budweiser glassware. ~ 407-396-6445. **Magic Max** carries an enticing collection of tricks and magic books, with a free lesson for every trick purchase. ~ 407-396-6884.

One of the largest gatherings of factory outlets is **Belz Factory Outlet World.** Over 160 stores sell discounted books, jewelry, electronics, clothing and dinnerware. One shop at Belz called **Everything But Water** (407-363-9752) sells swimwear and accessories. ~ 5401 West Oakridge Road, Orlando; 407-352-9611; www.belz.com.

At **Mercado Mediterranean Village,** shoppers are entertained while they browse the brick streets and Mediterranean-style storefronts filled with over 50 specialty shops and restaurants. **Faxon's** (407-363-1444) sells casual Florida-style resortwear and accessories. Collectible crystal figurines and Swarovski jewelry are available at **The Looking Glass** (407-351-1261).

Also located in the Mercado is **Del Sol** (407-354-0711), where you can watch any item from baseball caps to tote bags change color in the sun. Spiffy clothing and gifts for the car enthusiast await at **One For the Road** (407-345-0120). ~ 8445 International Drive, Orlando; 407-345-9337; www.themercado.com.

UNIVERSAL ORLANDO   Universal's imaginative shops make for some interesting browsing.

Universal Studios   Stop by **Cyberimage,** featuring unique merchandise for *Terminator* fans. If you're in the market for a knock-'em-dead casual wear, **Studio Styles** (Hollywood) has the latest in minuscule neon styles. Top it off at **Brown Derby Hat Shop** (Hollywood), where black and whites of the stars decorate the wall.

Young children can spend an afternoon in the **Cartoon Store** (World Expo), where they get to wade through stuffed Pink Panthers, Woody Woodpeckers and other cartoon favorites. Planning a trip to the Hawaii? Stop in **Quint's Surf Shack** for beach wear. Hitchcock fans should head for **The Bates Motel Gift Shop** (Production Central), which stocks plastic knives, terry cloth robes and shower curtains (without the bloodstains).

Universal CityWalk   In addition to being a food and drink mecca, Universal CityWalk is chachka heaven. Apart from the obvious (the **Universal Studios Store**), there are nearly a dozen retailers. At **All-Star Collectibles,** there's enough sports memorabilia to fill a ballpark, whether you're rooting for a college team or the pros. **Cartooniversal** will satisfy your urge for the funky and funny, from silly T-shirts to oddly entertaining toys. Some of the more unusual retail entries include **Fresh Produce Sportswear** (clothes "in the vibrant colors of your favorite fruits and vegetables"), **Glow!** (yup—everything glows, or seems to) and **Quiet Flight** (customized surfboards and the duds to go with them). If you absolutely must have the latest in Lava lamps, head to **Dapy**. And you can accessorize your stogie for the evening nightcap at **Cigarz at CityWalk**, which also features cordials and coffees.

Universal Islands of Adventure   There's no shortage of opportunities for nabbing souvenirs of your adventure. In Port of Entry, **Island Market and Export Candy Shoppe** features a global selection of exotic foods. Find whatever you need for your Betty Boop collection at Toon Lagoon's aptly named **Betty Boop Store**. Need to add to your comic book collection? Peruse the wares of Marvel Super Hero Island's **Comic Shop**. The Lost Continent's **Dragon's Keep** has an interesting selection of toys and games. Any title you need for your Dr. Seuss library can be found in **Dr. Seuss' All the Books You Can Read** in Seuss Landing. The term "plush Grinch" sounds like an oxymoron, but that's exactly what you'll find—and then some—at the **Mulberry Street Store**.

SEAWORLD   SeaWorld's handful of shops are of the souvenir variety, and offer little in the way of interesting browsing. For those who insist on a campy memento, there are stuffed Shamus, dolphins and sea lions and an assortment of ocean-themed T-shirts.

Nightlife

The Disney area, so resplendent with sightseeing gimmickry, has debuted its own brand of entertainment.

The biggest night game in town is Downtown Disney, a flashy playground of bars, restaurants and shops. Nearby, area restaurants take dinner theater a step further, to "dinner arena." Beware, the entertainment is usually more noteworthy than the food at these extravaganzas. Most require advance reservations, especially on weekends. Included here are most of the major dinner attractions, along with a sampling of more low-key gathering spots and watering holes.

EPCOT   Epcot's **IllumiNations: Reflections of Earth** is a must-see. This grand finale could easily be the highlight of your Disney visit. Staged at 9 or 10 nightly (depending on the seasonal closing time of Epcot) over the World Showcase lagoon, the program is a stunning visual concert of colored fountains, stirring music and laser lights that dance across the pitch-black sky (Epcot turns its lights off). IllumiNations goes much further than most laser shows, creating powerful images across shooting streams of water, the Spaceship Earth globe and the World Showcase countries.

The largest and most sophisticated laser show in the world, IllumiNations uses two types of lasers: argon for green and blue light and krypton for red. Some of the lasers are mounted on World Showcase pavilions, while others rest on a 50-ton barge in the lagoon. The show's pyrotechnic finale features some 650 fireworks in six minutes—nearly two fireworks per second!

Over at the Germany pavilion, the **Biergarten** inspires good times with a Bavarian beer garden atmosphere. An oom-pah-pah band and yodelers entertain. Japan's relaxing **Matsu No Ma Lounge** has bonsai planters, teakwood tables and splendid views across Epcot. The sushi platters and exotic rum fruit drinks are excellent.

Among other lively watering holes, the **Rose & Crown Pub** at Epcot's United Kingdom pavilion is a prime place to toss back a brew. The architecture reveals three pubs in one: a country pub with wood shingles, a city pub with turrets and etched glass, and a maritime pub. On the waterfront, it's warm, clubby and beautifully designed with polished oak, leaded glass and brass. You can always count on a jolly crowd.

DISNEY-MGM STUDIOS 50's **Prime Time Café** makes you feel like you stepped into a '50s television sitcom. Fashioned like a cozy living room, the place has cushiony couches, TV trays and waiters dressed like the Beave.

DOWNTOWN DISNEY Bordering the south shore of Buena Vista Lagoon, Downtown Disney is *the* nightlife destination in Disney World. Filled with exciting nightclubs, Downtown Disney also offers family-oriented entertainment, Cirque du Soleil and Disney Quest, an interactive virtual adventureland.

Pleasure Island The Magic Kingdom of nightlife, **Pleasure Island** plays to virtually every nighttime entertainment fantasy. The six-acre pleasure palace cranks with seven themed nightclubs and outdoor stages where singers and dancers reel with energy. A New Year's Eve–type celebration, complete with fireworks, laser lights and confetti, happens every night around midnight. One cover charge gets you into every club. Anyone under 18 must be accompanied by a parent or guardian, and you must be at least 21 to order alcoholic drinks. ~ 407-934-7781. The exception is **Mannequins Dance Palace**, where you must be at least 21 to enter.

> If you don't want to be in the Comedy Warehouse show, avoid the seats next to the telephones. (Otherwise, expect a phone call.)

Every Pleasure Island club has its own style of show, from country and western two-steppers to psychedelic gyrators.

The reason people flock to the **Comedy Warehouse** is its hilarious improvisational comedy; no two shows are ever alike. The warehouse decor is appropriately loony, with Mickey Mouse drums, giant crayons, fake palm trees and other kitschy stuff strung about everywhere. It has several shows that fill up fast each night. Plan to see the first comedy show (usually at 8:15 p.m.) or the last one (around midnight); the shows in between typically have a 30- to 45-minute wait.

Pleasure Island's **Adventurers Club** looks like a safari gone mad. Everywhere you look there's African-style weirdness: shrunken heads, propellers, a barstool with elephant legs, gargoyle sculptures, a hippopotamus head. One entire room is filled with masks that, every hour or so, come alive. Besides the talking mask shows, eccentric "travelers" tell tall tales to tourists.

While parents are visiting Pleasure Island's nightclubs, teenagers will find entertainment at the West End Stage with live bands and arcades.

The beat pounds so loud and hard at **Mannequins Dance Palace** it shakes your ribs. Billed as a "high-tech" nightclub, the steel-and-strobe palace pulsates in an atmosphere accented by cool fog. Waitresses tote trays of test tube shooters, and Madonna-style dancers strut their stuff on a revolving dancefloor. You must be 21 to enter.

The Pleasure Island Jazz Company is another step in this nightlife theme park's attempt to have something for everyone. The sit-down atmosphere here features musicians playing the latest and greatest in jazz's history. Appetizers and specialty drinks are served.

Aaah! Just listen to the mellifluous sounds of the Bee Gees, the Village People and Donna Summer living again at **8TRAX**, Pleasure Island's '70s-era club. Complete with a comfortable beanbag sitting area and rotating mirror ball, this is the place to don those bell bottoms and cure that dance fever.

Motion is sure to please all tastes with a variety of tunes that range from Top 40 to Alternative.

The **BET SoundStage Club**, owned by Black Entertainment Television, showcases live jazz, rhythm and blues, soul and hip-hop performances.

The **Rock & Roll Beach Club** has psychedelic carpets, black padded rails, fishing nets and parking meters. You can dance to everything from recorded "Mony Mony" to "Old Time Rock and Roll" and live bands, or shoot some pool upstairs.

You could go to **Planet Hollywood** just for a cocktail, but most people don't. There are several crowded bars inside this big blue ball of Hollywood kitsch, but hundreds of tables are where everyone hangs out having lunch, dinner and late-night eats. Most nights, there's at least an hour wait—if you're not eating. Add another half-hour for a table. On the plus side, you can visit Planet Hollywood with paying admission to Pleasure Island.

West Side   There seems to be no end to Disney World nightlife now that the resort has opened its own fashionable West Side. Under bright lights and blinking neon signs, the West Side (one third of the Downtown Disney complex—the other two pieces are Pleasure Island and the Marketplace) brings a number of trendy restaurant/clubs, many featuring live entertainment. The sound of Latin rhythms can be found at **Bongos Cuban Cafe** owned by singer Gloria Estefan. **House of Blues**, owned by Dan Aykroyd, Jim Belushi, John Goodman and members of Aerosmith, rocks with live music seven days a week. For something completely different, buy a ticket to see **Cirque du Soleil**. The renowned theater/acrobatic troupe has pitched a permanent tent on the West Side. The show is spectacular, but at $28 to $72 a pop depending on the seat, admission is on the expensive side, especially if you're bringing the whole family. ~ Tickets, 407-939-7600. For your movie-viewing pleasure, there's also a mammoth **AMC Theater** showplace (this place is huge—the largest in Florida) with 24 screens and more than 6000 seats (many of them stadium-style).

You've ridden all the banks and curves Disney's roller coasters have to offer: now design your own—and ride it. **Disney Quest** is 100,000 square feet of virtual entertainment where you can shoot the rapids, fly a magic carpet and engineer the coaster of your dreams—all without leaving the room. It's not just a grown-up playground. Young children who haven't grown quite big enough for the real rides will be especially happy here since there are few height requirements. Computer-savvy kids will not only love the games, they'll probably put mom and dad to shame. The four zones (Explorer, Score, Create and Replay) are only limited by your imagination—and your wallet. Unfortunately, the price rivals that of the real theme parks (about $33 for unlimited play). Look for occasional discounts on late-night admission.

DISNEY RESORTS   Every night, the tranquil, pitch-black Seven Seas Lagoon gets a jolt of electricity. Like someone flipping on a big light switch, the waters come alive with the **Electrical Water Pageant**. This 1000-foot caravan features thousands of tiny lights arranged to resemble sea creatures. As they weave around the lagoon, the shimmering "creatures" reflect across the water and appear to be swimming. You can see the beautiful pageant from the Polynesian Resort, Grand Floridian Beach Resort, Wilderness Lodge, Contemporary Resort, Fort Wilderness Resort and the Magic Kingdom when it's open until 11 p.m. The parade usually starts at 9 p.m. but travels past each site at various times. ~ 407-824-4321. If you're not staying at any of the resorts, simply ride the monorail or Disney bus to one. My favorite spot is the twinkling lakeside gazebo at the Grand Floridian Beach Resort.

Of all the Disney World activities, few get higher ratings from families than the **Fort Wilderness Campfire**. The old-fashioned gathering, open only to those staying at a Disney resort, is held nightly at a wooden trading post enveloped in mossy slash pines. It's a people event, with marshmallow roasting and sing-alongs where everyone joins in on camping classics like "My Bonnie Lies Over the Ocean." Kids go crazy when Chip and Dale show up and beg for chocolate chip cookies (bring a handful). For the finale, a full-length Disney movie is shown on an outdoor screen. ~ 407-824-2788.

At the **Spirit of Aloha**, the dinner show appeals to adults and children with an outdoor South Seas motif. Hula dancers and fire jugglers entertain while diners enjoy tasty barbecue fare. ~ Polynesian Resort, Disney World, 1600 Seas Drive, Lake Buena Vista; 407-824-8000.

Laughing Kookaburra Good Time Bar lists 99 varieties of beer and features live dance music in a down-under Australian-theme setting. ~ Wyndham Palace Resort & Spa, Walt Disney World Village, Lake Buena Vista; 407-827-2727.

At the **Hoop-Dee-Doo Musical Revue**, the Pioneer Hall Players crack corn in an Old West setting with appropriate chow. By far the most popular Disney revue (it can take several months to get a seat), it is also, in my opinion, the least entertaining. The dancing and singing are average at best, and the jokes are just plain silly. Worse yet, it costs big bucks. My advice: Skip this one and see the Magic Kingdom's Diamond Horseshoe Saloon Revue. ~ Fort Wilderness Resort; 407-934-7639.

A few of the newest alternatives to Pleasure Island nightlife are "seaside" at Disney's BoardWalk.

Dueling pianos play the night away at **Jelly Rolls** where you can sip a cocktail while listening to the tunes of two talented and quick-witted pianists. The entertainment is always a crowd pleaser, often erupting into audience-wide sing-alongs of old favorites.

Sports fans will find heaven with a brew, a hot pretzel and 80 TV screens perpetually broadcasting sports at the ESPN **Club**. During major sporting events, the club occasionally provides live commentary. A full menu at the bar and in the basketball-court dining room.

JUST OUTSIDE DISNEY WORLD The **Arabian Nights** dinner attraction features chariot races, Arabian horse dancing and white

DINNER AND A SHOW

Staking out your seat for **Fantasmic!** can indeed be a chore. During peak season, folks start their vigil a good hour before show time—and sometimes still don't get a seat. Skirt the lines by signing up for a dinner and Fantasmic! package. Dine at either Mama Melrose, the Brown Derby or Hollywood & Vine and get a voucher for a guaranteed seat. The catch: you'll probably end up with a late-afternoon (as opposed to evening) dinner hour—not necessarily a bad thing if you're toting young kids. Prices range from moderate to deluxe depending on the restaurant. Guests of a Disney resort can purchase tickets in advance at the hotel; others will have to wait and buy tickets at the park.

Lipizzan shows. ~ 6225 West Route 192, Kissimmee; 407-239-9223; www.arabian-nights.com.

A dining novelty, **Medieval Times**, brings back the Middle Ages. Here you eat fowl with your fingers and watch jousting. ~ 4510 West Vine Street, Kissimmee; 407-396-1518, 800-229-8300; www.medievaltimes.com.

The entertainment at **Mark Two Dinner Theater** is more traditional theater with local troupes performing Broadway classics. Reduced rates for children. Closed Monday and Tuesday; matinees on Wednesday, Thursday and Saturday. Admission. ~ 3376 Edgewater Drive, Orlando; 407-843-6275, 800-726-6275; www.orlandobroadway.com.

UNIVERSAL ORLANDO Dance at **The Groove**, enjoy reggae at **Bob Marley-A Tribute to Freedom,** or grab a cold one at **Pat O'Brien's**. Whatever your idea of nightlife, you're bound to find it at Universal's CityWalk. Opportunities for carousing, in fact, have multiplied tenfold since this 30-acre grownup theme park came to town. Big-name performers have begun making regular appearances at the **Hard Rock Live Orlando**, a 2200-seat Roman-style colosseum. The world's largest **Hard Rock Cafe** is attached. There's live entertainment of a smoother sort (or not) at **CityJazz**. If you're looking for a few good laughs, **Bonkerz Comedy Club** will supply them. If all of that is overwhelming, you can choose from 20 screens at the **Universal Cineplex.**

SEAWORLD SeaWorld has joined the dinner show circuit with its **Makahiki Luau**. Held nightly at 6:30 at a lakeside restaurant, it showcases hip-swinging island women, fire-eating men and a tropical menu of sweet 'n' sour chicken, seafood and hula pie. The food and entertainment more than satisfy, and the community seating is perfect for families who like to socialize. ~ 407-351-3600.

You can groove to a different beat over at Shamu Stadium in SeaWorld. The nightly show, **Shamu Rocks America**, features the killer whale getting down to the beat of popular rock tunes. Though you may have seen some of these tricks at the day show, they're never tired, particularly under the guise of this lively format. One neat addition: the outtake reel showcasing trainers at some of their less-than-graceful moments. Splash alert: the show's grand finale features the largest whale in captivity. One thump of his giant tail splashes all the way up into the stadium's second tier. In summer, end your stay at the park at the nightly laser and fireworks spectacle.

ELEVEN

Orlando Area

Orlando. Mention the word and most people envision Mickey Mouse, Cinderella's castle or perhaps even an imaginary town on Main Street U.S.A. But this is no imaginary town. In fact, like the Disney World "community," Orlando is growing at a rapid pace that makes it the boomtown of the South.

With the stream of new residents and jobs, the city of Orlando is spilling over into an ever-expanding metropolitan area. The population of the three counties that make up Orlando and its environs has mushroomed to more than one million. More than 25.6 million passengers arrive at Orlando International Airport every year. New factories are booming, with high-tech companies creating jobs at three times the national average. The Patriot missile and infrared sights for night warfare—two of the stalwarts of the Persian Gulf War's Desert Storm offensive—are made just a few miles from Disney's Star Wars fantasy ride.

Nicknamed "Hollywood East" because of the influx of movie-industry theme parks, the Orlando area is attracting some real-life "beautiful people" as well, including the likes of director Steven Spielberg, who bought a home in the city.

Others are discovering the region, too. Campus Crusade for Christ, whose stated ambition is to bring the gospel to billions by the next century, moved its headquarters from San Bernardino, California, to the Orlando area. Social worker Jerry Schall claims to have discovered the Fountain of Youth in a forested area 35 minutes from Disney World.

Since the 19th century Orlando has captured the imagination of entrepreneurs, dreamers and zealots alike. Together with the area's other residents, they have molded it into the quintessential American town. During the 1880s, a group of New England pioneers rode a one-way train to Orlando and began working their architectural charm. Around the gin-clear lakes they built crisp, white Colonial estates and graceful frame homes trimmed by verandas. Among the moss-covered trees they built a Spanish-style college, the first in Florida. Then they seasoned the city with art, introducing theater, painting, sculpture and literature. In 1908, locals proclaimed Orlando "The City Beautiful." It was perhaps the earliest attempt at national promotion.

The Great Depression set Orlando back, but not for long. Through the '30s and '40s, wealthy Northerners and Midwesterners arrived and built stately winter homes. Others, too, poured on the architectural charm. Famous families such as the Sears and the Edisons created sumptuous winter hideaways in the northern suburb of Winter Park. Spanish Mediterranean estates were the home of choice for many.

By the 1950s, Orlando began to feel real growth. The opening of Cape Canaveral, only 45 miles away on the coast, launched a wave of industry. But it did little to prepare the city for the tidal wave that rolled in 20 years later: Walt Disney World.

The 1971 opening of the Magic Kingdom gave Orlando a jolt and propelled it into one of the fastest-growing vacation centers in the world. With the "magic" of Disney came big-time highways and mega shopping malls, overnight tourist attractions and hundreds of new restaurants, and eventually more hotel rooms than any other city in the nation. It meant national attention and brought people from every walk of life—major investors and get-rich-quick entrepreneurs, religious zealots and drifters, and vacationing middle America—who transformed this New England–style sleepy town.

The rapid growth has carried a price. Typical big-city problems like traffic jams and air and water pollution are beginning to crop up in the greater metropolitan area. Long-time residents lament the invasion of neon and road signs and the loss of some city treasures. The last orange grove on Orange Avenue, for example, disappeared in 1977. From pastures where cows are grazing you now can see condos and fast-food restaurants. Interstate 4, which runs through the heart of Orlando, is the focus of ambitious improvement plans to clear gridlock. Right now, all you can plan on is traffic. Lots of it.

But all in all Orlando has handled its newfound fame well. Away from the theme parks that bring travelers to Orlando's door still beats the heart of a real city. Downtown Orlando boasts imagination indeed: Mirrored towers angle toward the sky. Fountains stream a rainbow of colors. Lakeshores flourish with museums, galleries, science centers and blocks of historic buildings. Away from downtown, turn-of-the-20th-century neighborhoods seem timelocked in a setting of ivy-wrapped pines and carpets of manicured greenery.

As it copes with the demands of a boomtown, the Orlando area is striving to retain its charm. There's an old-fashioned trolley that runs in the downtown area. Residential subdivisions, instead of the ubiquitous tract homes, try to instill a bucolic atmosphere.

But without question, the city's true character lies within its people. For this is still very much a hometown, a genuine place where people go to raise families. Maybe this is why vacationing families find so much in common with Orlando. Activities and sights, restaurants and shops are all geared toward family life. And where else do you find urban nightclubs designed with kids in mind?

While you're here, take time out from the theme parks and tune in to Orlando. Paddle a swan boat across downtown's Lake Eola. Stroll a brick street that was laid in the 19th-century. Tour an old home brimming with antiques, then linger in the rose gardens outside. Once you've seen what the city truly has to offer, you can say you've had the "real" Orlando experience.

▼ ▼ ▼ ▼ ▼ ▼ ▼ ▼ ▼
Orlando Area

Orlando may be an hour's drive from either Florida coast, yet the city possesses some of the state's most picturesque waters. The 1200 lakes that speckle Orlando range from small wading ponds to vast waters whose dark bottoms reach impossible depths. All across town, these silvery-blue mirrors reflect a mix of historic and modern architecture and perpetuate a lifestyle of water-skiing, bass fishing and careless walks along the shore.

SIGHTS

One of the prettiest and best-known lakes is **Lake Eola** (pronounced YO-la), which rests in the heart of downtown. The lake's **Centennial Fountain** was built to commemorate the city's 100th anniversary in 1975 and features a modern sculpture and a rainbow of lights at night. More than five millions gallons of water flow daily through the fountain. When the fountain was dedicated, waters were added from fountains in Spain, England, France and the United States—all nations that have ruled Florida. A lovely lakeside park, with moss-covered oaks and an Oriental pagoda, provides a spectacular view of the fountain.

The historic Orlando neighborhood known as Loch Haven Park offers three fine museums. The **Orlando Museum of Art** spotlights 18th century to present American works, art of the ancient Americas, African art and rotating exhibits from around the world. It also offers summer camp and classes in painting and sculpture for children ages 6 to 12, so adults can spend some leisure time viewing the exhibits while the kids prepare to be artists of the future. Closed Monday. Admission. ~ 2416 North Mills Avenue; 407-896-4231, fax 407-896-9920; www.omart.org, e-mail info@omart.org.

The **Orange County Historical Museum** travels back 12,000 years with the display of a Timucuan Indian canoe, then takes visitors to the Florida frontier days, and finally rolls into the early-20th-century era of boom and depression. Admission. ~ 65 East Central Boulevard; 407-836-8500, 800-965-2030; www.thehistorycenter.org.

Facts are flavored with fun for both kids and adults at the **Orlando Science Center**. The center's ultramodern facility practices its motto, "'Do Not Touch' is not in our vocabulary." Here you can touch amphibians and reptiles in the NatureWorks section of the Museum, while other exhibit sections such as Science City and Tech Works offer many types of hands-on exhibits (a couple of sure pleasers include ShowBiz Science: Entertainment Technology and the Inventors Workshop). There's also a KidsTown just for preschoolers. Adjoining theaters feature large-format films, planetarium and laser light shows and live performances. Closed

Orlando Area

Longwood
434 Winter Springs

Semoran Blvd
436
441
Orange Blossom Trail
Bear Lake
Forest City
434
Forest City Rd

Altamonte Rd

Lake Howell

Maitland
Lake Maitland
436
Semoran Blvd

Lockhart
17
92

423

Winter Park
426

426 ● Rollins College

Lake Virginia

Silver Star Rd
438
Lake Fairview
424
Lake Sue

435
441
50
Colonial Dr
423
Colonial Dr
50

4
● Lake Eola Park

Lake Mann
408
Holland East West Expwy

17
92
527
Clear Lake
435
Orange Ave

Turkey Lake
15

4
Little Lake Conway
436
551

Florida's Turnpike
John Young Pkwy
506

Universal Orlando ●
Oak Ridge Rd
Lake Conway
506

● Wet 'n Wild
482
Sand Lake Rd

International Dr
Orlando/Orange County Convention & Visitors Bureau
Extension
Orlando International Airport ✈

● Bee Line Expwy
528
527

● Central Florida Pkwy
17
N

SeaWorld Adventure Park
92
4 to Disney World
441

0   2 miles
0   2 kilometers

Monday in winter. Admission. ~ 777 East Princeton Street; 407-514-2000, fax 407-514-2277; www.osc.org.

The kooky, upside down–looking building is not a mistake, but the inventive shell for **Wonder Works**. Part arcade, part science museum (although it carefully bills itself as an "interactive attraction"), Wonder Works is a gadget-lover's playground with more than 100 things to do. Virtual experiences range from hoops to hang gliding. A simulator lets you concoct your own roller coaster and ride it. Kids can blow off theme-park over-stimulation with Laser Tag. The Outta Control Magic dinner show seems aimed at more than just kids by virtue of the fact it advertises "unlimited pizza, beer, wine and soda." ~ 9067 International Drive; 407-351-8800.

If you didn't get your fill through the Academy Award–winning film, you can peruse Titanic fact and fiction at **Titanic the Exhibition**. The 25,000-square-foot attraction re-creates some of the doomed vessel's rooms, as well as the famous grand staircase. Look for movie memorabilia (one of Leo's costumes, for instance), as well as original Titanic artifacts including china, deck chairs and letters penned by those on board. There are guided tours led by actors in period costumes. Admission. ~ 8445 International Drive; 407-248-1166, fax 407-248-1925; www.titanicshipofdreams.com.

Orlando's botanical fantasyland is **Leu Gardens**, where a nearly-50-acre profusion of bamboo, orchids, roses, camellias and other flowering flora border a picturesque lake. Kids feel right at home in this wild setting, where they can run free on soft grass and smell the flowers. Parents will want to join the guided tour of the handsome 1880s frame home, which showcases the lifestyle of a wealthy early-20th-century family. Admission. ~ 1920 North Forest Avenue; 407-246-2620, fax 407-246-2849; www.leugardens.org.

Who says Orlando isn't a religious experience? The "Living, biblical museum" **Holy Land** offers a trip back 3000 years to biblical times where you can visit the Walled City, interact with natives of the time, and tour the Temple of the Great King and the Wilderness Tabernacle. Holy Land aims to be something more than just empty consumerism, but judging by the fact that the shop sells a necktie with "The Story of the Crucifixion" on it, they're not totally averse to it. ~ 4655 Vineland Road; 407-367-2065, 866-872-4659.

A fantastic way to see Orlando is from the clouds. Hot-air ballooning has soared in popularity in the area, particularly with families. Several ballooning enterprises offer sunrise flights with spectacular views of the city and outlying lakes and theme parks. Cinderella Castle, Space Mountain and Spaceship Earth are highlights. **AirSports Aviation Inc.** includes a champagne toast after you land. ~ AirSports, 11475 Rocket Boulevard; 407-438-7773, fax 407-438-5131; www.airsportsinternational.com, e-mail air-sport@magicnet.net. Or try a champagne excursion in a balloon decorated with flamingos and palm trees at **Rise & Float Balloon Tours**. To ride, children should be at least four feet tall, big enough to see over the edge of the balloon's basket. ~ 5767 Major Boulevard; 407-352-8191, fax 407-857-9292; e-mail rise andfloatballoons@hotmail.com.

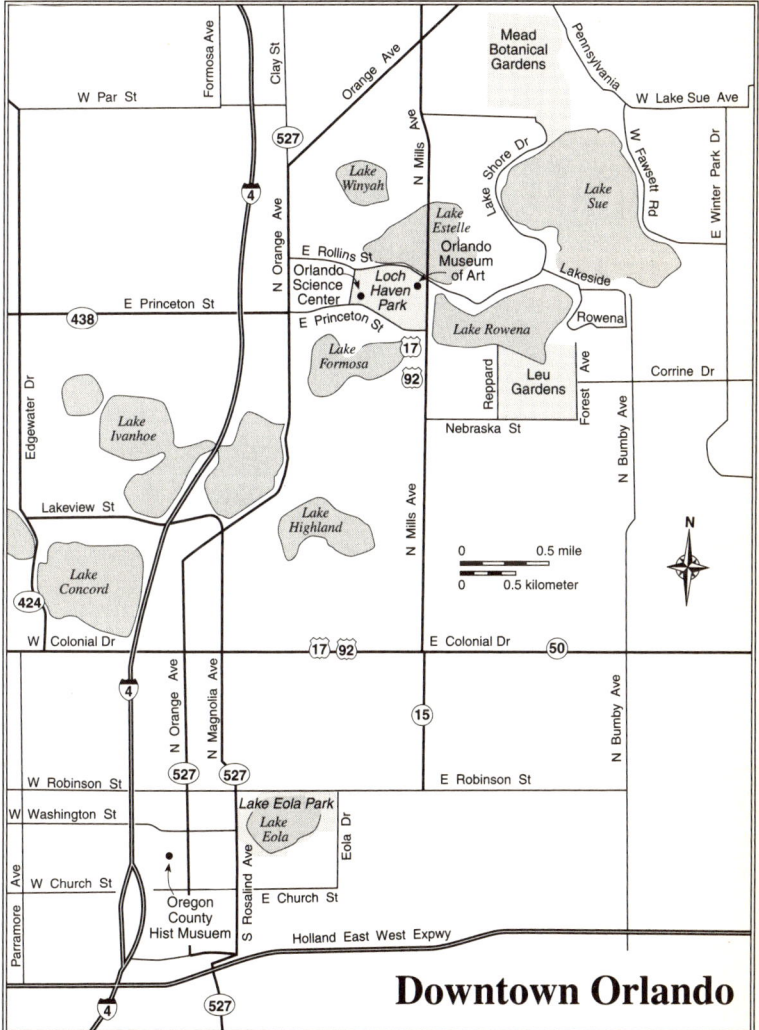

Downtown Orlando

Right outside Orlando on Route 426, the town of **Winter Park** delights families with its tree-lined avenues and lovely, old-time **Central Park** complete with benches, fountains and a stage. Folks here like to say that Winter Park is not a suburb of Orlando but the "superb" of Orlando. They're referring, of course, to the town's picture-book setting of winding brick streets, palatial turn-of-the-20th-century homes, blue jewels of lakes, hidden court-yards and grand oak and cypress trees dripping with Spanish moss. Here, expensive foreign cars populate the streets, and art galleries are nearly as plentiful as shops. ~ Park Avenue, between New England and Canton avenues.

HIDDEN ▶   Families can explore Winter Park's pretty scenery aboard the **Scenic Boat Tour**. The peaceful, one-hour cruise weaves through canals draped in vines and across lakes where perfect lawns slope to the water's edge. Children enjoy the tame ride and the abundance of native water birds, and adults get to relax amid Florida scenery at its undisturbed best. Admission. ~ 312 East Morse Boulevard, Winter Park; 407-644-4056, fax 407-695-9067; www.scenicboattours.com.

Just north of Winter Park lies the lovely bedroom community of Maitland. Here the **Maitland Art Center** hosts a changing array of contemporary sculpture, photography and paintings that appeal to adults and children. Most interesting, though, are the buildings themselves: a cluster of Mayan and Aztec designs built singlehandedly in the 1930s by an artist named André Smith. Over the years, the six-acre spot has become a retreat for artists and actors. Today, the lovely Garden Chapel on the grounds is a popular spot for weddings. ~ 231 West Packwood Avenue, Maitland; 407-539-2181, fax 407-539-1198; www.maitartctr.org.

Getting a bird's eye view of big and beautiful birds of prey is the highlight of a visit to the **Audubon Center for Birds of Prey**. Children are particularly intrigued by the bald eagles, owls, falcons, vultures and other fascinating feathered fliers who live here

◆◆◆

PLAY ORLANDO'S PLAYGROUNDS

Nothing breaks up a rigorous day of sightseeing like an afternoon at the park. Orlando's many fine playgrounds feature state-of-the-art equipment, jumbo sandboxes, landscaped surroundings and shady benches for parents. Some of the best: **Delaney Park** (1055 Delaney Avenue; downtown Orlando), **Dartmouth Park** (822 Dartmouth Street) and **Dover Shores Playground** (1450 Gaston Foster Road). In Winter Park, try **Lake Baldwin Park** (South Lakemont Avenue and Glenridge Way). For more information, call Orlando's Community and Youth Services at 407-246-2287; www.cityoforlando.net.

in a huge aviary. As one docent noted, "How often does a child get to stand five feet from a bald eagle and look him dead in the eye?" The society also offers an instructional area where the whole family can brush up on their bird sense. Guided tours given with advance reservation only. Closed Monday. Admission. ~ 1101 Audubon Way, Maitland; 407-644-0190, fax 407-644-8940; www.adoptabird.org.

A little farther north in Longwood, the **Bradlee-McIntyre House** exemplifies the mansions that heralded the golden days of the railroads that brought the tourist industry to Florida. Built in 1885 in nearby Altamonte Springs, it was moved to its present location in the early 1970s. The architecture and appointments have been restored to their Queen Anne style. Limited hours; call ahead. Admission. ~ 130 West Warren Avenue, Longwood; 407-332-6920.

Who's the oldest resident in Central Florida? Most likely it's the enormous cypress tree in **Big Tree Park**, which is thought to be 3500 years old. Kids can't climb the cypress, but they can marvel at its enormous size. With a height of 138 feet and diameter of nearly 18 feet, the nubby giant is the largest bald cypress tree in the nation. ~ General Hutchinson Parkway, north of Longwood; 407-788-0405, fax 407-788-7790.

For more information on area sights, visit the **Orlando/Orange County Convention & Visitors Bureau, Inc.** ~ 8723 International Drive, Orlando; 407-363-5872, 800-646-2087, fax 407-354-0874; www.orlandoinfo.com, e-mail info@orlandocvb.com.

Unlike the array of family-style lodging in the Disney World area, Orlando's accommodations are geared more toward corporate visitors and adults traveling without children. Still, a few places really do make families feel at home while at the same time providing the welcome surroundings of a "real" city.

LODGING

With its sleek, curving concrete and glass tower, the **Radisson Plaza Hotel** is one of the showcases of downtown Orlando. Like the outside, the inside is an eye-catcher. Sunshine streams through a dramatic glass atrium in the lobby, and rose-colored marble floors create a stylized look. Families will appreciate the extra space offered in the 337 guest rooms, outfitted with plush carpets and oak furnishings. Most rooms afford panoramic views of the city and adjacent Lake Ivanhoe. ~ 60 South Ivanhoe Boulevard; 407-425-4455, 800-333-3333, fax 407-425-7440; www.radissonorlando.com. DELUXE.

Downtown's other signature sleeping address is the **Four Points Hotel by Sheraton Downtown Orlando**. This 250-room hotel enjoys a superb location along Lake Eola. Its new decor has a Mediterranean flair, and among the many amenities are a fitness center and a heated outdoor pool. Despite the Four Point's standing as a corporate hotel, many families find it an inviting place to stay. ~ 151 East Washington Street; 407-841-3220, 800-321-2323, fax 407-648-4758; www.sheraton.com. MODERATE TO DELUXE.

The **Holiday Inn at the Orlando Arena** has a noisy but convenient location right next to Route 4. A 14-story building with a cozy yet modern appearance, its 276 guest rooms proffer contemporary appointments and fine city or lake views. Families will appreciate the heated outdoor pool, exercise room, laundry facilities and restaurant with children's menu. ~ 304 West Colonial Drive; 407-843-8700, 800-523-3405, fax 407-996-0103; www. holidayinn.com. MODERATE.

The **Courtyard at Lake Lucerne** offers 30 suites in four beautiful homes. One building, the Norment-Party Inn, is the oldest existing home in Orlando. Sitting on Lake Lucerne, it offers guests loveliness indoors and out. Ornate Victorian embellishments are complemented with American and English antiques throughout the six character-filled guest suites, parlor and other rooms. ~ 211 North Lucerne Circle East; 407-648-5188, 800-444-5289, fax 407-246-1368; www.orlandohistoricinn.com. MODERATE TO ULTRA-DELUXE.

DINING

Orlando may as well have invented the term "surf and turf." Only an hour from the Atlantic coast and plopped in the middle of the state's beef locker, local restaurants can proudly offer the freshest of both worlds. Many hotels offer coupons for restaurant discounts, and you'll find coupons in the telephone book as well.

Kitsch, Civil War style, is what you get at the **Dixie Stampede**. Dolly Parton's own restaurant performs nightly dinner shows that have a not-surprising Southern theme and feature trick riding, buffalos and costumed armies representing both sides of the American Civil War. Over the top? Sure. But Dolly's always been an infectious type of gal, and you'd be hard-pressed to leave without a smile. Come early (after 10 a.m. up until showtime) and meet the horses. ~ 8251 Vineland Avenue, Orlando; 407-866-4943.

The food at **Race Rock Orlando**—tasty if unoriginal chain-style fare—seems secondary to the important stuff, namely cool memorabilia from the race-car world. Some of the biggest names in the biz are purportedly behind it. And with tons of cars to look at, the place seems to amply live up to its self-styled billing as the "Shrine to Motorsports." ~ 8986 International Drive, Orlando; 407-248-9876.

Animatronic pirates are cast aside in favor of real ones (real actors, anyway) at the lively **Pirate's Dinner Adventure**. Dine aboard ship and watch the show with elaborate sets, swinging pirates and swashbucklers dueling for their fair maidens. Pirates interact with the galley, so be prepared to come with your best "aargh matey." ~ 6400 Carrier Drive, Orlando; 800-866-2469.

Plush and panoramic, **Lee's Lakeside** overlooks Lake Eola and the Centennial Fountain downtown. The menu does surf and turf superbly, with such specialties as châteaubriand bouquetière, tournedos, king crab and lobster. If it sounds a bit too elaborate for the kids, don't worry: The children's menu features everything from burgers and hot dogs to fried chicken and grilled cheese. No lunch; Sunday brunch. ~ 431 East Central Boulevard, Orlando; 407-841-1565, 407-841-7256; www.leeslakeside.com. DELUXE.

Número Uno is held in high regard among Orlando residents for its Cuban cuisine. The family-run eatery offers simple decor and a menu of standard Cuban specialties such as rice and beans, roast pork, paella and bean soup. Weekday lunch specials and half portions are available for children at dinner. Closed Sunday. ~ 2499 South Orange Avenue, Orlando; 407-841-3840, fax 407-422-1007. BUDGET TO DELUXE.

Unpretentious surroundings and dependably fine French fare draw the locals to **Coq au Vin**. The seasonal and regional menu changes every two months and features such favorites as eggplant *bayou têche*, with fresh crab and shrimp and a Cajun hollandaise sauce. Closed Monday. ~ 4800 South Orange Avenue, Orlando; 407-851-6980, fax 407-248-0658. MODERATE TO DELUXE.

If you're hankering to quietly eat a steak away from tourists, **Chaparral Ranch Steak House** is the place. Thick cuts are tossed onto a blazing orangewood fire for extraordinary flavor. Cowpoke elegance describes the ambience; down-home good describes the food. Small portions are guaranteed to make the kids happy. Closed Monday. ~ 6129 Old Winter Garden Road, Orlando; 407-298-7334, fax 407-290-9753. BUDGET TO MODERATE.

Standing waterfront in historic Winter Park, **Houston's** has become popular among Central Floridians for its dependable meat,

THE LEGEND OF ORLANDO REEVES

No one knows for sure how Orlando got its name, but many believe it comes from a brave but ill-fated soldier named Orlando Reeves. In 1835, Reeves joined a posse scouting for central Florida Indians. He was on sentinel duty one night when some Indians, disguised as pine tree logs, snuck into the soldiers' camp. Reeves spotted the intruders, fired his gun and saved his companions. Unfortunately, he was pierced by an arrow and died on the spot. Soon people started calling the town Orlando, and eventually that became the official name.

fish and vegetarian fare. The ambience is casual, the food grilled with hickory flair. Menu items include salads, fish, meat and chicken as well as a veggie burger, and a renowned apple walnut cobbler for dessert. ~ 215 South Orlando Avenue, Winter Park; 407-740-4005, fax 407-740-4005; www.houstons.com. MODERATE TO DELUXE.

If authentic Mexican food in a packed *casa* is your style, try the homemade guacamole, refried beans and burritos at **Paco's**. Kids usually go for the tacos, or the chef will fix them a special quesadilla (minus onions, peppers and other "yucky" stuff). Don't be turned off by the shabby look of this place—it's the real McCoy. No lunch on Saturday. Closed Sunday. ~ 1801 West Fairbanks Avenue, Winter Park; 407-629-0149. BUDGET.

SHOPPING   Save a few bucks on your souvenirs at **Orlando Premium Outlets**. Universal and Disney each have a shop here and both sell souvenirs (many discontinued items) for a lot less than at the park prices. Disney's store has some current merchandise as well—but you'll have to pay full price. There are dozens of other stores so you can pick up that Polo shirt, Giorgio Armani blouse or Coach bag you simply can't go home without. ~ 8200 Vineland Avenue, Orlando; 407-238-7787.

Caribbean One Stop offers Jamaican take-out, groceries, music and jewelry. ~ 2117 West Colonial Drive; 407-423-7552.

Madge Elaine's World has been an Orlando fixture since the mid-'70s. Wigs, stage and theatrical makeup, gag gifts and novelty items are all for sale here for thespians or the merely curious and costume inclined. Closed Sunday. ~ 5105 East Colonial Drive; 407-281-9333; www.madgeelainesworld.com.

Orlando has no lack of shopping malls. **Florida Mall**, while conventional, stands out because of its huge size and its pastel fairy-tale setting. Children naturally enjoy the imaginative surroundings, which feature lots of arches and toy stores including **Kay-Bee Toy and Hobby** (407-859-4822). Over 260 retailers, including several department stores, make this one of the largest malls in the southeast United States. Check out **Gap Kids** (407-856-7188) and replace clothes you left behind. ~ 8001 South Orange Blossom Trail; 407-851-6255; www.simon.com.

◆◆◆

ICE CREAM BIRTHDAY PARTIES

It's tough to throw a big birthday bash for your child when you're on vacation, but why not celebrate with a little ice cream? Try **Tropicana Smoothies and Swenson's Ice Cream**. ~ 8001 South Orange Blossom Trail, in the Florida Mall; 407-857-7271.

When locals say they're going shopping on "The Avenue," they of course mean Park Avenue. This Winter Park thoroughfare, considered *the* place to shop, is lined with the savviest of stores that can coax some serious dollars from your pocket. Even if you don't have a bundle to spend, it's always fun to look.

The Black Sheep specializes in handpainted needlepoint canvases, imported wools, silks, fabrics and accessories. Closed Sunday. ~ 128 Park Avenue South, Winter Park; 407-644-0122.

Not surprisingly, this posh town boasts an exclusive toy shop. The European collectibles at **Rune Stone** include such pricey items as Brio trains and Mohair Steiff teddy bears. ~ 326 Park Avenue North, Winter Park; 407-644-9671.

Winter Park Stamps stocks several hundred thousand stamps, some dating back to the 1840s. Closed Sunday. ~ 325 South Orlando Avenue, Winter Park; 407-628-1120; www.winterpark stampshop.com.

For a cozy pub atmosphere, go to **Bull & Bush**, have a Guinness and play some darts. ~ 2408 East Robinson Street, Orlando; 407-896-7546.

NIGHTLIFE

◄ *HIDDEN*

For a taste of culture, check out what's happening on stage at the **Bob Carr Performing Arts Center**. The elegant 2500-seat theater hosts major dance, opera, symphony and touring Broadway performances throughout the year. ~ 401 West Livingston Street, Orlando; 407-849-2577; www.orlandocentralplex.com.

The **Theatre for Young People** showcases favorite fairy tales and kid-style musicals and comedies from October through June. Shows are staged at the **Orlando Repertory Theatre**, which also presents regional and community theater for adults. ~ 1001 East Princeton Street, Orlando; 407-896-7365; www.orlandorep.com.

A family-friendly comedy club, SAK **Comedy Lab** hosts comedians who perform improv suitable for kids and grown ups. Cover. ~ Corner of Amelia and Hughey streets, Orlando; 407-648-0001; www.sak.com.

Located at Rollins College, the **Annie Russell Theatre** hosts theater performances from September through May. ~ 1000 Holt Avenue-2735, Winter Park; 407-646-2501; www.rollins.edu.

LAKE EOLA PARK 🏃 Charming Lake Eola Park is a fine place for simply strolling the lakeshores. Draped around downtown's Lake Eola, it's the quintessential city park, with fountains and luxuriant gardens and paddleboats shaped like swans. A tot lot makes the youngsters happy, while adults can relax in the Asian-style gazebo. Facilities include restrooms, picnic areas and a playground. ~ Rosalind Street and Washington Avenue; 407-246-2827.

BEACHES & PARKS

TURKEY LAKE PARK 🏃🚲🛶 Turkey Lake Park centers around a lake known as the headwaters of the Everglades.

Designed for family pleasure, the park features two sandy stretches along the lake (though swimming is not allowed because of the alligators), a picnic area, a swimming pool, nature and bike trails and flora that thrive here in the midst of the metropolis. Kids will enjoy the re-created cracker farm and petting zoo. You can camp here and catch pan fish in the lake. Day-use fee, $4 per vehicle. ~ 3401 South Hiawassee Road; 407-299-5594, fax 407-290-2423.

▲ There are 36 sites, all with RV hookups, and a primitive campground; $7 to $18 per night. Five rustic cabins, sleeping up to ten guests, are also available; $35 per night.

HIDDEN ▶ **MOSS PARK** 🏃 🚣 ⛵ 🚴 🛶 🚤 ⛴ This 3500-acre county park is sandwiched between two lovely lakes. Shadiness and a nice sand beach give this metropolitan fringe park its oasis feel. Much of its acreage remains in a natural, undeveloped state. It's not well-advertised, but the locals know it well. Swimming is good here and anglers try for perch, bass and other local freshwater fish. Facilities at the park include picnic areas, restrooms, pavilions, a playground, a softball field, volleyball courts and a nature trail. Take note: no pets are allowed here. Day-use fee, $1. ~ Located off Route 15 on Moss Park Road, southeast of Orlando's Route 528; 407-273-2327, fax 407-249-4498.

▲ There are 44 sites, 16 with RV hookups, and a primitive campground; $10 to $18 per night.

▼▼▼▼▼▼▼▼▼▼▼▼▼

Outdoor Adventures

The whole family can drop hook, line and sinker in one of Orlando's many lakes. Several guides guarantee fish, including half-day and full-day trips. Try **Ole Mossy Back Bass**. ~ 407-299-0071. Or call **Bass America**. ~ 398 Grove Court; 407-281-0845. Also consider **Bass Challenger Guide Service**. ~ P.O. Box 679155, Orlando, FL 32867; 407-273-8045, 800-241-5314; www.basschallenger.com.

SPORT-FISHING

GOLF

Orlando's gentle, green terrain and wide-open spaces make it a perfect place to tee off. Try the 18-hole, semiprivate **Meadow Woods Golf Club**. ~ 13000 Landstar Boulevard; 407-850-5600. Or check out the 18-hole, public **Hunter's Creek Golf Course**. ~ Route 441, located four miles south of Florida's Turnpike; 407-240-4653. Just north of Orlando you'll find the 18-hole, public **Winter Pines Golf Club**. ~ 950 South Ranger Boulevard, Winter Park; 407-671-3172. Also nearby is the 18-hole, semiprivate **Sabal Point Country Club**. ~ 2662 Sabal Club Way, Longwood; 407-869-8787.

ICE SKATING

As unlikely as it may seem, steamy Orlando actually sports an ice rink—the **RDV Sportsplex Ice Den**. ~ 8701 Maitland Summit Boulevard; 407-916-2550.

TWELVE

Side Trips from Orlando

There is a saying among Floridians that the farther you go from Disney World, the closer you get to the true wonders of their state. Truth is, however, you need not venture far from Disney's door to find the poetic scenery that the theme parks can only try to imitate: billowing green hills, lakes framed with bulrushes and tiny historic towns that seem plucked from a fairy tale.

These rural rhythms start just outside the Orlando metropolis and head in every direction, creating a circle of splendid sightseeing for the family that wants to take in the "magic kingdom" of Florida. The circle takes in both Florida coasts, from the technological Space Coast and fast-paced Daytona Beach to metropolitan Tampa and sun-washed St. Petersburg and Clearwater. Except for the West Coast cities, everything is within an easy hour's drive of Orlando. For some of these adventures, just an afternoon (or morning) of your time will be plenty. For others, you'll want to consider staying overnight to enjoy all the sights and sounds.

Let's go!

Northeast of Orlando, the towns of Sanford and DeLand recall the 19th-century steamship era with riverboat attractions and mansions that rich visitors left in their wake, in styles ranging from spiffed-up cracker to Victorian Gothic. Sand pine forest and spring waters still refresh travelers tired of resort hubbub. Remember the magic number 72: it's the temperature of these springs, as well as the average temperature of upper central Florida.

State parks and national forests in this area also offer refuge to the crowd weary—and to alligators, Florida panthers, deer, wild turkeys and migratory birds. Fishing camps take the place of towering hotels, and fried catfish pushes steak au poivre off the plate.

In the hills south of Orlando, citrus reigns. Here temperatures average in the high 70s and the climate is generally rainier than along the coast. Blossom-scented tranquility settles in between pretty little towns named either for the many nearby lakes or for the escape from cold they offer: Winter Haven, Lakeland, Lake Alfred, Frostproof, Lake Wales.

West of Orlando, sleepy towns such as Clermont, Bushnell and Howey-in-the-Hills paint a portrait of rural quaintness. The Withlacoochee River winds toward the Gulf above a state forest bearing the same name. Like the areas north and south of Orlando, this western region boasts countless waters: crystal springs, lakes and rivers that gush and gurgle and teem with fish, aquatic realms that have given life to fertile agricultural lands. Those acres have produced still another side of central Florida—rows of citrus trees that lie like neatly plaited hair, as well as farms of winter vegetables and miles of cattle scrub.

Over on the East Coast, the beaches are launching grounds for vehicles that rocket people into outer space. Epcot may provide a glimpse into the future, but the Space Coast *is* the future. Since NASA established a space center here in the 1960s, the area has turned into a bedroom community for astronauts, scientists and their support staff. A beautiful stretch of beach offers sensational viewing points for space launches.

On the other end of the technological spectrum, this area contains some of the finest beaches and wildlife refuges in the state. For 40 miles north to Daytona Beach, the Atlantic Ocean alternately laps and crashes against a seemingly endless wide ribbon of sand. This giant sandbox contains great surfing spots as well as beaches where the waves are gentle enough for small children. Virtually all of this coast is separated from the ocean by a series of lovely barrier islands. Between these islands and the mainland is the Intracoastal Waterway (called a river in some locales), where calmer inland waters provide safe passage for pleasure craft everywhere on the coast. Most of the fun, a lot of the area's history and even a glimpse into the future can be found on the islands.

No single focal point highlights this region, but it is bound by one sensibility—an overwhelming consciousness of the ocean's proximity. The salt air, casual atmosphere, emphasis on water sports and abundance of exquisite seafood provide constant reminders. And, although development has obstructed views in some areas, particularly Daytona Beach, virtually every square foot of beach is open to the public.

The geography in this region is fairly consistent: flat, sandy beaches fringed with palm trees and imported Australian pines (not true pines, by the way). The climate is, on the whole, temperate.

Oddly enough, the best sightseeing route here is not well known. It is possible—and recommended—for visitors to drive the entire coast along Route A1A. This beach-hugging road lopes through resort towns and retirement enclaves and villages not much bigger than intersections. Route A1A runs through the barrier islands, often within earshot of the surf.

The most developed of east Florida's resort towns is Daytona Beach. Daytona is now known as spring-break capital for the college crowd, but during summer it becomes a haven for families. Younger folks love this high-energy beach town for its boardwalk, amusement-park atmosphere and concessions and great swimming. Automobile traffic is still tolerated on the beach, but professional racing has been removed inland to the tracks at the Daytona Beach Speedway. In fact, all beach driving is hotly disputed and may end soon, as environmentalists argue that the cars interfere with Mother Nature, especially the sea turtles who come up to lay their eggs on Florida's beaches in the early summer.

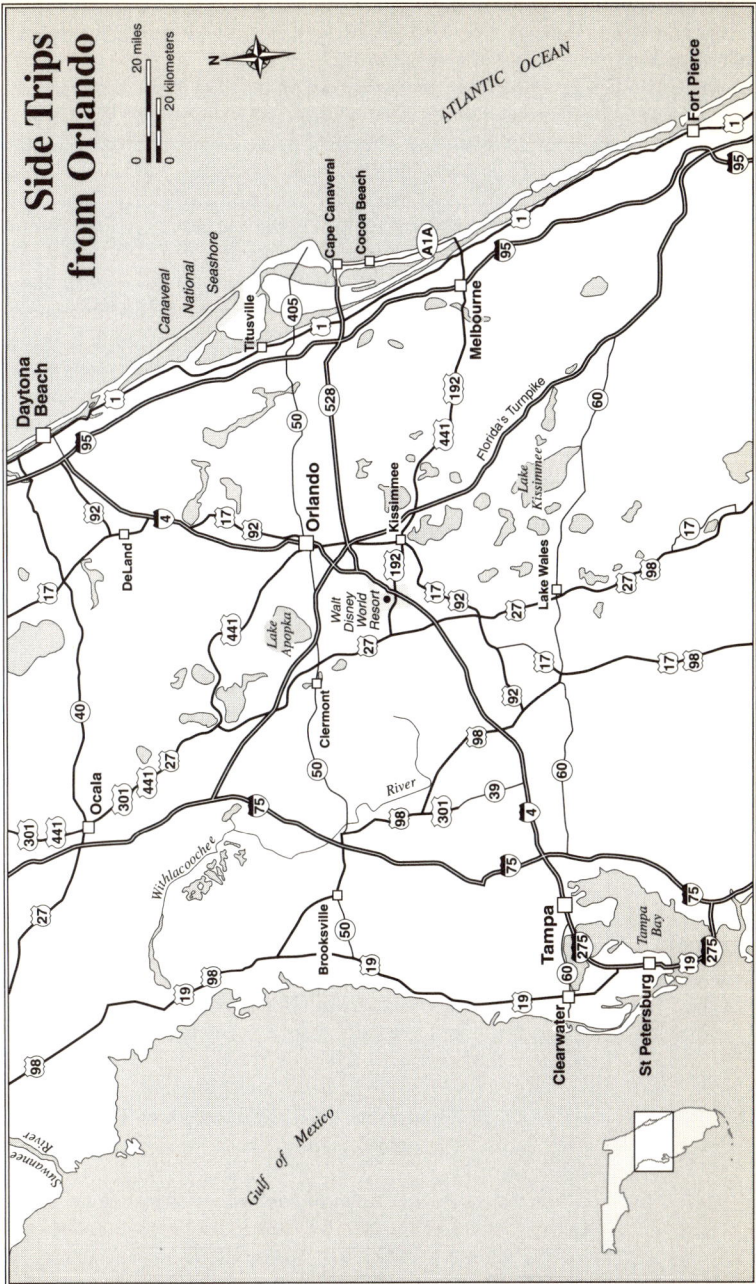

Side Trips from Orlando

N

20 miles

20 kilometers

0

0

ATLANTIC OCEAN

Fort Pierce

1

95

Cape Canaveral

Cocoa Beach

A1A

1

Melbourne

95

1

Canaveral National Seashore

Titusville

405

1

528

192

441

Florida's Turnpike

60

Daytona Beach

95

1

50

Orlando

Kissimmee

Lake Kissimmee

17

92

92

4

17

DeLand

441

192

17

Lake Wales

27

98

17

Lake Apopka

Walt Disney World Resort

27

92

27

Ocala

441

Clermont

17

92

98

17

98

40

27

50

River

98

301

60

17

301

441

27

39

4

75

75

Wichlacoochee

75

Brooksville

50

Tampa

275

Tampa Bay

75

19

98

19

19

60

275

19

St Petersburg

Clearwater

98

Suwannee River

Gulf of Mexico

Whether or not the cars disappear, plenty of pristine areas remain in the Space Coast and Daytona Beach area. And where else can you take your children from outer space to the deep ocean in a single day?

Certainly such paradoxes exist across the state on the West Coast, where visitors find a pleasing balance between the wild and the wilds. In big-city Tampa, skyscrapers seem to shoot up overnight. The town's pace is set by whizzing jai alai orbs, zooming corporate successes and neon nightlife. Yet wildlife can be found even in this soaring metropolis, on the Serengeti Plains of Busch Gardens Tampa Bay, where thousands of exotic animals roam freely. The old ways are preserved in parks, the renovated downtown area and at shrimp docks.

Across Tampa Bay lie two gleaming jewels, St. Petersburg and Clearwater, whose spirits are stoked by the gorgeous Gulf of Mexico. Once the butt of retirement-home jokes, St. Petersburg now enjoys a livelier image, thanks to the beautiful young people who populate its shell-strewn sands. But the heart of the beach action still throbs in Clearwater, just north of St. Petersburg. A futuristic pier, restored downtown and dynamic, sun-soaked beaches make this the Gulf Coast's most popular playground. True to its name, the city's shores are lapped by see-through waters tinted a pale jade.

The Gulf Coast is blessed with the same semitropical climate and flora as Florida's burgeoning East Coast. Plus it has something the Atlantic side doesn't: seaside sunsets.

But whether your intention is to see a spectacular sun or an enthralled son, take a day trip or stay over, you can only experience these wonders if you travel away from the theme parks and into the real Florida. A side trip will help you discover the state's true character, the character that is held sacred by those who call Florida home.

Day Trips

There is so much to explore within an easy drive of Orlando that it's possible to visit a crowded theme park in the morning, then spend the afternoon in the country. No matter which direction you take out of town, getting there is half the fun as you discover bucolic byways that lead to a slower, crowdless dimension.

SIGHTS

Traveling north of Orlando takes you through a pastoral profile of folded green hills, plantation homes, boiled-peanut shacks and lakes that dip into the horizon. Along the way here, where agriculture is still king, you can stop at a roadside vegetable stand and shoot the breeze with a farmer. You can drive a narrow road through citrus groves, or wade (gingerly) through a cactus farm.

To find all this and much more, head north on Route 17-92, which leads into Sanford. Route 441 north will take you to Mount Dora.

The old steamboat town of **Sanford** is today known as the "Celery Capital of the World." Still retaining its riverside personality, Sanford also blends agricultural, historic and metropolitan characteristics.

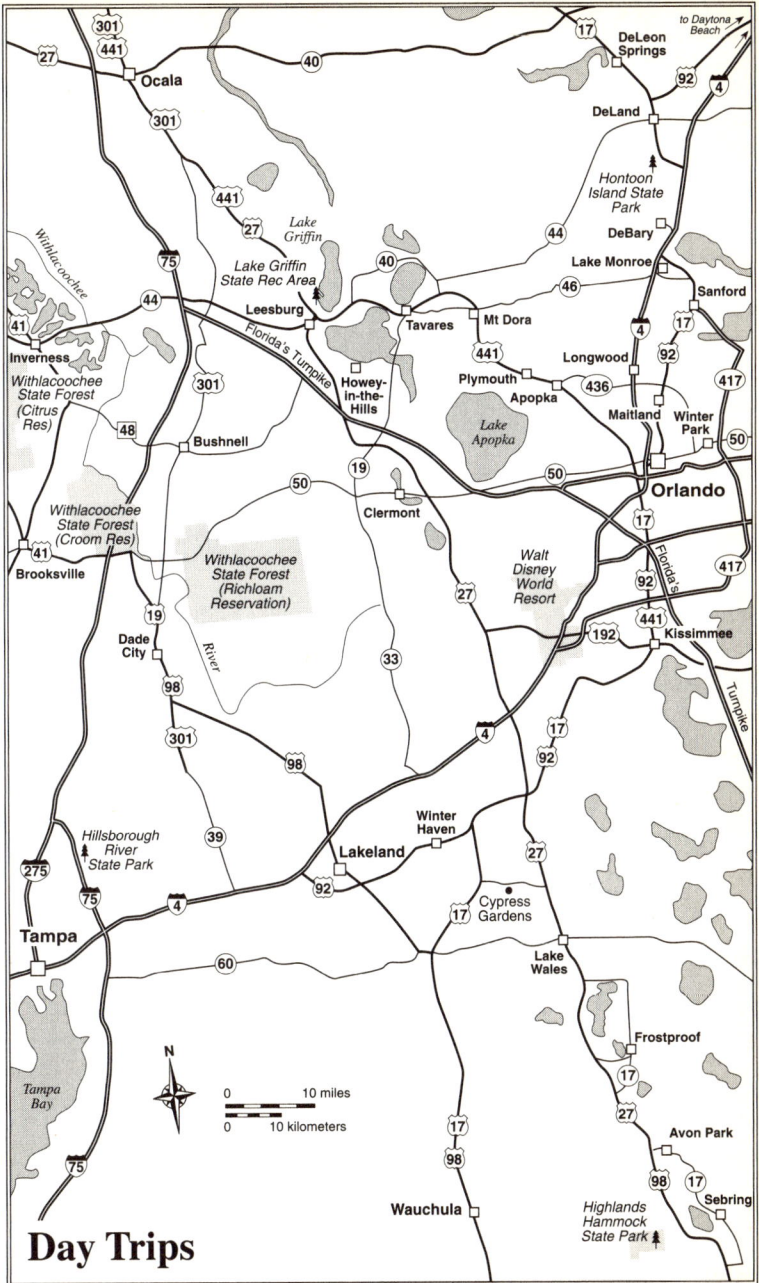

Day Trips

The **Museum of Seminole County History** depicts the town's diversity with exhibits covering settlement, the citrus industry, cattle ranching and vegetable farming. Railroad and steamboat memorabilia and furnished rooms of a typical steamboat-era mansion are also featured. Closed Sunday and Monday. ~ 300 Bush Boulevard, Sanford; 407-665-2489.

For a narrated tour of St. Johns River wildlife and a peek at its great steamboat days, ride aboard **St. Johns River Cruises and Tours**. Alligators, osprey, manatees and bald eagles will greet your passage as they did a century ago. (It's wise to call a few days in advance as trips often fill up.) Admission. ~ 2100 West French Avenue, Orange City ; 407-260-8813; www.sjrivercruises.com.

Rivership Romance leaves out of Monroe Harbor Marina on a popular lunch or dinner river sightseeing trip aboard a 100-foot 1940 steamboat. Every cruise includes lunch or dinner, live music and dancing. Admission. ~ 433 North Palmetto Avenue, Sanford; 407-321-5091, 800-423-7401, fax 407-330-7043; www.rivershipromance.com.

More information on Sanford awaits at the **Greater Sanford Chamber of Commerce**. ~ 400 East 1st Street, Sanford; 407-322-2212, fax 407-332-8160; www.sanfordchamber.com; e-mail info@sanfordchamber.com.

As you follow Route 1792 out of Sanford, along glistening Lake Monroe, you will come to the **Central Florida Zoological Park**. This 116-acre zoo may well be the highlight of your northern day trip, as the kids gape at the llamas and 300 other exotic animals on display. Thatched-roof shelters make ideal spots for a family picnic. Admission. ~ 3755 Route 1792, Lake Monroe; 407-323-4450; www.centralfloridazoo.org, e-mail centflzoo@totcon.com.

A few miles west of Sanford lies one of the prettiest towns in Florida. **Mount Dora** is a storybook village of gingerbread mansions, lakeside inns and 19th-century ambience. The downtown boasts brick and wrought-iron structures, New England touches, one of the state's proudest antique store districts and a "mountainous" Florida elevation of 184 feet. Stop in at the **Mount Dora Area Chamber of Commerce**, housed in a restored railroad station, for a guide to the area's antique shops and historic homes. ~ 341 Alexander Street; 352-383-2165, fax 352-383-1668; www.mountdora.com, e-mail chamber@mountdora.com.

Among the showiest of these regally preserved mansions is the **Donnelly House**, an ornate fantasy castle in Steamboat Gothic style, accented with stained glass and hand-carved trim. Built in 1893 for one of the city's founders, it is now used as a Masonic Lodge. ~ Donnelly Street between 5th and 6th avenues, Mount Dora. Across the street, shady **Donnelly Park** provides shuffleboard and tennis courts.

Housed downtown in the old city jailhouse, **Royellou Museum** features historic photographs and temporary exhibits. Closed Monday through Thursday. ~ 450 Royellou Lane, between 5th and 4th avenues off Baker Street, Mount Dora; 352-383-0006; www. historicmountdora.com, e-mail info@historicmountdora.com.

The **Miss Dora** takes tours out of Gator Inlet Marina into the Dora Canal, the channel that runs between Lake Dora and Lake Eustis. These lovely cypress-studded waters have been preserved from logging to provide refuge for various waterfowl and migratory birds. Admission. ~ 1505 Route 441, Tavares; 352-343-0200; http://captaincharlie.home.vol.com.

Florida Cactus, Inc. will change any preconceived notions   ◄ *HIDDEN* about cactus being merely green, prickly plants that grow in desert wastelands. Families can see the amazing plants growing: red, yellow and pink ones; cacti that form a 16-foot-circumference electric clock; small cacti, gigantic cacti—Florida Cactus does more with cactus than you ever cared to imagine. Closed Sunday. ~ 2542 South Peterson Road, Plymouth; 407-886-1833, fax 407-886-5661.

South of Orlando lies a peaceful, countrified world where grazing cattle speckle the horizon and townsfolk spend lazy afternoons on the front porch. Here in Florida's heartland, citrus scents the air with its blossoms in spring and ripe juices in winter. This gentle landscape also harbors some singular Sunshine State oddities—spooky hills, singing towers and human pyramids on skis—guaranteed to liven up the family outing.

Known as the Highlands area, this section lies along Florida's central spine. From the Orlando area, take Route 4 to Route 27 and follow it south. Soon you'll come to the town of Winter Haven, home to one of Florida's oldest and most popular destinations:

THE PLACE WHERE IT'S ALWAYS CHRISTMAS

While you're exploring central Florida, make sure you show the kids Christmas. Christmas, Florida, that is. This peaceful, rural town, about 25 miles east of Orlando, features humble frame homes, moss-covered woods and a three-story Christmas tree that twinkles year-round. At the **Fort Christmas Historical Park**, children can climb stairs and wooden walkways and peek out rifle holes. Learn how 2000 soldiers built the fortress in two days, starting on December 25, 1837. There are also pioneer houses furnished in period styles; guided tours are offered daily. The original fort rotted, and the current replica opened in 1977, on Christmas Day. The museum is closed Monday, but the grounds stay open for picnickers. ~ 1300 Fort Christmas Road, Christmas; 407-568-4149, fax 407-568-9790.

Cypress Gardens. Here, you can lose yourself in vast botanical gardens or watch the famous aquatic shows that feature hoop-skirted Southern belles, human pyramids on skis and air dancing on the high wire. Visitors can stroll through the gardens or board canal boats, while the "Island in the Sky" takes you on a ride to a revolving platform towering 16 stories above the botanical gardens. On the grounds you'll also find an old Southern town that harks back to the antebellum era, and **Lake Eloise**, where the world-famous water-ski revue is staged. The park's **Plantation Gardens** includes "Wings of Wonder," a 5500-square-foot Victorian-style butterfly conservatory where you mingle with a thousand of these free-flying insects. This precursor of modern amusement parks offers at least a day's worth of entertainment. Admission. ~ Route 540, Winter Haven; 863-324-2111, fax 863-324-7496; www.cypressgardens.com.

HIDDEN ▶ Also in town is the **Water Ski Museum and Hall of Fame**. The memorabilia, photos and literature trace the development of water-skiing from 1922, when the sport was born in Minnesota, to modern times. The dramatic videos of barefoot and trick skiing are favorites here with children. Closed weekends. ~ 1251 Holy Cow Road, Polk City; 863-324-2472, fax 863-324-3996.

The quirkiness of **Lake Wales** can be seen by the town's main attractions: an eccentric dollhouse-like country inn, a singing tower and a "spooked" hill. Start exploring the area north of town at the first of these, **Chalet Suzanne**, and have a peek at the quaint Old World restaurant, inn, gift shops and ceramic studio. Tours can be arranged through the soup cannery, where the restaurant's trademark dishes are canned. In the tiny ceramic studio in the midst of the meandering cobblestone village, you can watch craftspeople making dishware and personalized gifts. ~ 3800 Chalet Suzanne Drive, Lake Wales; 863-676-6011, fax 863-676-1814; www.chaletsuzanne.com, e-mail info@chaletsuzanne.com.

> Chalet Suzanne's signature romaine soup was sent to space with Apollo 16.

HIDDEN ▶ A trip to **Historic Bok Sanctuary** is a treat for the senses: exotic blossoms scent leaf-paved paths and squirrels chatter atop towering oaks. Here, in 1928, Dutch immigrant Edward Bok built a 205-foot carillon tower of Georgia marble and St. Augustine coquina stone to show his appreciation for the beauty he felt America had brought into his life. He planted the 157 acres around the singing tower in magnolias, azaleas and plants from Asia to create an atmosphere of peace. The carillon, a registered historic structure, rings out classic harmonies every half-hour to add a special magic to this place. Small children love hand-feeding the birds and fish here. Admission. ~ 1151 Tower Boulevard, Lake Wales; 863-676-1408, fax 863-676-6770; www.boksanctuary.org, e-mail info@boksanctuary.org.

The thing I found spookiest about **Spook Hill** was the convoluted route you must take to get there if you follow the signs. To make it simpler, take a left on North Avenue. At the bottom of the hill, you must turn around to experience the mystery here: "spooks" power your car back up the hill. A legend accompanies the mystery, and kids are guaranteed to love it. ~ North Avenue and 5th Street, Lake Wales.

Lake Wales itself is a pretty little town that lassoes a lake. For a scenic view of the water and its lakeside mansions and park, follow **Lakeshore Boulevard**. The history of the area, including the building of the railroad that settled inland Florida, can be seen at **Lake Wales Depot Museum**. The museum, housed in the Atlantic Coastline Depot, sits next to a number of historic railroad cars. Closed Sunday. ~ 325 South Scenic Highway, Lake Wales; 863-678-4209, fax 863-678-4299; www.cityoflakewales.com, e-mail thedepot@cityoflakewales.com.

Sebring is best known for its **Sebring International Raceway**, where the 12-Hour Endurance Race is held each March. For racing enthusiasts who want hands-on experience, the Raceway's **Panoz Racing School** offers one-, two- and three-day classes. ~ 113 Midway Drive, Sebring; 863-655-1442, fax 863-655-1777; www.sebringraceway.com, e-mail sirmktg@sebringraceway.com.

Aside from the roar of engines, this is a pretty, lake-mottled town blending a sense of heritage, a touch of sophistication and a dash of the outdoors. For more information on the area, stop at the **Greater Sebring Chamber of Commerce**. Closed weekends. ~ 309 South Circle, Sebring; 863-385-8810, 877-844-6007, fax 863-385-8810; www.sebringflchamber.com, e-mail information@sebringflchamber.com.

The area west of Orlando is known as the Green Swamp and is an important underground aquifer system in Central Florida. Typical Green Swamp terrain includes cypress marshes, sandhills, pine forests and hardwood hammocks.

View one of Florida's younger enterprises—winemaking—at **Lakeridge Winery & Vineyards**. The winery opened in 1989 and uses all Florida-grown grapes. Families can view a short video, take a guided tour of the facilities, and sample some vintages (kids get grape juice). Most children enjoy learning about winemaking, but those who don't can watch cartoons. Sweeping views of the vineyards can be enjoyed from the picnic pavilions. Kids of all ages get to participate in grape stomping from late-June through mid-August. Call for monthly festival schedules. ~ 19239 Route 27 North, Clermont; 352-394-8627, 800-768-9463, fax 352-394-7490; www.lakeridgewinery.com, e-mail lakeridgew@aol.com.

History can be fun for the kids over in bucolic Bushnell. Here you can view the site where the Second Seminole War began at the **Dade Battlefield Historic State Park**. The museum and nature trail commemorate December 28, 1835, when a tribe of American Indians ambushed troops under Major Francis L. Dade. The Dade Massacre began seven more years of bloody and costly battles in Florida. Day-use fee, $2 per vehicle. ~ 7200 County Road 603 or South Battlefield Drive, off State Road 476, Bushnell; 352-793-4781, fax 352-793-4230; www.dadebattlefield.com.

From there you can forge into the **Withlacoochee State Forest**, which lies between Inverness and Brooksville (see the "Beaches & Parks" section). Stop at the **Hernando County Welcome Center** to find out more about the area. ~ 30305 Cortez Boulevard, Brooksville; 352-754-4405, fax 352-754-4406; www.fl southern.edu.

DINING

Several delightful restaurants reflect the pastoral flavor of the region north of Orlando:

Seafood with Southern flair is what you'll find at **Catfish Place**, a restaurant set in an antique railroad depot. Freshwater catfish is the specialty, but you can also select from frogs' legs and alligator as well as flounder, clams and scallops. The children's menu features hamburgers and grilled cheese sandwiches. Closed Sunday and Monday. ~ 311 South Forest Avenue, Apopka; 407-889-7980, fax 407-884-6070. BUDGET TO MODERATE.

The homestyle cooking at **Original Holiday House** has drawn crowds since the late 1950s. Guests serve themselves buffet style in this well-preserved old home. Choices include leg of lamb, fish, roast beef and salad. Special children's prices. ~ 704 North Woodland Boulevard, DeLand; 386-734-6319, fax 386-736-6668; www.holidayhouserestaurant.com. BUDGET.

Rocking chairs sit on the wide front porch of Lakeside Inn's **Beauclair Dining Room**. Formal elegance reigns inside, where heavy curtains drape the windows overlooking the pastoral inn grounds. The tasty menu offers nouvelle entrées such as sirloin steak with portobello mushrooms and Georgia bourbon chicken. Despite such culinary formality, children are regular diners and get their very own menus. ~ 100 North Alexander Street, Mount Dora; 352-383-4101, 800-556-5016, fax 352-735-2642. MODERATE TO ULTRA-DELUXE.

South of Orlando, four restaurants enjoy local and statewide acclaim:

Tasty seafood and steaks have given **Christy's Sundown** its top billing with locals and critics. Antiques and works of art combine to create a Mediterranean mood. Lobster, stone crab, chicken, pasta and Kansas City steaks are the fare here. A children's menu is available. No lunch on Saturday. Closed Sunday. ~ Route 17 South, Winter Haven; 863-293-0069, fax 863-298-0979. MODERATE TO DELUXE.

For a romantic tryst without the kids, don't miss **Chalet Suzanne Restaurant**. A premier Florida restaurant and inn, it is legendary for its fine cuisine served in a Swiss-style chalet. Its signature romaine soup is canned on the premises as are other soups bearing the Chalet Suzanne label. The tables, set with fine European china, offer either a stunning overlook of the lake or seclusion behind stained-glass windows. Chicken Suzanne, curried shrimp, shad roe and lobster Newburg are among the proffered entrées in their six-course dinners. A children's menu is available. ~ 3800 Chalet Suzanne Drive, Lake Wales; 863-676-6011, 863-324-0391; www.chaletsuzanne. com, e-mail info@chaletsuzanne.com. ULTRA-DELUXE.

> Having a shopping attack? Sanford's Flea World–Fun World offers bargain prices. ~ 4311 North Orlando Avenue, Sanford; 407-321-1792.

One of the loveliest places to eat in all of Florida is on the patio of the **Carillon Café** at the Historic Bok Sanctuary. Here, surrounded by green-and-floral alfresco decor, you feel cut off from modern tempos. The fare is nothing more than counter-service sandwiches, salads, soup and hot dogs, but the pastoral ambience and serenades from Bok Tower can't be beat by the swankiest restaurant. No dinner. ~ 1151 Tower Boulevard, Lake Wales; 863-676-1355, fax 863-453-2308. BUDGET TO DELUXE.

A spot of great local repute, the **Olympic Restaurant** seems to serve the entire town at lunchtime. The dining area is a couple of sprawling rooms with Greek pictures on the wall. The food is plain good eating: sandwiches, country-fried chicken, fried seafood platter, barbecue spare ribs and Alaskan king crab. Smaller portions are available for kids. ~ 504 Route 27 North, Avon Park; 863-452-2700, fax 863-453-2308. BUDGET TO DELUXE.

West of Orlando, **El Conquistador** matches the Spanish flavor of the Mission Inn resort where it is located. The menu is as simple as the surroundings are elegant. Featured dishes include veal with Gulf shrimp, artichoke and lemon, and potato-encrusted salmon. Non-smoking. Smaller portions are available for kids. ~ Howey-in-the-Hills; 352-324-3101, fax 352-324-2636; www. missioninnresort.com. MODERATE TO DELUXE.

BEACHES & PARKS

Just outside Orlando, dense forests and an abundance of rivers, lakes and springs create some of the state's most appealing parks. And in case you want to take more than a day trip to absorb all of this beauty, I have noted the parks that permit camping.

KELLY PARK 🚶 ⛺ 🛶 The 245-acre Kelly Park features highly productive clear-water Rock Spring, which has created a large swimming pool. The park shows off some of the area's loveliest natural attire of oaks and palm trees. Boardwalks have been built on some of the nature trails. Swimming's great, and you can camp here. Day-use fee, $1 per person. ~ Located on Kelly Park

Road, one-half mile off Route 435 near Apopka; 407-889-4179, fax 407-889-3523.

▲ There are 24 sites, most with RV hookups; $13 to $18 per night, with a minimum stay of two nights. Reservations must be made in person.

WEKIVA SPRINGS STATE PARK 🏃 🚴 🐎 🏇 ⛵ 🛶 🚣 At Wekiva Springs State Park you'll find sand pine forest and wetlands on an extensive springs system. These spring-warmed waters have created a popular swimming spot for Orlando refugees. The area around the spring swimming pool is cemented, with a wooden bridge that crosses the crystalline waters and leads to a nature trail. Trails take you through wet forests along the springs and to various other plant communities. Day-use fee, $4 per vehicle. ~ Located off Wekiva Springs Road between Apopka and Route 4; from Route 434 take exit 49 (Longwood); 407-884-2009, 409-884-2008 (main office), fax 407-884-2039.

Camping out? The Florida Association of RV Parks and Campgrounds can help you find a place. ~ 1340 Vickers Road, Tallahassee, FL 32303; 850-562-7151; www.floridacamping.com.

▲ There are 60 sites, all with RV hookups; $15 to $17 per night. Primitive camping allowed; $3 per night.

LAKE MONROE PARK 🛶 🚣 🚤 At the spot where the St. Johns River bulges into a lake, Lake Monroe Park maintains natural charm beneath tunnels of spreading oak. Used mostly for boating and fishing by locals, it is quiet and secluded. ~ Located on Route 17-92 between Sanford and DeBary; 386-668-3825, fax 386-668-3826.

▲ There are 44 sites, all with RV hookups (ten accommodate tents); $15 to $17 per night. The park is undergoing extensive renovations, to be completed in summer 2004. Call for more information.

HONTOON ISLAND STATE PARK 🏃 🚴 🚣 🚤 🛶 At Hontoon Island State Park, you'll see Indian mounds, bald eagles, cypress trees and a replica of a Timucuan Indian totem that was found here. But no cars or motorcycles: this 1650-acre spit of land lies in the middle of St. Johns River and requires boat transportation to reach. A ferry comes here daily. You can fish for bass, crappie and other freshwater panfish. Day-use fee, $2 per vehicle or vessel. ~ The ferry landing is located at 2309 River Ridge Road near DeLand; 386-736-5309, fax 386-822-6395; www.dept.state.fla.us/parks.

▲ There are 12 tent sites; $8 per night. Also available are six rustic cabins, each accommodating up to six people; $20 to $35 per night. There is a two-night minimum stay on weekends and holidays. Overnight boat camping is also available; $13.28 (water and electric hookups included). Reservations required: 800-326-3521.

DELEON SPRINGS STATE RECREATION AREA 🏃 🐾 🛶 🏊
🚤 🛶 DeLeon Springs State Recreation Area promised a fountain of youth to wintering visitors as far back as the 1890s and
was named for the original seeker of anti-aging waters. A great
deal of wildlife can be spotted along the nature trails here, and
there's good swimming and fishing. Remains of an old Spanish
sugar mill stand near the spring, a favorite local swimming hole.
Day-use fee, $4 for two to eight people and $2 for single drivers.
~ Off of Route 17, six miles north of DeLand; 386-985-4212;
fax 386-985-2014.

LAKE GRIFFIN STATE RECREATION AREA 🏃 🚲 🛶 🏊
🚤 🛶 Lake Griffin State Recreation Area is a natural boating
and fishing haven on the shores of a large lake. Much of the park
is marshy and swimming is not allowed, but there is a playground.
Locals will tell you this is the place to see "floating islands," a
phenomenon caused by chunks of shoreline breaking away into
the lake. Day-use fee, $3.25 per vehicle. ~ Located on Route 441-
27 about two miles north of Leesburg; 352-360-6760, fax 352-
360-6762.

▲ There are 40 sites, all with RV hookups; $10 per night.

TRIMBLE PARK 🏃 🚲 ⛺ 🛶 🚤 🛶 A bird sanctuary and   ◄ *HIDDEN*
county recreational area, Trimble Park lies on a peninsula jutting
into Lake Beauclair. The lake, known principally to locals, is huge
and beautifully trimmed in mossy oaks and cypress. You'll have
to watch closely for an inconspicuous sign on Route 441 that signals the turnoff for the park, which takes you down a winding,
scenic road. Mainly an angler's mecca, the park is also a satisfy-
ing find for privacy-seeking campers. The park has a picnic area,
restrooms, showers, pavilions, a playground and nature trails. ~
5802 Trimble Park Road off Earlwood Road near Mount Dora;
352-383-1993, fax 352-735-1748.

▲ There are 15 sites, all with RV hookups; $13 to $18 per
night. Discounts available for seniors. Reservations must be
made in person.

LAKE ARBUCKLE PARK 🏃 🚲 🛶 🚤 🏊 🛶 A secluded,   ◄ *HIDDEN*
rustic fishing and camping haven, Lake Arbuckle Park features
seven acres of cypress- and oak-studded grounds on Lake Arbuckle. Fishing's good here. ~ Located 3.3 miles off Lake Reedy
Boulevard east of Frostproof; 863-635-2811.

▲ There are 38 sites with RV hookups; $9.50 to $12 per night.

HIGHLANDS HAMMOCK STATE PARK 🏃 🚲 🐎 Alligators and
orchids can be seen from a "trackless train" that tours the cypress swamps and semitropical jungles in popular Highlands
Hammock State Park. Hiking trails also meander through its
9000-plus acres, and an eight-mile paved bicycling loop traverses

the hammock. The park is named for the high, forested terrain found on Florida's central ridge. Children love spotting the white-tailed deer that reside here, as well as the otters, Florida scrub jays, red-shouldered hawks, occasional bobcats and the extremely rare bald eagle and Florida panther. Day-use fee, $3.25 per vehicle. ~ Located west of Sebring off Route 27 at the end of Hammock Road (County Road 634); 863-386-6094, fax 863-386-6095.

▲ There are 138 campsites, 113 with RV hookups; $8 to $13 per night.

LAKE LOUISA STATE PARK   A preserved segment of Green Swamp, Lake Louisa State Park lies over an important underground aquifer system. The park skirts the shores of Lake Louisa and also encompasses Bear Lake. Typical Green Swamp terrain is found here: cypress marshes, sandhills, pine forests and hardwood hammocks. Good swimming and fishing in the lakes. Day-use fee, $2 per vehicle. ~ Located off Route 561 south of Clermont on Lake Nellie Road; 352-394-3969, fax 352-394-1318.

▲ There are 60 sites, all with RV hookups; $10 to $12 per night.

WITHLACOOCHEE STATE FOREST   The second-largest state forest in Florida, Withlacoochee State Forest encompasses 156,000-plus acres. Several tracts are designated, including Forest Headquarters, Croom, Richloam, Citrus, Two-Mile Prarie and Jumper Creek. These are subdivided into various recreation areas and forestry stations. The park focuses on the Withlacoochee and Little Withlacoochee rivers, which flow through a variety of indigenous Florida landscapes. Hiking trails penetrate the forest in several areas, allowing visitors a look at the region's diverse flora and fauna. There are several campgrounds, plus good fishing. Trails are available for hikers and bikers. ~ Main entrance off Route 75 near Brooksville; 352-754-6896, fax 352-754-6751.

▲ There are nine main campgrounds (some with hookups available); $10 to $13 per night. Primitive camping is allowed off the hiking trails.

▼ ▼ ▼ ▼ ▼ ▼ ▼ ▼ ▼ ▼ ▼

The Space Coast

Disney World may be the stuff of every kid's fantasy, but head 50 miles east to Florida's Atlantic shore and you'll find the stuff that real dreams are made of—the launching pads that hurtle rockets and shuttlecraft toward other worlds. Space Mountain, after all, is just a ride. A peek of authentic exploration awaits eager young minds and their parents alike. So strap yourself in and journey to Kennedy Space Center on Merritt Island.

Once on the East Coast, scenic Route A1A hugs the shoreline on its way north toward Cape Canaveral. Except for a few condominium complexes, virtually nothing lies between the roadway and the beach as the two-lane highway cuts through small residential communities.

SIGHTS

While you can't actually blast aboard one of the space shuttles at the **Kennedy Space Center Visitor Complex** (at least I wouldn't recommend it), you can experience the next best thing. Exhibits and tours here fuel the imagination, recapturing the history of America's space exploration and giving a glimpse into its future. ~ Route 405, Kennedy Space Center; 321-449-4444; www.kennedyspacecenter.com.

Launch into the adventure at the main complex, a concentrated universe of space matter including the aptly named **Rocket Garden** (where you'll find rockets from each stage of America's space program), the *Early Space Exploration* exhibit highlighting the fledgling Mercury and Gemini space programs, and the *Exploration in the New Millennium* display looking at travels of tomorrow. Virtual space adventures are available via a duo of space-themed IMAX films, and you can peer into a full-size replica of a shuttle orbiter. To get the lowdown on the latest missions, check into the hourly presentations at the **Launch Status Center**. The Center has started catering to children with additions such as the Mad Mission to Mars 2025 stage show. And budding as-

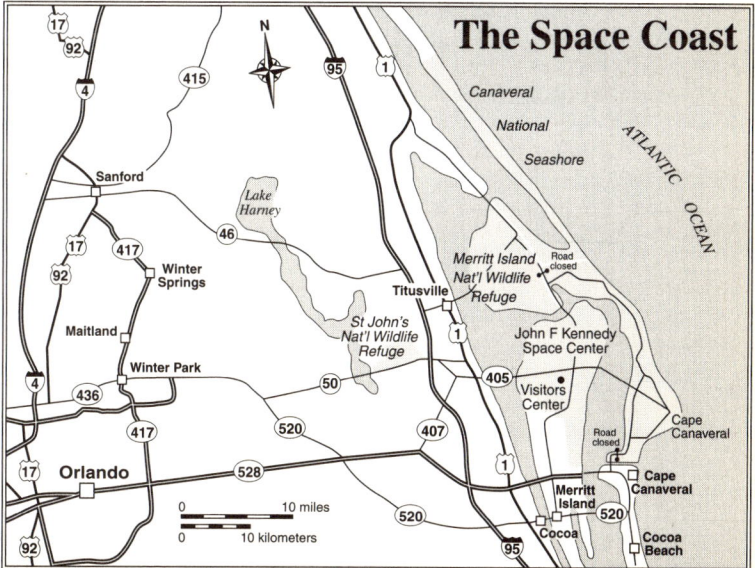

The Space Coast

tronauts can hear first-hand accounts of space travel at daily Astronaut Encounters.

You'll get closer to the real action on in-depth tours taken by bus. Motor coaches roll through restricted areas alongside the enormous crawlway used to transport shuttles from the hangar to the launch pad. Visitors get out at three stops along the way for breathtaking perspectives on the past, present and future of NASA's adventures.

From the **LC-39 Observation Gantry** (stop 1 on the tour), you'll get a vista of much of the Space Center terrain. At a mile away, the four-story tower is too close to be safe during an actual launch, but it's perfect for appreciating the famous takeoff site. The full girth of a space vehicle (in this case, a rocket from the Apollo program) can be appreciated at the **Apollo/Saturn V Center** (stop 2) where an actual Apollo/Saturn V Moon Rocket is on display. The huge—*huge*—vessel is one of only three such rockets in existence, left over after the demise of the Apollo program. Here, too, NASA shows its flair for drama in a re-enactment of the Apollo 8 launch. You know the happy outcome, but the event, set in a "working" control room assembled from original equipment, is nail-biting nonetheless.

Buses depart the main complex regularly throughout the day beginning at 9:45 (the facility closes at dusk, so check on arrival for the last parting tour) and make stops roughly every ten minutes at each of the three centers. Be sure to keep your eyes open between stops as buses cruise within feet of such landmarks as the enormous Vehicle Assembly Building (where the shuttle is put together) and the countdown clock and observation bleachers familiar to anyone who's watched a launch on TV. Bus drivers even point out such important icons as where Major Anthony Nelson (of *I Dream Of Jeannie* fame) went to work every day (the building front used in the series is here), and the homes of other creatures that fly, such as some eagles. Ever mindful of its location, the center pays homage to its wildlife neighbors at the *Nature and Technology—Merritt Island National Wildlife Refuge* exhibit at the main complex.

Though a visitor center of sorts has been around nearly as long as the space program (formerly under the name Spaceport USA), the place has been spiffed-up of late into a full-fledged attraction. There's even a kitsch quotient in the number of souvenirs for sale, as well as the quirky restaurants (The Lunch Pad) and regular appearances by the "space man" during "Astronaut Encounter."

There's so much here, you'll want to leave a full day for it—that is, unless you have a child under age eight, in which case you'll probably want to abbreviate your visit to under four hours (although there is a **Children's Play Dome** with climbing areas to distract them). It's all amply entertaining, and you can count on learning a thing or two thousand. I, for one, didn't know that Kennedy Space Center was actually a city (yes indeed, folks, it's got its own zip code, post office and fire station) or that the Florida crew handles ground, launch and land duties; once in the air, control gets handed over to Houston. If familiarity with space travel makes any of us ho hum, the **Astronaut Memorial**, a stunning monument to the 17 astronauts who died in the line of duty, is a poignant reminder of the hazards of the job.

If simply touring NASA isn't enough, now you can break bread with an astronaut. Lunch with an astronaut is offered daily at 12:30. Space is limited and advance reservations are recommended. Call **321-449-4400** for tickets.

Also on Merritt Island are the offices of the **Cocoa Beach Tourism and Convention Council**, a good place to pick up maps and brochures. Closed weekends. ~ 400 Fortenberry Road, Merritt Island; 321-459-2200, fax 321-459-2232; www.cocoabeachchamber.com.

The remainder of Merritt Island, north of the Kennedy Space Center, is largely devoted to the Canaveral National Seashore (see the "Beaches & Parks" section) and the **Merritt Island National Wildlife Refuge**. Within the refuge, an auto tour route guides visitors to prime viewing sites. The **Black Point Wildlife Drive** leads into habitats for such unusual species as the anhinga, a bird that swims in the canals with only its snakelike head visible above the water. The refuge is closed four days prior to shuttle launches, visitors should check for closures. ~ 321-861-0667, fax 321-861-1276.

◀ *HIDDEN*

On the mainland, the coast's attractions include the **Astronaut Memorial Planetarium and Observatory**, offering several perspectives on natural history and the space age. The comfortable theaters here screen a changing roster of educational skyscape shows and full-dome motion pictures. The observatory boasts a lobby filled with space memorabilia. Admission. ~ 1519 Clearlake Road, Cocoa; 321-634-3732, fax 321-634-3744; www.brevard.cc.fl.us/~planet.

A short drive away, the **Brevard Museum of History and Natural Science** takes visitors back in time through exhibits of early settler furniture, American Indian tools and pottery, and the remains of extinct animals. As for natural history, the museum maintains an extensive shell collection and 22 acres of nature trails. Closed Monday. Admission. ~ 2201 Michigan Avenue, Cocoa; 321-632-1830, fax 321-631-7551; www.brevardmuseum.com, e-mail bmhs@brevardmuseum.com.

The wildlife that inhabits the upper reaches of the St. Johns River (one of the few North American rivers that runs south to north) is best viewed from a boat. Half-hour and one-hour airboat rides at the **Lone Cabbage Fish Camp** cruise the inland

◀ *HIDDEN*

marshes for a close-up look at exotic flora and fauna. ~ 8199 Route 520, four miles west of Route 95, Cocoa; 321-632-4199, fax 321-638-0059; www.twisterairboatrides.com, e-mail captaintwister@aol.com.

At the **American Police Hall of Fame and Museum**, 50,000 square feet of exhibit space showcase the history of villain nabbing, including a jail cell replica, a real gas chamber and guillotine, and a video crime clock with up-to-the-second statistics. Admission. ~ 6350 Horizon Erive, Titusville; 321-264-0911, fax 321-264-0033; www.aphf.org.

Mother Nature and the trappings of the space age exist side l y side in the Cape Canaveral area. Every time a space shuttle blasts off in a cloud of steam and smoke, the waterfowl and other wildlife on surrounding Merritt Island are momentarily disturbed before returning to the peaceful routine established by their kind over the centuries.

LODGING   Most of the accommodations in the area are near the ocean, and the better ones can be found in Cocoa Beach. The city of Cocoa, separated from the beach by the Banana River, Merritt Island and the Intracoastal Waterway, is a few miles closer to the Kennedy Space Center.

The **Pelican Landing Sunshine Villa Resort** is a find—a beachfront hotel with 18 rooms; most are efficiencies with equipped kitchens. Behind the hotel is a deck you can lounge on before traipsing down the boardwalks that lead to the beach and the endless stretch of the Atlantic. Children under 12 stay free. Reservations strongly advised from January through March. ~ 1201 South Atlantic Avenue, Cocoa Beach; 321-783-7197. MODERATE.

Within easy walking distance of the Cocoa Beach Pier, the **Ocean Suite Hotel** makes up in room size what it lacks in proximity to the ocean. The pleasant building offers light and airy rooms. ~ 5500 Ocean Beach Boulevard, Cocoa Beach; 321-784-4343, 800-367-1223, fax 321-783-6514; www.oceansuiteshotel.com. MODERATE.

The **Inn at Cocoa Beach** offers the best of everything. All the rooms in this T-shaped inn are beautifully decorated with fine furniture, plush carpeting and little touches like throw pillows, stools and framed artwork. Attractive drapes cover sliding glass doors that open onto private patios and balconies. There are gorgeous views of the ocean right out front, and it's possible to witness space launches from the third-floor observation deck. This place has a residential charm all too rare in an area dominated by chain hotels. ~ 4300 Ocean Beach Boulevard, Cocoa Beach; 321-799-3460, 800-343-5307, fax 321-784-8632; www.theinnatcocoabeach.com. DELUXE.

One of the biggest surprises in Cocoa Beach is the **Doubletree Oceanfront Hotel** with its Southwestern theme. Upstairs, its 148 luxurious rooms feature tropical-beach decor in peaches and blues, each with a private balcony, refrigerator and microwave. ~ 2080 North Atlantic Avenue, Cocoa Beach; 321-783-9222, 800-552-3224, fax 321-799-3234; www.cocoabeachdoubletree.com. DELUXE.

The **Best Western Oceanfront Resort** strikes me as a bargain only if you insist on a second-story room facing the courtyard. Otherwise, you could pay top dollar to stay in the oceanfront tower. The peach and seafoam green decor is contemporary in a bare-bones kind of way. Several units are equipped with modest cooking facilities. ~ 5600 North Atlantic Avenue, Cocoa Beach; 321-783-7621, 800-962-0028, fax 321-799-4576; www.best western.com. MODERATE TO ULTRA-DELUXE.

If you'd rather sleep where you can smell the ocean breezes, consider camping at the **Oceanus Mobile Village and RV Park**. The tidy RV park enjoys a superb location along the Banana River, a stone's throw from the Atlantic Ocean. After you park your RV, you can fish off a 240-foot pier or take a dip in the heated pool. Of course, the glistening white beach, waiting across the river, is sure to be the highlight of your stay. ~ 152 Crescent Beach Drive, Cocoa Beach; 321-783-3871. BUDGET.

DINING

Most towns have one restaurant revered as a local institution. On the Space Coast, that place is **Bernard's Surf**. It's been on the same corner since the 1940s, boasting the freshest crab, lobster and fish in the county. Bernard's is divided into three parts: a raw bar, a formal, dimly lit dining room and a bar and grill rimmed by red leatherette booths. An oversized menu is required to list the

LUXURIOUS CAMPING

The place to camp on the Space Coast—or perhaps anywhere in Florida—is **The Great Outdoors RV/Golf Resort**. This 2800-acre retreat combines outdoor living with resort luxury. Carpeted with soft grass and sprinkled with palms and pines, it boasts an 18-hole championship golf course, 22 freshwater fishing lakes, a department store–size recreation center, tennis and croquet courts, and a state-of-the-art health club. Children delight in the nature trails lined with animal feeders. Deer, wild turkey and even bobcats reside here. You can bring your own RV (no tent or pop-up campers permitted). RV sites are budget-priced—a real family deal. ~ 125 Plantation Drive, Titusville; 321-269-5004, 800-621-2267, fax 321-269-0694; www.tgoresort.com.

steak, rib and chicken offerings as well as dozens of seafood dishes, all in a variety of combinations. There's also a generous menu for the small fry in the family, as well as early-bird specials with prices guaranteed to make the big fry happy. Dinner only. ~ 2 South Atlantic Avenue, Cocoa Beach; 321-783-2401, fax 321-783-0418; www.bernardssurf.com. MODERATE TO DELUXE.

Families will feel right at home in **Alma's Seafood & Italian Restaurant**. This old-fashioned Italian eatery feels warm and inviting with its maze of small rooms. The moderately priced surf and turf menu also lists classics such as spaghetti and veal and kid-pleasing pizza, while the wine cellar boasts 200 vintages. Arrive early for dinner and enjoy early-bird specials. Dinner only. ~ 306 North Orlando Avenue, Cocoa Beach; 321-783-1981. BUDGET TO DELUXE.

Comfort food doesn't get any better than what you'll find at **Simply Delicious**. The restaurant serves breakfast, lunch and dinner and everything is made fresh, from the sandwiches served on homemade bread to the sumptuous turtle pie. It's best advised for families with older kids, though, since the restaurant doesn't have high chairs. ~ 125 North Orlando Avenue, Cocoa Beach; 321-783-2012. BUDGET TO MODERATE.

HIDDEN ► It's a good idea to tuck a meal under your belt before setting out for the Kennedy Space Center. Cheap and convenient is the **Kountry Kitchen**. In this big, friendly joint, an honest country breakfast of bacon, eggs, grits and biscuits is laid out as early as 6 a.m. Or on the way back, stop in for home-style lunches: spare-ribs, salmon patties, chicken and dumplings, chicken-fried steaks and other hearty meals. Children's plate available. No dinner. ~ 1115 North Courtenay Parkway, Merritt Island; 321-459-3457. BUDGET.

On the main thoroughfare leading to the Kennedy Space Center is **Victoria's Family Restaurant**. Within the brick-and-wood interior you will find *moussaka* and its country cousins, as well as seafood and chops. Victoria's fun, simple fare is sure to

FLORIDA'S BEST SURFIN' SHOP

Ron Jon Surf Shop qualifies as a tourist destination. Calling itself the world's largest surf shop, this kaleidoscopic, warehouse-size store is open 24 hours a day and feels like a neon beach party. Rock fountains gush beside a glass elevator that glides between two floors. It's a haven for local teenage "dudes," though all kids love sifting through the thousands of T-shirts, swimsuits, water toys and other get-me-to-the-beach stuff that paint this store with electric color. ~ 4151 North Atlantic Avenue, Cocoa Beach; 321-799-8888; www.ronjons.com.

please younger palates. Early-bird specials. No dinner on Sunday. ~ 370 North Courtenay Parkway, Merritt Island; 321-459-1656. MODERATE.

When the kids start screaming for ice cream, head for **Village Ice Cream and Sandwich Shop**. The hole-in-the-wall town fixture, located near posh boutiques, serves a variety of the creamy stuff as well as light sandwiches. No dinner. ~ 120-B Harrison Street, Cocoa; 321-632-2311. BUDGET.

Between Cocoa and the Merritt Island Wildlife Refuge, a delightful mainland stop near Route 1 is **Dixie Crossroads**. Despite its size (about 400 seats), this family-style favorite made me feel right at home, with waitresses refilling my iced tea every time they passed by my windowside table. And everything edible that swims in nearby waters can be found here in plentiful helpings. Don't miss the rock shrimp, succulent and tasty thumb-size delicacies that go well with rice. Budget-priced lunch specials. ~ 1475 Garden Street, Titusville; 321-268-5000, fax 321-268-3933; www.dixiecrossroads.org, e-mail mrrockdcr@aol.com. MODERATE TO ULTRA-DELUXE.

BEACHES & PARKS

CANAVERAL NATIONAL SEASHORE   It took an act of Congress to set aside the last 24-mile stretch of undeveloped beach in eastern Florida for Canaveral National Seashore on Merritt Island. In 1975, the government acted to preserve some 58,000 acres of water and wilderness stretching north from the Kennedy Space Center. In this pristine setting, kids delight at the sight of alligators, turtles and even manatees that live in some of the shallow lagoons. Some 301 species of birds have been observed at the seashore, including threatened ones such as the brown pelican and the bald eagle. The barrier island, consisting mostly of pure shell sand, was formed more than a million years ago. Evidence of ancient residents has been found stacked into a number of mounds, most notably Turtle Mound, a 35-foot-tall pile of oyster shells assembled by the Timucuan Indians sometime between A.D. 800 and 1400. ~ 321-267-1110, fax 321-264-2906; www.nps.gov/cana.

APOLLO BEACH   At the north end of Cape Canaveral Seashore, Apollo Beach is accessible by dune walkovers. It is a long strip of white quartz sand, and the swimming and surfing are great. ~ Take Route A1A south from New Smyrna Beach.

KLONDIKE BEACH   Klondike Beach is the central of the three distinct beaches at Canaveral National Seashore. Klondike is a totally undeveloped area at the end of a hike through saw palmettos and Spanish bayonets. Angel wings, sand dollars and smooth, rounded moon snails are among the shells found on the area beaches.

PLAYALINDA BEACH ⚓ 🏃 🛶 🚣 Five miles of pristine white sand form a narrow ribbon between the high-water line and the delicate sand dunes. In June and July, kids over eight can watch a nightly ritual: Turtles come ashore here to lay their eggs in the sand (reservations are required to view the laying; for information, call 386-428-3384 ext. 18). The swimming here is excellent, and surfing is good, but currents can be strong. Within sight of NASA's launch pads, Playalinda is usually closed for three days prior to a launch (call 321-867-2468 for NASA's launching schedule). ~ Located east of Titusville off Route 402.

MERRITT ISLAND NATIONAL WILDLIFE REFUGE 🏃 🚣 Egrets, herons, gulls and terns form a welcoming committee on the 140,000-acre Merritt Island National Wildlife Refuge north of the Kennedy Space Center. A diverse habitat includes salty estuaries, dense marshes, pine flatwoods and hammocks of hardwood where armadillos are as common as grey squirrels. The portions of the refuge that are not marsh consist of dense vegetation that helps protect such exotic species as air plants and indigo snakes. Several species of migratory waterfowl retreat to the refuge during the coldest months of the year, making this one of Florida's prime birdwatching areas. The best times to visit are spring, fall and winter. Closed Sunday from April through October. Also closed four days prior to a shuttle launch. Call for closures. ~ Take Exit 80 from Route 95 and head east on Route 406; east of Titusville, continue on Route 402; 321-861-0667, fax 321-861-1276; merrittisland.fws.gov.

TURKEY CREEK SANCTUARY 🏃 🚣 Thick with palmettos and pines and flowering vines and bordered by a meandering creek,

---

BAHAMAS BOUND

One of the very best side trips a family can take is a cruise to the Bahamas, with **Disney Cruise Lines**. Three- and four-day cruises sail to the Bahamas and Disney's own Castaway Cay, a palm-filled island fringed in white sand. Once on board, there's no lack of activities. Younger children can dance with Snow White or whip up a batch of Flubber. Teenagers can take a moviemaking class or do what teens do best—hang out with other teens. For the adults, there's babysitting services so they can enjoy a night out sans children. There are also many opportunities throughout the trip to take pictures with favorite Disney characters. Cruises can be combined with three or four nights at a Disney World hotel. Packages include admission to all Disney theme parks along with Downtown Disney, the Disney water parks and the Wide World of Sports. ~ Port Canaveral; 800-951-3532; www.disneycruise.com.

Turkey Creek Sanctuary is truly a purist's sanctuary. Families can roam the boardwalks through hardwood hammocks and along the bluffs overlooking the creek, using the park's signs to identify plants. The favorite kid activity is spotting the fish, turtles and occasional manatees that thrive in the warm creek. There's also a hands-on interpretive center, where you can learn about snakes, plants and animals. Picnic creekside or in a lovely gazebo. Boardwalk paths are wheelchair accessible. ~ 1502 Port Malabar Boulevard, Palm Bay; 321-952-3433, fax 321-726-9767.

Daytona Beach Area

The best-known resort town on the central East Coast, Daytona Beach is famous for its 23-mile-long beach, a marvel of sparkling sand packed so hard you can easily drive a car on it. And that's what people started doing in the early 1900s, gradually developing the beach into a natural race track where speed records were set as early as 1903.

Today, automobile racing and sunshine are still the paramount attractions up and down the strip of sand that stretches from Ponce Inlet north to Flagler Beach. There is history here, too, in archaeological remains and the ruins of old plantations, and in the gracefully aged lighthouses.

SIGHTS

Poised near the inlet separating New Smyrna Beach from Daytona Beach, the second-tallest brick lighthouse on the East Coast, the 175-foot-tall **Ponce de León Inlet Lighthouse** affords a breathtaking view of the inlet as well as the surrounding communities. Built in 1887, the so-called "Beacon at Mosquito Inlet" is still a working lighthouse, and the entire facility, including the keeper's cottages (which were converted into museums), is open to the public. The lighthouse was designated a National Historic Landmark in 1999. Admission. ~ 4931 South Peninsula Drive, Ponce Inlet; 386-761-1821; www.ponceinlet.org.

The centrally located **Daytona Beach Area Convention and Visitors Bureau** offers tips and guidance for area visitors. ~ 126 East Orange Avenue, Daytona Beach; 386-255-0415, 800-544-0415, fax 386-255-4872; www.daytonabeach.com.

Another way to get your bearings in Daytona Beach and nearby communities is by leaving the driving to someone else—such as a riverboat captain. **Coastal Cruises** maneuvers on the Indian River and offers lunch, dinner and sunset cruises. ~ 800-881-2628; volusia.com/cruise. **Tiny Cruise Line** plies the Halifax River and offers waterview cruises of riverfront estates and the Intracoastal Waterway. 386-226-2343.

Housed in a former bank that is Daytona Beach's finest example of beaux-arts design, the **Halifax Historical Museum** is best known for the six murals depicting local attractions such as the Ponce de León Inlet Lighthouse. But more fascinating is a highly detailed model of the Boardwalk area circa 1938, with hundreds of miniature people filling the bandshell. This elegant museum's historical displays range from prehistoric Indian tools to artifacts retrieved from nearby plantation ruins to a smattering of memorabilia from the early days of car racing. Closed Sunday and Monday. Admission. ~ 252 South Beach Street, Daytona Beach; 386-255-6976, fax 386-255-7605; www.halifaxhistorical.org, e-mail mail@halifaxhistorical.org.

A single stretch of International Speedway Boulevard near the Daytona Beach Municipal Airport constitutes a sporting paradise in itself. The famous **Daytona International Speedway** replaced the beach as the prime racing locale in 1959. Today, families can travel the banked, two-and-a-half-mile, tri-oval race track that drivers like Cale Yarborough and Richard Petty helped put on the map. Unless you're a qualified racer, however, you won't be driving, but riding in a tour bus. You'll also find an interactive racing attraction. The most renowned of many events hosted here is the Daytona 500, which attracts hundreds of thousands of visitors each February. Admission. ~ 1801 West International Speedway Boulevard, Daytona Beach; 386-253-7223, fax 386-257-1914; www.daytonainternationalspeedway.com.

Things in Daytona Beach didn't always move so fast, as you can see at one of the city's most interesting museums where a giant ground sloth is displayed next to contemporary Florida artworks. Far from the beaten track, in a forested setting in Tuscawilla Park, the **Museum of Arts and Sciences** boasts an eclectic collection including 19th-century drawings and one of the largest displays of Cuban artwork in the United States. What children enjoy most, though, are the museum's planetarium and a natural science exhibit. Children under six are free. Closed Monday. Admission. ~ 1040 Museum Boulevard, Daytona Beach; 386-255-0285, fax 386-255-5040; www.moas.org, e-mail moas@n-jcenter.com.

HIDDEN ▶   You can show the kids the days of Southern plantations at **Bulow Plantation Ruins State Historic Site.** There are canoes for rent and a mile-long unpaved road that leads through dense undergrowth to a picnic area (bring your lunch); the ruins lie another quarter-mile away to the left. Looming out of the jungle like a movie prop from *Raiders of the Lost Ark* is a series of crumbling coquina shell ruins, all that remains of a 19th-century sugar mill. An interpretive center nearby tells the story of the plantation's development by slave labor, its prosperous production of sugar cane, cotton, rice and indigo, and its ultimate destruction by the Seminole tribe who burned plantations in anger over being displaced by settlers. Admission. ~ Off King's Road north of the Old Dixie Highway, Bunnell; 386-517-2084.

About 40 miles north of Daytona Beach, Route A1A runs right by **Marineland**, a roadside attraction that was built in 1938 to facilitate underwater filming. Though nowhere near the scope of newer oceanariums, there's something endearing about this seaside complex, now listed on the National Register of Historic Places. The most enduring feature is the dolphin show, performed twice daily by well-trained sea mammals in an oceanview ampitheater. There is almost always entertainment of some kind, whether it's a special-effects film called *Sea Dream* or divers hand-feeding sharks in a huge tent sporting hundreds of portholes for underwater viewing. Marineland also boasts an impressive 35,000-gallon re-creation of a Florida freshwater spring, and wildlife exhibits featuring live alligators, caimans, iguanas and other reptiles. Admission. ~ 9600 Oceanshore Boulevard, Marineland, 940-460-1275, 888-279-9194, fax 940-461-1056; www.marineland.net.

LODGING

Route A1A is one long canyon of hotels and motels that try to differentiate themselves with decorative themes ranging from Polynesian to Mayan. In fact, many of them are very much alike on the inside, and almost all are equidistant from the beach.

A few stoplights south of the frantic midtown action, the beach has the same sun, the same clean sand, but fewer people. In front

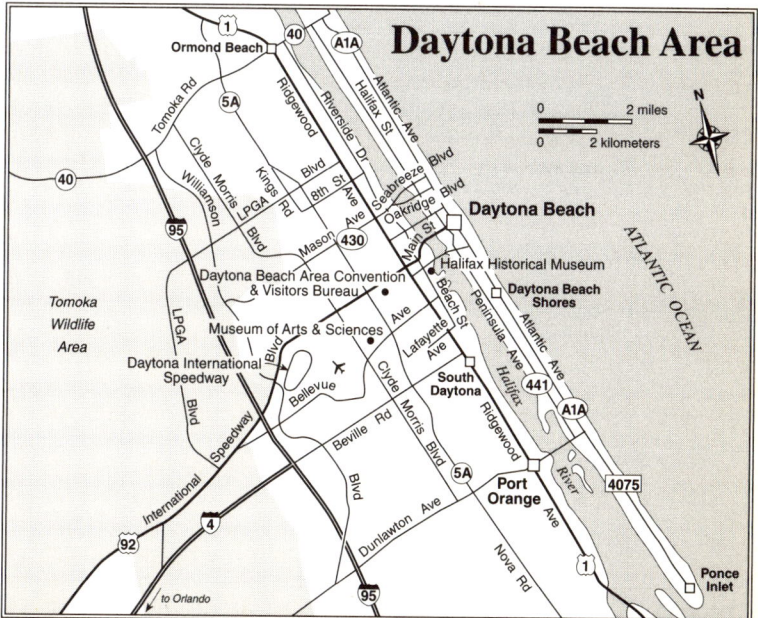

Daytona Beach Area

of the **Day Star Motel,** you can at least find a square of sand to call your own. For reasonable prices, you get two double beds and a full kitchen. For a little more, you get a large oceanfront efficiency. Also on the grounds is a heated pool. These accommodations aren't beautiful, but they are clean and well maintained. Children under 12 stay free. ~ 3811 South Atlantic Avenue, Daytona Beach; 386-767-3780, 800-506-5505; www.daystar motel.com. BUDGET TO MODERATE.

The tropically themed **Beach Quarters** is a comfortable place for the whole family. Every room at the five-story inn is a spacious suite, and there's an on-site restaurant. End the day by enjoying your private balcony furnished with rocking chairs. ~ 3711 South Atlantic Avenue, Daytona Beach; 386-767-3119, 800-332-3119, fax 386-767-0883; www.thebeachquarters.com. MODERATE TO DELUXE.

One of the most unusual hotel configurations I've ever seen belongs to **Perry's Ocean-Edge,** a complex of 204 units. You can rent an oceanfront motel room or enclosed garden room, but families will find the most space in an apartment suite or garden efficiency. Three swimming pools—including a huge solar-heated one with a retractable roof—a toddler pool, whirlpool, playground, shuffleboard courts and small putting green are among the many amenities. ~ 2209 South Atlantic Avenue, Daytona Beach; 386-255-0581, 800-447-0002, fax 386-258-7315; www. perrysoceanedge.com, e-mail reservations@perrysoceanedge. com. MODERATE.

Families who don't mind a 15-minute drive to the beach should consider staying at **Indigo Lakes Holiday Inn.** A lush oasis of velvet green fairways, sharp blue lakes, ponds and trees, it boasts all-weather tennis courts and an Olympic-size pool. This self-contained resort also harbors fitness trails and volleyball courts. The focus here is on the outdoors; the rooms are spacious, very comfortable and equipped with a private patio or balcony. Kitchenettes are available. ~ 2620 West International Speedway Boulevard, Daytona Beach; 386-258-6333, 800-465-4329, fax 386-254-3698. BUDGET TO ULTRA-DELUXE.

A wooded oasis amid city surroundings, the **Nova Family Campground** features 200 sites for RVs, pop-up campers and tents, and offers cabins too. True to its name, the facility attracts vacationing families to its shady environs. There are a swimming pool, game room, recreation hall and convenience store. The beach lies ten minutes away. ~ 1190 Herbert Street, Port Orange; 386-767-0095, fax 386-767-1666; www.gocampingamerica.com/ novacamp.com. BUDGET.

DINING   **Kelsey's Riverview Restaurant** has a waterfront location and does best with its seafood, including local shellfish as well as grouper and mahimahi. Chicken and ribs are also available. Children particularly like it here because they can watch the dolphins playing in the water outside. Plus, they get their own menu. ~ 101 Flagler Avenue, New Smyrna Beach; 386-428-1865, fax 386-428-4843. MODERATE TO DELUXE.

The question at one spot is not so much *if* you want catfish, but *how* you want it: fried, Cajun-style, baked or broiled with lemon-pepper. But **Aunt Catfish's on the River** also dishes up flounder and plenty of other seafood. In this rustic riverfront restaurant, entrées come with sweet rolls, hushpuppies and a salad buffet, just the kind of meal you'd expect in such a friendly place. Great for families, Aunt Catfish's features a good children's menu and budget-priced early-bird specials. They also offer Sunday brunch. ~ 4009 Halifax, Port Orange; 386-767-4768. BUDGET TO DELUXE.

LIGHTHOUSE POINT COUNTY PARK When the locals tire of the crowds in central Daytona Beach, they head south to the less well-known beach at Lighthouse Point Park. Bypassed by Route A1A, **Ponce Inlet Park** is often overlooked except by travelers in search of the Ponce de León Inlet Lighthouse. The southern portion of the park has five pavilions where you can enjoy a picnic while watching the fishing boats in the inlet, or you can cast a rod from the fishing pier on the jetty walkway. To the east is a particularly beautiful stretch of pale sandy beach where it's possible to take long walks in relative peace and quiet. The swimming is good here, especially for young beginners. Day-use fee, $3.50. ~ Located at the end of Atlantic Avenue south of Daytona Beach; 386-756-7488, fax 386-322-5177.

BEACHES & PARKS

◄ *HIDDEN*

DAYTONA BEACH The promotional brochures proclaim Daytona Beach to be 23 miles of hard-sand beach, but technically only four miles of that lie within the city limits of Daytona Beach. To the south is Daytona Beach Shores, to the north, Ormond Beach, both virtually indistinguishable from Daytona Beach. Aside from the expanse of clean beige sand (500 feet wide at low tide), the most striking aspect of the beach is the presence of automobiles. Motorists are required to park perpendicular to the ocean, in single file, and to restrict their beach driving to poorly marked "lanes." A speed limit of 10 mph is enforced, but it is still distracting to have to look both ways before proceeding into the surf, and parents, of course, should keep careful watch over their children. The swimming, however, is excellent here, with shallow, sandy shelves perfect for the short stuff. You can surf at the north end of the beach. ~ Located between Ocean Dunes Road and Plaza Boulevard off Route A1A.

TOMOKA BASIN GEO-PARK The approach to the 2000-acre preserve is along a driveway worthy of

◄ *HIDDEN*

an antebellum plantation (which it once was), with magnolia trees and moss-draped oaks threatening to overtake the road. Flanked by the Halifax and Tomoka rivers, this park has lush, coastal hammocks dense with shrubs and trees. A quarter-mile nature trail leads through the hammocks. You can camp here, and there's plenty for a family to do—have a picnic, go saltwater angling (permit required), rent canoes or visit the interpretive center. Day-use fee, $3.25. ~ 2099 North Beach Street, Ormond Beach; 386-676-4050, fax 386-676-4060. Reservations: 800-326-3521.

▲ There are 100 sites, two-thirds with RV hookups; $10 to $17 per night.

GAMBLE ROGERS MEMORIAL STATE RECREATION AREA AT FLAGLER BEACH With frontage on the ocean as well as on the Intracoastal Waterway, the windswept Gamble Rogers Memorial State Recreation Area at Flagler Beach offers close encounters with a variety of wildlife. A short nature trail winds through tall sand dunes, where scrub oaks and shrubs make an excellent habitat for cardinals and mockingbirds. On the inland side of the park, fiddler crabs and wading birds wander through the marsh grasses and shallow waters near the boat basin. On the ocean side, sea turtles lay eggs (in early summer) in the rough coquina-shell sand above the high water mark on this narrow, undeveloped beach. The swimming and fishing here are excellent. Day-use fee, $3.25. ~ 3100 South Route A1A, Flagler Beach; 386-517-2086, fax 386-517-2088.

▲ There are 34 sites with RV hookups, water and electricity; $19 to $21 per night.

Tampa

To many, Tampa means Busch Gardens and Buccaneer football. But to those who take the time to explore, and to the accelerating numbers who are making this Florida West Coast hub home, Tampa is seen as a sophisticated network of growth stemming from carefully nurtured agricultural and fishing roots. Located about 75 miles from Orlando, this thriving city boasts dazzling corporate towers that rub elbows with spruced-up historic buildings and re-created street markets. The result is sophistication with a homey feel.

SIGHTS
One of the biggest renovation projects undertaken has been **Harbour Island**. Once weed infested, today its cobblestone streets lead to a world-class hotel. ~ 813-229-5000. The PeopleMover monorail carries passengers to and from the island and around the downtown area.

The neighborhood across the water from the island is also looking up. The **Franklin Street Mall** allows pedestrian outdoor shopping among restored boutiques that sit in contrast with Tampa's skyscraping and skyrocketing downtown commercial image.

The newest attraction to open at Tampa's Garrison Seaport Center is **The Florida Aquarium**, a 152,000-square-foot behemoth that encourages harmony between people and their natural environment. Boasting over one million gallons of water, the aquarium is home to 10,000 plants and animals native to Florida, and showcases four of the Sunshine State's environments (wetlands, bays and beaches, coral reefs and offshore) by tracing the path of a drop of water from the ground in the northern part of the state to the open ocean of the keys. There are also hands-on exhibits, including enormous touch tanks inhabited by mollusks, anemones and other invertebrates. There's also an educational playground called Explore A Shore, an interactive attraction where kids can climb on mangrove roots, dig in a sandy beach and crawl through coral reefs. Admission. ~ 701 Channelside Drive, Tampa; 813-273-4000, fax 813-273-4160; www.flaquarium.org.

The 450 "hands-on" displays at MOSI **Museum of Science and Industry**, mean experiencing a hurricane and riding a high-wire bicycle. The largest science center in the southeastern United States, MOSI is home to the world's two largest articulated dinosaur skeletons, and also shelters a butterfly garden, an IMAX screen, a planetarium and a public library. This is a facility that has fun with scientific phenomena. Admission. ~ 4801 East Fowler Avenue; 813-987-6300, 800-995-6674, fax 813-987-6310; www.mosi.org, e-mail blittlej@mosi.org.

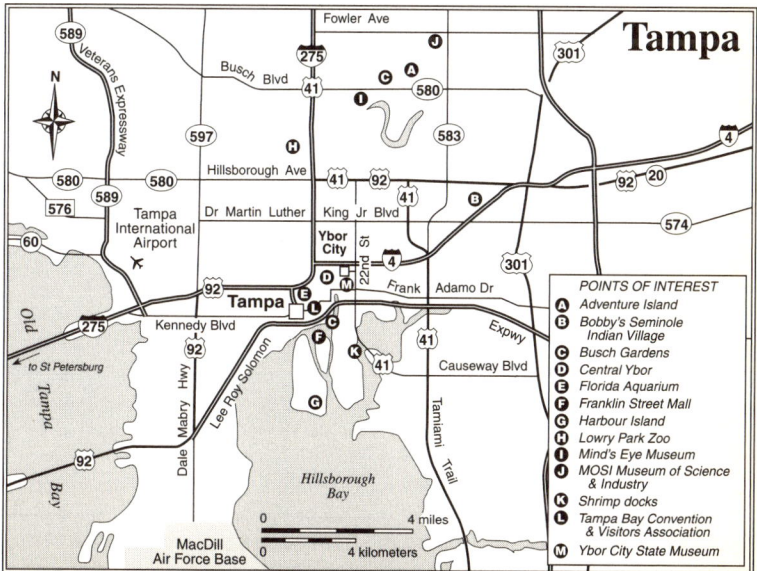

Another pastime is watching the occasional shrimp boats come in to unload their catches at the **shrimp docks**. If you don't catch any activity from the shrimpers, it's still a good place to watch waterfront activity and see gargantuan sea craft passing by. ~ 22nd Street Causeway.

Visitors to Ybor City, once a well-known cigar-making center, can still see the cobblestone streets, Spanish-tiled storefronts and wrought-iron detailing reminiscent of the days when Cuban, Jewish, Spanish, German and Italian immigrants lived here.

The **Ybor City State Museum**, once a Cuban bread bakery, depicts the history of the area near Preservation Park, an early-20th-century cobblestone street. Three renovated structures demonstrate typical cigar workers' homes. Guided walking tours of the area start from the museum every Saturday at 10:30 a.m. Admission. ~ 1818 East 9th Avenue; 813-247-6323, fax 813-242-4014; www.ybormuseum.org, e-mail info@ybormuseum.org.

Stop by the **Visitor Information Center** at Centro Ybor for a self-guided walking tour map of Ybor City. ~ 1600 East 8th Avenue; 813-248-3712, fax 813-247-1764; www.ybor.org, e-mail info@ybor.org.

Central Ybor is a shopping, dining and entertainment complex in the heart of Ybor City. ~ Seventh Avenue and Sixteenth Street; 813-241-8838; www.ybor.org.

For information on the Tampa area, stop in at the **Tampa Bay Convention & Visitors Association** Closed Sunday. ~ 400 North Tampa Street, Suite 2800; 813-223-1111; www.visit tampabay.com.

BUSCH GARDENS AREA The number-one attraction in the Tampa metropolitan area and one of the country's foremost zoos is **Busch Gardens Tampa Bay**. The 335-acre theme park takes visitors to 19th-century Africa via the 20th-century technology of a skyride. The wilds are juxtaposed with the wild; animals placidly roam the Serengeti Plains as thrillseekers get dunked, spun and set on their heads by different amusement rides. Tropical bird gardens, beer sampling and food and gift stands are all presented in exotic surroundings.

One thing you won't find too much at Busch Gardens is Disney-style lines. During summer and popular holidays, a few rides (roller coasters, river rapids, etc.) sometimes feature a wait of 30 to 45 minutes. During the rest of the year, you can usually walk right on. What you will find in Busch Gardens are nine themed sections:

Timbuktu, fashioned as an ancient desert marketplace, is home to the tortuous looping roller coaster called the Scorpion. Riders know it as the snake with a 62-foot plummet and curves banked from 0 to 60 degrees. If you survive the Scorpion, you can say you've pulled over 3Gs (gravitational forces). Kids familiar with R.L. Stein's wildly popular series of creepy kids' books will run to—or perhaps screaming from—the new **Haunted Lighthouse** 4D flick at the Timbuktu Theater. For the weak of stomach, several midway-style rides offer tamer encounters. In **Morocco**, elaborate tiles and keyhole architecture re-create an exotic walled city. Roving sheiks perform in the streets, while indoors at the Moroccan Palace Theater, you can watch the World Rhythms on Ice show, a skating extravaganza that offers a Broadway-style tour of seven nations. At the 65-acre **Serengeti Plain**, offering visitors up-close views of African herds. Giraffes, zebras, gazelles, elephants, rhinoceroses and other exotic animals roam free on this veldt-like prairie. You can take the self-guided walk, or pay an extra $15 to ride in an up-close motor tour where you can see the animals from an open-air truck. You can also take a locomotive, skyride or promenade around the plain.

Children are enchanted by **Nairobi**. There's a petting zoo with goats and Nocturnal Mountain, where families can view animals in their own nighttime setting. Nairobi also features Myombe Reserve: The Great Ape Domain, a three-acre gorilla and chimpanzee habitat that replicates western lowland terrain in Africa. Over in the bustling African town of Stanleyville, the Tanganyika Tidal Wave sends thrill seekers over the edge in a boat, while the Stanley Falls log flume ride excites the whole family. The sight of King Tut's Tomb signals you've arrived in **Egypt**. The Middle Eastern marketplace features the "ruins" of ancient temples and a tourable tomb as well as contemporary carnival games where you can win homely but loveable plush toys. For thrills, soar on Montu, an inverted coaster that will turn you upside down seven times, or play it safe on Akbar's Adventure, a virtual roller coaster ride. More excitement awaits at **The Congo**. Here, the Python roller coaster rockets visitors along 1200 feet of track that corkscrews into two 360° spirals. But the biggest thrills are to be found at the Kumba roller coaster, where three different gravity-defying loops are part of this awesome ride. There's also the Congo River Rapids, a family-style raft ride through caves and under waterfalls. Walking on the **Edge of Africa** offers a different sort of experience entirely. Natural habitats in this "African Fishing Village" are enclosed with glass, providing encounters

MORE FOR LESS

In town for a while? Consider a **FlexPass**. Multi-park tickets come in four- or five-park versions. For $175.95 per adult, get unlimited admission for 14 days to both Universal parks, Sea World and Wet & Wild (another $35 gets you Busch Gardens Tampa as well). You'll save on club admission at CityWalk, too.

with the likes of lions, hyenas, hippos, ringtailed lemurs and an animal nursery cares for fledgling birds and delicate gazelle. In the area's popular **Rhino Rally**, customized Land Rovers travel both land and water. Some 2000 exotic fowl hoot, caw, flit and fly around the area aptly named **Bird Gardens**. Guests can partake of their own flight on Gwazi, a soaring, double wooden roller coaster billed as the Southeast's largest and fastest. In addition, the **Land of the Dragons** offers a giant three-story-tall treehouse and kid-size rides (including a ferris wheel and a flume ride). Nearby, **Crown Colony** is meant to imitate a British-African village. The area's highlight is a family-style restaurant, though the beautiful, renowned Clydesdale horses also make their home here. Admission. ~ 3000 East Busch Boulevard; 888-800-5447; www.buschgardens.com.

Next door to and owned by Busch Gardens, **Adventure Island** is a 25-acre water theme park featuring an endless surf pool, inner-tubing chutes and water slides with names like Calypso Coaster and Caribbean Corkscrew. The latter offers a high-speed journey through translucent braided slides. Check out Key West Rapids, a dipping, swooshing slide that can be ridden alone or by as many as four interlocking innertubes. Splash Attack is an aquatic jungle gym with rope swings, slides and lots of water. Parents will enjoy the leisurely "Rambling Bayou" float ride, while toddlers feel right at home in the kiddie pool at Fabian's Fun Port. When they're not on the speed slides, teens hang out at the video arcade. Admission. ~ 10001 Malcolm McKinley Drive (also known as 40th Street); 813-987-5660.

LODGING   Most of the accommodations in the city are chain hotels catering to the business traveler or overnight guest. Those looking for a fun-in-the-sun resort should head across the bay to St. Petersburg and the necklace of islands that adorn it. If you plan on staying awhile in the bay area, I recommend rooming there. For those seeking a few days of metropolitan stimulation and culture, I have found a few Tampa hotels that excel.

◆◆◆

SEMINOLES, SNAKES AND ALLIGATOR WRESTLING

While you're in the Tampa Bay area, you might consider a side trip to the nearby **Bobby's Seminole Indian Village**. It contains a Seminole Indian village of chickee (thatched-roof) structures and a museum demonstrating the way of life of these long-time Florida residents. Spectacular alligator wrestling and snake shows are sure to wow the kids during the annual pow wow in November. Call ahead for group arrangements. Admission. ~ 5221 North Orient Road; 813-620-3077, fax 813-620-1767.

The **Radisson Bay Harbor Inn** offers private balconies in 257 modern rooms overlooking the bay or the city. A tab buys you lots of extras: restaurant, lounge, tennis courts and pool. Children under eighteen stay free. ~ 7700 Courtney Campbell Causeway; 813-281-8900, 800-333-3333, fax 813-281-0189; www.radisson. com/tampafl. ULTRA-DELUXE.

On the outside, the **Doubletree Guest Suites on Tampa Bay** looks like a Mayan temple dedicated to the god of bay waters. Inside, the look is decidedly up-to-date, with subtle shades, dark woods and modern family conveniences. All 203 units are suites, and the facility provides swimming and hot tub facilities. Parasail and waverunner rentals are available. ~ 3050 North Rocky Point Drive West; 813-888-8800, 800-222-8733, fax 813-888-8743. ULTRA-DELUXE.

Holiday Inn City Centre sits downtown on the riverfront near the Tampa Bay Performing Arts Center. Its 316 units include plushly carpeted rooms and suites decorated in modern mauves and teals. Kids under 16 stay free. ~ 111 West Fortune Street; 813-223-1351, 800-513-8940, fax 813-221-2000. DELUXE.

On Harbour Island in the downtown hub, the **Wyndham Harbour Island Hotel** spells luxury in the form of 300 posh rooms with bay vistas, along with sophisticated clubs and restaurants. Dark woods panel the lobby areas. ~ 725 South Harbour Island Boulevard; 813-229-5000, 800-946-3426, fax 813-229-5322; www.wyndham.com. ULTRA-DELUXE.

More homey and less glitzy is the family-operated **Tahitian Inn**. You will find comfortable, clean rooms, a swimming pool and a café. ~ 601 South Dale Mabry Highway; 813-877-6721, 800-876-1397, fax 813-877-6218; www.tahitianinn.com. BUDGET.

The **Howard Johnson Busch Gardens Main Gate** takes its name from its proximity to Busch Gardens, located only 200 feet away. Modern decor here extends to its 99 rooms with contemporary steel accents. There are also a pool, restaurant and lounge. ~ 4139 East Busch Boulevard; 813-988-9191, fax 813-984-7880. BUDGET TO MODERATE.

Tampa offers little in the way of campgrounds. However, heading west toward Clearwater you will find **Bay Bayou RV Resort**, a tidy place with large grassy lots for parking an RV. Amenities include a heated swimming pool and jacuzzi. Families are the main summer customers; during winter, seniors frequent the park. Some sites are along a saltwater creek. ~ 12622 Memorial Highway; 813-855-1000, fax 813-925-0815. BUDGET.

Another good bet for camping is the **Hillsborough River State Park** (see the "Beaches & Parks" section).

Local seafood—pompano, grouper, shrimp and stone crab—makes a culinary splash at most Tampa restaurants, washed with the new

DINING

wave of American cuisine. Standing at the crossroads of Cuban, Spanish, Greek and Scottish subcultures, and influenced by its international port role, Tampa offers fare that tends to be Continental while maintaining the homespun flavor of its surrounding agricultural communities.

In the center of Tampa International Airport, **CK's** is a revolving rooftop restaurant overlooking the airport and the Tampa city skyline. The views are paralleled by the menu; the specialties include angus beef, vegetarian moussaka and fresh seafoods. The 5 p.m. to 6:30 p.m. early-bird specials make this pricey place affordable for more moderate budgets. Dinner only. ~ 7th floor of TIA, Tampa; 813-878-6500, fax 813-873-0945. DELUXE.

Saltwater aquariums, exotic music and articles that have washed ashore give **The Castaway** its South Seas ambience. The food is mainly steak and seafood with some pasta and chicken dishes. Families can enjoy budget prices with early-bird specials. ~ 7720 Courtney Campbell Causeway, Tampa; 813-281-0770, fax 813-281-2215. MODERATE TO DELUXE.

For a taste of what has now become an all-American tradition, go to **Hops Restaurant, Bar and Brewery**, a microbrewery where the suds ferment before your very eyes. The four copper brew tanks dominate the dining room that serves no-frills American fare including steak, filet mignon, a range of salads, chicken pasta and, of course, beer. ~ 327 North Dale Mabry Highway, Tampa; 813-871-3600. BUDGET TO MODERATE.

Bern's Steak House is the place you go *without* the kids. This is Tampa's top shelf, and the restaurant often pointed to as Florida's best steak house. The heavy, rococo decor gives it a slightly somber feeling, but be assured, things don't get any fresher than Bern's homegrown herbs and vegetables. It has outstanding steaks and the largest wine selection in the area; the phone book–size wine list here boasts 6500 labels from 19 different countries! For dessert, diners head upstairs, where they sit in hollowed-out wine casks with radios for after-dinner relaxation. Dinner only. ~ 1208 South Howard Avenue, Tampa; 813-251-2421, fax 813-251-5001; www.bernsteakhouse.com. ULTRA-DELUXE.

The Mexican food at **Don Pablos** is perfect for families looking for something a little different. The friendly atmosphere goes well with delicious homemade tacos and salsa. Non-adventurous kids need not go hungry: the place serves burgers and sandwiches as well. ~ 6001 Waters Avenue, Tampa; 813-882-3766. BUDGET TO MODERATE.

In the historic cigar-factory district of Ybor City, restaurants principally feature Cuban food. The Cuban sandwich, Ybor City's gastronomic mainstay, creates a sense of friendly rivalry among restaurateurs, who all claim theirs is the best. Basically, this is little more than a sub sandwich. The difference is the Cuban bread, baked in yard-long loaves using a time-honored method that produces something totally unrelated to a sub bun. Most importantly, they're made with stuff kids tend to like—ham, pork and Swiss cheese. Other area specialties include Spanish soup, black beans and rice, *paella*, flan and Cuban coffee.

Silver Ring Café holds the reputation as maker of the best Cuban sandwich. Seating is at a long mahogany counter, at tables or on stools facing little shelves along the wall. Lunch only. ~ 206 Morgan Street, Ybor City; 813-301-0200. BUDGET.

New Orleans ambience and food take Ybor City diners on a cultural departure at **Café Creole**. Once a popular Spanish club, the restored building swings with jazzy background music, lively atmosphere, architectural drama and spicy Creole concoctions. The prices are good for blackened fish, crawfish, jambalaya and crab cakes. Closed Monday. ~ 1330 9th Avenue, Ybor City; 813-247-6283, fax 813-248-3041. MODERATE TO DELUXE.

Latam at the Centro has incredibly inexpensive châteaubriand, as well as Latin American specialties with a heavy Cuban influence. Housed in a historic 1902 building with pressed tile ceilings and a fabulous onyx bar, Lantam exudes retro style. Lunch is served weekdays; dinner is served Thursday through Saturday. ~ 1913 Nebraska Avenue, Ybor City; 813-223-7338, fax 813-229-1934; www.latams.8m.com. BUDGET TO MODERATE.

◄ HIDDEN

HILLSBOROUGH RIVER STATE PARK 🚶 🚲 ⛵ 🎣 ⛵ Hillsborough River State Park includes 3000 forested acres and a suspension bridge that spans the placid river. Across Route 301 from the park entrance sits Fort Foster, a reconstructed Seminole War fort garrisoned by soldiers of the United States Second Artillery. The park includes canoe rental and camping facilities, and you can swim in a swimming pool. Day-use fee, $3.25 per vehicle. ~ Located on Route 301, eight miles southwest of Zephyrhills; 813-987-6771, fax 813-987-6773.

BEACHES & PARKS

FLAMENCO FOR FAMILIES

The **Columbia Restaurant** is both landmark and restaurant extraordinaire. The block-long building demonstrates a Spanish influence in its ornate tiling, archways, balconies and grand chandeliers. Although the waiters wear dinner jackets and there is live flamenco dancing every night, the Columbia is casual, reasonable and especially suited to families. Its menu includes traditional and inventive Spanish dishes: paella, steak *salteado, boliche* and filet mignon Columbia, for example. For children, there are chicken strips and fries. ~ 2117 East 7th Avenue, Ybor City; 813-248-4961, fax 813-248-1718; www.columbiarestaurant.com. MODERATE TO DELUXE.

▲ There are 106 campsites, 80 with hookups; $14 to $17 per night. Reservations: 800-326-3812.

BEN T. DAVIS MUNICIPAL BEACH ~ A stretch of sand lying along the Courtney Campbell Causeway, the nine-mile drive bridging Tampa and Clearwater has pretty landscaping, and the sand is soft and white. This is one of Tampa area's two saltwater beaches, and the locals swarm here. True beach lovers go the distance to the other side of the Pinellas County peninsula across the causeway to the beaches of Holiday Isles. ~ The park lies right on the Courtney Campbell Causeway's east end as it heads toward Rocky Point; 813-282-2909, fax 813-274-7429.

St. Petersburg Area

Resting on a peninsula across the bay from Tampa, St. Petersburg is about two hours from Orlando. What brings travelers here from all over Florida, and the world, are a dazzling thread of islands woven to the mainland by five bridges. This thread, often known as the Holiday Isles, has developed into highrise heaven thanks to its gorgeous beaches and lucid waters. Pleasure seekers of all ages are attracted to this paradise playground where the most strenuous activity is building sandcastles.

SIGHTS

Activity in downtown St. Petersburg centers around **The Pier**, an inverted pyramid-shaped structure that houses an aquarium (admission), shops, restaurants and an observation deck. ~ 800 2nd Avenue Northeast; 727-821-6443; www.stpetepier.com. One office of the **St. Petersburg Chamber of Commerce** is located in the lobby of The Pier. ~ 727-821-6164; www.stpete.com. Another can be found nearby. ~ 100 2nd Avenue North; 727-821-4069.

The view from The Pier overlooks the seaside city in all its splendor and is especially scenic at night.

The **Sunken Gardens** is a pleasant surprise, with its jungle-like ambience. The grounds were created in a sinkhole from which the water was drained. The fertile pit was then landscaped with exotic plants. You'll see tropical birds flitting among bougainvillea and hibiscus. Admission. ~ 1825 4th Street North, St. Petersburg; 727-551-3102.

From downtown, head west to the Gulf and comb the strand of sandy islands. To make the island tour, take Pinellas Bayway across the peninsula that comprises Pinellas County, to Fort de Soto Park. North of the five islands that form the park, the town of Tierra Verde eases into the holiday carnival scene that its neighbor, St. Pete Beach, begins. The sun and watersports action continues along this sandy rim all the way to Clearwater Beach—a splendid finale to the family's Gulf-front tour.

From St. Pete Beach, the **island chain** along Gulf Boulevard includes Treasure Island, Madeira Beach, Indian Rocks Beach,

Bellair Beach and Clearwater Beach. These Gulf-front islands are separated from the mainland by a narrow trickle of water that broadens at both ends.

Between Treasure Island and Madeira, a boardwalk with salty shops, restaurants and charter boats has cropped up at **Johns Pass Village and Boardwalk**. Patterned after a fishing community of yore, it pays tribute to the community's commercial fishing industry. ~ 150 128th Johns Pass at Gulf Boulevard, Madeira Beach; 727-394-0756; www.johnspass.com.

The **Suncoast Seabird Sanctuary** works to restore injured and crippled sky-dwellers. You may catch close-up views of many species here, including the native cormorant, great blue heron, brown pelican and snowy egret. ~ 18328 Gulf Boulevard, Indian Shores; 727-391-6211; www.seabirdsanctuary.org.

One colorful lodging option is the **Sunset View Motel**. For affordable rates, you can sleep with sea breezes wafting through jalousie windows. Refrigerators and microwaves come with each cozy room in this circa-1940 building that makes you feel right at home. Three-night minimum stay during weekends and holidays. Kids under seven stay free. ~ 34 North Gulf Boulevard, Indian Rocks Beach; 727-596-5771. MODERATE.

LODGING

◀ *HIDDEN*

A historic masterpiece in cotton-candy pink, the **Don CeSar Beach Resort and Spa** greets visitors to this beach town. It stands stately and fancifully to woo guests with complete resort services. Classic Florida resort style is embodied here. Built in the 1920s, when F. Scott and Zelda Fitzgerald supposedly visited, it was converted into an Army hospital during World War II. You'll find 275 rooms, plus restaurants, lounges, a conference facility and a grand ballroom, in prime condition. The Don's personality combines equal doses of Mediterranean, fairy castle and beach resort. Children ages 5 to 12 can take part in the "kids limited" program, with supervised arts and crafts and a host of other activities led by retired schoolteachers. There are also two swimming pools, one with an underwater sound system, and the resort is right on the beach. ~ 3400 Gulf Boulevard, St. Pete Beach; 727-360-1881, 800-282-1116, fax 727-367-6952; www.doncesar.com, e-mail doncesar@mindspring.com. ULTRA-DELUXE.

Long Key Beach Resort provides some architectural interest with its 44 beachfront guest rooms, efficiencies and apartments. Peaked roofs, a wooden observation sundeck and a rounded bay window front upgrade the hotel look. The rooms are pleasant, the efficiencies not without character. A pool and poolside lounge and 180 feet of expansive beach are other amenities. ~ 3828 Gulf Boulevard, St. Pete Beach; 727-360-1748, 888-566-4539, fax 727-367-9026; www.longkeybeachresort.com, e-mail lresort@tampa bay.rr.com. MODERATE TO DELUXE.

Guests can tour the grounds via gondolas at the exotic **Trade-winds Island Grand**. Housing 577 rooms, Tradewinds takes complete care of guests with four pools, a sauna, whirlpool, tennis and croquet courts, fitness center, sailing equipment, four restaurants, a wide beach and children's activities. Each room includes a wet bar, refrigerator and exclusive furnishings. ~ 5500 Gulf Boulevard, St. Pete Beach; 727-367-6461, 800-237-0707, fax 727-263-2221; www.justletgo.com. ULTRA-DELUXE.

A dramatic spiral staircase is the centerpiece of the elegant lobby at **Dolphin Beach Resort**. The rooms, 173 in all, spread in a jagged lowrise building fronted by white beach and brightened by colorful sails and cabañas. The rooms are spacious with separate dressing areas. The on-site restaurant serves Continental and American cuisine. ~ 4900 Gulf Boulevard, St. Pete Beach; 727-360-7011, 800-237-8916, fax 727-367-5909; www.dolphinbeach.com. DELUXE.

Clearwater Beach Motel lies low along blindingly white sands. Typically beach oriented, the various units (economy suites, efficiencies, deluxe suites and standard rooms) won't win awards for interior decoration but are clean and roomy and provide partial kitchen facilities. ~ 500 Mandalay Avenue, Clearwater Beach; 727-441-2425, 800-292-2295, fax 727-449-2083; www.clearwaterbeachhotel.com, e-mail cbhotel@msn.com. DELUXE TO ULTRA-DELUXE.

Fine resort style at **Adam's Mark** is defined with accommodations and location that create a Caribbean atmosphere. The 217 modern rooms corner a wide stretch of beach and are custom designed with elegant tropical touches. ~ 430 South Gulfview Boulevard, Clearwater Beach; 727-443-5714, 800-444-2326, fax 727-442-8389; www.adamsmark.com. DELUXE.

The St. Petersburg area also offers numerous family-oriented campgrounds. One of the finest is **St. Petersburg/Madeira Beach Resort KOA**, where 96 acres border a saltwater inlet dotted with islands. You can rent canoes and paddle across the inlet, or rent a bike and pedal around the palmy campgrounds. The 500 sites accommodate RVs or tents, but the real family deal is the 60 one- and two-room cabins. Best of all, there's plenty to keep you busy: a huge swimming pool, three hot tubs, miniature golf, a game room and volleyball. Of course, the Gulf beach is only two miles away. ~ 5400 95th Street North, St. Petersburg; 727-392-2233, 800-562-7714, fax 727-398-6081; www.koa.com, e-mail stpetersburg@koa.net. BUDGET.

Fort de Soto Park (see the "Beaches & Parks" section) is also an excellent place to camp.

DINING   Continental cuisine with a difference comes in affordable prices at **Good Times Continental Restaurant**. The Old World influence

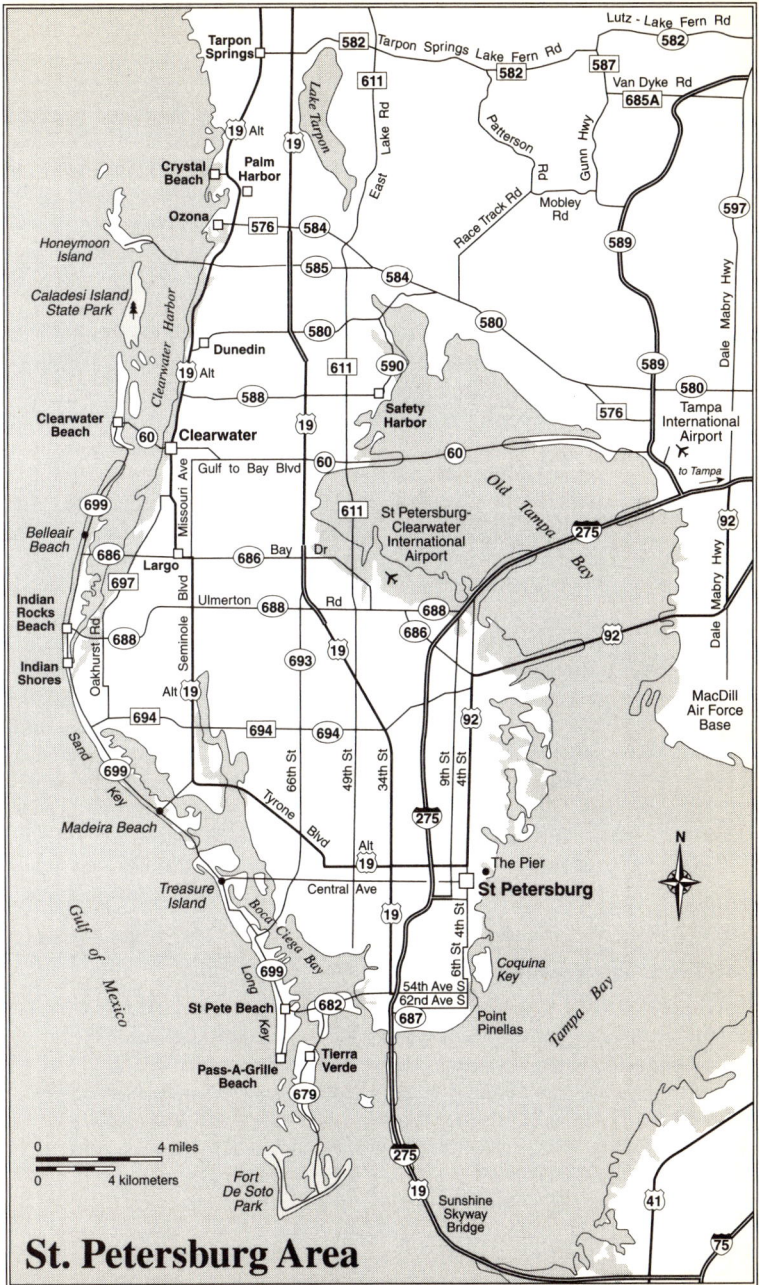

Tarpon Springs

Lutz - Lake Fern Rd
582
Tarpon Springs Lake Fern Rd
582
582
587
Van Dyke Rd
685A
611

Gunn Hwy
Patterson Rd
597
19 Alt
19
Crystal Beach
Palm Harbor
Ozona
Race Track Rd
Mobley Rd
589
Honeymoon Island
576
584
Caladesi Island State Park
585
584
580
580
589
Dunedin
611
590
576
Tampa International Airport
19 Alt
588
Safety Harbor
✈
to Tampa
Clearwater Beach
60
Clearwater
19
Gulf to Bay Blvd
60
60
699
Missouri Ave
611
St Petersburg-Clearwater International Airport
✈
Old Tampa Bay
275
92
Belleair Beach
686
Largo
686
Bay Dr
697
Seminole Blvd
Ulmerton
688
Rd
688
92
Indian Rocks Beach
688
686
Oakhurst Rd
Indian Shores
693
19
MacDill Air Force Base
Dale Mabry Hwy
Alt 19
694
694
694
92
66th St
49th St
34th St
9th St
4th St
Tyrone Blvd
699
275
Madeira Beach
Sand Key
Alt 19
Treasure Island
Central Ave
The Pier
St Petersburg
N
Boca Ciega Bay
19
699
Long Key
St Pete Beach
682
6th St
4th St
Coquina Key
Tampa Bay
54th Ave S
62nd Ave S
687
Point Pinellas
Pass-A-Grille Beach
Tierra Verde
679
Gulf of Mexico

0 _____ 4 miles
0 _____ 4 kilometers

Fort De Soto Park
275
19
Sunshine Skyway Bridge
41
75

St. Petersburg Area

takes a refreshing departure from France and Italy to offer taste-bud tantalization in the form of Hungarian chicken *paprikash*, beef stroganoff, filet mignon topped with glazed peaches and béarnaise, apple strudel and Czech and German beers. All is served in a plain-looking facility with vinyl chairs and pool-hall paneling. Half portions available for children. Dinner only. Closed Sunday and Monday; closed mid-July through mid-August. ~ 1130 Pinellas Bayway, Tierra Verde; 727-867-0774. MODERATE TO DELUXE.

On Pass-a-Grill Beach, **Hurricane Seafood Restaurant** seats you outdoors with a beach view, or inside its wood-accented, casual dining room. Seafood comes in every form imaginable at reasonable prices. Children's menu. ~ 807 Gulf Way, Pass-a-Grill Beach; 727-360-9558, fax 727-363-6428; www.thehurricane. com. BUDGET TO MODERATE.

Crabby Bill's is your basic beach seafood eatery where the food is terrific and the prices even better. The oyster stew is made to order, and the catfish, shrimp, crab and fish have earned the place a reputation that means long waits. Children's menu. ~ 401 Gulf Boulevard, Indian Rocks Beach; 727-595-4825, fax 727-596-3258; www.crabbybills.com. BUDGET TO ULTRA-DELUXE.

For more than a decade, folks across Tampa Bay have made faithful sojourns to the **Lobster Pot**, a place that can feed any lobster fetish. Maine, African and Florida lobsters, served unadorned or in creamy garlic or curry sauces, headline the menu. There are fish and prime steaks as well. Fresh flowers, candles and linens assure subtle formality amid fishing nets, mounted lobsters and other seaside decor. Children's menu and early-bird specials. Dinner only. ~ 17814 Gulf Boulevard, Reddington Shores; 727-391-8592, fax 727-393-2026. MODERATE TO ULTRA-DELUXE.

In Clearwater Beach, **Heilman's Beachcomber** is known for its bargain Southern-style dinners of fried chicken, gravy and mashed potatoes. Locals will also tell you that this is the best

◆◆◆

OYSTERS, EVERY WHICH WAY

To get the true flavor of Florida's Gulf Coast, dine at **P.J.'s Oyster Bar**. Rolls of paper towels hang on coat hangers above the tables at this ultracasual beach nook, which doles out oysters, clams, crab and shrimp in their unadulterated state (raw and/or steamed, hold the sauce). The menu also offers fried, broiled, baked or steamed seafood, sandwiches and blackened specialties. Grilled cheese and chicken fingers are available for young, picky eaters. P.J. the parrot runs the show. ~ 500 1st Street North, Indian Rocks Beach; 727-596-5898, fax 727-593-2774. BUDGET TO DELUXE.

place in the bay area to get good stone crab in season. The ambience is simple, the menu diversified, the quality consistent. There's a children's menu. ~ 447 Mandalay Avenue, Clearwater Beach; 727-442-4144, fax 727-441-8982; e-mail heilmans@earth link.net. MODERATE TO DELUXE.

Twenty-eight miles of sugar sand sweetens Pinellas County's Gulf front. Its public beaches spread wider than anywhere else along the coast.

BEACHES & PARKS

FORT DE SOTO PARK A precious natural respite from the beach crowds lies at Fort de Soto Park on five road-connected islands at the southern tip of Pinellas County. Hiking trails take you to mortars marking a disassembled Spanish-American War fort and around quiet paths shaded by Australian pines and live oaks dripping with Spanish moss. Secluded areas are available at both East Beach and North Beach. The sand is coarse, shelly and booby-trapped with sand spurs. Natural vegetation along the beaches grows low to the ground: cactus, sea grape shrubs and sea oats. You get a true deserted feeling with none of the development on the northern islands to clutter the view. Fishing is excellent, and a three-mile area of the seven-mile-long beach is approved for swimming. At the north end and southwest tip, currents are dangerous. ~ Off Pinellas Bayway, south of Tierra Verde; 727-582-2267, fax 727-552-1863; www.fortdesoto.com.

◄ HIDDEN

▲ There are 233 sites, all with RV hookups; $27.75 per night. Reservations must be made at the camp office in person at the St. Petersburg County Building, at 150 5th Street North, Room A 116, St. Petersburg.

PASS-A-GRILL BEACH A popular gathering place for young sunbathers, Pass-a-Grill Beach is a strand of fluffy sand that loops around the southern point of the island of St. Pete Beach. The long, wide beach is flanked by quaint homes and low-rises. The swimming is good, and facilities include showers, dressing rooms, a snack bar and picnic area. ~ Located on Gulf Way on southern St. Pete Beach; 727-367-2735, fax 727-363-9249; www. stpetebeach.org.

SAND KEY PARK Like most of the parks in Pinellas County, Sand Key Park is beautifully landscaped. The facility looks more like a resort than a county park, with lush greenery and beautiful, blond sands. There are picnic tables under the pines, restrooms, dressing rooms with indoor/outdoor showers, playgrounds and a boardwalk that stretches out along the sand. The swimming is good here. Parking is $.75 an hour. ~ Located at the northern end of Belleair Beach at 1060 Gulf Boulevard; 727-588-4852, fax 727-588-4854; www.pinellascounty.org.

CLEARWATER BEACH Clearwater Beach is the reason thousands cross the big bridge from Tampa every weekend. The most popular West Coast beach, Clearwater combines fast-paced action and gentle surf with ribbons of shells, wavy dunes and fine sun-bleached sands. Even the name sounds rejuvenating. The beach rambles for three miles, from the wall-to-wall hotels and crowds in the south to remote spots in the north. Families usually prefer the northern end, though swimming and fishing are excellent everywhere. ~ Located at the west end of Route 60; 727-562-4800.

Index

249–90; sights, 223, 224, 238–43; visitor information, 243
Orlando FlexPass, 279
Orlando International Airport, 32
Orlando Museum of Art, 238
Orlando Science Center, 238, 240
Oscar's Classic Car Souvenirs & Super Service Station, 93; shopping, 227

Pacific Point Preserve, 179, 180
Package pickup: (Disney World) 38–39, 67, 91, 111, 225; (SeaWorld) 176, 225; (Universal Orlando) 140, 160
Packing, 18
Pangani Forest Exploration Trail, 116
Panoz Racing School, 257
Parking: (Disney World) 36, 66, 89–90, 110, 125, 128, 131, 137; (SeaWorld) 174; (Universal Orlando) 139
Pass-a-Grill Beach, 289; dining, 288
Penguin Encounter, 178, 180
Peter Pan's Flight, 51
Pets, 24; (Disney World) 24, 38, 67, 91, 111, 125, 129, 132; (SeaWorld) 24, 176; (Universal Orlando) 24, 140, 160, 171
Pets Ahoy, 184
Petting Farm (Fort Wilderness), 126
Photography, 24–25; (Universal Orlando), 153, 167
The Pier (St. Petersburg), 284
Pirates of the Caribbean, 44
Plantation Gardens, 256
Playalinda Beach, 270
Playhouse Disney, 98
Pleasure Island, 135; nightlife, 231–32; shopping, 228
Plymouth: sights, 255
Pocahontas and Her Forest Friends, 122
Polk City: sights, 256
Ponce de León Inlet Lighthouse, 271
Ponce Inlet: sights, 271
Ponce Inlet Park, 275
Popeye & Bluto's Bilge-Rat Barges, 169
Port of Entry, 161; dining, 220; shopping, 230
Port Orange: camping, 274; dining, 275
Poseidon's Fury, 163–64
Price ranges used in book: dining, 26–27, 203; lodging, 26, 186
Primeval Whirl, 118
Production Central, 153–55; dining, 219; shopping, 229
Pteranodon Flyers, 167

Rafiki's Planet Watch, 116–17
Raft rides, 130, 133
Rainfall, 15

Reddington Shores: dining, 288
Reflections of China (film), 81–82
Reign of Glory (exhibit), 80
Restaurants. *See* Dining; *see also Dining Index*
Revenge of the Mummy, 154
Richard Petty Driving Experience, 135
The River of Time: El Rio del Tiempo, 80
Rivership Romance (boat tour), 254
Rock 'n' Roller Coaster, 96
Rocket Garden, 263
Royellou Museum, 255
Rudder Buster (slide), 130
Runoff Rapids (water slide), 133

Safety, 10
St. Cloud: camping, 202; vistor information, 200, 222
St. Johns River Cruises and Tours, 254
St. Pete Beach (town): lodging, 285–86
St. Petersburg area, 284–90; beaches & parks, 289–90; camping, 286, 288, 289; dining, 286, 288–89; lodging, 285–86; map, 287; sights, 284–85; visitor information, 284
San Francisco/Amity, 149–50, 152; dining, 219
Sand Key Park, 289
Sanford: sights, 252, 254; visitor information, 254
Scenic Boat Tour (Winter Park), 242
Sea Base Alpha, 77
Seasons, tourist, 14–15
SeaWorld Adventure Park, 173–84; dining, 221; discounts, 22–23; game plan, 174; guest services, 174, 176; hours, 20; map, 175; nightlife, 235; nuts & bolts of visiting, 174–76; shopping, 230; tickets, 22; transportation in, 176; transportation to, 32–33, 174; visitor information, 20. *See also specific areas, attractions and services*
SeaWorld Sleepovers, 179
Sebring: sights, 257; visitor information, 257
Sebring International Raceway, 257
Senior travelers, 28, 30; discounts, 23, 30
Seuss Landing, 161–63; dining, 220; shopping, 230
Shamu Stadium, 182; nightlife, 235
Shamu's Happy Harbor, 182
Share a Dream Come True (parade), 41–42
Shark Encounter, 181
Shark Reef Snorkeling Tank, 130
Shoes, 18, 129, 132
Shopping, 224–30. *See also* Shopping *in specific areas and cities*

Lodging Index

Summerfield Suites, 197
Sunset View Motel, 285
Swan, 188–89

Tahitian Inn, 281
Thrift Lodge, 199
Tradewinds Island Grand, 286
Tropical Palms Resort, 200

Villas at Wilderness Lodge, 191

Wilderness Lodge, 191
Wyndham Harbour Island Hotel, 281
Wyndham Palace Resort & Spa, 192–93

Yacht Club Resort, 190

LODGING SERVICES
Central Reservations Service, 194
Kissimmee–St. Cloud Convention and
   Visitors Bureau, 200
Kissimmee–St. Cloud Reservations, 194
Walt Disney World Central Reservations
   Office, 186

Dining Index

HIDDEN GUIDES

Adventure travel or a relaxing vacation?—"Hidden" guidebooks are the only travel books in the business to provide detailed information on both. Aimed at environmentally aware travelers, our motto is "Where Vacations Meet Adventures." These books combine details on unique hotels, restaurants and sightseeing with information on camping, sports and hiking for the outdoor enthusiast.

THE NEW KEY GUIDES

Based on the concept of ecotourism, The New Key Guides are dedicated to the preservation of Central America's rare and endangered species, architecture and archaeology. Filled with helpful tips, they give travelers everything they need to know about these exotic destinations.

PARADISE FAMILY GUIDES

Ideal for families traveling with kids of any age—toddlers to teenagers—Paradise Family Guides offer a blend of travel information unlike any other guides to the Hawaiian islands. With vacation ideas and tropical adventures that are sure to satisfy both action-hungry youngsters and relaxation-seeking parents, these guides meet the specific needs of each and every family member.

Ulysses Press books are available at bookstores everywhere. If any of the following titles are unavailable at your local bookstore, ask the bookseller to order them.

You can also order books directly from Ulysses Press
P.O. Box 3440, Berkeley, CA 94703
800-377-2542 or 510-601-8301
fax: 510-601-8307
www.ulyssespress.com
e-mail: ulysses@ulyssespress.com

HIDDEN GUIDEBOOKS

____ Hidden Arizona, $16.95

____ Hidden Bahamas, $14.95

____ Hidden Baja, $14.95

____ Hidden Belize, $15.95

____ Hidden Big Island of Hawaii, $13.95

____ Hidden Boston & Cape Cod, $14.95

____ Hidden British Columbia, $18.95

____ Hidden Cancún & the Yucatán, $16.95

____ Hidden Carolinas, $17.95

____ Hidden Coast of California, $18.95

____ Hidden Colorado, $15.95

____ Hidden Disneyland, $13.95

____ Hidden Florida, $18.95

____ Hidden Florida Keys & Everglades, $13.95

____ Hidden Georgia, $16.95

____ Hidden Guatemala, $16.95

____ Hidden Hawaii, $18.95

____ Hidden Idaho, $14.95

____ Hidden Kauai, $13.95

____ Hidden Maui, $13.95

____ Hidden Montana, $15.95

____ Hidden New England, $18.95

____ Hidden New Mexico, $15.95

____ Hidden Oahu, $13.95

____ Hidden Oregon, $15.95

____ Hidden Pacific Northwest, $18.95

____ Hidden Salt Lake City, $14.95

____ Hidden San Francisco & Northern California, $18.95

____ Hidden Southern California, $18.95

____ Hidden Southwest, $19.95

____ Hidden Tahiti, $17.95

____ Hidden Tennessee, $16.95

____ Hidden Utah, $16.95

____ Hidden Walt Disney World, $13.95

____ Hidden Washington, $15.95

____ Hidden Wine Country, $13.95

____ Hidden Wyoming, $15.95

THE NEW KEY GUIDEBOOKS

____ The New Key to Costa Rica, $18.95

____ The New Key to Ecuador and the Galápagos, $17.95

PARADISE FAMILY GUIDES

____ Paradise Family Guides: Kaua'i, $16.95

____ Paradise Family Guides: Maui, $16.95

____ Paradise Family Guides: Big Island of Hawai'i, $16.95

Mark the book(s) you're ordering and enter the total cost here ➥ [_____]

California residents add 8.25% sales tax here ➥ [_____]

Shipping, check box for your preferred method and enter cost here ➥ [_____]

❏ BOOK RATE   **FREE! FREE! FREE!**

❏ PRIORITY MAIL/UPS GROUND   cost of postage

❏ UPS OVERNIGHT OR 2-DAY AIR   cost of postage

Billing, enter total amount due here and check method of payment ➥ [_____]

❏ CHECK   ❏ MONEY ORDER

❏ VISA/MASTERCARD _____EXP. DATE_____

NAME _____PHONE_____

ADDRESS _____

CITY_____ STATE _____ ZIP_____

MONEY-BACK GUARANTEE ON DIRECT ORDERS PLACED THROUGH ULYSSES PRESS.

ABOUT THE AUTHORS

LISA OPPENHEIMER and her seasoned team of researchers—Alexis, 13, Melissa, 10, and Steve, 45—have embarked on numerous Disney World fact-finding missions, braving the perils of the Jungle Cruise, the peaks of Space Mountain and the virtual dog slime of Honey I Shrunk the Audience. Working at Disney and elsewhere, she's earned bylines in several travel books, as well as on the pages of *Disney Magazine*, *Parents* and *Family Life*.

CATHERINE O'NEAL is the author of *Hidden Belize* and *Hidden Carolinas* and co-author of *Hidden Florida* and *Hidden New England*. She contributes regularly to *Travel & Leisure*, *Outside* and *Bride's*, and has been published in more than 30 magazines and newspapers, including *Parents*, *Country Living*, the *Washington Post* and the *New York Post*. A native of Florida, she currently resides in the Florida Keys.

ABOUT THE ILLUSTRATOR

GLENN KIM is a freelance illustrator residing in the San Francisco Bay Area. His work appears in numerous Ulysses Press titles including *The New to Key Ecuador and the Galápagos*, *Hidden Southwest* and *Hidden Arizona*. He has also illustrated for the National Forest Service, several Bay Area magazines, book covers and greeting cards, as well as for advertising agencies that include Foote Cone and Belding, Hal Riney and Jacobs Fulton Design Group.